Investigating Abnormal Behaviour

Weidenfeld Modern Psychology

Series Editors:

Dr Alan Baddeley (Director, Psychology Research Unit, Cambridge), Professor Peter Bryant (Watts Professor of Psychology, University of Oxford), and Professor Nicholas Mackintosh (Professor of Psychology, University of Cambridge).

Already published:

Cognition and Cognitive Psychology, Anthony J. Sanford
The Psychology of Language and Communication, Andrew Ellis and Geoffrey Beattie

Investigating Abnormal Behaviour

Edgar Miller
District Psychologist, Cambridge Health Authority

Stephen Morley
Lecturer in Clinical Psychology, University of Leeds

Weidenfeld and Nicolson · London

George Weidenfeld and Nicolson Ltd
91 Clapham High Street, London SW4 7TA

ISBN 0 297 78847 7 cased
ISBN 0 297 78848 5 paperback

Filmset by Deltatype, Ellesmere Port

Printed by Butler & Tanner Ltd
Frome and London

Contents

Preface

This book has its origins in a series of lectures given to under-graduates at Cambridge as part of the Natural Sciences Part II course in Psychology. Being forced to try to convey an appreciation of a large field within only twelve lectures, and starting virtually from scratch, demanded a radical appraisal of what should be covered and how it should be conveyed. Our answer was to try to base the course around the key issues that arise in dealing with abnormal behaviour rather than to present a comprehensive coverage of everything from schizophrenia to mild stress reactions. The specific material presented could then be selected so as to illustrate the basic questions and how they might be resolved. Although our approach was forced on us by particular local circumstances, we found it a satisfying way to teach. We believe that it has a general validity even for courses which are not as cramped as ours then was. Whether other teachers share our enthusiasm for this approach remains to be seen.

Books are not written in a vacuum and this one is no exception. Our thinking has been influenced and enriched by many teachers and colleagues to whom we owe a considerable debt. In particular, we would like to thank Myra Hunter, Geoff Shepherd, Iain Wilkinson and Mark Williams who read and commented on sections of the manuscript. Nevertheless we remain responsible for any confusions or inaccuracies that remain.

The early stages of planning were facilitated by the excellent coffee and generally pleasant ambience of Martin's Coffee House. In the final stages the process of production was greatly enhanced by Sheila Turner's willingness to transcribe our generously overscored drafts. We are very grateful to her for this. Finally, and most particularly, we would like to record our gratitude to our wives, Sally Miller and Alison Morley, and families who have helped, supported and tolerated us through this book's long period of gestation.

Ed Miller
Stephen Morley   *Cambridge and Leeds, 1985*

Acknowledgements

Figures 2 and 4 are reproduced, by permission of the Association for Advancement of Behavior Therapy and the authors, from Edward S. Shapiro, Rowland P. Barrett and Thomas H. Ollendick, 'A comparison of physical restraint and positive practice over-correction in treating stereotypic behavior', *Behavior Therapy*, *11*, pp. 227–33 (copyright 1980 by the Association for Advancement of Behavior Therapy). Figure 3 is reproduced, by permission of Pergamon Press and the authors, from C. Bilsbury and S. Morley, 'Obsessional slowness: a meticulous replication', *Behaviour Research and Therapy*, *17*, pp. 405–8 (copyright 1979 by Pergamon Press Ltd). Figure 6 is reproduced, by permission of the Royal College of Psychiatrists and the authors, from C. E. Vaughn and J. P. Leff, 'The influence of family and social factors on the course of psychiatric illness', *British Journal of Psychiatry*, *129*, pp. 125–38 (copyright 1976 by the Royal College of Psychiatrists). Figure 12 is reproduced, by permission of Academic Press, from N. R. Ellis, 'Memory processes in retardates and normals' in N. R. Ellis (ed.), *International Review of Research in Mental Retardation*, *4* (copyright Academic Press). Table 3 is reproduced, by permission of W. H. Freeman & Co., from M. E. P. Seligman, *Helplessness: On Depression Development and Death* (copyright 1975 by W. H. Freeman & Co.).

1 Introduction

Abnormal psychology often has a particular appeal for those studying psychology at an undergraduate level. There is a general fascination for student and layman alike in the problem of 'mental illness'. Abnormal psychology also links with the applied area of clinical psychology and therefore appears to have some credibility in terms of possible applications to 'real life' problems. In this it contrasts with some other aspects of psychology which, to students at least, can sometimes come across as being rather dry and often of purely academic interest. Some students may also see a course in abnormal psychology as something that can act as a possible testing ground for a later career choice and the desirability of seeking postgraduate training in clinical psychology.

Regardless of the reasons for its popularity with undergraduates, abnormal psychology is a fascinating field of study in its own right. It presents many challenging problems, both theoretical and methodological. More than most areas of psychology, it has been subjected to (or suffers from – according to taste) a plethora of different approaches and underlying models. As if this were not enough, it has attracted more than its fair share of rather superficial, offbeat, and even frankly dotty contributions. This can make it difficult for the newcomer to distinguish the sensible from the purely fatuous.

The very diffuseness of abnormal psychology raises problems for anyone trying to write an introductory text. An all-embracing comprehensiveness is not possible if the length of the text is to be kept within reasonable bounds. Choices have to be made about the kind of material selected for inclusion and the way that it is to be organized and presented. These choices will of course be dependent upon the aims that the authors have in mind. The solution attempted in this book differs quite radically from that adopted in most other texts on abnormal psychology. In order that the reader is not misled into thinking that he or she is being offered something that they did not anticipate, or into failing to realize that what is covered is necessarily limited in certain ways, it is appropriate to set out exactly what is being attempted. An understanding of this will also assist the reader in integrating the material presented here with information gained from other sources.

There are two major approaches that could be taken in a text of this nature. The most popular for texts in abnormal psychology is to organize the material around various clinical conditions (schizophrenia, obsessional neurosis, mental handicap, etc.) so that one or more chapters are devoted to each major disorder or group of disorders (e.g. Davison and Neale, 1982: an excellent text). Although comprehensive in one sense this approach suffers disadvantages. To keep within a reasonable length, it is difficult to consider many of the disorders in anything other than a superficial way. In any case a single author, or small group of authors, cannot be fully familiar with the full range of work relating to a very varied range of clinical conditions.

An alternative that has been more extensively canvassed than actually followed in practice is to subdivide the material in terms of disturbances in different aspects of psychological functioning (attention, memory, language, etc.). This is alleged to help psychologists get away from a medical or clinical system of classification which, it is argued, is of dubious validity. Despite the urge to dispense with medical terminology, this has a nasty habit of creeping back into the discussion. Thus a chapter on, say, disorders of attention will end up with sections dealing with attentional disturbances in schizophrenia, in severe mental handicap, etc. Since the material presented in this way is basically that provided by the text structured around clinical categories but broken up in a different way, there is still the problem of keeping the length of the book within bounds whilst trying to be both comprehensive and cover the material at a suitable depth. The few texts written in this way (e.g. Costello, 1970; Eysenck, 1973) tend to be multi-authored and directed at a more advanced level than is envisaged here.

A different approach is being taken in this book. The aim of the text is to introduce the reader to the major types of question that arise in abnormal psychology and to consider the ways in which these questions might be answered. In addition we intend to illustrate the ways in which psychology can contribute to the understanding and management of clinical conditions characterized by abnormal behaviour. As a result we hope that basic issues will be articulated more clearly and possible ways of resolving them covered in greater depth than is usual in introductory texts. This approach gives much greater emphasis to abnormal psychology as a branch of the overall discipline of psychology rather than as a mere description of strange and exotic phenomena. This gain has to be paid for in other ways. The main cost lies in the fact that the range of abnormalities dealt with, whether these are defined in terms of clinical conditions or of psychological functions, will be much more limited than that covered in the more conventional texts. Most of the major disorders will in fact get some mention but some will be covered very much more intensively than others. For example, the selection of depression as the main means of illustrating certain basic issues means that affective disorders will be examined in some detail. In contrast, only limited aspects of the work on schizophrenia will receive any sustained attention.

If it is desired to emphasize the basic questions that arise in abnormal psychology, it is also important to be clear at the outset as to just what these questions are. As a preliminary there are a number of basic conceptual issues. These relate to such things as what constitutes 'abnormality', how abnormal behaviour can best be described and classified, and the very vexed question as to whether there is such a thing as 'mental illness'. These questions will be dealt with in the next chapter. They are also quite contentious and no final answer to them will be offered. Nevertheless the kind of position that is adopted in response to them colours the handling of the material to be considered in this book.

Having established a workable and defensible position with regard to these basic conceptual issues, a number of more empirical and theoretical questions arise with respect to specific manifestations of abnormal behaviour. It is necessary to be able to identify, describe and classify the different behavioural abnormalities. For example, is it sensible to separate mood disorders like depression from other kinds of abnormality and, if so, is depression a unitary entity or are there different sorts of depression? Just what criteria need to be used in order to answer questions of this kind? Abnormal behaviour, just like normal behaviour, needs to be explained. A very wide range of explanatory models have been used in abnormal psychology and these need to be examined.

Despite the extreme positions taken to the contrary by a few authorities, the position adopted here is that abnormal behaviour can only be fully understood when it is considered against a background of information that can be provided by other disciplines. The conditions that give rise to abnormal behaviour are also, to varying degrees, biological and social phenomena. Non-psychological approaches need to be considered if the particular benefits and limitations of psychological explanations are to be seen in their proper context. These questions of description, classification and explanation, as well as the general issue of the nature of psychological impairments that might occur, will be dealt with in Chapters 3 to 7 of this book. They will use depression as the main example because this is the single condition that best illustrates these basic points. Nevertheless some reference will occasionally be made to other disorders.

As commonly defined, abnormal behaviour is almost always regarded as undesirable and as something to be changed or modified if at all possible. In studying normal behaviour the concern is usually to understand and explain the phenomena that are observed. Any manipulation that is carried out is generally with the aim of enhancing that understanding by means of experiment. Those interested in studying abnormal behaviour have a similar desire to understand but may also have a strong interest in trying to find ways of modifying the basic phenomena. Chapters 8 to 13 aim to describe some of the major psychological approaches to the treatment or management of behavioural abnormalities, with a particular emphasis on comparing the different types of therapeutic model and the ways in which the effects of treatment can be evaluated. Detailed discussion of the therapeutic techniques themselves will be avoided since this belongs more properly to post-graduate training in clinical psychology.

In order to broaden the material covered and provide some different examples of the issues identified earlier, Chapters 14 and 15 will offer a discussion of some further topics. These have been selected partly because they illustrate particular questions or psychological approaches, but also partly because they represent problems of general social concern at present. In some writings on abnormal and clinical psychology there appears to be what can be described as a 'reverse utility' law. This can roughly be stated as 'the number of papers published on a given abnormality or clinical condition is inversely related to the frequency with which that abnormality or condition is encountered in the general population'. Common problems of major concern do present interesting psychological questions and it is good to emphasize these sometimes, at the expense of the rare exotica which can dominate discussion all too often.

This is not to argue that rare conditions may not rightly be studied much more extensively than their relative frequency might indicate. One important reason for studying abnormal behaviour that has not been mentioned so far is that abnormality can assist in the understanding of normal behaviour and the processes that govern it. If a function, like memory or reading, tends to break down in certain ways then this can give useful clues as to how this process operates under normal circumstances. Rare but relatively pure forms of psychological malfunctioning can therefore be of considerable theoretical interest and in consequence attract a disproportionate amount of attention.

A good example of this is the rather rare form of acquired dyslexia known as 'deep dyslexia'. (For most people the term 'dyslexia' conjures up the image of the child who has undue difficulty in learning to read. Technically this is 'developmental dyslexia' and needs to be clearly distinguished from acquired dyslexia which occurs in adults who could once read with normal facility but whose reading becomes impaired as a result of cerebral lesions.) People whose reading is disrupted following brain lesions most commonly exhibit 'surface dyslexia'. Errors that are made in reading are then typically of the form that the word 'house' is read as 'mouse' (i.e. a word that may look like the real thing or at least shares some sensory or 'surface' characteristics with it). They do not make errors in which an incorrect word is read which is linked with the one supplied in terms of its meaning rather than any sensory characteristic. An example might be when 'house' is read as 'dwelling'. The rare cases of people suffering from 'deep dyslexia' make this sort of error without being prone to the surface dyslexia kind of error (e.g. Coltheart *et al.*, 1980). Furthermore the surface dyslexic can use ordinary spelling rules to read and pronounce nonsense words like 'sut', whilst this causes considerable difficulties for the deep dyslexic, presumably because nonsense words have no meaning that he can access.

This example gives evidence of what is sometimes referred to as a 'double dissociation'. In other words the two quite different types of reading error can occur entirely independently of one another. Thus it is not possible to argue that one kind of disturbance might be merely a more extreme manifestation of the other (at least not without considerable theoretical contortions). This is then quite strong evidence that in normal reading the material to be read is processed in two quite different ways: in terms of its sensory characteristics and in terms of its meaning. Clear and isolated examples of disturbances in one particular aspect of functioning, such as deep dyslexia, are rarely encountered but can yield important theoretical insights that may be difficult to obtain by studying normal individuals.

To return to the choices facing the authors, the large range of models encountered in abnormal psychology has already been mentioned. Again not all of these can be considered in a book of this nature. Attempts at understanding the phenomena of concern can be very crudely placed into two categories. On the one hand are those models that claim to be oriented towards explanation in a scientific sense and which are capable of producing hypotheses that can be tested empirically. At the other extreme are models which are more concerned with a subjective understanding of what is observed. Many psychodynamic formulations fall into this latter category and their proponents not infrequently regard experimental approaches as, at best, superficial and any attempt to derive testable hypotheses from their theorizing as totally misguided.

In the following pages the emphasis will be very much upon empirical approaches to abnormal behaviour. To some degree this is because it is the way that is favoured by the authors. Also of significance is the fact that it is the empirical approach that links abnormal psychology to the mainstream of experimental psychology with which the student will already have some familiarity.

2 Some Basic Issues

As indicated in the previous chapter, there are a number of fundamental issues that need to receive some attention before we proceed to the main topics of concern. These issues are important because the position that is adopted with regard to them very much colours the way in which more specific topics are covered in the following chapters.

The questions raised by the clinical classification systems and by arguments concerning the fundamental nature of behavioural abnormalities are extremely contentious and have received no general consensus. Like many hotly disputed issues, they are complex and are better considered in a calmer atmosphere than that which typically surrounds acrimonious debates. A thorough discussion of them would also take up a great deal more space than can be afforded here. In this chapter the goal is fairly modest. This is just to set out the nature of the problems and give some indication of the kinds of argument that have been offered in support of the major positions that have been adopted.

Because these issues are so basic, and because very varied opinions are held, it is important that the authors should clearly set out their own position. This is done at the end of each section. These positions reveal some of the underlying assumptions behind the selection of material to be encountered in the rest of the book and the way that this is handled. It is suggested that readers consult at least a few of the cited references to get a first-hand account of alternative positions.

What is abnormal?

The use of the term 'abnormal psychology' implies that there is a branch of psychology for which this is a reasonably apt description and which can be more or less clearly differentiated from other aspects of psychology. In practice the subject matter of abnormal psychology is as easy, or as difficult, to separate from what might be

regarded as mainstream experimental psychology as is developmental or social psychology. Unlike developmental and social
psychology, the basis of this differentiation is less clear-cut. What
constitutes 'abnormal' in this context can be defined in many ways
and none of these is entirely satisfactory as a single basis for defining
the subject matter of abnormal psychology. For convenience,
definitions of abnormality can be considered under three main
headings which constitute the statistical, departure from cultural
norms and subjective definitions.

Statistical definition

This assumes that psychological characteristics can be viewed as
dimensional. The average level, or a range about the average, is
then regarded as normal and the extremes are defined as abnormal.
An immediate question is how deviant from the population mean an
individual needs to be to be considered abnormal? Any chosen cut-
off point is necessarily arbitrary, assuming a continuous variation in
the characteristic under consideration, although it is possible to be
more sophisticated and have degrees of abnormality.

The obvious situation in which the statistical concept of abnormality applies is that of mental handicap. The lowest 2 per cent
of the population in terms of intelligence (i.e. those with an IQ
below a cut-off point somewhere in the region of 70 to 75) are
usually considered to be mentally handicapped. The study of the
psychological characteristics of this group is usually considered to
fall within the scope of abnormal psychology.

On the other hand, the statistical definition has severe limitations. Those with an IQ above 130 are equally as deviant in a
statistical sense as the mentally handicapped but are not regarded as
'abnormal' in the sense that this word is used in the phrase
'abnormal psychology'. The authors know of only one, rather
dated, textbook of abnormal psychology that mentions those of
superior intelligence, whereas most say at least something about the
mentally handicapped. In addition, rare phenomena like eidetic
imagery or subjects with phenomenal powers to carry out mental
arithmetic (e.g. Hunter, 1962) are not considered under abnormal
psychology.

Departure from the cultural norm

Probably the best definition of abnormality in this context is in terms of some departure from the cultural norm. Seeing things that no one else can see, or hearing things that others cannot hear, is not considered socially appropriate or ideal in a Western European culture, nor is being afraid of things like spiders which can do no harm. Not surprisingly, departures from the cultural norm are almost always unusual in the statistical sense but this is not a necessary feature. Despite the fact that most people may have the symptoms of influenza in the middle of a particularly virulent epidemic, this is not considered ideal.

The problem with this type of definition of abnormality is that it can be arbitrary and can vary both between and within cultures. Anthropologists have described cultures (e.g. of certain North American tribes) where seeing visions of a kind that would be readily classed as hallucinatory in Britain is considered entirely normal, at least under certain circumstances.

Views as to what is considered abnormal also vary within cultures over time. Within a quarter of a century, views about the nature of homosexuality have changed very considerably and it is now generally not considered to be 'abnormal' in the sense that it once was. Homosexuality also illustrates the arbitrariness of ideas as to what is a deviation from norm or ideal. Whilst female homosexuality may not have been considered normal or ideal it was never regarded as quite such a large departure from the ideal as male homosexuality.

Subjective definitions

Since abnormal psychology is largely concerned with clinical groups, it is worth pointing out that people do not come to clinics because they feel that they have met some abstract definition of abnormality. For the most part they come because their feelings or behaviour cause them distress, or because their behaviour causes distress and difficulty to those with whom they come into close contact. This is a highly individual and subjective definition, but it is one of considerable practical importance. People's subjective impressions of what is abnormal and undesirable obviously overlap appreciably with the other two criteria but this overlap is by no means perfect.

Comment

In general there is no satisfactory definition of what is abnormal in 'abnormal psychology'. Somebody was once inspired to define intelligence as being what intelligence tests measure. Unsatisfactory though it may be, this book will define abnormal psychology as being the study of the kind of issues that are commonly covered in texts on abnormal psychology – in other words the study of the types of behavioural abnormality encountered in people with psychiatric and neurological disorders and the mentally handicapped.

Classification

The field of abnormal psychology covers a very wide range of behavioural abnormalities. These are much wider than those associated with psychiatric disorders although the bulk of abnormal psychology is based on the study of phenomena that also form part of psychiatry. In dealing with this work it is extremely difficult to avoid using the psychiatric classification system. This is far from being wholly satisfactory and its limitations will be described later in this section. Nevertheless it is the only classification system for abnormal behaviour that is in common usage and it will no doubt retain its pre-eminence until something better is proposed.

Table 1 *An outline of contemporary psychiatric classification.*

	Functional		Organic
Psychoses	*Neuroses*	*Miscellaneous and personality disorders*	
Schizophrenia	Phobias	Psychopathy	Senile dementia
Manic-depressive psychosis	Anxiety states	Addictions (drugs, alcohol, etc.)	Arteriosclerotic dementia
Depression (psychotic)	Depression (neurotic)	Sexual deviations (e.g. paedophilia)	Toxic confusional states
	Obsessional disorders	etc.	Huntington's chorea
	Hysteria		Myxoedema (hypothyroidism) etc.

It is therefore essential to have some idea of the psychiatric classification system. The basic outline of this is set out in Table 1, although different authorities tend to vary slightly with regard to details. A number of national and international organizations have drawn up very detailed classification systems for statistical and research purposes. These will not be described here but the best known at present are the ninth revision of the International Classification of Diseases (ICD-9), introduced by the World Health Organization (1978), and the American Psychiatric Association's (1980) third edition of its Diagnostic and Statistical Manual (DSM-III). In passing it should be noted that some classification systems, like DSM-III, are 'multi-axial' in that they base classification not only on alleged clinical disorders but also bring in judgements about personality characteristics, presence of psychosocial stressors and the developmental history of the individual.

It can readily be seen that the system set out in Table 1 is a hierarchical one. The bases for splitting up specific disorders into groups will be described but it is not possible to describe all the different clinical conditions. The reader is strongly advised to read the chapters giving clinical descriptions in one of the elementary psychiatric texts written for medical students such as Curran *et al.* (1980), Linford-Rees (1976) or Trethowan (1979).

The most fundamental distinction is between organic and functional disorders. The basis for this distinction is quite clear. As the term suggests, the organic disorders are those which have a known physical base, usually involving some form of pathology of the central nervous system. Probably the most commonly encountered are the dementing diseases (senile dementia, arteriosclerotic dementia, Alzheimer's disease, etc.), but there are also a large number of fairly rare conditions. These include Huntington's chorea (a genetically linked disease characterized by sudden, jerky 'choreiform' movements and accompanied by a progressive dementia) and myxoedema (hypothyroidism). Psychiatric disturbances can also accompany physical disease which does not primarily affect the nervous system. This is particularly so in old people where 'confusional states' can be produced by such things as urinary tract or chest infections or even the injudicious overprescribing of drugs. Similar states can also result in young adults who abuse non-prescribed drugs.

The functional disorders are, of course, those with no established physical cause. Occasionally disorders thought to belong in the functional group are discovered to be the consequence of physical pathology and are transferred into the organic camp. The best known of these is GPI (general paresis of the insane) which was eventually discovered to be a manifestation of the tertiary stage of syphilis, although this is by no means the only example. It is possible that other functional disorders will eventually be shown to have an organic basis but it is unreasonable to expect that this will be the case for all.

The functional disorders are subdivided into two main groups, the psychoses and the neuroses. However, it is possible to delineate a third group, the so-called personality disorders, as has been done in Table 1. The psychoses include such things as schizophrenia, manic-depressive psychosis, and some forms of depression. These are disorders which may, but do not necessarily always, show such bizarre features as hallucinations, delusions and disorders of thinking. The neuroses include such things as anxiety states, phobias, hysteria, obsessions and compulsions, and a form of depression. (Whether or not there really are two forms of depression is an issue which will be taken up in Chapter 3.)

Although psychiatrists commonly distinguish between the psychoses and the neuroses, it is difficult to find clear lines of demarcation. At least three possible criteria have been suggested. The first is severity, and it is suggested that the psychoses are the most severe forms of mental disorder. This may be generally true but it also begs the question as to what is meant by 'severe'. According to at least some definitions of 'severe', there are exceptions. For example, obsessional compulsive disorders can be extremely handicapping. The person who continually has to wash his hands, the housewife who has to clean the whole house carefully from top to bottom each day, and the individual who cannot escape from elaborate checking rituals can all be extremely handicapped. In practical terms they may be much more at a disadvantage than some psychotic patients with delusions or hallucinations.

Another possible criterion for differentiation lies along the lines that neurotic behaviour can be seen as an extension or exaggeration of normal characteristics, whilst psychotic manifestations are qualitatively quite different from anything within normal experience. This again has some immediate validity. Few people would be regarded as having a spider phobia of the kind that would bring them to a psychiatric clinic (see Chapter 10 for a case example), yet many experience some uneasiness when encountering a spider. In contrast the hallucinations and delusions of the schizophrenic cannot be matched to normal reactions in the same way. This criterion also breaks down under closer examination. The phenomena associated with conversion hysteria (a neurotic disorder), such as paralysis of the limbs with no physical cause, seem to be equally as foreign to normal experience as hallucinations.

Finally, it has been suggested that neurotic patients show 'insight' into their problems whilst psychotics do not. It is true that many neurotic patients show what the psychiatrists describe as 'resistance' to their symptoms, in that they will try to combat them and make statements indicating insight such as 'I know that it is ridiculous to be afraid of spiders because they cannot harm me'. In general psychotics do not show such features. However once again there are important exceptions to the rule. The person with hysterical paralysis does not show insight and the deluded psychotic may occasionally indicate that ideas pop into his head which, on a moment's reflection, he realizes are silly and nonsensical.

There is thus no entirely adequate basis for the conventional distinction between psychosis and neurosis. This leaves the 'personality disorders' as the final subgroup within the functional disorders. These are probably best described negatively as psychological problems which do not fit into the other categories and include such things as alcoholism and other addictions. The best known of the personality disorders is probably psychopathy. The classical picture of the psychopath is the young adult male who can be socially attractive at a superficial level but who does not make deep relationships with others. He tends to use other people as tools or objects by which to gain his own ends and he not infrequently commits antisocial acts, often of a criminal nature. The natural 'con man' is one possible manifestation of psychopathy.

Problems of classification

Two general problems have been raised with regard to psychiatric classification. The first, which can be dealt with quite quickly, has been raised by those who have argued that classification is impossible due to the inherent heterogeneity of people. The second problem relates to the validity of the particular classification system in use. A particular aspect of this latter problem is the question as to what kind or type of classification system is most appropriate. These issues have been discussed extensively by Kendell (1975; 1983), who covers the issues in very much greater detail than is possible here.

Although different authorities have argued from time to time that the classification of behavioural abnormalities is pointless, a little reflection reveals that some form of classification is virtually inevitable. If not all mental disorder is the same, and the evidence lies overwhelmingly in the direction of assuming that it is not, then its features within any given individual need to be described. The use of different descriptive terms for different people immediately provides some sort of basis for a classification unless it is assumed that the same term cannot be applied to more than one individual.

Kendell (1983) points out that every psychiatric patient has attributes at three levels:

A. those he shares with all other psychiatric patients;
B. those he shares with some other patients, but not all;
C. those that are unique to him.

Classification is feasible providing there are attributes at level B, and to a considerable degree the value of classification depends upon the relative size and importance of attributes at level B compared with those at levels A and C. It is certainly the conventional view of most psychologists and psychiatrists that there are important attributes at level B.

In any case, it can be argued that the issue can be examined in empirical terms. If a useful classification system can be developed then this implies that there is a logical basis for the classification of psychological abnormalities. The answer to this problem then becomes partially dependent upon the answer that is given to queries about the validity of the present classification system. However, the reverse argument does not apply. If existing systems are shown to be invalid, this does not mean that a valid system cannot be developed.

The psychiatric diagnostic system has been strongly attacked on the grounds that it lacks reliability. Several studies (e.g. Beck *et al.* 1962; Kreitman, 1961; Zubin, 1967) have taken samples of psychiatric patients and looked at the diagnostic agreement between two or more psychiatrists who have examined the same patients. General discriminations between organic and functional disorders can be made quite well, but reliability can be very poor for specific psychiatric diagnoses. In Kreitman's (1961) study, agreement between two diagnosticians was only 28 per cent for neurotic disorders, 61 per cent for the functional psychoses and 75 per cent for organic disorders.

On the face of it these reliability studies are not very impressive and suggest that the traditional diagnostic categories cannot be used with great reliability. As Cooper (1983) points out, little attempt was made in many of these studies to ensure that the people making the diagnosis used agreed criteria so there is some scope for improving reliability even within the bounds of the present system. Ley (1972) has also carried out a more sophisticated analysis of data from some of the reliability studies and suggests that psychiatrists are about 75 per cent accurate in their diagnoses. A further point is that the kind of study described so far typically takes a varied sample of psychiatric patients and forces the diagnostician to fit them into one category or another. It could be that a good proportion can be diagnosed reliably but that there is a subgroup that just does not fit into the system. Ley's (1972) analysis did not find strong support for this possibility but was certainly not sensitive enough to rule it out.

When attempts are made to devise special instruments or interview procedures for reaching diagnoses based on operational criteria, and psychiatrists or other raters are trained to use the procedures, then fairly impressive levels of reliability can be achieved, especially for the major psychoses (schizophrenia and depression). Examples of such developments are the Present State Examination (Wing et al., 1974), the Feighner Criteria (Feighner et al., 1972) and the Research Diagnostic Criteria (Spitzer et al., 1978). In a study reported by Murphy et al., (1974), it was found that inter-rater reliability was 94 per cent for the presence of depressive symptoms and 80 per cent for specific diagnoses. In fact most of the unreliability in this last figure could be attributed to diagnosticians disagreeing about the level of certainty with which they accorded the diagnosis rather than which diagnosis they actually chose. Of their original sample, a subset of forty-three who had initially been considered to have 'primary affective disorders' was given a blind re-evaluation five years later. The level of agreement at follow-up was 86 per cent. Basically similar results were found over a four-year follow-up by Faverilli and Poli (1982).

It thus appears that at least some psychiatric categories can be used with good levels of reliability and certainly well enough for research purposes. The reliability is not perfect but can be made to be more than adequate as far as such things as the major functional psychoses are concerned. Whether the system is valid in the sense that it relates meaningfully to other significant features like aetiology or response to treatment, is difficult to assess. There is a relationship between psychiatric diagnosis and treatment but this could be contaminated by the fact that psychiatrists believe that diagnosis is related to treatment response. The classic study of Roth (1955) demonstrated that, as far as certain diagnostic categories in psychogeriatric patients are concerned, diagnosis can be a reasonably powerful predictor of outcome.

The standard psychiatric diagnostic system (or set of related systems) is based on categories. It is generally assumed that these are mutually exclusive and defined by a set of necessary and sufficient features. From this it follows that every psychiatric patient can be slotted into one of them, much like categorizing an assorted collection of items of fruit such as apples, pears, bananas, etc. Contemporary work in cognitive psychology suggests that categories used in natural language are not exclusively defined. Instead there is a prototype for each category and membership is determined by how well an individual approximates to the prototype with respect to the number of shared features. On this basis one would expect to find less than perfect reliability in allocating individuals to categories, some within-group heterogeneity and some overlap between group membership. Also the diagnosticians' confidence and accuracy of allocation will be a function of the number of features an individual shares with the prototype. Cantor *et al.* (1980) have applied this argument to psychiatric diagnosis and showed that this model fits reasonably well.

Others, like Eysenck (1970), have argued for a dimensional system. Possibly psychiatric disorder lies along several dimensions and the individual is best described as lying at a set of points along these dimensions. Although a dimensional approach has a considerable appeal, especially for psychologists, it does, as Kendell (1983) indicates, have some disadvantages. It is difficult for the clinician to cope with more than one or two dimensions, and in fact dimensional systems often end up by being converted into categories before the information that they convey can be usefully related to individuals. On top of this, no dimensional system has ever gained wide acceptance and so dimensional classification is not suitable for use in an introductory text like the present one.

The main part of this book will therefore go along with the standard psychiatric diagnostic system. This is not because the authors regard it as ideal or beyond improvement. It is the only generally used system and it is difficult to avoid using it without going to very elaborate and artificial lengths. Nevertheless this necessary reliance on the standard system is not quite such a dreadful imposition as some would claim. Used carefully, and with proper safeguards, the system is workable and there is no viable alternative.

The Nature of Psychological Abnormality

The position taken so far has not seriously deviated from the standard medical or psychiatric approach to abnormal behaviour. This is a stance that has attracted considerable, and often justified, criticism. It is appropriate therefore to take a rather more careful look at the nature of the phenomena that are going to be discussed in the greater part of the book. It is also likely to be helpful if the authors indicate the kind of position that they have adopted. In order to cover the various issues fully it would be necessary to expound at considerable length. The present aim is merely to give some idea of the basic arguments.

Many books on abnormal and clinical psychology or related areas (e.g. behaviour therapy or psychotherapy) contain a routine condemnation of what is described as 'the medical model'. This medical model is sometimes set up as an Aunt Sally to be quickly and comfortingly knocked down by the particular kind of psychological or social model favoured by the writer concerned. In these arguments a simple dichotomy is outlined between one kind of model and another where one is clearly outdated and wrong whilst the other is self-evidently correct, especially when viewed through the author's pair of rose-coloured spectacles. It is part of the argument being advanced here that the real situation is very much more complex than this and that the simple adversarial view of the different models as being in direct competition with one another is often mistaken. In other words, it is not a simple issue of *either* one model *or* the other, and this is so even when discussion is confined to those disorders with no known organic cause.

In many discussions the 'medical model' is considered to be essentially that which regards psychological abnormalities as diseases, with the archetypical disease being a bodily malfunction caused by some infectious agent such as a bacterium. It is highly likely that schizophrenia and obsessional neurosis are not diseases in this sense. However, as will be shown later, this is a particularly narrow view of disease and it is not really helpful to use the term 'the medical model' since medicine, like all other scientific enterprises, incorporates a number of different models. The alternative types of model may be psychological (e.g. the behavioural model which postulates that maladaptive behaviour is learned just like normal adaptive behaviour) or social in nature. The biggest attack on 'the medical model' has come from the exponents of social models invoking such processes as labelling, scapegoating and the notion that it is the family or society that is disturbed rather than the individual. In this latter case the argument goes that the individual's apparently abnormal or deviant behaviour is not the consequence of anything that can be considered to have gone wrong with the individual. Rather it is that any individual will behave unusually if the outside stresses upon him are abnormal in nature. Some advocates of social models, like Laing (see Siegler *et al.*, 1969), have also made things difficult by slipping from one social model to another.

It is just not possible to go through all the evidence that has been put forward, or even to give a reasonably representative sample of it. However, it is instructive to look at one of the studies that is most frequently cited with regard to explaining 'mental illness' as a purely social phenomenon. Rosenhan (1973), in a famous paper entitled 'On Being Sane in Insane Places', reported what happened to a number of subjects without genuine psychiatric symptoms who, for the purposes of this investigation, managed to get themselves admitted to psychiatric units in the USA. When going to see the psychiatrist, subjects gave false names and claimed to suffer from one of the alleged symptoms of schizophrenia which was auditory hallucinations. Subjects tried to answer all other questions truthfully.

A number of Rosenhan's subjects were admitted to institutions and were typically given the diagnosis of schizophrenia. On discharge they were given such labels as 'schizophrenic in remission'. Despite the fact that subjects tried to behave entirely normally after admission, none was detected as an imposter by the staff; although it is interesting that the subjects recorded that their fellow patients often had suspicions. Whilst subjects were in the hospital, staff observations were very much coloured by their perceptions of them as psychiatric patients. For example, one subject seen to be writing notes (to record his impressions as part of the study) was described by a nurse as indulging in 'writing behaviour' in a way that indicated that the nurse considered this activity as a manifestation of pathology. When asked ordinary, everyday questions by subjects hospital staff tended to react in a way that was quite different to the normal response to such questions outside the institution.

Rosenhan, and others very much impressed by this study, have drawn certain conclusions from it. One of these is the importance of labelling. Once the subject is categorized as 'schizophrenic' his behaviour, even quite innocent and otherwise normal behaviour, is perceived and described in different terms. This attitude persists beyond the point where the subject's behaviour is considered to have returned to normal in that he is discharged with the description 'schizophrenic in remission'.

This study is a significant one and gives cause for concern to anyone working in the mental health field. The following comments are not in any way intended to detract from this. The present concern is with whether it can really bear the full weight of the particular interpretation that has been placed upon it. This is the interpretation that so-called 'mental illness' has been shown to be merely the consequence of a labelling process. Clearly labelling is an inadequate account on its own since it does not explain why some individuals get labelled in the first place. However, it is possible to appeal to other social phenomena such as scapegoating to get round this. Even leaving this point aside, the study loses some of its conviction under closer scrutiny. (For a critical account see Spitzer, 1976.)

Rosenhan's account of what actually transpired between the subjects and the psychiatrists at the initial interview is second-hand and there is no direct record of what was actually said. Such a record would have been difficult to obtain without running the risk of giving the pseudo-patients away. There is no doubt that the psychiatrists were fooled into making a faulty diagnosis. Rosenhan implies that this happened absurdly easily, but proper supportive data is lacking. Even if the psychiatrists were fooled as readily as is suggested then this does not prove that the concept of schizophrenia is merely an empty label, although it might say something about the gullibility of these psychiatrists.

An important question raised by this study is just how easily a psychiatrist should be fooled if it is the case that 'schizophrenia' is something more than a label. A little reflection on the kinds of factors that might bias a psychiatrist's decision-making reveals, as Scheff (1966) has pointed out, that there may be powerful inbuilt tendencies that go against finding that a potential patient is normal. Psychiatrists, just like other medical practitioners, probably prefer to err in the direction of incurring false positives as opposed to false negatives. It is usually considered a much more serious error for a physician to fail to identify disease when faced with someone who is really ill (i.e. a 'false negative') than to investigate and treat someone who appears to be ill but really is not (i.e. incur a 'false positive'). On top of this is an expectation, not at all unreasonable under most circumstances, that by far the great majority of people who present with symptoms do so because they have some genuine distress or concern. The deliberate malingerer may be a hazard under some unusual circumstances (e.g. in prisons or in military units in wartime) but is a very rare phenomenon in ordinary practice.

Given these strong biases to accept what the patient says as genuine and to presume the presence of illness rather than its absence, it is not all that surprising that it is relatively easy to fool psychiatrists into thinking that a normal person is mentally disturbed. Other types of physician can be similarly fooled. It is in fact relatively easy to fake a story suggestive of epilepsy and to fool a neurologist into making that diagnosis. This does not mean that genuine cases of epilepsy do not exist.

Rosenhan is also correct in drawing attention to labelling phenomena in his report. The description of 'writing behaviour' implies that the nurse was influenced by the label so as to regard otherwise normal behaviour as a manifestation of abnormality. The account also shows that hospital staff do not respond to patients in the same way as they presumably would to 'normal' people. At best, however, these observations just demonstrate that powerful labelling effects can occur. This is hardly surprising in view of what is known about studies of attribution in social psychology. It does not prove that everything can be attributed to labelling.

Again the example of epilepsy brings this point out very clearly. Once the label 'epileptic' has been applied to an individual, it can then cause others to act towards that person in a different way that is sometimes quite irrational and which bears no relation to his actual behaviour or handicap. That a labelling effect can occur with epilepsy does not prove that epilepsy is merely a label and few would doubt that it is a genuine physical disorder.

This brings up a general point about claims to the effect that so-called 'mental illness' can be entirely accounted for in terms of particular social mechanisms like labelling or scapegoating. In order to make such claims it is not sufficient to show that such phenomena do occur. It is necessary to achieve a much stronger goal, which is to show that these mechanisms can account for all the variation in the situation. This of course also applies to any other exclusive claims whether they be in terms of medical, psychological or social mechanisms. To question the exclusive role of social mechanisms is clearly not the same thing as denying that they have any importance at all. In fact they may be very significant factors under some circumstances. For example, Blaxter (1978) showed that the diagnosis of alcoholism was a function of several social variables like local record-keeping practices, local medical customs, cultural definitions of alcoholism and whether the person was seen by casualty officers or psychiatrists. The presence of symptoms and signs of alcohol abuse was not a significant contributor to diagnosis.

The importance of labelling in schizophrenia has been examined in another investigation which contrasts with Rosenhan's work. Having obtained videotape recordings of subjects alleged to have schizophrenia and similar recordings of normal controls, Lindsay (1982) showed these to a sample of ordinary people (actually patients in a general hospital) who acted as raters. These observers were asked to rate each subject shown in the videotapes for certain characteristics. One set of raters was told nothing about the subjects being rated. The other two sets were told which subjects were psychiatric patients and which were not. For one set the information given was accurate but for the other the indicated attribution was the complete reverse of what was really the case.

If Rosenhan, and those who think like him, are correct then certain predictions follow. Where information about the psychiatric status of the subjects was withheld, ratings should not differ according to whether the person rated was actually a patient or not. This is especially so as the videotapes were carefully collected in order not to contain certain expressions of overt symptoms. For the other two sets of raters the ratings should emerge as being more abnormal for subjects identified as schizophrenic regardless of whether this attribution was correct. Some small effect attributable to labelling was found, but the overwhelming thrust of the results was to show that the true psychiatric patients were rated as more abnormal regardless of any information provided. The results of this investigation do not deny that labelling effects occur but they strongly indicate that the label is far from wholly an empty one and that there is a reality of some kind behind it.

An extreme supporter of the labelling hypothesis could still argue that labelling effects also influence the person who is labelled. Knowing that one has been categorized as a 'schizophrenic', or at least that one is being treated as a 'psychiatric patient', may itself induce altered behaviour. The altered behaviour of others towards the person who is so labelled may further enhance the change. This possibility cannot be excluded on the basis of the data presented so far and it is a hypothesis that has yet to be put to the test. One slight point against it is that the patients videotaped by Lindsay were fairly new cases and had not had a very long time to adapt to the label.

Also, in looking at other psychiatric conditions it is difficult to see how the ceaseless and exhausting overactivity of the hypomanic or the perpetual involvement of the obsessional in distressing and pointless rituals could be merely the consequence of applying a label.

Another influential and much-cited figure in these debates is Thomas Szasz. In his best-known work, entitled *The Myth of Mental Illness*, Szasz (1961) argues that the term 'mental illness' implies that the phenomena involved are 'basically similar to bodily diseases'. In rejecting this view he argues that psychiatrists are really dealing with 'personal, social and ethical problems in living'. He also dislikes the notion of 'mental illness' because it undermines the concept of personal responsibility in that it can then be argued (as sometimes happens in the courts) that people are not responsible for certain actions because they were 'mentally ill' at the time. The idea that mental disorders might be reduced to 'problems of living' has a certain superficial attractiveness. One major difficulty is that the notion of a 'problem of living' is itself a rather slippery concept that is inadequately defined.

The concept of 'mental illness' also requires a closer examination. Of course the kinds of phenomena under discussion are not illnesses like infectious diseases, and to this extent Szasz and those who think like him are correct. Does this mean that a disease model of mental abnormality is definitely wrong or inappropriate? This all depends upon what is considered to be a disease model. A little thought makes it very clear that medicine uses a wide range of models to explain physical disease and it is therefore impossible to settle on a single 'medical model'. The infectious diseases model is just one of many, and the particular disease models underlying medical accounts of closed head injury, diabetes, cancer of the lung and spina bifida are all different from one another and not the same as the infectious diseases model.

Medicine basically deals in explanations of abnormality that operate on anatomical, physiological or biochemical levels. When considered in this light it is difficult to divorce psychological abnormalities entirely from medical approaches to understanding them. Even a disturbance that is clearly best defined in psychological terms, like a phobia or anxiety state, which probably has no organic cause, does have physiological and biochemical manifestations (e.g. Gray, 1982). In attempting to give a full account of such phenomena it is therefore sensible to look at these levels of explanation as well as dealing with the psychological and social aspects. It is just not possible to ignore explanations at the 'medical' level even though these may not be fundamental in any given case.

To summarize, the position adopted here is that any complete account of abnormal behaviour needs to take into account explanations at levels other than the purely psychological. It must be recognized that psychological abnormalities do have social aspects on the one hand just as they have physiological and biochemical aspects on the other. The general approach which contrasts the 'medical model' on one side with explanations in terms of social processes, such as labelling, on the other, is really drawing a false antithesis as though these things were necessarily incompatible. Factors at a number of different levels may be important and the extent to which they are significant or offer a causal mechanism in any given context is a matter for empirical investigation rather than ideological argument.

3 Description and Classification of Depression

In this and the chapters that immediately follow it is intended to look at a number of the basic questions in abnormal psychology which were outlined in the first chapter. In doing so, depression will be used as the major example although from time to time some reference will be made to other disorders. Another point briefly made in Chapter 1 also bears repetition. The discussion will focus on fundamental questions and ways of resolving them rather than concentrating on giving a comprehensive account of depression. In passing, it is expected that a good coverage of the significant work on depression will be achieved. However, since the main emphasis is on the kinds of question that arise and the possible ways in which they might be answered, this means that the particular details selected for discussion and the relative importance that is attached to them may depart a little from what might otherwise be the case if the basic aim had been the typical and rather more straightforward one of providing a comprehensive examination of depression.

Immediately the question arises as to what is meant by the term 'depression'. It is a term that can be used in a number of different ways even within the sense of referring to a mood state rather than to, say, a meteorological phenomenon. It is possible to delineate at least three uses of 'depression'. The first is its everyday use to indicate the lower end of the normal variation in mood. Thus the worker faced with a tedious and boring job may claim to feel depressed on a Monday morning. Here there is no implication that there is anything abnormal in this variation of mood. It is a simple fact of life that we all have things that make us happy and experiences that push us in the opposite direction.

A second usage is that of 'depression' as a symptom. In this case it is assumed that there is a lowering of mood that has no real environmental precipitant or which is in excess of what might be considered a normal response to a precipitant if one is present. Depression as a symptom is encountered in a wide range of disorders, like Parkinson's disease and obsessional neurosis, where it is part of another clinical syndrome rather than an alleged disorder on its own.

The dominant use of the term 'depression' in psychopathology is to refer to alleged clinical syndromes or disorders of which lowered mood is the main, but by no means the only feature. It is in this sense that depression is now being used as a major example in this book. In taking it further it is easiest to begin by describing the conventional clinical picture of depression, assuming for the moment that it is an identifiable syndrome.

The clinical picture

The classic features of depression are described in the psychiatric textbooks. The reader may benefit from perusing the account of depression or 'affective disorders' given in one of the major psychiatric texts such as Slater and Roth (1973). Such a source will give the traditional psychiatric picture of depression together with some account of other aspects, like epidemiology and biochemistry, which are not covered in any detail in this book.

The main feature of depression is of course a markedly lowered mood, although this is not always the patient's major complaint on presentation. This lowered mood is expressed in the way the person talks, the way that he moves and holds himself, and his general demeanour. Activity level is usually reduced but so-called 'agitated depression' can also occur in which the patient may be overactive, continually walking up and down, with wringing of hands and other signs of distress.

Thought content is gloomy and morbid. Everyday events are often interpreted as indicating the individual's incompetence or inadequacy. For example, the clerk whose boss is not his usual cheerful self may interpret this as a reaction to his poor performance despite the presence of alternative explanations which, under the circumstances, others would regard as much more plausible (e.g. the fact that the boss's marriage is apparently on the verge of breaking up). In extreme cases there are suicidal ideas, with a real risk of these being put into effect. Sometimes there can even be frank delusions. Depressive delusions are characterized by being morbid and associated with guilt. The schizophrenic may believe that he is being persecuted; the depressive feels that he is getting the just punishment for the dreadful sins that he has committed.

Sleep is typically disturbed, with patients waking early and being unable to get off to sleep again. However, the pattern can be the reverse with a difficulty in getting off to sleep in the first place. Little response is achieved by things that would normally have aroused interest, the appetite for food and libido are usually lowered; almost paradoxically, some people overeat when depressed. Anxiety can also be a prominent feature of some depressions.

Depression is a disorder that often occurs and then shows good remission after a while even with no special therapeutic intervention. In those who have experienced one episode of depression there is an appreciable chance that it will recur. Sometimes it shows a course where it alternates with bouts of mania or hypomania. Most people who have attacks of depression never become hypomanic, but the vast majority of these who become hypomanic also get periods of depression. Because of this relationship between depression and mania, some description of mania is also required.

Mania

In many ways the picture is the reverse of depression. Mood tends to be elated or euphoric and it is quite typical for those affected to claim that they have never felt better in their life. There is considerable overactivity, with the person rushing hither and thither, passing from one activity to another and not finishing one thing before starting another. This overactivity can be of such a degree that little or no sleep is taken and it can result in a state of complete physical exhaustion.

There can also be an incessant flow of speech. This is often referred to in the psychiatric textbooks as 'pressure of speech' because there is the impression that the production of speech just cannot keep up with the flow of ideas that lie behind it. Thought processes seem to be disturbed in that conversation jumps from one topic to another, sometimes with little rational link as far as the listener is concerned.

The patient with mania or hypomania is impossible to live with yet raises problems of management since, unlike the individual in a state of depression, he does not think that anything is wrong. In fact from his point of view things are quite the reverse and he does not see the basis for everyone else's concern. Full-blown mania is quite obvious and clearly represents an abnormal state. The lesser degrees (i.e. hypomania) can also lead to real difficulties. Because the individual's judgement is impaired he may do silly things such as entering into extensive financial commitments that he cannot possibly manage to honour in pursuit of some hare-brained idea. For these reasons, manic patients are often compulsorily admitted to psychiatric hospitals.

Classification of affective disorders

The affective disorders, and particularly depression, illustrate more clearly than most other psychiatric conditions a number of basic issues involved in classification. Firstly, is it possible to ask whether it is really appropriate to delineate a group of people who can be regarded as having depression? Can people with depression be clearly distinguished from those who have no mental abnormality and can depression be reliably distinguished from other alleged mental disorders? If these questions can be answered in the affirmative then a second set can be examined. These relate to whether depression is a unitary phenomenon as opposed to there being two or more different types of depression.

The kind of evidence very briefly reviewed in Chapter 2, in discussing the psychiatric classification system in general, indicated that depression could be identified with a good degree of reliability. Studies particularly looking at the identification of affective disorder when using clearly defined operational criteria have produced fairly impressive levels of reliability (Murphy *et al.*, 1974; Faverilli and Poli, 1982). Whilst good reliability in differentiating depression is an essential point, there is no guarantee that what is reliably differentiated is of any real significance. To take an analogous situation, it may be possible to classify people as having blue or brown eyes with considerable accuracy. This does not prove that the individuals concerned have been separated into groups that bear any useful relation to anything else. To show that the concept of depression is valid it is additionally necessary to show that the category meaningfully relates to other factors that might be of interest. In the case of psychiatric disorders this means showing that the kinds of explanation and treatment that apply to depression are different from those applying to other types of disorder.

It is difficult to attempt to deal with this further point at this stage because to do so would presume much of the evidence that is covered in later chapters. The assumption for the moment is that the concept of depression does have sufficient validity to make it meaningful to use it as a central concept. For example, the kinds of models of depression described in Chapter 6 have not been found useful in attempts to explain schizophrenia or the many forms of neurotic disorder.

The subclassification of depression

Whilst psychiatrists have generally accepted that depression is a separate disorder, there have been considerable disputes about whether it constitutes a single disorder or is best subdivided into different types. The most common view is that there is more than one kind of depression and the alternative viewpoints have been conceived as a set of dichotomies (endogenous versus reactive, unipolar versus bipolar, etc.). Despite this there has always been a significant minority view to the effect that the various manifestations of depression form a continuum and do not reflect entities. Lewis (1938), in a classic paper, suggested that the alleged different forms 'are nothing more than attempts to distinguish between acute and chronic, mild and severe; and where two categories only are presented, the one – manic depressive – gives the characteristics of acute severe depression, the other of chronic mild depression'. Whatever view may be taken on the basis of evidence available today, it is still difficult to refute Lewis's position categorically although many authorities would feel that the balance of evidence runs against him.

In fact a number of different subclassifications have been suggested and many of these are outlined below.

Endogenous vs. reactive (or exogeneous). This has always been a major distinction and its basis lies in the presumed causal factors. Endogenous depression is considered to be produced by something that has gone wrong within the individual (e.g. genetic predisposition or malfunctioning biochemistry). Reactive (or exogenous) depressions are, as the name implies, presumed to occur as a response to external events.

Psychotic vs. neurotic. Here the distinction is in terms of the clinical features. It is assumed that some depressions have psychotic features like delusions and a quality (as well as extent) of mood change that take them right outside the range of normal experience. Neurotic depression is more like an extension of normal mood changes and is associated with other neurotic features such as anxiety.

Although the assumptions underlying the endogenous vs. reactive distinction are logically distinct from those underlying the psychotic vs. neurotic distinction, the two dichotomies do show considerable overlap in practice. For this reason these two dichotomies will not be kept as separate as they otherwise might be when the evidence for them is considered later.

Unipolar vs. bipolar. This distinction is based on the long-term course of the disorder. To a considerable degree it cuts across the two dichotomies already described. Some people with depression have a clinical history which includes episodes of hypomania interspersed between periods of depression. (Naturally, the afflicted individual is not either depressed or hypomanic all the time and long periods of relatively normal mood levels may occur between the periods of abnormality.) Such disorders are often now described as bipolar disorders. Other individuals just experience bouts of depression with no indication of hypomania and these are regarded as having unipolar disorders.

One problem with this subclassification is that patients have to be followed for some time before they can be safely categorized. A person who has one hypomanic and one depressive episode in either order is obviously bipolar. It is usually considered necessary to wait until an individual has had three or more episodes of depression with no indication of hypomanic swings before the label 'unipolar' can be applied reliably. Since many people with affective disorders have several episodes but with long periods of relatively normal mood levels in between, the classification of unipolar or bipolar can usually be made eventually. However there are people who only appear to have a single bout of clinically significant depression and these cannot be satisfactorily described as unipolar or bipolar. Cases with only hypomanic episodes are very rare.

Other distinctions. Other subclassifications have been developed and are desribed by Andreasen (1982), but these are of less concern in the present context. One of these is the distinction between primary and secondary depression (e.g. Woodruff *et al.*, 1967). Primary depression is a depressive syndrome occurring in a person who has no history of any other psychiatric disorder. If another psychiatric syndrome has occurred previously then the depression is regarded as secondary. The main purpose of this distinction is to take out all patients whose depression might be the accompaniment or consequence of something else. In these terms our present concern is mainly with primary depression.

Winokur *et al.* (1971) have presented another subdivision which is related to age at onset. It has been noted by Winokur's group that patients whose onset of depression occurred before 40 years of age differed in certain respects from those whose first depressive episode became manifest later in life (see also Winokur, 1979). The early onset group contained more females. Male relatives of depressed females in this early onset group had a raised prevalence of antisocial behaviour and alcoholism, whilst female relatives had an increased tendency to experience depression. The implication from this is that there is a familial or genetically transmitted disorder that tends to manifest itself as depression in females but in antisocial behaviour and alcoholism in males.

Winokur's group defines as 'pure depression' the disorder found in males over 40 years who also had a family history of affective disorders. The predominantly female group with onset before 40 years of age is then described as 'depression spectrum disorder'. Whilst these two categories of 'pure depression' and 'depression spectrum disorder' account for a good proportion of the people who develop affective disorders, they say nothing about women with a late onset, men who have a family history of antisocial behaviour and alcoholism or people who have no family history of psychiatric disorder at all. To cope with these, another category of 'non-familial depression' was introduced. Andreasen and Winokur (1979) then combined this classification system with others to form a complex hierarchical model. This divides affective disorders initially into primary and secondary groups, with the primary group being further subdivided into bipolar and unipolar disorders. The distinctions between depression spectrum, pure depression and non-familial then apply to the unipolar group.

This classification system developed by Winokur's group is interesting in that it is based on a systematic set of familial and genetic studies. It will not be specifically examined in the following sections of this chapter but a good idea of the basic evidence on which it is based can be obtained from the cited references.

Evidence relating to subclassifications

The possible subclassifications of depression have attracted considerable debate and a large number of empirical investigations. This is especially so for the distinctions between endogenous and reactive depressions (which as we have seen overlap considerably with the psychotic/neurotic distinction). The traditional psychiatric approach to resolving this question is to select two well-defined groups with one containing, say, clear cases of alleged endogenous depression and the other clear cases of reactive depression. The two are then compared on a particular variable, such as response to electroconvulsive therapy (ECT), and if they differ with respect to this variable it is then assumed that the classificatory distinction is justified.

The logical flaw in this procedure is that it is based on looking at the extremes and it does not allow for the possibility that an unbiased series of depressed patients might contain every gradation from endogenous to reactive. It could then be that the variable chosen for examination, like response to ECT, is more manifest at one end of the spectrum than the other. Studies of this kind cannot therefore prove the existence of two types of depression in the absence of something further. A simple example can make this point very clear. A visitor from another planet anxious to make a catalogue of all the different life forms on earth whose experience of dogs is restricted to St Bernards and chihuahuas could readily be forgiven for listing these as very different species. Only when seen against the vast panorama of canine variation is it possible to view these two very different breeds as part of the same family of 'dogs'.

One way to strengthen the argument from extreme groups would be to try to establish what neuropsychologists describe as a 'double dissociation'. If features can be found that are associated with one type of depression and not the other (e.g. a good response to ECT), and yet other features are found which go in the reverse direction (e.g. showing a better response to another form of treatment in the group not most susceptible to ECT), then this considerably strengthens the grounds for regarding the two subtypes as being really different and not just the extremes of a single distribution. Unfortunately studies of this kind have generally not been done.

A number of other methodological points have been made by Ni Bhrolchain (1979). She points out that studies tend to have been carried out on hospital samples and that this could bias the results since only a small proportion of those who develop depression actually get admitted to hospital. In addition, she argues that the type of variable that is fed into any analysis needs to be considered much more carefully. Often studies aiming to discriminate between two types of depression will use symptoms, possible aetiological factors (e.g. whether there is an obvious environmental precipitant) and response to treatment. This assumes that there is a one-to-one relationship between aetiology and clinical symptomatology and between symptomatology and treatment. In particular she elaborates on the possible relationships between aetiological factors and clinical symptomatology, demonstrating that the relationship may not be such that different aetiologies lead to different symptoms. If this is the case, it becomes important to separate out the different types of variable and not to confound possible aetiological variables with clinical features.

The studies published so far generally fail to meet the kind of rigorous methodological requirements just described. Many of these are summarized in Andreasen (1982). A number of studies have given results consistent with the notion that there is some basis to the distinction between endogenous and reactive depression. For example, endogenous depressives appear to have a good response to antidepressant medication (Rao and Coppen, 1979) and to ECT (Carney and Sheffield, 1972). Endogenous depression is also associated with good long-term outcome (Paykel et al., 1974).

The difficulty is that most of these studies could be explained in other ways without too much difficulty. If the sole difference between endogenous and reactive is one of severity then the 'endogenous' group, being more severe, has more room to improve with treatment and so appears to respond better. If Lewis (1938) is also correct in relating this distinction to chronicity as well then the 'endogenous' depressions, being the severe but acute cases, might be expected to have a better outcome than the more chronic 'reactive' depressions. In addition, there are other group comparison studies that have given negative results. For example, Ni Bhrolchain et al. (1979) compared groups of alleged psychotic and neurotic depressions based on a discriminant function analysis of symptoms and concluded that the only difference was one of severity.

An alternative approach to the subclassification of depression has been by the use of multivariate techniques. The problem in discussing studies based on multivariate analyses lies in the fact that they rely on complex statistical models and it is impossible to provide a discussion that is entirely adequate without going into technicalities which go beyond the reader's presumed (and possibly the authors' actual!) level of statistical sophistication. The following account which attempts to avoid anything but the simplest of statistical notions therefore runs the risk of some distortion.

What can be said with confidence is that the use of multivariate statistical procedures in the field of diagnostic classification is shrouded in controversy. Various allegedly competent authorities simply do not agree on what is the most appropriate form of analysis, whether the data fed into the analyses conform to the assumptions of the statistical models, and what the results all mean. The account given here cannot reflect all the differing points of view which inevitably lays it open to the charge of being biased.

One of the clearest and least technical discussions of the various multivariate methods has been provided by Maxwell (1971). The reader who wishes to follow the statistical argument further might be well advised to begin with this paper. As might be expected after this statement, the present authors have been strongly influenced by Maxwell's views.

One of the most commonly used techniques, or family of techniques, is factor analysis. (Here this term is being used in a generic sense to include such things as principal components analysis.) In essence the question this procedure tries to answer is how many 'dimensions' are needed to describe the data? Just as it takes two dimensions in space to describe figures like a square or a triangle, so a factor analysis of the different features associated with depression might suggest that these features can be subsumed into two superordinate dimensions (or 'factors') which might be labelled, say, severity of mood change and psychomotor features (agitation as opposed to retardation). It is important to note that the presence of two factors or dimensions does not mean that there are two types of depressed patient (such as are implied by the endogenous vs. reactive distinction). Rectangles of different sizes still need to be described in two spatial dimensions as do triangles and pentagons. Knowing that we need two dimensions to describe shapes does not tell us whether all the shapes being considered in a given set are essentially of the same type (e.g. all rectangles of different sizes) or whether there is a mixture of different *types* of shapes including rectangles, triangles and circles. It is this latter type of question that is of concern in searching for evidence for different types of depression.

There is one possible way in which factor analysis techniques (in practice usually principal components analysis) could yield evidence of different types. Each factor (or dimension) produced by the analysis consists of a set of 'weightings' which are numbers between +1 and −1 which indicate the degree to which each of the original measures fed into the analysis contributes to this factor. For each subject the data from the original measures can be combined using these factor weightings to give a subject score on each factor. The distribution of these scores on the factors derived from each subject can then be examined. Because of the nature of the statistical model this distribution of scores is almost always normal, and where it deviates significantly from normal this usually indicates that the statistical assumptions on which the model is based have been violated. The results of the analysis are then invalid.

It is possible to get a bimodal distribution of factor scores. Such a bimodal distribution has been looked for by Kendell (1968), amongst others, and it could be that such a bimodal distribution is legitimate (in the sense of not being due to a violation of the statistical assumptions) and therefore reflects two types of depression. According to Maxwell (1971), by far the most likely cause of a bimodal distribution is a violation of the assumptions and this is made much more probable by the often unsatisfactory nature of the clinically derived data that are fed into the analysis in the first place.

Because factor analysis starts from the results of applying a number of measures to a large group of subjects and deriving a correlation matrix based on the intercorrelation of each possible pair of measures, it obviously, as a minimum requirement, depends upon the same assumptions as the product moment correlation coefficient. Scores on the measures are expected to be normally distributed. In clinical studies, various features relating to subjects are often listed as present or absent. At best they will be rated on a four- or five-point scale. It is possible to derive indices of correlation from data of this type which can be legitimately used as the basis for factor analyses. However, other technical problems arise (Maxwell, 1971) and it would be highly unlikely that the typical clinically based study would cope with these entirely satisfactorily.

To summarize, factor analytic techniques basically deal with the question as to whether it is possible for symptoms or other features to be reduced to a smaller number of more basic dimensions. These techniques cannot directly answer the question of immediate concern which is whether there are different types of depression. This issue can only be tackled by looking for a bimodal distribution of scores on one of the factors. According to Maxwell (1971), the most likely interpretation of a bimodal distribution is that there has been a violation of the assumptions on which factor analysis is based, thus making it very difficult to derive any sensible conclusions. The considerable technical problems surrounding factor analysis mean that it is difficult to derive any reasonable consensus of opinion with regard to interpreting the results of these studies.

Several factor analytic studies have yielded a factor which corresponds more or less to a combination of features commonly associated with endogenous depression. Seven such studies are reviewed by Mendels and Cochrane (1968). The features associated most strongly with the endogenous factor include such things as severity, retardation, visceral symptoms, absence of precipitating stress, weight loss, self-reproach or guilt, and suicidal ideation. A number of more recent investigations have also found evidence of a factor corresponding to endogenous features (Kiloh *et al.*, 1972; Paykel, 1971). Although a factor corresponding to endogenous depression does often emerge, there is much less agreement as to the nature of other factors, particularly one that could correspond to reactive or neurotic depression. Kiloh *et al.* (1972) suggest that this might be because neurotic depression is often diagnosed by exclusion in that it is depression but without endogenous features. Neurotic depression may therefore be a heterogenous subgroup that possibly needs further differentiation. In another factor analytic study, Carney *et al.* (1965) found indications of a bimodal distribution of scores on a relevant factor.

There have also been important investigations that have failed to obtain findings matching the endogenous/reactive distinction. In a major study, Kendell (1968) looked for a bimodal distribution of scores on a bipolar psychotic/neurotic factor. Kendell (1976) acknowledges that the data fed into his first analysis might have been of less than adequate reliability but claims that a further factor analytic study based on data from careful structured interviews is not so readily open to such a criticism (Kendell and Gourlay, 1970). The findings were again negative.

A rather different position has been advanced by Eysenck (1970), who is convinced that the factor analytic studies have demonstrated that two dimensions are necessary to account for the variation in symptomatology. These he equates with the psychoticism and neuroticism of his own personality theory. In effect he rejects the notion of a typology as implied by the endogenous/reactive distinction and opts for a dimensional model. As Kendell (1976) indicates, even if it is agreed that Eysenck is correct in advocating a dimensional model of depression rather than a typology, it is hardly clear that two is the right number of dimensions. The nature of at least one of these dimensions is also rather more obscure than Eysenck would allow.

Even if studies like those of Kendell and Gourlay (1970) are discounted and it is agreed that there is some degree of consistency in the factor analytic studies, they are still of dubious value in relation to the endogenous/reactive distinction. Some consensus can be claimed for an endogenous factor but the nature of the other is obscure. Much more serious is the point that there are at the very least real grounds for doubting the suitability of the technique for answering the question under discussion.

If factor analysis is of dubious value in this context, are there other multivariate techniques that might be of use? The family of techniques with the potential to reveal different types of depressed patient, such as might correspond to the endogenous/reactive distinction, is that referred to as cluster analysis. Cluster analysis is again described by Maxwell (1971). The starting point is also the subject's status on a number of different variables or features. Indices of similarity between different pairs of subjects are then derived and individuals sorted into groups in terms of some predetermined criterion. Most forms of cluster analysis are non-parametric and therefore it is legitimate to use data that violate the assumptions of normality on which factor analytic techniques are based.

Everitt (1972) has provided a more extensive discussion of cluster analysis which avoids the deeper statistical technicalities. As he indicates, there are many unresolved problems in cluster analysis. In order to derive clusters or groups it is necessary to have good criteria for what constitutes a 'group' in the context of these procedures. If satisfactory criteria do exist, they have proved very elusive to determine and the criteria actually in use are far from ideal. It is also difficult to resolve the question as to how many groups should be extracted. Everitt indicates that if data from a single well-established group are fed into a cluster analysis then the technique will happily produce a set of pseudo-groups. Given these problems it is hardly surprising that several different forms of cluster analysis exist and that when the same data is fed into different procedures the results are often far from consistent. Everitt's own suggestion for getting out of this impasse is only to rely on the results of cluster analyses when a number of different forms of analysis give broadly similar results. In further correspondence relating to Everitt's paper, Paykel (1972) argues that such techniques are better regarded as hypothesis-generating than hypothesis-testing. Paykel may have a point but the problem is that most investigators are searching for a means to test the validity of pre-existing hypotheses about the subclassification of depression. Only rarely are they trying to derive new hypotheses.

Only a small number of investigators in this field have actually used cluster analysis. Paykel (1971) arrived at four categories which he identified as psychotic depressives, hostile depressives, anxious depressives and young depressives with personality disorder. Subjects falling in the hostile group and those with personality disorder tended to be young and to have milder degrees of mood disturbance. The other two groups were older with more severe depression.

Andreasen et al. (1980) arrived at three clusters in an analysis based on seventy-one items of information derived from structured interviews applied to a substantial sample of depressed patients. One of their clusters showed some correspondence with the classical concept of endogenous depression and another approximated to a neurotic or reactive group. Andreasen et al.'s third cluster consisted of subjects with milder depressions that was reasonably consistent with the group identified by Paykel (1971) as young depressives with personality disorders.

Yet another study by Pilovsky et al. (1969) also arrived at three groups one of which was considered to correspond to endogenous depression. Of the other two groups one was clearly non-depressive, which is not surprising since a substantial minority of the subjects used were not originally considered to have depression. The final group were depressed but with very mixed pictures.

Given the considerable practical and methodological problems involved, it is difficult to arrive at firm conclusions. With regard to the endogenous versus reactive distinction, a number of studies of different kinds do give some support to the notion of endogenous depression although it must also be acknowledged that there are equally well conducted investigations that give negative results. Even if the concept of endogenous depression is accepted, the appropriate basis for subclassifying those depressions that remain once the endogenous cases have been taken out remains obscure. At best only one half of the endogenous/reactive distinction is validated.

Unipolar vs. bipolar depression. At first sight it might seem that there is a clear basis for this distinction in that bipolar cases have one clear feature (hypomanic swings) that readily differentiates them from unipolar cases. A little further thought shows that the distinction need not be as unequivocal as it appears at first sight. It could be that both unipolar and bipolar disorders represent cases where there are cyclical changes in mood with both periods of depression and periods of relatively elevated mood. All that may distinguish the unipolar cases is that their upswings are not quite high enough to take them beyond what is the normally acceptable range of variation in mood. In this way unipolar and bipolar disorders are not separate subtypes but manifestations of the same thing, with bipolar cases possibly having wider-ranging mood swings which puts their highest mood level into the hypomanic range.

The exact definition of putative bipolar and unipolar cases can also cause difficulty and the issue is discussed by Perris (1982). An individual who has been treated for both depressive and hypomanic episodes is no problem and is readily classified as bipolar. Cases with clear episodes of depression are not so easy to categorize because they could produce a hypomanic episode some time in the future. The more depressive episodes there have been without any sign of hypomania, the less likely the latter becomes. Perris has himself used the criterion of three depressive episodes without any evidence of hypomania for unipolar depression, but other researchers have adopted different criteria. In any case there is also the problem that certain cases are unclassifiable by this system. These are the cases with only a single depressive episode.

One way in which attempts have been made to distinguish between these two types is in terms of genetic linkage. The classic study is that of Perris (1966). Perris looked at the rates for affective disorder in first-degree relatives of probands with either unipolar or bipolar disorders. Although the results did show a little overlap, there was an extremely clear trend towards showing that where an affective disorder was present in relatives it followed the nature (i.e. bipolar or unipolar) of the disorder in the proband. This suggests a clear distinction between the two types of affective disorder which is probably genetic in nature. (The question as to whether results like these really reflect a genetic influence, as opposed to some form of familial social transmission, will be dealt with in the next chapter.)

Perris (1982) reviews a number of other studies looking at the risk of affective disorders in the first-degree relatives of subjects with either unipolar or bipolar disorders. When tabulated, the combined results are not as straightforward as those from the Perris (1966) study. The overall risk of an affective disorder of any kind seems reasonably comparable regardless of whether the probands are unipolar or bipolar, with a possible trend to a slightly greater risk for the relatives of bipolar cases. When considered in terms of the nature of the affective disorder in the relative (where such a disorder occurs), the relatives of unipolar probands show a heavy preponderance of unipolar disorders and this confirms the results of Perris (1966).

The picture for the relatives of bipolar cases is more confused.

The risk for bipolar disorders in the relatives of bipolar probands is very much higher than for unipolar probands. Nevertheless it does seem that there is still an appreciable risk of unipolar disorders in the relatives of bipolar cases. In some studies this is even greater than the risk for bipolar disorders.

Aggregating the results of a number of studies gives some support for the separation between unipolar and bipolar disorders, but this is far from perfect. Perris (1982) argues that there are other reasons why the confusion should arise in the case of bipolar probands. One of these is that in classifying a relative known to have had an affective disorder as bipolar or unipolar some relatives will have had only one or two recorded depressive episodes. Such cases are liable to be classed as unipolar but will carry a certain risk of developing a later hypomanic episode. Thus true bipolar cases can get mis-classified as unipolar whilst the reverse error is very much less likely. Factors like this could work to obscure the trends in the data, but there is no means of judging whether they could account for most of the allegedly unipolar relatives of bipolar probands. In fact, given the relatively low proportion of the total number of affective disorders usually judged to be bipolar, it is unlikely that a very large proportion of the unipolar relatives or of bipolar probands could be explained away by this kind of mechanism. It seems best to conclude that studies of this kind suggest some degree of support for the distinction between unipolar and bipolar disorders, but the discrimination is certainly not perfect.

Bipolar and unipolar disorders can also be distinguished in terms of the age of onset of the first episode. Again the studies are reviewed by Perris (1982) and there is a fairly consistent trend for bipolar cases to have their first episode of affective disorder in early adult life (i.e. usually with a median age in the twenties). First episodes of unipolar disorders are typically fifteen to twenty years later. This raises an important point with regard to the kinds of study of risk in relatives described immediately above. It could be that the true separation in these family studies is between early and late onset disorders. It could then be that there is some other factor that predisposes early onset cases towards having hypomanic episodes. (The age factor here could also be related to Winokur's distinction between 'pure depression' and 'depression spectrum disorder' – see page 30.)

Response to treatment is another factor that might be used to discriminate between the two alternative forms. Lithium (in the form of lithium carbonate) has been used quite extensively with patients who have affective disorders. Mendels (1976) reviewed the then existing published studies of the effects of this drug. In general the findings indicate that a high proportion of bipolars and only a relatively small proportion of unipolars respond favourably.

More psychological variables have been used in an attempt to distinguish the two types of affective disorder. In at least two types of study, fairly consistent results have been obtained. Binney and Murphy (1973) looked at psychomotor activity in depressed unipolar subjects and in bipolar subjects during a depressive episode. Bipolar cases when depressed seemed to exhibit a prolonged period of psychomotor retardation whereas agitation was more common in the unipolar cases. Similar results have been obtained by others. For example, Kupfer et al. (1974) made telemetric recordings of activity in drug-free unipolar and bipolar cases (the latter in a depressive phase). During waking hours the unipolar cases showed about twice as much activity as the bipolar subjects.

Sleep patterns also seem to differ with regard to these two types of subject. Bipolar subjects in a depressive phase tend towards hypersomnia (i.e. sleeping more than eight hours per night) whilst unipolar depressives tend towards hyposomnia. Again this is a finding that emerges with some consistency (see Detre et al., 1972; Kupfer et al., 1972). Other findings relevant to the unipolar/bipolar distinction have been reviewed by Depue and Monroe (1978).

Final comment on the subclassification of depression

When the evidence is considered overall it still remains a defensible position to opt for the null hypothesis and claim that there is no overwhelming evidence in favour of subdividing depression into different types. The best support comes for the distinction between bipolar and unipolar cases, and here the evidence is probably good enough to support Depue and Monroe's (1978) conclusion to the effect that this distinction can be used as a reasonable working hypothesis. The position with regard to the endogenous/reactive distinction remains confused, with far too much contradictory evidence for comfort.

4 Epidemiology, Genetics and Biochemistry

In a sense this chapter deals with the more specifically medical aspects of depression. As was explained in Chapter 2, there are very good reasons for not seeing mental disorders as being purely medical or purely social or even purely psychological phenomena. Explanations at different levels are not necessarily mutually exclusive and it is not possible to appreciate fully the extent or the limitations of psychological approaches to a problem of this nature without setting these in the perspective of the medical and social aspects. It is therefore necessary to take some cognisance of such things as epidemiology, genetics and biochemistry.

As will become clear, epidemiology is one place in which the medical and social sciences do meet. It will be seen that epidemiological evidence about depression both points to questions that require further investigation and can also contribute to the resolution of theoretical issues about the causation of depression (see Chapter 6). Genetics and biochemistry will be considered in rather less detail although they are both essential to providing a complete picture of depression.

Epidemiology

An important question in relation to any problems or difficulty to which people may be prone is its frequency of occurrence. In medical circles this comes under the heading of 'epidemiology'. In fact, although the term may seem a little exotic, the methodological aspects of epidemiology are very similar to those that arise in the social sciences with respect to such things as social surveys. In this sense epidemiology can be seen not as a medical discipline but as part of a family of methods of social investigation that happens to be concerned with diseases or related conditions rather than with such things as voting patterns or attitudes to immigration. A brief, readable and straightforward guide to epidemiology has been provided by Rose and Barker (1979). Anyone looking for a fuller account of the principles of epidemiology than can be offered here would be well advised to start with this admirable little book.

Epidemiologists usually deal in 'rates' which express the frequency of occurrence of a particular state or event as a function of the population at risk for this state or event. Thus the birth rate of 13.48 per 1000 in 1980 for the UK represents the proportion of live births in that year as a function of the total population. It should also be noted that rates typically apply for a period of time (although this need not always be the case) and the birth rate just cited refers to the period of a year.

There are two particular kinds of rate of common concern. One of these is the incidence or inception rate. This gives the proportion of new cases arising in a given population per unit length of time (usually a year). Studies of incidence can be difficult to carry out and because incidence rates are often very low may require the study of very large populations. For these reasons the most commonly cited rates are typically not those of incidence but prevalence.

Prevalence is the proportion of a given population having the condition or characteristic of interest at any one time. Prevalence rates are always bigger than incidence rates because they include all who have the condition and not just those who present as new cases who make up the incidence rate. Prevalence rates can refer to a single point in time (so-called point prevalence) or can refer to anyone in the stipulated population that might have the condition during a set time period (period prevalence). Although easier to conceptualize, point prevalence rates are often less accurate than period prevalences and can seriously underestimate the true situation. Rose and Barker (1979) describe a study of angina in middle-aged men where the point prevalence was 4 per cent. Extending the investigation over a five-year period covering the same population gave a period prevalence of 10 per cent. The reason for this large difference was not that a further 6 per cent developed angina over the five years of the study. It was largely due to the fact that the symptoms of a chronic condition like angina can fluctuate considerably and a single application of the questionnaire encountered a large number of people who had had symptoms, and would again experience symptoms in the future, but who were symptom-free at the critical time. Even though the questionnaire was apparently designed to ask if respondents had experienced the critical symptoms in the past, it failed to detect many such cases with a single administration. Another limitation of point prevalence, particularly in relation to some conditions, is that it is sensitive to short-term fluctuations in prevalence.

As explained above, incidence rates are often fairly low and always less than the prevalence. An important point to note is that in conditions that tend to run a long, chronic course, like some of the major psychiatric disorders, a relatively low incidence can slowly accumulate a large number of cases and so result in an appreciable prevalence. There are a number of problems surrounding the collection of epidemiological data and their interpretation. These are outlined by Rose and Barker (1979). Many of these become quite obvious given a little thought and a basic knowledge of the principles of experimental design. Only two will receive any further attention here.

One of the problems that arises concerns the definition of the 'population at risk' and one of the commonest errors in attempting to utilize epidemiological data lies in confusing the nature of the population involved. Rates can be given for the population as a whole and these are known as 'crude rates'. Often it is more appropriate and sensible to subdivide the population. Thus it can be less informative in predicting, say, the likely need for maternity beds to give the birth rates as the figure per 1000 of the population as a whole rather than as the figure per 1000 women within a certain age range related to the childbearing years. Other conditions, e.g. cancer of the prostate or of the uterus, have even less meaning when expressed as rates for the population as a whole.

A crucial issue in epidemiology concerns the definition of a 'case'. If a population is being surveyed to determine the prevalence of something like depression then there is a need to have some reliable means of determining just who has depression and who does not. Ideally such a study may wish to cast its net wide enough to include all those who might be considered as having a clinically significant degree of depression, but not so all-inclusive as to register those who are just experiencing the kinds of mood fluctuation that might be considered part of everyday normal life. Various fairly reliable means of identifying the major psychiatric disorders havé now been established, such as the Present State Examination (Wing *et al.*, 1974) and the Research Diagnostic Criteria (Spitzer *et al.*, 1978). Having widely agreed criteria makes things easier, but clearly the rates obtained in any epidemiological study will be appreciably influenced by the kind of criteria that are used. This is especially so with psychiatric disorders where there is considerable scope for disagreement as to what are the right criteria to use.

Epidemiology of depression

Several authorities have discussed the epidemiology of depression in some detail (e.g. Boyd and Wiessman, 1982; Slater and Roth, 1973). For the major depressive disorders Boyd and Weissman (1982) cite a number of studies which offer estimates of the point prevalence rates. These give a median value of around 2 to 3 per cent for men and 4 to 5 per cent for women, although including milder depressions could increase these figures considerably. Estimated incidence rates are of the order of 100 per 100,000 per year for men, with the corresponding figures for women being more than twice as high.

When rates are examined in relation to other factors there is a very consistent tendency for prevalence and incidence to be higher in women. This will be discussed separately below. Rates also relate to age. In women they reach a peak in the 35 to 45 age range with a possible further tendency to increase with advancing age. Despite the fact that older psychiatric authorities claimed a relationship between the menopause and depression in women, as exemplified by the term 'involutional depression', there is little evidence of an increased risk of depression in the menopausal years. In fact some have even reported that the rate actually falls at this time (e.g. Grad de Alarcon et al., 1975). The relationship with age is less clear in men, but, if anything, the tendency is for the risk of depression to increase with age.

In general, rates for depression are not related to social class. One of the few possible exceptions is, as Brown and Harris (1978) have claimed, that women with children have a higher risk of depression if they come from the working class as compared with middle-class women. The same authors found no such trend for women without children. Despite this, some communities have been claimed to be prone to particularly high or particularly low rates of depression (Slater and Roth, 1973). The parts of Sweden north of the Arctic Circle are alleged to have low rates of depression and high rates of schizophrenia. The reverse pattern occurs in the Hutterite communities in North America (the Hutterites, who tend to live in isolated communities, are a religious group with rather strict puritanical beliefs).

The sex ratio. As already noted, there is an excess of females over males in almost all epidemiological studies that have attempted to look at rates for the two sexes separately. It has also been suggested that there may be certain biases that could produce a spurious excess of women psychiatric patients. For example, doctors (who more often than not tend to be male) may be more prone to detect depression in their female patients. Conversely depression is more likely to go undetected in men. Another possibility is that women are more ready to go to the doctor when they feel distress and to admit to having disordered feelings. The plausibility of biases of this kind in the diagnosis of depression is increased when it is realized that many patients considered to have depression do not actually complain of this as such when they present to the doctor. They may complain of vague physical symptoms and it is then necessary for the doctor to detect that the patient appears to be low in mood and then to elicit the signs and symptoms by further questioning. It is for this reason that people who are quite markedly depressed may emerge from a consultation with a prescription for, say, something to deal with their indigestion, and with their mood state overlooked or merely seen as the consequence of physical discomfort rather than its real cause.

A number of studies have aimed to get at the possibility that the adverse sex ratio for women is merely an artifact of presentation patterns of diagnostic biases (e.g. Byrne, 1981; Weissman and Klerman, 1977). Byrne argued that if there is a bias in recognition or diagnosis then the sex difference should disappear if an objective and standard method of detecting depression is applied to a random sample of the population. Furthermore if the sex difference results from men emphasizing physical symptoms rather than mood changes, then asking separately about physical and psychological features would enable this effect to be revealed.

Byrne (1981) studied a population sample from the city of Canberra in Australia. Each case completed the Zung (1965) scale for depression. This is a reasonably well standardized self-rating scale containing twenty items which covers somatic symptoms often associated with depression (e.g. fatigue and constipation) as well as the more psychological aspects such as low mood. Even with a self-report scale of a fairly objective nature, the proportion of women giving high scores was much greater than for men. Analysis of the types of symptom scored positively did not reveal any sex differences, thus failing to confirm the hypothesis that men might be less willing to complain about changes in feelings. Weissman and

Klerman (1977) similarly failed to find evidence of biasing effects in the diagnosis of depression that would artificially increase the rate for women.

It thus seems likely that the higher risk of depression in women is not the consequence of artifacts of the kind just encountered. This does not mean that women are necessarily more prone to depression than men because of something inherent in their biological make-up, although this does remain a possibility. It could be that women have no greater inbuilt tendency to depression than men but that they are more likely to encounter the kinds of adverse social circumstances that can precipitate or even cause depression (see Chapter 7 for a discussion of the effects of adverse events on depression).

Suicide. This is a phenomenon that will not be discussed in any detail but needs to be mentioned because of its association with depression (see also Hankoff, 1982). In Britain about ten people per 100,000 commit suicide each year. It is related to depression in that there is a higher risk of suicide in people with depression and that retrospective studies suggest that many who commit suicide are depressed at the time.

In discussing suicide it is important to distinguish between true suicide, where there is a definite and determined attempt by the individual to take his own life, and attempted suicide, sometimes known as 'parasuicide'. Attempted suicide is very common and its rate is increasing to such a degree that the typical District General Hospital in Britain will admit several 'overdoses' per week. Only a minority of attempted suicides have any marked psychiatric disorder and they typically occur in circumstances which lead to real doubt as to whether the individual concerned seriously intended to threaten life. For example, the overdose of drugs that is taken (drug overdose being by far the most common method used by attempted suicides) is well below lethal levels, and, unlike the true suicide, the overdose is often taken under such circumstances that it will quickly be discovered by someone else. The individual may even take a token overdose and then telephone for an ambulance immediately afterwards.

Although true suicides and attempted suicides will clearly overlap in that the person who really intends to take his own life may fail or the person intending a token overdose may misjudge the situation and die, the two populations are quite different. As already indicated, males predominate in true suicides whilst many more women make suicide attempts. Suicide is also more prevalent with increasing age and higher socioeconomic status. The reverse is true for attempted suicides. In Britain in recent years there has been a period where the true suicide rate has declined whilst that for attempted suicides has increased. The case for regarding these two things as separate is therefore quite strong.

Genetics

There is general agreement amongst those who have looked for possible genetic factors in depression that there is some form of genetic transmission (see reviews by Nurnberger and Gershon, 1982; Slater and Roth, 1973; Zerbin-Rudin, 1979). It is clear that the relatives of those that suffer depression have an increased risk of becoming depressed themselves and that this risk increases with the closeness of the relationship. That depression runs in families does not of course prove a genetic transmission. It could be that the experience of living in contact with someone who is depressed acts as a predisposition to depression. In other words, families can transmit psychological effects by means of the environments they create as well as through their genes.

In order to show a genetic link it is necessary to look at much more specific data. If there is a genetic link then monozygotic ('identical') twins who have a common genetic endowment should have a high concordance for depression and much higher than dizygotic or fraternal twins who are no more alike genetically than ordinary siblings. All seven of the twin studies cited by Nurnberger and Gershon (1982) found a higher concordance for depression in monozygotic than dizygotic twins.

Possible snags with the twin data are that the concordance for monozygotic twins was far from perfect in most studies (the range being from 33 per cent to 93 per cent). However, less than perfect concordance rates for monozygotic twins are quite compatible with a genetic basis as long as it is acknowledged that heredity is not the sole cause of depression. It can also be argued that identical twins, who look alike, are more likely to be treated similarly than dizygotic twins who are typically no more similar than other siblings. This means that environmental influences operating through the family could then result in a greater concordance for monozygotic twins. The crucial thing would be to study twins reared apart from an early age, but such cases are difficult to find. Other technical difficulties can arise in research using twins. For example, multiple births are more hazardous than single births and any damage is unlikely to affect both twins equally. This could mean that twins are not quite as comparable as is usually assumed.

An alternative approach which has become more popular in recent years is to look at children adopted early in life. If a familial characteristic, like a tendency to become depressed, is passed on by environmental influences then an adopted child would be more likely to develop depression if one or both of the adoptive parents is susceptible to depression. If the transmission is truly genetic then depression in the adopted child will be more related to depression in the natural parents.

Mendlewicz and Rainer (1977) looked at the adoptive and natural parents of twenty-nine adoptees who had suffered bipolar affective disorders and who had been adopted before the age of 1 year. In comparing the biological and adoptive parents there was no difference in the frequency of psychiatric disorder other than affective disorder. However 31 per cent of the biological parents had experienced affective disorder as opposed to only 12 per cent of the adoptive parents. This is evidence in favour of genetic transmission but, as Zerbin-Rudin (1979) points out, 12 per cent is still a rather high figure for the adoptive parents. This suggests that the mode of transmission from parent to child may not be solely genetic.

In another adoption study, Cadoret (1978) looked at biological parents with affective disorder whose children had been adopted. Of eight such children, three developed unipolar depressive illnesses. In the case of adopted children whose biological parents had either a non-affective psychiatric disorder or no psychiatric disorder at all, only eight from a total sample of 118 developed an affective disorder. This again points in the direction of a genetic influence but the findings are complicated by the fact that there was a raised incidence of psychiatric problems in the adoptive parents of children whose biological parents had been depressed.

The final adoption study has been reported by Von Knorring *et al.* (1983). Their initial sample consisted of 115 adoptees with either affective disorder or 'substance abuse'. They also had a control group of 115 subjects matched with the 115 adoptees. There was a fivefold increase in psychiatric problems amongst the adoptive parents of the adoptees with psychiatric disorder compared with the parents of the control group. This suggests environmental influences but there was also a threefold increase of psychiatric morbidity in the biological mothers of female adoptees, as against the controls. There was no clear effect for males. There was also no appreciable degree of concordance between the particular disorder found in the biological parents and that found in their children. This is not so surprising in view of the two conditions that were selected for examination, since others have claimed a genetic relationship between depression and alcoholism (see Winokur *et al.*, 1969). If this is true, then one would expect a low degree of association between the same disorder across two generations, because the same genotype can be expressed either as depression or alcoholism and there will not be a unique association between the same disorder across two generations.

Von Knorring *et al.* (1983) interpret their data as showing some degree of genetic determination, but the genetic effect is small and much less than that suggested by Mendlewicz and Rainer (1977). The fact that adoptive parents had a high level of psychiatric morbidity indicates a familial relationship mediated by non-genetic means. However, they also raise the important methodological point that the direction of this transmission is not clear. It is tempting to assume that the relationship must occur because abnormal parents induce abnormal behaviour in the children that they rear. This is not necessarily so and it could be that having an abnormal child induces psychological problems in the parents. Alternatively, some form of interactive process might be involved with a combination of vulnerable parents and a vulnerable child acting to the detriment of both.

When all is considered there does appear to be some degree of genetic transmission in depression. It must equally be acknowledged that depression is by no means wholly determined by genetic factors, since the genetic data are not strong enough to suggest that other processes are of only minor importance. Having got this far, two questions remain. These concern the nature of the specified genetic mechanism involved and the possible relationship between genetic and other factors.

At one time, specific genetic models were canvassed for affective disorders. For example, it has been suggested that 'manic-depressive psychosis' (i.e. bipolar disorder) was transmitted by an autosomal dominant gene. The more recent evidence, as reviewed by authorities such as Nurnberger and Gershon (1982) or Zerbin-Rudin (1979), is difficult to match with any particular model.

With regard to the possible relationship between genetic and non-genetic factors, it is possible to enquire about the relative importance of genetic influences. In practice it is extremely difficult to quantify the contribution made by hereditary as opposed to other forms of influence, as the debate concerning the extent to which variations in intelligence can be ascribed to heredity has shown. Even if a figure could sensibly be given, it would be specific to the particular population from which it was derived and any general environmental changes affecting that population could invalidate the figure. In any case, to search for such a figure assumes that genetic and other influences that might affect the incidence of depression operate in a simple additive manner and this assumption may well prove to be unjustified. All that can safely be concluded for the moment is that genetic influences are likely to be partially, but far from totally responsible.

It is possible to look at the relationship between genetic and other factors in another way. It is possible that in producing depression the right kind of genetic endowment is a necessary but not sufficient condition. In other words, people can only develop depression if they possess a certain kind of genetic endowment but other influences are also required before depression becomes manifest. Alternatively, the right set of genes may be a sufficient but not a necessary condition. Here it is assumed that depression can be inherited, and in such cases its occurrence is largely or wholly determined by heredity; however, depression can also be produced by other causal mechanisms and these other mechanisms operate in a good proportion of cases. The data obtained so far do not allow these possibilities to be separated out.

Another possibility, which is at least as plausible as the two just described, is that hereditary influences do not act to produce depression in any direct way. They may act like a catalyst in a chemical reaction to enhance or potentiate the influences that do have a causal effect on depression. Thus the basic causes of depression may be non-genetic (i.e. psychological, biochemical or social) and possessing the right kind of genetic endowment may just make the individual more vulnerable to the effects of these other causal mechanisms. The idea of genetic influences working in this indirect way would be the most congenial from the point of view of trying to fit in genetics with models of depression which implicate psychological or social influences as the basic causes. Nevertheless this does not guarantee that genetic influences actually do operate in this way.

Biochemistry

There is considerable literature on the biochemistry of depression. This is an extremely complex field and only a brief summary of the most prominent current models can be offered. As a preliminary point it should be noted that if it is accepted that there is any genetic influence on depression, of whatever kind, then this can only act by biochemical means. Thus looking for biochemical abnormalities is a corollary of investigating genetic influences. The reverse is of course not true. Biochemical abnormalities can occur without necessarily being produced by genetic means. Finally, it should be noted that biochemical research is intertwined with the pharmacological treatment of depression. Establishing biochemical abnormalities provides a possible rationale for drug treatment. Drugs known to have an antidepressant effect can also give clues as to the biochemistry of depression.

Research into the biochemistry of psychiatric disorders is beset with a number of difficult methodological problems. The biochemical reactions that go on within the brain are very complex, involving long chains of chemical reactions. Not only can these chains interact with one another but it is not equally easy to look at the many different stages within a long chain of reactions. The fact that a metabolite detected in urine or cerebrospinal fluid is lowered could be due to a breakdown in the system at a number of different points.

Gibbons (1968), in a review of the biochemistry of affective disorder, outlines three then-current areas of work. Firstly adrenocortical activity appears to be raised in a proportion of depressed patients, as revealed by raised corticosteroid secretion. According to Gibbons, this change is most likely to be the consequence rather than the cause of depression. Secondly, whilst plasma and cerebrospinal fluid concentrations of sodium and potassium are usually normal in depression, changes have been found in the total body content of water or electrolytes or in their distribution within the body (e.g. an increase in intracellular water and a decrease in extracellular water accompanied by a shift of sodium from one to the other). Again there is some good experimental support for these findings but it is not clear that changes of this type are not merely the consequence of depression. The final area identified by Gibbons (1968) is work based on the hypothesis that depression might be due to a decreased concentration of monoamines at receptor sites in the brain. The three monoamines found in the brain are dopamine (DA), noradrenaline (NA) and 5-hydroxytryptamine (5HT). The evidence implicating monoamines was derived by analogy from investigations on animals.

Approximately a decade and a half after Gibbons's review the field is largely dominated by the amine hypothesis or particular variants of it (Eccleston, 1982; Zis and Goodwin, 1982), although there has been a resurgence of interest in neuroendocrinological changes (Sachar, 1982). There are several lines of evidence that point to the involvement of amines in depression (Eccleston, 1982; Zis and Goodwin, 1982). The use of reserpine in the treatment of hypertension produced depressive disorders in a number of patients, and reserpine is a drug that depletes amines in the brain. Analysis of the cerebrospinal fluid of depressed patients has shown low levels of a metabolite of 5HT, which is one of the three monoamines found in the brain. There is also a relationship between the effects of drugs on the catecholamine system (noradrenergic or dopaminergic) and their effect on mood. Drugs that enhance the output of this system, such as the tricyclic antidepressants among many others, tend to have an antidepressant effect and to precipitate manic features. The reverse is generally found for drugs that depress catecholamine output. Although the general trend is definitely there, it is also the case, as Zis and Goodwin (1982) point out, that the relationship between these drugs and their effect on affective state is by no means a perfect fit.

If the biogenic amines are involved in depression the question then arises as to which of the three is the crucial one? This has proved difficult to answer because the systems associated with all three tend to interact. Eccleston (1982) suggests from his review that the NA system may be involved in mood whilst the DA system is more concerned with psychomotor activity and motivation. These two systems might then be under the inhibitory control of 5HT neurons. Antidepressant drugs might then act directly by increasing activity in the mood or psychomotor activity/drive-related systems, or indirectly by releasing these systems from the inhibitory effects of 5HT.

Finally, it should be noted that there has been a recent growth of interest in the neuroendocrinology of depression. This is related to the use of the dexamethasone suppression test as a possible biological marker for certain forms of depression. Administration of dexamethasone suppresses plasma cortisol levels for some time afterwards. A number of investigators (e.g. Carroll *et al.*, 1976) have shown that there is a rapid release from this depression, especially in subjects with the more endogenous type of depression. This in turn implies overactivity of the hypothalamic-pituitary adrenal axis.

Just why this should be so has not been elucidated. Carroll (1982) states that there is no evidence that this overactivity of the hypothalamic-pituitary adrenal axis is of any aetiological significance. It may well be secondary to other things and Eccleston (1982) suggests that this system is affected because a biogenic amine may normally exert some inhibitory control over it. Carroll's (1982) suggestion is that it could be a consequence of abnormal limbic system functioning.

Looking at the biochemical work as a whole, it does seem to be the case that certain biochemical changes can be identified in a reliable and repeatable way in some kinds of depressed patients. Whether any of the biochemical systems discussed here represents the fundamental biochemical disturbance in depression, assuming that there is such a fundamental disturbance, has yet to be decided. The extent to which the phenomena are the cause or the consequence of depression is also still unknown. What does seem clear is that biochemical changes can produce depressive symptoms in some patients, e.g. those with myxoedema (hypothyroidism), but this does not mean that all depressions are biochemically determined and that biochemical disturbances cannot also be the consequence of depression. Similarly the fact that drugs which can influence appropriate biochemical systems, such as the tricyclic antidepressants, do have a therapeutic effect in depression is by no means firm proof that the ultimate cause of depression is biochemical. Indeed the fact that these changes do not occur in all who suffer depression suggests that even if biochemical factors do play some causal role in depression, and it is quite possible that they may, then they do not provide the whole story.

Pharmacology and physical treatments

It would be quite logical to follow a discussion of the biochemistry of depression with some account of its pharmacology. As it happens, the general issue of treatment and its evaluation will be taken up in Chapter 8 and those that follow, using disorders other than depression to illustrate the main issues. In this very brief section it is intended to give the barest outline of pharmacological and physical treatments of depression for the sake of completeness. Psychological work leading on to psychological forms of treatment of depression will be covered in Chapter 6.

Discussions of the various forms of treatment used for depression can be found in Paykel (1982). The two most effective groups of antidepressant drugs are the tricyclic antidepressants (e.g. Amytriptyline) and the monoamine oxidase inhibitors (e.g. Phenelzine), both of which affect the catecholamine system. In general the tricyclics are usually used as the drugs of first choice because they do not share the potentially dangerous side effects of the monoamine oxidase inhibitors. Lithium salts are also used especially for patients with bipolar disorders. Lithium appears to have a prophylactic effect and is therefore used in people with repeated bouts of affective disturbance. Its main problem is that the therapeutic dose is quite close to the toxic dose and so the use of this drug requires careful monitoring.

Another major medical treatment for depression is electroconvulsive therapy (ECT). Its use has been reviewed by Kiloh (1982) and Berriòs (1983). In essence ECT involves the applying of an electric current across the head in order to induce an artificial epileptiform fit. In practice it is always given with a muscle relaxant and with the patient anaesthetized. ECT is a purely empirical treatment in that it seems to have an antidepressant effect for which no rationale can be offered. In this it is unlike most forms of drug treatment which can be linked to biochemical hypotheses about the nature of depression. Although once very widely used in psychiatry, ECT is now generally restricted to people with severe depression. As a treatment it has certainly proved controversial and capable of arousing considerable public concern. Its indiscriminate use in the past, and even abuse in some places, undoubtedly fuelled this concern, as did its side effects on memory. Possibly the most defensible position at the moment is that it does have a definite but limited value in the treatment of a small number of depressed patients. This is at the price of some minor disruptions of memory but this side effect is transitory (Weeks et al., 1980).

Other medical treatments, like psychosurgery, have been used in the treatment of depression. These are of only minor importance and the main medical forms of treatment remain the various types of antidepressant medication and ECT.

5 Deficit and Assessment

This chapter deals with two major issues which are not necessarily closely interlinked but which are put together for organizational convenience. A prominent concern in abnormal psychology has been the presence of 'psychological deficit', which can be defined as a decrement in psychological functioning, usually as assessed by intellectual or laboratory tasks, as a result of a particular clinical disorder. Present-day research in abnormal psychology, at least as far as the functional disorders are concerned, is much less concerned with the question of deficit than it used to be. Nevertheless the issue is still an important one.

The second topic to be covered in this chapter is that of assessment. There is a need for instruments that will identify a disorder like depression and which will measure the degree to which subjects possess this attribute. Severity may well be a significant variable when looking at the psychological changes produced by the disorder. It is also of considerable importance in evaluation treatments. Trials of different types of therapeutic regimen presuppose the ability to measure change in the degree of depression, level of paranoia, strength of phobia, etc.

Psychological deficit in depression

In looking at psychological deficit, interest will be confined to tests of intellectual functioning and performance on the types of task often studied in the laboratories of experimental psychologists. There is an area of research into depression which deals with 'cognition' in the sense of the way in which the depressed person construes himself and the world and what attributions he makes. For example, it has often been claimed that when the depressed person experiences failure he is more likely than a 'normal' person to see this as a consequence of his own inadequacies rather than as the operation of events outside his control. Thus if he fails to obtain a job that he has applied for then this is attributed to his own worthlessness rather than the presence of a large number of other similarly qualified candidates. This latter area of research has strong links with some of the major psychological theories of depression and will therefore be covered in the next chapter.

As in many of the previous discussions, it is helpful to look at the methodological problems first. In doing so, it is simplest to stick to a single example from within the range of variables that might be investigated. The example taken here will be the problem of trying to establish that a clinical condition such as depression results in a decline in IQ as measured by one of the standard intelligence tests such as the Wechsler Adult Intelligence Scale.

The easiest way to prove a drop in IQ is to apply an intelligence test to a well-defined group of depressed subjects and to see if their mean IQ is less than the population mean of 100. Not all measures that might be of interest come with established population norms like the major intelligence tests. In any case these population norms may not be entirely appropriate since there could be biases in the population from which the experimental subjects are drawn. The clinic in which the study is done may have a catchment area with a social distribution that does not match the sample on which the test was developed. This is an important consideration when any observed differences are rather small.

A much more satisfactory arrangement is to introduce a control group matched with the experimental group for potentially relevant variables such as level of education and social class. Even this may not be wholly adequate. If the experimental group do not do as well as the controls, this does not automatically rule out the possibility that the disorder in question tends to occur more often in those who were originally less able with respect to the attribute in question. There is in fact evidence that patients diagnosed as having hebephrenic schizophrenia come from a subpopulation whose premorbid intelligence level is lower than average (Payne, 1973).

Ideally investigations aiming to show deficits should study subjects before they develop the condition and then at a later date when they have become depressed, schizophrenic, or whatever else is of interest. This is obviously very difficult in practice because it could involve testing a very large number of normal subjects and then re-examining the small proportion who later became depressed or schizophrenic. Some subjects who did not develop a psychological disorder could also be retested after a similar interval to act as controls for such things as the effects of ageing and of practice effects on the measures.

Given the obvious practical difficulties, it is not surprising that studies of this kind are not attempted. On the other hand, it is sometimes possible to capitalize on the fact that an investigator can sometimes find samples of subjects who have been tested previously for some other reason. Children in some school systems and inductees to the armed services may be routinely given tests of intelligence and other abilities. Those later developing psychiatric disorders can then be retested together with suitable controls drawn from the same initial sample. This also presupposes that the investigator can gain access to the previous test data and that the original testing was done long enough before the onset of psychiatric disorder to have been uncontaminated by it. Given the insidious onset of some disorders the latter complication may be difficult to exclude with complete conviction. Some studies of this kind have been reported in relation to schizophrenia with evidence of decline in some, but not all instances (see Payne, 1973).

A less satisfactory strategy that is easier to use in practice is to test subjects when they are depressed or schizophrenic and then to retest them after they have recovered. Again, controls who can be retested after a similar interval are necessary to take factors like practice effects into account. This assumes that any deficit is necessarily reversible. Since some disorders can run a chronic course, often with fluctuations in severity, there is also the problem of deciding which subjects have recovered.

There has also been a tradition of trying to measure intellectual decline indirectly. It has been found that in ageing and in certain kinds of brain pathology there is a tendency for performance on certain intellectually related tests to decline to a relatively large degree whilst performance on others remains relatively static. For example, many vocabulary tests and certain subtests of the Wechsler Adult Intelligence Scale hold up fairly well. These can be used to estimate premorbid IQ. Present IQ can then be assessed in terms of tests that are more susceptible to decline and the difference between the two is then assumed to reflect the extent of intellectual deterioration.

The argument behind the use of indirect measures of decline is superficially attractive but the method depends upon certain assumptions. These assumptions have been examined in detail by E. Miller (1977; 1980) and they turn out to be, at best, only rough and ready approximations to the real world. For example, it is necessary to assume that in the premorbid state subjects' IQs as assessed by the two different types or sets of tests would have been equal. This is often not the case. When the method is extended, as it has been, to measuring decline in the functional psychiatric disorders like schizophrenia, there is also the further gratuitous assumption that the pattern of decline will necessarily mimic that occurring in ageing or certain kinds of brain damage. This has yet to be shown. For this reason the use of indirect methods should be regarded as highly suspect.

A final problem lies in the fact that performance on a particular measure may decline for a number of reasons. Even if it could be unequivocally demonstrated that measured IQ deteriorates as a result of depression then this is far from being proof that depression has a deleterious effect on intellectual functioning. It could be that performance declined as a result of lowered motivation or the fact that the subjects were so preoccupied with their gloomy thoughts that they could not attend adequately to the task in hand, or for a number of other reasons. Ruling out these alternative explanations, which certainly do have a degree of plausibility in the case of a condition like depression, may not be impossible, but it is certainly very difficult. It is possible that even admitting a patient to a hospital may be a disturbing enough experience to have an effect on intellectual performance and treatments such as drugs or electro-convulsive therapy can certainly have at least a temporary effect on performance.

It follows from this that demonstrating psychological deficits and delineating their nature can be extremely difficult. This is especially so where any deficits that do occur are small and fairly subtle. Where deficits are much more gross, as in mental handicap or the effects of brain lesions, then it is possible to establish the presence and nature of deficits with much greater confidence.

General intellectual functions

In general the possibility of intellectual decline in the affective disorders has not attracted the same interest as intellectual functioning in schizophrenia. The then available evidence was exhaustively reviewed by Payne (1973). Payne gives a table showing the mean IQ levels of different abnormal groups when tested during their illnesses. Subjects with affective psychoses had a mean IQ of about 95. This data is contrasted with another table taken from data reported by Mason (1956), which gives the IQs of groups of American servicemen at induction into the services but who later developed a psychiatric disorder. The premorbid mean IQ of those who later developed manic-depressive disorder is above that of Mason's normal controls. Putting these two pieces of information together does suggest the possibility of some intellectual deterioration but, as W. R. Miller (1975) points out, the argument is rather tenuous. The tests used were different and the samples may not have been comparable in other ways. There is also some more recent evidence that the mean IQs of groups of patients whilst depressed can be on the upper side of average (Donnelly *et al.*, 1982).

Investigators using indirect methods of measuring deterioration have also claimed to find evidence of intellectual impairment in depression. M. B. Shapiro and Nelson (1955) employed the Babcock-Levy Test, which is based on the principle that a vocabulary test can give an indication of premorbid intelligence and that other types of test can indicate the present level. On this test, manic-depressive patients exhibited significant impairment. The logic of using indirect methods, exemplified on this occasion by Babcock-Levy, has already been questioned and evidence of the kind provided by Shapiro and Nelson can no longer be regarded as carrying any conviction.

Better evidence is provided by test-retest studies. Although there have been reports like that of Mason (1956) of the premorbid IQs of people who later became depressed, no investigators with access to premorbid test results appear to have managed to compare these with performance on similar tests when the subjects had actually become depressed. What has been done is to compare results from depressed samples with test findings after the subjects had recovered. Davidson (1939), with a gap of about six months between testing when depressed and retesting when recovered, found a gain of around one year in mental age on the Binet scale in manic-depressives. As already indicated, Donnelly *et al.* (1982) found that depressed subjects, tested whilst they were off all drugs, had a mean IQ that was a little above normal on the Wechsler Adult Intelligence Scale. When in remission the mean IQs were found to have increased by a few IQ points. Neither Davidson nor Donnelly *et al.* had control groups but the latter rightly point out that other research with the same test indicates that the observed gains are quite in line with those expected as a result of practice effects on retesting over a similar interval. Suitable evidence on which to base a similar judgement about Davidson's (1939) findings is not readily available. However, test-retest gains due to practice can be quite large on some tests and so practice effects must be considered as being at least a possible explanation for the whole of the observed improvement on the Binet test.

Neuropsychological tests

There has been a recent fashion for taking neuropsychological tests, or test batteries, and applying them to patients with functional psychiatric disorders. These are tests particularly devised to be sensitive to changes produced by damage to or organic disease of the brain. This work has recently been reviewed by Goldstein (1984). Just why this kind of exercise has become so popular is difficult to discern since the underlying reasoning is not above criticism.

In general there has been some tendency for subjects with depression to give mean scores below what would otherwise be expected on the basis of normative data when batteries of neuro-psychological tests are administered (e.g. Rush *et al.*, 1983). Although low scores are obtained they are not as low as those derived from groups of subjects with known brain damage (Heaton and Crowley, 1981). A variety of different explanations for such findings is possible and there is no need to invoke an explanation along the lines that affective disorders are associated with a mild brain dysfunction of the kind encountered in patients with neuro-logical disease.

What has aroused some interest is a fairly well replicated finding that subjects with depression do worst on those neuropsychological tests most sensitive to damage in the non-dominant (usually right) hemisphere of the brain (e.g. Fromm and Schopflocher, 1984; Goldstein *et al.*, 1977; Taylor *et al.*, 1981). There is similar evidence that subjects with schizophrenia may be likely to do relatively badly on tests associated with dominant, or left hemisphere damage (see Goldstein, 1984). Whilst such findings could be of interest in themselves as indications of the kinds of cognitive malfunctioning likely to result from the two conditions, there is, of course, a temptation to go beyond this and draw assumptions for the pathological base of the functional psychoses. Thus schizophrenia is linked to an alleged left hemisphere disturbance and depression to right hemisphere malfunctioning.

Although such conclusions are tempting, they are not entirely justified by the data. Similar kinds of evidence have also been used to suggest that one hemisphere of the brain might be more affected than the other in normal ageing (Goldstein and Shelly, 1981), dementia and Parkinson's disease (Bentin *et al.*, 1981). E. Miller (1983) has argued that alternative explanations are possible and, under some circumstances at least, may be more likely. Because damage to the right hemisphere produces a deficit on certain kinds of test (often those with a visuospatial component), it does not mean that all who do relatively poorly on such tests have right hemisphere brain damage. For example, it could be that depressed patients are poorly motivated or have difficulties in sustaining attention and that alleged 'right hemisphere tests' are also particularly prone to distorted results for these other reasons. Similarly, given the association between schizophrenia and various verbally related phenomena (e.g. thought disorder), it is possibly not surprising that schizophrenics do not do well on the heavily verbally dependent left hemisphere tests. For this reason the performance of depressed patients on neuropsychological tests may not be of great interest except where the tests themselves are related to specific psychological functions and not just measures that happen to correlate with different types of brain damage.

Memory and learning

These two functions can be difficult to separate and are probably best regarded as the two sides of the same coin. For this reason they will be dealt with together.

Patients with depression not infrequently complain of memory impairments and a large number of clinical studies have found that depressed patients can sometimes do rather badly on clinical tests of learning and/or memory (e.g. Kendrick *et al.*, 1965). This causes problems in clinical practice because older psychiatric patients with either depression or dementia can present with a very similar picture in that they are withdrawn, neglected and rather low in spirits. The differential diagnosis between depression and dementia in such cases is rather difficult and yet is important because these two disorders have very different implications for treatment and prognosis. Clinical psychologists have tried to use tests of learning/ memory in order to discriminate between the two possibilities. This is on the basis that patients with dementia do have real memory impairments, whereas most depressed patients will perform much better than those with dementia despite their subjective complaints of memory loss. This clinical work is extensively reviewed elsewhere (E. Miller, 1980; 1984), but there is one problem that emerges in using tests of learning/memory in this way. This is because some patients whose subsequent history and response to treatment clearly suggests that they may have been depressed may be erroneously regarded as being demented because they actually perform as badly as demented subjects on these tests. This is now often referred to as the problem of 'depressive pseudo-dementia'. As far as present purposes are concerned, the important lesson that can be drawn from this work is that depression can result in lowered performance on tests of learning and memory (see also McAllister, 1981).

A further question that can be asked is what characterizes this apparent memory impairment? One set of authors who have reported a small series of studies relating to this point is Henry *et al.* (1973). They gave various tests of learning/memory to subjects with bipolar disorders (in both the hypomanic and depressive phases) and to subjects with unipolar disorders. All subjects were then retested after improvement in their clinical condition had taken place. One of the tests used involved serial learning whereby a list of eight words was read out to the subject who had to give an immediate recall of the words in the same order as they were presented. A total of six consecutive trials was given with each list.

The number of words correctly recalled from the first present-ation of each list did not increase significantly on retesting after clinical improvement as far as the depressed groups were con-cerned. There was an improvement in the number of words recalled from trials 2 to 6. Henry *et al.* then related the recall on the first trial to short-term memory and that from the later trials to long-term memory, and suggested that depressed subjects had an impaired ability to transfer material from short- to long-term memory. Apart from any theoretical difficulties in working with this rather old-fashioned model of memory which distinguishes between short- and long-term memory, there are also other difficulties with this evidence. For example, in the absence of appropriate control groups it is not possible to rule out practice effects as a possible source of the change on trials 2 to 6 which occurred with retesting. The number of words recalled from the first presentation may not have shown a significant gain on retesting simply because short-term memory (or whatever process underlies recall after a single presentation) is less capable of benefiting from practice or because aggregating the data from five trials as opposed to just one gives a better chance for small practice effects to be revealed. It is also interesting that others have claimed that LTM is intact in depres-sion but STM is impaired (Sternberg and Jarvik, 1976).

In general there has not been much interest in examining the alleged memory impairments occurring in depression in terms of the kinds of models of memory formulated by experimental psychologists, e.g. the levels of processing model following Craik and Lockhart (1972) or the Baddeley and Hitch (1974) working memory model. In contrast there has been some interest in looking at memory for different types of material and a good example of such a study is provided by Lishman (1972a; 1972b). Subjects were presented with a list of eighteen topics such as 'the countryside' and 'atomic warfare'. These were then rated on a semantic differential (Osgood *et al.*, 1957) to indicate the subjects' feelings about each of these topics. Two weeks later, subjects were asked to recall as many of these topics as they could. There was a general tendency for normal subjects as well as depressed patients who had recovered to recall many more of the topics rated as having a positive hedonic tone. This trend was very much reduced in subjects who were depressed. As well as this the investigation confirmed previous work in showing that depressed subjects also recalled fewer topics. In a further study of recognition memory, Dunbar and Lishman (1984) found that depressed subjects recognized unpleasant material better and pleasant material less well than controls. The overall recognition level for both groups was the same.

Comparable results have been obtained by others. Clark and Teasdale (1982) tested depressed patients who exhibited a marked diurnal variation in mood. Subjects were each tested twice, on occasions when their mood was relatively high and when it was relatively low. The test consisted in presenting the subjects with a list of twenty words and requiring them to retrieve an experience from memory relating to each of the words. Subjects showed longer response latencies when they were more depressed as well as recalling a greater proportion of unhappy memories at this time. When they were less depressed, unhappy memories formed a smaller proportion of the total. Work of this kind does seem to indicate that long-term recall in depressed patients is biased by the affective connotations of the material, with depressed subjects, not surprisingly, being more likely to recall material with gloomy or depressive connotations. In passing, it is also worth noting that the Clark and Teasdale (1982) experiment is a little unusual in that it found effects attributable to diurnal variation. Despite patients frequently claiming that they are more depressed at certain times of the day (e.g. in the morning), investigations seeking to gain objective confirmation of this pattern have often failed to find diurnal changes (e.g. Williams, 1975).

Again it can be questioned whether the poor performance of depressed subjects on measures of learning and/or memory is really due to a disturbance in these functions or to some other more general cause such as lowered motivation. Miller and Lewis (1977) specifically addressed this issue. They suggested that subjects with depression might do badly on memory tests because they adopted a very conservative response strategy. Thus in a situation where subjects are asked to recall words presented previously, those with depression might be less willing than normal subjects to produce responses when they were not completely sure of the correctness of the response. In other words, they would get fewer correct by refusing to guess when there is a good chance that the guess will be correct. Miller and Lewis examined this possibility by using a recognition test that could be subjected to a signal detection analysis which permits the ability to discriminate or recognize previously presented stimuli to be distinguished from biases of the kind hypothesized. The results suggested that the depressed group did not differ significantly from the controls in terms of 'pure' memory, whereas the depressed subjects clearly operated a much more conservative response strategy (as if they were unwilling to indicate what they recognized as a stimulus until they were absolutely certain). A third group with dementia did give results suggesting a marked impairment of memory which goes some way to contradict the possible criticism that the depressed group performed similarly to the normal controls on the measure of pure memory simply because this test was not sensitive enough to reveal differences.

Cohen *et al.* (1982) attempted to look at the effect of motivation on memory performance. They required subjects to squeeze a bulb linked to a dynamometer to maintain 80 per cent of their maximum grip for as long as possible. They also used a memory test derived from the procedure used by Peterson and Peterson (1959). The results showed that depressed subjects were less willing to make an effort on the dynamometer task than normal controls and that the more depressed these subjects were the less willing they were to make an effort. There was also a correlation between their measure of effort and performance on the memory test. Thus it seems that motivational factors might at least partially explain the poor learning/memory in depressed subjects.

Further evidence that apparent deficits in learning and memory in depressed subjects are really a side effect due to other changes has come from Lang and Frith (1981). They looked at learning and reminiscence on the pursuit rotor using depressed subjects and carefully matched normal controls. Although the depressed group performed at a consistently lower level than the controls, they did appear to show similar amounts of improvement both within and between sessions. Further analysis showed that the depressed subjects had a particular difficulty in following high-frequency movements, thus suggesting slowed motor reactivity. Thus the difficulty seems to lie in the execution of the skill rather than its acquisition or retention.

Speed

Psychomotor retardation is a well-established feature of depression in the classical clinical description. It is not therefore surprising that many investigators have chosen to look at speed in depressed subjects as revealed by a range of different tasks. An early study is that of M. B. Shapiro and Nelson (1955), who administered a range of tests designed to assess both cognitive and motor speed to groups of female psychiatric patients and normal controls. In general the results showed that the clinical groups were slower than the controls and that the slower the patients were, the more severe their psychiatric disorder. Even neurotics were slower than controls, though they were faster than those with more psychotic disorders. Of the latter, the acute schizophrenics were the least retarded and the chronic schizophrenics the slowest of all. Manic-depressives came between the two schizophrenic groups.

The experiment illustrates certain general points. Firstly, slowness is to some extent a characteristic of all psychiatric subjects. Whatever the task involved, investigators looking at speed of performance almost invariably find depressed subjects to be slowed. Finally, where depressives have been compared with psychiatric subjects belonging to other diagnostic groups it is often the case that they are not as slowed as schizophrenics. Hall and Stride (1954) report just one other example of schizophrenics being more retarded than subjects with depression as assessed by reaction times.

Since impaired speed is not a feature that is peculiar to depression, it is a little surprising that psychiatric textbook descriptions particularly stress psychomotor retardation as a feature of depression. It could be that whilst the typical depressed patient is no more slowed than the typical schizophrenic, the range of variation in the degree of slowing is much greater in depression. This could result in depression producing the most extreme, and therefore the most memorable, cases with the clinical descriptions then emphasizing the extreme features. It is also possible that there is some discrepancy between the kind of behaviour studied by psychologists and that observed by psychiatrists in clinical interviews. Depressed patients could then be more retarded than most other groups with regard to behaviour that can be observed by psychiatrists. As far as the tendency for schizophrenics to be even slower is concerned, it is possible that it is largely the chronic rather than the acute schizophrenics who are slower than depressed subjects as indicated by M. B. Shaprio and Nelson (1955). Since the typical psychiatric descriptions stress the picture in the acute phase, this could again partly explain why retardation is alleged to be associated with depression rather than schizophrenia.

Although it is well established that depressed patients are slow on almost every measure of speed that has been tried (see W. R. Miller, 1975), this is not an area of research that has attracted a great deal of attention in recent times. One type of slowing that has been looked at relatively recently is 'speech pause time' (SPT). Szabadi et al. (1976), got a small number of depressed and normal subjects to count from one to ten and looked at the SPTs which he defined as the time intervals between successive phonations. The depressed patients had longer SPTs than the controls but these improved with recovery. Szabadi et al.'s depressed subjects were selected as showing little sign of psychomotor retardation and SPT showed an effect whereas other measures of retardation (e.g. tapping time and rating of the relevant item on the Hamilton Depression Rating Scale) did not. Thus the authors suggest that SPT might be useful as a sensitive indicator of retardation. Unfortunately the size of the sample was very small for the purpose of making this kind of claim.

Other investigators have subsequently looked at SPT in depression (Greden and Carroll, 1980; Greden et al., 1981). They used the same test as Szabadi et al., (i.e. the subject counting from one to ten at his preferred rate) and confirmed that SPTs are indeed longer in depressed subjects than in normal controls. Phonation times do not differ. With recovery, SPTs are reduced and Greden et al. (1981) found that after recovery their depressed subjects had SPTs that were indistinguishable from the normal controls. In some instances the improvement on recovery can be quite dramatic, with subjects reducing their SPTs by over 50 per cent (Greden and Carroll,

1980). These studies generally support the notion that SPT could be a useful measure of depression.

Why should depressed patients be slow? One of the most attractive hypotheses to explain depressive slowing was put forward by Foulds (1952), who suggested that this is the result of over-attention to internal stimuli (prominent gloomy thoughts, etc.). Foulds put forward this hypothesis because he found that con-currently doing a distracting task (with the subject repeating numbers spoken by the experimenter as the experimenter counted 1, 2, 3, etc.) actually improved the speed with which depressed subjects did the Porteus Maze Test. It was presumed that the distracting task took subjects' attention away from the internal stimuli. Foulds also showed that the improvement on testing with the accompaniment of the distraction task was not attributable to a practice effect. M. B. Shapiro *et al.* (1958) also confirmed the beneficial effect of distraction in depressed subjects (although they did not confirm some other speculations by Foulds about the relationship between the distraction effect and the effect of ECT).

Other psychological impairments in depression

The aspects of psychological functioning considered so far repre-sent only a few of the areas that have been examined in relation to depression. Nevertheless they illustrate the kinds of investigation that have been carried out and the difficulties that arise in trying to interpret the results. Some other aspects of functioning will be mentioned much more briefly. A more extensive, but slightly out-of-date review is provided by W. R. Miller (1975).

There have been studies that have looked at perceptual processes in depression. In more recent times these investigations have looked at dichotic listening tasks (e.g. Johnson and Crockett, 1982; Yozawitz *et al.*, 1979). Dichotic listening has been of interest because it is possible to look for asymmetries between the perception of material presented to the two ears and this is then related to theoretical ideas about possible selective dysfunction of one hemisphere. In general, studies like those cited do tend to show some deviations from the normal pattern of ear asymmetries and often towards the kinds of pattern that would be expected if right hemisphere functioning were disturbed. As with the discussion of the use of neuropsychological tests, the problem is that depressed patients may show different patterns of performance as compared with the normal for a whole variety of reasons. Dichotic listening is a complex task and it demands very little ingenuity to think up alternative reasons for the findings.

The use of language by depressed subjects has also been examined. Hinchliffe *et al.* (1971) looked at five-minute samples of speech from depressed subjects and controls (general surgical patients). The depressed subjects had lower rates of speech, made a greater number of personal references, used more negators (e.g. not and never) and more expressions of feeling. Andreasen and Pfohl (1976) carried out a linguistic analysis of speech samples taken from both depressed and manic subjects. In general they found that depressive speech was more vague and qualified as well as indicating considerable self-preoccupation. Both of these sets of investigators agree in showing that the speech of depressed subjects indicates considerable concern with the self, which is hardly an unexpected finding for anyone who has had contact with moderately to severely depressed psychiatric patients.

Comment

In discussing the material presented in his review, W. R. Miller (1975) reached a number of conclusions. Although a certain amount of work has been reported since, it does not appreciably affect the general picture and some of Miller's conclusions bear repetition here. The first of these is that depressed subjects do generally perform less well than normal controls. This is an important conclusion because some authorities have suggested that depression, and even quite severe depression, is not associated with impaired performance in psychological functioning (e.g. Beck, 1967; Yates, 1966). As W. R. Miller indicates, this appears to be because undue emphasis was given to a small number of rather atypical negative findings.

A second conclusion is that there do not appear to be any deficits that are specific to depression. Where comparative data are available, groups with other forms of psychopathology tend to be impaired on the same tasks. There are a number of possible explanations for this. One is that the different forms of psychopathology all share a common element and it is this common element that leads to deficit. Whatever the reason, there does not appear to be anything unique about depression that is revealed by this work. The possibility that different sorts of clinical groups may exhibit similar impairments but for different reasons has an obvious attraction in a situation like this but lacks any firm supporting evidence.

A final conclusion is that little progress has been made towards devising theories of depressive deficit. Here the situation contrasts with schizophrenia where there is an embarrassing profusion of theories to explain schizophrenic deficit (e.g. Buss and Lang, 1965; Lang and Buss, 1965; Neale and Oltmanns, 1980). Other than the psychological theories of the causation of depression to be discussed in the next chapter, only two explanations of deficit appear to have been offered. One is cognitive interference, whereby depressives are assumed to perform badly because of the intrusion of distracting worries and preoccupations. The other is in terms of motivational factors and it is assumed that depressives have either low motivation or an inability to sustain motivation. Of these two, cognitive interference has received some support from the work of Foulds (1952) and M. B. Shapiro *et al.* (1958). Poor motivation can be seen as a consequence of processes like learned helplessness which will be discussed in the next chapter.

In general, as indicated earlier, interest in the psychological deficit that results from depression has waned and little theoretical effort has gone into building and testing models that might explain these types of deficit. Instead psychological theorizing in relation to depression has developed on a broader front and has mainly been concerned with explaining the aetiology of the whole syndrome rather than the particular deficits that have been outlined above. This more general theoretical approach belongs in the next chapter.

Measurement and assessment

In investigating a problem like depression it is essential to have some means of identifying who can be considered to have the condition and also extremely useful in many areas of research to have an instrument that can measure the degree to which individuals possess the characteristic in question. The basic principles involved in devising and using such instruments are well illustrated by the appropriate work relating to depression.

Instruments to evaluate depression, or any other behavioural abnormality, can be devised with a number of different problems in mind. These include the identification of cases that can legitimately be considered to be depressed as opposed to those who can be regarded as normal or who have other types of psychopathology. Basically such instruments have a cut-off point (which can be determined by a simple score or by some combination of scores or features) which determines whether an individual falls into the category of 'depression' or not. Secondly, instruments may be used to determine the degree to which the individual possesses the given characteristic. The latter is not just a more sophisticated version of the former in that it treats the condition as a continuum rather than an all or none phenomenon. This is not necessarily the case in the conventional psychiatric nosology. For example, Endicott and Spitzer's (1978) Research Diagnostic Criteria for primary affective disorder require the presence of a certain number of specified criteria not all of which will be present in all depressed subjects and there is no implication that subjects possessing all of the criteria are necessarily the most depressed.

Scales may not only be required to indicate the degree of depression but to be sensitive to change in the level when applied on more than one occasion. Such instruments are of considerable importance when it is desired to detect change in the level of characteristic as a result of some experimental manipulation as in a trial of a treatment.

Instruments that are valuable in one of these roles are not necessarily ideal in others. For example, with instruments designed to indicate the presence or absence of a form of psychopathology high levels of reliability (in the psychometric sense of high test-retest reliability) are desirable. High reliability then tends to go with high stability and a lack of sensitivity to small changes in the level of the variable that is being assessed. On the other hand, if it is desired to apply a scale repeatedly to detect the extent to which the variable in question changes over time (e.g. in response to some form of treatment) then high reliability which brings in its train high stability and a relative insensitivity to change may be counter-productive. The characteristics of any instrument or scale need to be carefully matched to the job that needs to be done.

Another question with a presumed entity like depression is whether the scale is being used to indicate the presence or absence of the syndrome as a whole or is just being used to measure one aspect, typically the level of mood. In general a test that is used to identify an alleged clinical syndrome, or to measure the extent to which an individual conforms to that syndrome, will obviously have to cover the main aspects of that syndrome. Where a scale is being used to detect change, this comprehensiveness is less essential and it is possible for the scale to concentrate on a key feature like low mood.

In the case of a condition like depression the key feature, which is mood, is a subjective experience and only directly accessible to the individual concerned. The observer can only infer the presence of a depressed mood in the subject from what the subject says or does. This leads to a split in scales of depression between those that require an observer (typically a professional such as a psychiatrist or psychologist) to rate the subject in some way and those that require the subject to rate himself. Advantages and disadvantages are attached to both these approaches.

Self-rating scales (i.e. those filled in by the subject) do offer a more direct rating of subjective feelings such as the level of mood. On the other hand depressed patients may be so depressed by their gloomy thoughts that they find it difficult to concentrate adequately on any tasks that makes demands upon them. In addition the person who is depressed may just not be aware of certain aspects of his behaviour in the way that an observer is. The agitated patient may not realize how agitated he is and the depressed patient with delusions may not rate his thought content as being in any way abnormal. Such features can be rated by the observer and observers can be trained to apply the criteria to be used in making judgements in a fairly standard way. Inter-observer reliability can be calculated for observer-based scales but no comparable form of reliability can be obtained from self-rating scales.

Whether observer-based ratings or self-ratings are best depends upon circumstances. As far as depression is concerned, the fact that depressed subjects need not necessarily be aware of all the clinical features of depression that they possess means that observer-based scales are generally best for identifying depression and measuring the degree to which the individual exhibits the features associated with the syndrome. Self-rating scales are better when attempting to measure changes in mood but observer-based scales can be used in this context as well.

Empirical research comparing the value of self-rated as opposed to observer-rated scales is conflicting. There are studies (e.g. Arfwidsson *et al.*, 1974; Prusoff *et al.*, 1972) that have come down in favour of observer-rated scales. On the other hand, Kearns *et al.* (1982) found no difference. It is highly likely that the answer to a question like this will depend on such factors as the particular scales being compared, the subject populations involved and the purpose for which the scales are being used. It is probable that a sensible general answer to this question cannot be given.

Particular scales in common usage

It is not intended to describe those techniques specifically devised for the classification of subjects as depressed or not. Most modern research tends to use such things as the DSM III criteria or the Spitzer *et al*. (1978) Research Diagnostic Criteria. These have been briefly dealt with in an earlier chapter (pages 00–00). Present discussion will centre on measures of the degree to which subjects can be considered depressed.

The two most commonly used scales of depression are undoubtedly the Beck Depression Inventory (Beck, 1961; 1967) and Hamilton's (1960) rating scale. Both of these have been reasonably well developed from a psychometric point of view, have useful levels of reliability and a proven ability to discriminate between subjects with different degrees of depression (e.g. Kearns *et al.*, 1982). Their repeated successful use in clinical trials of anti-depressant treatments attests to their ability to detect change in levels of depression at least to a degree of sensitivity that is required for the typical clinical trial.

The Beck Depression Inventory considers depression under twenty-one different headings (e.g. sadness, guilt, insomnia and loss of appetite). Under each heading are four or more statements scored on a four-point scale (0, 1, 2 or 3) which relate to the characteristic concerned. It is a self-rating scale in that the subject is asked to select, for each heading, the particular statement that most corresponds to his state. It is, however, tester-assisted in that the tester is encouraged to read the statements to the subject rather than just relying on him to read them for himself.

The Hamilton Rating Scale for Depression (HRSD) is an observer-rated scale in that the observer rates each of twenty-one items on a scale covering either three or five points (this varies from item to item). Both the BDI and the HRSD deal with both the subjective and somatic symptoms of depression. They have been criticized in that neither of them deal with anxiety which can also be a prominent feature of some patients diagnosed as having depression (Snaith *et al.*, 1971). A number of other investigations have attempted to modify and improve the BDI and the HRSD but these attempts will not be described here. In general these scales have been successful and have stood the test of time.

Other self-rating scales for depression that turn up with some frequency in research are the Zung (1965) scale and what is essentially a British modification of this, the Wakefield Scale

(Snaith *et al.*, 1971). Both these scales are based on a set of statements (twenty for the Zung and twelve for the Wakefield), with the subject having to rate the extent to which each of the statements applies to him on a four-point scale. Further items have been added to the Wakefield Scale to make the Leeds Scale for the Self-Assessment of Anxiety and Depression (Snaith *et al.*, 1976). There is evidence from the original development of these scales and from elsewhere (e.g. Kearns *et al.*, 1982) that these scales have useful levels of reliability and validity.

As far as observer-rating scales are concerned, there have been few serious rivals to HRSD. A promising recent development is the Montgomery and Åsberg (1979) scale. This is shorter than the HRSD, in that it is based on only ten features of depression. Each feature is well described and has to be rated on a seven-point scale with fairly clear descriptions of what is required to score at different levels on the scales. High inter-rater reliabilities can be achieved with all those reported being 0.89 or better. There is also additional support for Montgomery and Åsberg's contention that their scale discriminates between depression of different degrees of severity at least as well as the HRSD (Kearns *et al.*, 1982). Since it is about half the length of the HRDS and does the job just as well, the Montgomery and Åsberg scale might well start to supersede the HRSD.

Personal questionnaires

As already indicated, many of the symptoms of depression are subjective and involve feelings of sadness, guilt, etc. Although these feelings tend to have common themes like low mood, despair for the future, and a concern for past sins or misdemeanours, these can be expressed in many different ways. Especially where single-case research is being carried out, or it is desired to follow the course of an individual patient's problems, it is useful to have some form of scale that can be used to measure the individual subject's own particular symptoms or worries.

Whilst several techniques are available for getting at an individual subject's problems, a method of particular value in the measurement of depressive symptomatology has been devised by M. B. Shapiro (1961). This Shapiro called the 'Personal Question-naire'. In fact it has been shown that Shapiro's original Personal Questionnaire is not just a single technique but one example of a whole family of techniques that can all be described as 'Personal

Questionnaires'. From the point of view of simplicity of exposition, only Shapiro's original version will be described in any detail although more sophisticated versions do exist (e.g. Mulhall, 1976).

Shapiro's (1961) Personal Questionnaire starts with a structured interview which covers most aspects of psychopathology. (The technique can be used to deal with the patient's subjective feelings in relation to any kind of condition, and not necessarily just psychiatric disorders, but is particularly applicable to people with depression because of the nature of depressive symptomatology.) This interview is used to derive a set of 'illness statements'. These consist of statements by the patient, in his words, describing his problem. In the case of someone with depression, they will be things like 'I always feel very sad', 'I cannot sleep properly at night', and 'I feel very guilty about things that I have done wrong'. Typically the procedure will yield something in the order of fifteen to twenty statements of this kind but there is no fixed number of statements to be derived. The general aim is to get a set of statements that will adequately represent the range of the patient's problems and the actual number of statements necessary to do this may be very small or very large. (One of the weaknesses of Personal Questionnaire techniques is that there is no clear rule for determining what are a reasonable representative set of statements for each subject and the decision has to be based on clinical judgement.)

Each of the illness statements then forms the basis of an item in the final scale. Taking the statement 'I always feel very sad' as an example, two further related statements are derived. One of these is a 'recovery statement', which may be something like 'I no longer feel sad'. This is often worded so as to negate the illness statement rather than to indicate the reverse of the illness statement (e.g. 'I now feel happy'). The third, or 'improvement statement', is worded so as to represent the mid-point on a subjective scale between the illness and recovery statements. That the suggested improvement statement is at the mid-point between the other two is checked by getting the subject to scale the statements using a special procedure. If necessary, the working of the improvement and recovery statements can be adjusted to achieve the correct relationships to the illness statement in terms of the perceptions of the subject (rather than those of the scale constructor). The same procedure is followed for all the illness statements.

Having got the three statements for each item, the final version of the questionnaire can now be produced. For each item, pairs of statements are written one above the other on cards (often 127 ×

7.6 mm record cards are used). The three statements for each item yield three possible pairs: illness statement with recovery, improvement with recovery and illness with improvement. When all the cards from each item have been prepared they are shuffled and presented to the subject in a deck to be sorted as to whether the upper or the lower statement best corresponds to how he feels at that time. For each item the three responses can normally be allocated to a four-point scale. If considered appropriate, a total score can be derived by adding the scores from each item.

The system contains an inbuilt check on reliability (in the sense of internal consistency). The three cards from each item can be sorted in eight possible ways. Of these, four are mutually consistent and four are inconsistent. Experience in using this form of the Personal Questionnaire suggests that inconsistent patterns of responses are very low (of the order of 2 to 3 per cent and even less), which suggests that subjects find sorting the cards to be a meaningful and easy task. Although this form of the Personal Questionnaire takes time to develop, once this has been done the questionnaire can be used over and over again with the same subject, and subjects rapidly learn to sort the cards quite speedily.

One problem with an ideographic technique like the Personal Questionnaire is that it is difficult to get external validation. It is, of course, possible to apply it several times to a depressed subject and show that it varies in line with other indices (e.g. alternative measures of depression). The value of this is limited since it applies to only that particular Personal Questionnaire with that particular subject and the validation is only achieved after the questionnaire has been used quite extensively. In something like a single-case experiment, putting in additional measures to validate the Personal Questionnaire is counter-productive since the investigator might just as well have relied upon these other measures in the first place.

The other argument for the validity of the Personal Questionnaire is that it deals directly with the patient's own statements about his problems. It is precisely these same statements that tend to be used in deciding that the patient is depressed in the first place. In effect the Personal Questionnaire is getting quite close to the 'raw data' of depression. Other than this it is only possible to fall back on the claim that Personal Questionnaires typically appear to yield useful and meaningful data although there are obvious weaknesses with this kind of argument.

As already mentioned, there is a whole family of Personal Questionnaire techniques. One of the most useful alternative versions is Mulhall's (1976) 'Personal Questionnaire Rapid Scaling Technique' (PQRST). Like the original M. B. Shapiro (1961) version, this starts from illness statements derived from the patient. In this case an illness statement like 'I feel depressed' is put in the form 'My feeling of depression is . . .'. These statements are written on a form and put in a special answer booklet. Again the subject is asked to choose each time between two alternatives but in this case he is offered pairs of adjectives to complete the statement (e.g. 'considerable' and 'mild') such that the statement would then come closest to applying to him. A number of different pairs of adjectives are presented for each item, thus enabling the PQRST item scores to cover ten or even fourteen points rather than just three in Shapiro's (1961) version. The other big advantage of the PQRST is that it cuts out the time required to develop recovery and improvement statements and to go through the scaling exercise.

Conclusion

Researchers in the field of depression are fortunate in that there are a number of well-established scales for the measure of depression that are of proven value. The BDI and HRSD are extensively used but alternatives for these do exist. When it comes to following the fortunes of the individual depressed patient or in carrying out single-case research, the Personal Questionnaires are of considerable potential value.

6 Psychological Models

Psychological models of behavioural abnormalities have been derived from a number of sources. One rich source of models has been psychodynamic thinking as it has developed from the original ideas of Freud. The study of animal and normal human behaviour by experimental psychologists has provided another source of explanatory models. Finally, models may be derived directly from investigations of the particular disorder itself without borrowing too deeply from other sources. Explanations of depression have been derived in all three ways and prominent examples will be examined below.

Before looking at particular theories of depression it is useful to deal with two preliminary points. It is sometimes assumed that explanations are always causal in that they set out just how the particular phenomena of interest came to be produced. Causal models are useful, especially in relation to certain issues such as possible methods of prevention. They are not the only, or even the most frequent form of explanation. Scientific laws generally describe relationships between certain critical variables. Ohm's Law is a good example. This functional model describes the relationships between voltage, resistance and current flow in simple electrical circuits. It says nothing about why the particular relationship it describes comes to be as it is. Functional models of this kind can be extremely useful, just as Ohm's Law is very valuable in designing electrical circuits. In the same way explanations of abnormal behaviour need not say anything about causation in order to be useful in other ways which can include suggesting manipulations that might be useful in treatment.

The second point is that many theorists putting forward psychological models of depression, including major figures like Freud and Seligman, have specifically refrained from claiming that their particular model offers an explanation for all cases of depression even where these models are alleged to be causal in nature. In this way psychological theories of depression differ from those attempting to explain phobias or anxiety, where it is assumed that psychological factors offer the only possible form of causal mechanism. If it is allowed that depression may result from mechanisms of quite a different kind from those posited by the theory, and often assumed to be biological in nature, then certain things follow. There must be at least two types of depression and the endogenous/reactive distinction described in Chapter 3 would fit nicely since it has implicit within it the assumption that some depressions are internally caused while others are a reaction to environmental events. As was seen in Chapter 3, the evidence for this distinction is hardly compelling. Alternatively, it could be the case that all depressions exhibit the same range of features but that this clinical syndrome represents the final common pathway of a number of different causal chains.

Psychodynamic models

Psychodynamic thinking, which has largely developed from the original work of Freud, has tended to diversify as well as change and develop. There is thus no single psychodynamic model of depression and there is certainly no space within this book to describe all the many variants. Nevertheless, there is a common theme that has tended to run through much psychodynamic thinking about depression and it is this theme that will form the focus for this section. It should also be remembered that Freud did not just devise explanations for different forms of psychopathology. He created an important school of psychological therapy and this aspect of Freud's thinking will be examined in some detail in Chapter 8.

The classic psychoanalytic paper on depression is that of Freud (1917) entitled 'Mourning and Melancholia'. In this paper, as the title suggests, Freud uses bereavement as an analogy for depression. In passing it is worth noting that this is one of Freud's writings that merits reading in the original for the student who wishes to get some more direct insight into the nature of Freudian thinking. Within a relatively few pages it conveys a much better impression of Freud's mind at work than the 'Introductory Lectures in Psychoanalysis'. From the title the latter would seem to be the ideal introduction but they are extremely prolix and devoid of clearly enunciated ideas.

According to Freud, 'the distinguishing features of melancholia are a profoundly painful dejection, abrogation of interest in the outside world, loss of the capacity of love, inhibition of all activity, and a lowering of the self-regarding feelings to a degree that finds utterance in self-reproaches and self-revilings, and culminates in a delusional expectation of punishment.' Apart from the loss of self-esteem, these features are found in the grief of those who have been bereaved.

In the case of someone who has been bereaved there is an identifiable loss (the husband, mother, child, etc.). Freud then suggests that the depressed person may also have undergone a loss. The object that is lost may be an internal representation rather than something that is external or it could be that the object is still there but lost to the person as an object of love. Just as the loss that has occurred in depression is of a kind that is not obvious to the observer, it is similarly not obvious to the sufferer.

In these circumstances the ambivalence which Freud claimed to be part of all love relationships comes to the fore. The positive feelings are absorbed back into the person by a narcissistic identification whereas the negative feelings (hate, anger, etc.) are turned back on the person himself. This leads to a loss of self-esteem, to self-reproach and other similar features which form part of the outward signs of depression.

This general line of thinking was developed by Freud and others (e.g. Abraham, 1911; 1916; 1924; Freud, 1921; 1923). In his 1923 paper, 'The Ego and the Id', Freud elaborated on the processes like those alleged to underlie depression at greater length. The negative, inwardly turned aspects of depression were linked to strong, internally directed feelings of aggression. This leads to a common feature of most psychodynamic interpretations of depression which is an alleged link between depression and aggression and specifically aggression of certain kinds or exhibited under certain circumstances.

As already indicated, psychodynamic explanations are very complex with many interlocking facets. This means that any concise description, such as that given above, is likely to involve some simplification or distortion. It also means that the theories do not lead to clear-cut and readily testable hypotheses. What is much more realistic with psychodynamic theories is to use them as a springboard to develop much simpler and testable hypotheses. This is the direction that will be taken in the rest of this section which will now examine the relationship between depression and aggression. Two slightly different hypotheses have been derived. One is that depression results from self-directed aggression and the other is that it arises as a consequence of unexpressed aggression. The latter especially is a hypothesis which, if true, could have wider implications. For example, getting the depressed patient to express aggression could help to reduce the level of depression.

In general, two approaches have been used to look at the relationship between depression and aggression. The first is epidemiological where it is predicted that depression will vary in different populations as a function of their alleged ability to express aggressive feelings. The second is by attempting to apply independent measures of aggression to see if the expected evidence of high levels can be found in depressed groups.

Epidemiological evidence

The prevalence of depression can vary quite appreciably between different populations. Within the general population it is generally supposed that it is more socially acceptable for certain subgroups to express their aggressive feelings (either verbally or physically) than it is for others. Depression should be more prevalent when agression is least tolerated.

Kendell (1968) reviewed the existing epidemiological evidence with just this sort of prediction in mind. Depression is encountered more frequently in the old than the young and in women more than men. This is in line with what might be expected, in that society is generally less tolerant of overt expressions of hostility in women and those who are older. There are also specific groups where the cultural norms make the expression of aggression highly unacceptable. One example is formed by the Hutterite communities in North America (see also page 44). As Kendell shows, the evidence definitely indicates that there is an increased prevalence of depression in Hutterite communities (although the rate for schizophrenia is lowered).

Of the extensive evidence considered by Kendell (1968), by far the greater part is consistent with the notion that depression is linked to suppressed aggression. The steady accumulation of epidemiological evidence since Kendell wrote this paper would not alter the general picture. On the other hand, not all the data considered by Kendell are consistent with the hypothesis. Studies of psychiatric disorder in submarine crews have not revealed a raised prevalence of depression despite the fact that living in very cramped conditions means that the expression of aggression has to be kept on a very tight rein. The rate for other disorders, particularly anxiety, is raised. The possible snag with this last source of evidence is that submarine crews are often carefully selected and it could be that the selection process is more efficient at excluding those with depressive tendencies than it is in weeding out other types of problem. Submarine crews also tend to be volunteers and the kind of person who volunteers for submarine service may not be the sort of person who is predisposed to depression.

Although the general run of evidence is certainly consistent with the notion that depression is caused by suppressed aggression, there is a limitation. As Kendell (1968) points out, epidemiological evidence is not very good at discriminating between competing hypotheses and it is relatively easy to think of other mechanisms that could account for the same findings. For example, if adverse life events play an important role in producing depression (see the next chapter), then women and the elderly may be more prone to experiencing such events, or more vulnerable to their effects when they occur.

An example of an epidemiological study that tries to make use of 'naturally occurring' changes is provided by Lyons (1972). He made use of the unrest and disorder in Northern Ireland to look at the impact of increased aggressive behaviour in the population on the rates for depression. He reported data for two periods of time (1964 to 1968 and 1969 to 1970) for two different areas. One of these was the city of Belfast and the other was a rural area (County Down). The significance of these times and places is that 1964 to 1968 represents the period just prior to major outbreaks of civil disturbance in Belfast during 1969 and 1970. In contrast County Down remained peaceful throughout the whole of the time being studied.

Table 2 *Results of Lyons's (1972) study of the effect of civil violence on the incidence of depression.*

| | Annual rate | |
	1964–68	1969–70
Belfast	1275	1109
County Down	904	941

$\chi^2 = 8.37$ $p < 0.01$

Lyons based his analysis on the mean number of new cases of depression being seen per year by the psychiatric services within the two areas. This data is reproduced in Table 2. The main point to note is that the figures for the two periods showed no significant change (in fact a small increase) in County Down. In Belfast the occurrence of riots and other disturbances in 1969 and 70 was associated with a significant drop in the annual rate of new cases of depression. Thus it seems that social unrest involving increased expression of aggression within a population does result in lowered rates for depression just as the hypothesis derived from psycho-dynamic thinking would predict.

Whilst the rationale behind this study may be sound, the data need to be interpreted with caution. In particular it could be that the rioting could have other effects which would make the lowered rate for depression more apparent than real. The numbers cited refer to cases encountered by the psychiatric services. Contrary to expectations, evidence suggests that experience of war and other major upheavals means that the numbers presenting to psychiatric services for disorder may actually decline (see Slater and Roth, 1973). One possible reason for this is that with troubles on the streets people may be less willing to go to their doctors or out-patient clinics to seek help. Alternatively such circumstances may create increased social cohesion as people unite against a common enemy and this could mitigate against the precipitation of psychiatric disorder. Regardless of the reason for this wartime decline it could be that a similar phenomenon occurred in Belfast in 1969 and 1970. Lyons could have checked on this by examining similar data relating to other types of psychiatric disorder. If it was only the rate for depression that had gone down in 1969 and 1970 then this would have considerably enhanced the case for interpreting the study as supporting a hypothesis linking depression to suppressed aggression. If other disorders declined as well and to a similar degree then the findings could not be regarded as supporting this hypothesis unless it is assumed that other disorders also result from suppressed aggression.

The measurement of aggression in depressed patients

An alternative way of looking at the relationship between depression and aggression is to obtain, if possible, an independent measure of aggression and apply it to depressed subjects and suitable controls. There are many studies of this kind. A good example of an investigation that is more extensive than most and which illustrates the difficulties involved is provided by Blackburn (1974). For this reason it is worth describing in a little detail.

In her series of investigations Blackburn has used Fould's 'Hostility and Direction of Hostility Questionnaire' (HDHQ) as described by Foulds *et al.* (1960). In essence this questionnaire aims to measure 'extrapunitiveness' and 'intropunitiveness' as two distinct aspects of hostility. It can thus be used to test the alternative version of the aggression/depression hypothesis which supposes that depression is particularly associated with inwardly directed aggression.

In this particular experiment Blackburn (1974) used six groups of subjects. For one group, the subjects were patients with bipolar affective disorders tested during a phase when they were depressed. The second group was similar but the subjects were tested after recovery from a depressive episode. The next two groups again had bipolar affective disorders, but they were tested either during a manic episode or after recovery from such an episode. The final two groups had unipolar depressions, again with one being tested whilst they were depressed and the other after recovery. This design enables changes between illness and recovery to be examined as well as the effects of hypomania and depression.

The results suggested that manic patients were extrapunitive when compared with the depressed groups and also when compared with normal subjects for whom scores on this test had been reported by other investigators. The key groups from the present point of view were those with depression and both actively depressed groups had high levels of intropunitiveness. Recovered depressed patients had significantly lowered levels of intropunitiveness and this confirms what Blackburn had predicted on the notion that high levels of internally directed aggression are a feature of depression.

In another study of the same general type Cochrane and Nielson (1977) used a measure of 'undischarged drive' (a subscale derived from Cattell's IPAT Anxiety Scale) and one of aggression based on the Object Relations Test (a form of projective test). Separate groups with endogenous and reactive depressions were used as well as two control groups. Only the endogenous group exhibited higher levels of aggression but both depressed groups had higher drive levels. The authors suggest that depressives of all types have inhibited drives but only in those with endogenous depression do these take the form of aggression.

Others have suggested that aggression may only be a feature of certain subgroups of people with depression. Fava *et al.* (1982) looked at subjects with a recent onset of unipolar depression. Using a special symptom questionnaire with a scale for hostility it was found that hostility was only related to depression in those subjects who lacked an apparent precipitating loss. Conventional wisdom with regard to the classification of depression would imply that this same subgroup would probably be the ones most likely to be regarded as endogenous if the endogenous/reactive distinction was being used. To this extent the results of Fava *et al.* (1982) are consistent with those of Cochrane and Nielson (1977).

The results of studies of this kind generally appear to support the notion that aggression is associated with depression and there are results that could be claimed to fit both versions of the aggression/depression hypothesis. Unfortunately, there are problems in interpretation that have not so far been mentioned that weaken the significance of this work. Firstly, the studies may show a general association between aggression and depression but do not indicate the direction of causation. The original hypothesis implies that suppressed or inwardly directed aggression produces depression. Investigations like those described leave it open as to whether aggression produces depression, or the causation goes the other way round. Alternatively the aggression and depression could both be produced by a third factor. A possible way of resolving the direction of causation is to do longitudinal studies in which samples of subjects were followed over time to see if the increase in aggression (either suppressed or inwardly directed) antecedes the occurrence of depression.

Another important limitation lies in the measures that have been used. Cochrane and Nielson used a measure of aggression based on a projective test and projective tests are notorious for producing measures of poor reliability and validity (Vernon, 1964). The questionnaire measures like the HDHQ also raise problems. Foulds *et al.* (1960), in commenting on the development of this questionnaire, describe the selection of items to measure intropunitiveness as relating to 'self-criticism and guilt'. Self-criticism and guilt are of course features that can be encountered in the more severe forms of depression. If these are also defined as examples of internally directed aggression then intropunitiveness is a feature of depression by definition; this is the problem of criterion contamination. In other words the whole issue becomes one of semantics and outside the realm of empirical verification or refutation. If it is desired to go beyond this, as the hypotheses under consideration appear to in claiming that certain forms of aggression produce depression, then it is necessary to avoid 'criterion contamination' by having measures of aggression that are independent of the criteria that are used to define depression. This does not appear to have been achieved.

Looking at the evidence as a whole with regard to the relationship between aggression and depression, the general trend in the findings is certainly consistent with the idea that the two processes are linked. The problem is that it is very weak evidence that is either readily open to other interpretations or which does not overcome major methodological problems such as ensuring that the measures of depression and aggression are not mutually contaminated.

Learned helplessness and other behavioural models

Psychologists interested in abnormal behaviour have often derived theoretical models directly or indirectly from laboratory research into different aspects of learning in animals. A number of explanations of depression have been derived in this way and the best-known and most extensively developed is undoubtedly the learned helplessness model. This section will largely concentrate on the learned helplessness model but before turning to this some cruder and less satisfactory behavioural formulations will be mentioned. These are more extensively reviewed by Eastman (1976).

Reinforcement is a central concept in many of these models. Lazarus (1968) largely set the scene by suggesting that depression might be produced by 'inadequate or insufficient reinforcement'. Lazarus was not specific as to what constitutes an inadequacy or insufficiency and a number of other theories can be seen as more specific elaborations of this general theme. Lewinsohn *et al.* (1970) have surmised that depression might result from a reduced frequency of social reinforcement. A slightly different approach is taken by Ferster (1973), who inclines to the view that there is a reduction in the repertoire of reinforceable behaviour. In other words the individual fails to receive reinforcement because there is a loss of the responses that would elicit it. Costello (1972) rings yet another variation on the basic theme by allowing that the behaviour may still occur, and be followed by the same reinforcers, but that the reinforcers have lost their reinforcing properties for the depressed subject. Costello offers a number of speculations as to why this might happen.

Williams (1984a) draws attention to a final theory in this group which is based on aversive control. Behaviour could be reduced and depression result because certain responses become associated with aversive punishing outcomes or stimuli linked with aversive outcomes. For example, after bereavement the widow comes into contact with cues that would otherwise have been associated with her husband such as the chimes from the clock that the husband used to make a minor ritual of rewinding every night. These no longer signal the presence of the husband and produce frustrative non-reward.

These theories are all open to the general criticism of being rather limited and simple-minded. Doubts can be raised as to whether the behaviour concerned can be related directly and in the way intended to basic operant procedures with animals. Such thinking also does not take into account more recent and more sophisticated analyses of animal learning (e.g. Dickinson, 1980; Mackintosh, 1983). Whilst notions like reduced reinforcement might explain some aspects of depressive behaviour (e.g. retardation), they are much less credible as explanations of other features of the depressive syndrome such as sleep disturbances. These models will therefore not be taken any further.

As already indicated, the most important and best-known behavioural explanation of depression is the 'learned helplessness' model. It is a model that has been fairly directly developed from animal research and the single best account of the original animal research and its initial application to depression is probably that of Seligman (1975).

The concept of learned helplessness emerged from experiments on animals of which a good example is provided by Seligman and Maier (1967). These authors used three groups of dogs which received different treatments during the initial phase of the study. The first group were strapped into a hammock where they were given electric shocks which could be switched off by pressing a pad with their noses. The second group was yoked to the first and received an identical pattern of shocks but could not terminate the shock by pressing the pad. The final group acted as a control and received no shock in the hammock.

The following day all subjects underwent training in a two-way shuttle box. In the shuttle box a light went on which was followed by footshock ten seconds later. In the usual way of shuttle box training the subjects could learn to escape or avoid shock by jumping the barrier into the other side of the box. The group that could terminate shock in the initial phase by pressing the pad and the control group that received no shock did well in the shuttle box and readily learned to jump the barrier. About 75 per cent of the yoked group which had been unable to control shock in the first phase of the experiment completely failed to escape shock in the shuttle box. This kind of result has been obtained in several experiments (see Seligman, 1975) and appears to be quite robust.

When initially placed in the shuttle box most dogs will rush around frantically when they experience shock. The normal dog will eventually get over the barrier and escape. Learning proceeds on subsequent trials and the normal dog learns to avoid shock. Dogs from the yoked group similarly rush around to begin with but may then lie down and become very passive. Even if such a dog does escape on one trial it is less efficient in making use of this information to escape on the following trials. It appears generally 'depressed' and 'anxious'. Seligman claims that dogs in this group have 'learned helplessness' in that they have learned that outcome is independent of responses as a result of the experiences gained in the initial phase of the experiment. Such learning of independence between response and outcome then interferes with performance in the shuttle box.

Seligman (1975) suggests that learned helplessness has a number of aspects. These are cognitive, motivational and emotional. The animal has the expectation that responding and reinforcement are unconnected, its motivation is reduced and it becomes anxious and depressed. Seligman then argues that learned helplessness and depression have much in common. The features of both are summarized in Table 3 which is reproduced from Seligman's book. Some of the alleged features of learned helplessness given in this table have not been described in this account and some of the listed features of depression are debatable. Nevertheless there is at least some degree of correspondence between the two conditions. This led Seligman to suggest that reactive depression in man might be a manifestation of learned helplessness, with learned helplessness in man being regarded as an expectation that responding and re-inforcement are independent or unrelated.

A large amount of research effort has gone into testing this version of the learned helplessness model of depression. It has also had to involve a switch from animal research to mainly human research. A good illustrative study is that of W. R. Miller and Seligman (1975). A number of student volunteers were used as

Table 3 *Summary of features common to depression and learned helplessness (from Seligman, 1975, reproduced with permission of W. H. Freeman & Co., from* Helplessness).

	Learned helplessness	Depression
Symptoms	Passivity	Passivity
	Difficulty learning that responses produce relief	Negative cognitive set
	Dissipates in time	Time course
	Lack of aggression	Introjected hostility
	Weight loss, appetite loss, social and sexual deficits	Weight loss, appetite loss, social and sexual deficits
	Norepinephrine depletion and cholinergic activity	Norepinephrine depletion and cholinergic activity
	Ulcers and stress	Ulcers (?) and stress; feelings of helplessness
Cause	Learning that responding and reinforcement are independent	Belief that responding is useless
Cure	Directive therapy: forced exposure to responses that produce reinforcement	Recovery of belief that responding produces reinforcement
	Electroconvulsive shock	Electroconvulsive shock
	Time	Time
	Anticholinergics; Norepinephrine stimulants (?)	Norepinephrine stimulants; anticholinergics (?)
Prevention	Immunization by mastery over reinforcement	(?)

subjects. These were assigned to 'depressed' or 'non-depressed' groups on the basis of whether their scores on the Beck Depression Inventory exceeded a previously established mean score for college students. As indicated in the previous chapter, the Beck Depression Inventory is a commonly used instrument to measure depression in clinical research. The experiment then followed a fairly standard paradigm for learned helplessness studies.

In the first part of the experiment about a third of the subjects in each group were exposed to white noise which they could escape by pressing a button. Another third were exposed to white noise which they could not escape, whilst the rest experienced no noise at all. In the main part of the experiment all subjects were required to try to solve anagrams. The anagrams followed a standard letter pattern so that it was possible to look at the subjects' ability to learn this pattern as well as their overall success rate.

Although the results did not come out entirely perfectly, they were definitely very much as might be predicted by the model. The non-depressed subjects showed poor anagram solution and learning after being exposed to inescapable noise, as opposed to those who could escape the noise or who experienced no white noise at all. In other words they showed the learned helplessness effect. Depressed subjects under the no-noise pretreatment condition performed worse than the non-depressed group under the same condition and the introduction of inescapable noise did not further affect the performance of subjects in the depressed group. It was as if depressed subjects had already experienced a learned helplessness-inducing pretreatment. It should also be remembered that the so-called 'depressed' group in this experiment were not psychiatric patients but had been selected as scoring above the average for student samples on the Beck Depression Inventory. It is quite possible that none of them would have been regarded as clinically depressed within the context of a psychiatric clinic.

Such was the impact of the learned helplessness model that it quickly inspired interest and research. This was so much so that one whole issue of the *Journal of Abnormal Psychology* for 1978 was devoted to papers evaluating and refining the model. Many of these merit reading. Some carried detailed criticisms of the application of learned helplessness to human depression, especially Costello (1978) and Depue and Monroe (1978). Because the model has been refined and adapted there is no need to look more widely at studies relating to the original version or at criticism only applicable to that version. On the other hand, some of the points in the two critical papers already referred to are worth outlining because they raise issues of general relevance to a much wider range of research in abnormal psychology.

One of the most obvious features of the learned helplessness research in general is that it is heavily based on 'analogue' experiments. By 'analogue' studies in this context is meant the use of subjects who are not directly taken from clinical samples but who are assumed to have some features in common with them. Thus in the paper by Miller and Seligman that was described above the subjects were students and not depressed patients. In this case the students were classified as 'depressed' on the basis of having scores above the student mean on the Beck Depression Inventory.

The value of analogue research in general will be examined in a later chapter (Chapter 11). For the present all that needs to be done is to point out that analogue research does have limitations. One of these is that non-clinical student subjects who share a particular feature in common with depressed patients (a relatively high score on a particular inventory in this case) may also however differ from patient samples in other important respects. It is thus incumbent upon those making extensive use of analogue research to show either that their analogue subjects do really represent clinical samples in all potentially relevant ways or to go on and show that their findings do generalize to clinical samples. This has often not been done extensively enough in research on learned helplessness and especially that pertaining to the original learned helplessness model.

In testing out a model like this as a possible explanation of depression, it is important to examine all aspects of the model and not just the kind of predictions examined by Miller and Seligman (1975). One important prediction of the model is that procedures inducing learned helplessness ought also to result in some tendency towards depression. This prediction has not been examined very extensively although there are one or two reports of relevance. Gatchel *et al.* (1975) carried out a rather similar experiment to that of Miller and Seligman (1975), using inescapable aversive tones as the learned helplessness-inducing procedure and anagram-solving as the main task to be affected by the learned helplessness. In general the effect on anagram-solving was pretty much as Miller and Seligman had found. In addition Gatchel *et al.* got their subjects to fill in adjective check lists as indicators of mood to yield scores relating to depression, anxiety and aggression. Again the induction procedure appeared to alter mood in the direction that would be expected. On the other hand, it could be argued that being exposed to uncontrollable aversive noises is likely to lower any person's mood (or result in anxiety and aggressive feelings). This is not necessarily the same thing as being depressed in the clinical sense. It still remains an open question as to whether factors that induce learned helplessness can also result in clinical depression.

It is also important to show that alternative explanations of the same data do not hold. One possible criticism of the early learned helplessness work on human subjects was that the procedures to induce helplessness might just have produced low motivation and not the emotional and cognitive aspects that Seligman claimed were present. Since depression can also result in poor motivation and low rates of responding the two things can look alike in experiments without depression being specifically associated with learned helplessness.

A final important point with regard to testing models of this kind experimentally is that it is often assumed that the relationships which hold for a narrow range of experimental situations are representative of what is true over a very wide range of 'real-life' behaviour. This is by no means necessarily the case. The generalization of findings needs to be demonstrated rather than just anticipated.

Further discussion of the learned helplessness model as already described is unnecessary since the theory has undergone a major revision. Seligman and his colleagues (e.g. Abramson *et al.*, 1978) acknowledged that the original formulation was inadequate in that it failed to take account of certain features of clinical depression. It is now argued that it is not exposure to learned helplessness contingencies *alone* that produces depression but the kinds of attributions that are made as a result of this experience. It is hypothesized that depression results when the individual makes attributions that are internal, stable and global in relation to negative events. By *internal* is meant that the individual attributes responsibility for what has gone wrong to himself rather than to some external agent. The attribution is stable because it is regarded as being a manifestation of a long-lasting characteristic as opposed to being, say, a mistake that is not likely to occur too often in the future. It is *global* because the tendency to make a mess of things applies to all kinds of situations and not only that of immediate concern. In the same way any positive events that happen to occur will get the reverse kind of attribution. They will be attributed to an external cause, as being unstable (i.e. not likely to happen again) and specific to the set of circumstances that held at that particular time.

The reformulation also states that the individual who becomes depressed expects that aversive circumstances are likely to obtain and that he will be unable to do anything about them when they occur. These different features are interrelated in that the greater the certainty that aversive circumstances will arise and the less that these are seen as controllable, the greater the motivational and cognitive deficits that will emerge. The more important these uncontrollable events are to the individual the more mood and self-esteem will be lowered.

Abramson et al.'s (1978) reformulated learned helplessness model differs significantly from the original version. It is in some ways quite a different kind of model. Although the experience of being in a situation involving helplessness (i.e. where responding and reinforcement are unrelated) still remains as a necessary condition for depression, the emphasis has shifted very much to the making of certain attributions about such situations. The theory has therefore become much more 'cognitive' in the sense that Beck's model (to be considered next) is described as cognitive. In other words, it is very concerned with the individual's thought processes.

In moving in this direction, the theory has also become less causal in nature. The straight analogue of the animal experiments implies that experiencing situations in which the individual is helpless will cause him to become depressed. The reformulated version describes the individual's expectancies and the kinds of attributions that he will make. The account says very little about what causes the person to have these expectancies or to make attributions of the kind that have been described.

As Williams (1984a) has pointed out, most work on the re-formulated model has concentrated on the alleged attributional style associated with depression rather than such things as the expectancy of highly aversive events. As an example, Seligman's own group (Seligman et al., 1979) has compared student subjects with relatively high scores on the Beck Depression Inventory with those having low scores. On a special measure designed to elucidate attributional style which describes situations (both positive and negative) and asks subjects to indicate their likely reactions, the 'depressed' group tended to attribute bad outcomes to internal, stable and global causes. The results are very much in line with expectations, but it is an analogue study using student volunteers as subjects and the authors rightly point to the need to extend this work to clinically depressed groups.

Where clinical groups have been used, the results are not always so encouraging although generally positive. Hargreaves (1982), in the thesis described by Williams (1984a), used Seligman *et al.*'s (1979) Attributional Style Questionnaire and could find no difference in patterns of attribution between clinically depressed patients and normal control subjects. On the other hand, a study by Raps *et al.* (1982) found evidence of a maladaptive attributional style in depressed, but not in schizophrenic patients. Fennell and Campbell (1984) also found that depressed patients exhibited the predicted kind of cognitive style when compared with recovered depressives and normal controls.

The reformulated version of the learned helplessness model has much in common with Beck's theory of depression. In fact Seligman (1981) suggested that the later version of his model could largely subsume Beck's theory. To be fair the same assertion could equally well be made the other way round. For these reasons, present purposes can be served quite well by leaving learned helplessness and passing on to Beck's theory. It should be remembered that many of the issues to be covered in the discussion of Beck's ideas will also have a bearing on the reformulated learned helplessness model. Those seeking a more extensive discussion of the later developments in the learned helplessness view of depression can consult reviews by Coyne and Gotlib (1983) or Peterson and Seligman (1984). The former paper, which is concerned with cognitive approaches to depression in general, concludes that the learned helplessness model is inadequate. As might be expected, Peterson and Seligman (1984) are more favourably inclined.

Beck's cognitive theory of depression

Although this theory has similarities with the reformulated learned helplessness model, its antecedents are very different. The learned helplessness approach to depression arose from an extension of animal research in experimental psychology into human and clinical problems. In contrast Beck's theory is based on clinical observations.

Beck's theory is set out in a number of publications (e.g. Beck, 1967; 1976; Beck *et al.*, 1979). Essentially it regards the key features of depression as being certain forms of negative and illogical thinking. Hence the common description of 'cognitive' that is applied to the theory in order to indicate that the primary disturbance lies in cognitive processes. The other features of depression, such as low mood, then follow from these cognitive disturbances.

Beck has characterized depressive thought in terms of a 'cognitive triad'. There is a negative view of the self (e.g. 'I am a failure'), the world (e.g. 'the things that go on are terrible') and the future (e.g. 'things will always go badly and never get better'). Thoughts of this nature arise more or less automatically and without real consideration in the mind of the depressed person.

In addition the depressed individual is prone to make systematic logical errors in thinking. These are of several kinds, such as selective abstraction when the person notes only the negative aspects of his behaviour and the things that go on around him. Other errors are overgeneralization or drawing conclusions to the effect that because one thing has not gone well then everything else will go wrong; magnifying the significance of negative events and minimizing the importance of positive ones; and personalization where bad things are related to the self even when there are no real logical grounds for this attribution.

In passing it can be seen that these logical errors show considerable overlap with the maladaptive attributions identified by the reformulated learned helplessness model. Beck's personalization is almost identical with the notion of internal attribution of negative events. Making stable and global attributions about negative events relates to Beck's concept of overgeneralization in that stable attributions imply a generalization over time and global attributions a generalization across situations.

A final major aspect of Beck's theory is that he regards depressed people as exhibiting certain kinds of schema. A 'schema' in this sense is a relatively consistent or habitual way in which the individual makes sense of and interprets his experiences. Those people who become depressed will have schemata that impart a depressive flavour or bias in how they see the world. Again this bears some relationship to the assumption in the reformulated learned helplessness model, that depressed individuals have a high expectation of negative or aversive states of affairs.

A major feature of this kind of theorizing is the primacy accorded to cognitive processes or styles of thinking (in this sense it can almost be seen as going a little way beyond the reformulated learned helplessness model in the importance accorded to cognitive processes). The theory is not fully causal in that it does not describe how the disturbed cognitive processes arise in the first place although Beck has speculated on background factors, such as certain kinds of childhood experience, that might predispose to the development of depressive schemata. However, there is a clear implication in Beck's theory (as in the reformulated learned helplessness model) that it is the disturbed thought processes that render people vulnerable to lowered mood and other features of depression.

If this is the case, it would be expected that people who later become depressed will show evidence of some disturbance in thought processes prior to becoming depressed. Lewinsohn *et al.* (1981) applied measures designed to reveal such cognitive processes to a large sample of subjects some of which later became depressed. Those who became depressed were not especially prone to cognitive distortion at initial testing. In this investigation the gap betwen initial testing and the occurrence of depression in those subjects who became depressed was of the order of several months. It could be argued that had this interval been shorter then the style of thinking might have been more predictive of who would become depressed. In fact Golin *et al.* (1981), using a more complicated design (a 'crosslagged panel correlational design'), obtained indications that attributional style could predict depression one month later. The problem here is that if cognitive style is to be proved to act independently to produce depression then it needs to be manifest some time beforehand. With short gaps of the order of a few weeks it could be that the change in cognitive style is merely the first feature of depression that appears as the disorder develops.

Studies in which allegedly normal subjects are assessed and then followed up to see who develops psychopathology later are difficult to carry out in practice. As an alternative some researchers have argued that if already depressed patients are followed up into remission then it should be the case that recovered depressives would show distorted thinking if it is the presence of certain patterns of thinking that lead to depression (and if these patterns of thinking are not just a part of depression). Experiments along these lines could run into problems of interpretation, especially if the results turn out to be positive. For example, it could be argued that thought processes take much longer to revert to normal than mood and other features of depression, or that once depression has occurred thought processes tend to be more or less permanently biased towards a depressive mode. These possibilities could occur without cognitive processes having the kind of primacy that is maintained by the theory. Negative results are much less open to alternative hypotheses.

A number of relevant investigations have been reported but that of Wilkinson and Blackburn (1981) is not atypical. They studied four groups of subjects consisting of depressed patients, recovered depressed patients, recovered patients with other diagnoses (mainly neurotics) and normal controls. In the two depressed groups, all had unipolar major depression in terms of the Research Diagnostic Criteria (Spitzer et al., 1978). In addition to the Beck Depression Inventory, three measures alleged to tap different aspects of depressive cognitive processes were used. The currently depressed patients were differentiated from the other three groups on the cognitive measures but the recovered depressed group did not differ from either of the control groups. These findings are therefore negative.

Eaves and Rush (1984) carried out an experiment somewhat similar to that of Wilkinson and Blackburn (1981). The main difference of significance was that, instead of having separate groups of currently depressed and recovered depressed subjects, they tested the same group of subjects twice: once while depressed and again when recovered. Like Wilkinson and Blackburn they found that on remission the depressive forms of thinking tended to return to control group values. However, they also ran a correlational analysis and found that depressive attributional biases were correlated with the length of the depressive episode. Eaves and Rush suggest that attributional biases either result from long-term depression (thus reversing the originally suggested causal relationship) or that they lead to greater time being spent in depressive episodes. It is interesting that Lewinsohn et al. (1981) found a closely related phenomenon. In their study the subjects with the most deviant attributional style whilst depressed had the poorer outcome.

The results cited immediately above have been largely negative from the point of view of Beck's theory of depression and its implications for the role that cognitive processes play in predisposing people to become depressed. As is often the case, apparently contradictory findings have been obtained although the general trend remains negative rather than positive. Two studies by Wittenborn and his associates (Altman and Wittenborn, 1980); Cofer and Wittenborn, 1980) have looked at women who had recovered from depression in comparison with subjects who had never been depressed. The once depressed subjects were more likely to respond positively to questionnaire items indicating such things as low self-esteem, a pessimistic outlook and a preoccupation with failure. The subjects were younger than those used in the other studies just described, and so Wittenborn's group may have got positive results because they were looking at a different subtype of depression. Another possibility is that they were just picking up the consequences of having been depressed. Since those who have been depressed once have a much increased risk of future episodes of depression, it could be that the findings are also due to some of the subjects moving into a phase of being depressed again with the reported features being the first signs of the new episode.

When considered overall, the evidence that depressive ways of thinking predispose people to become depressed is not at all strong. Nevertheless there is a weaker version of the theory that suggests that moment-to-moment fluctuations in mood might be produced by depressive thoughts, images, etc. (Williams, 1980). Evidence for this comes from 'mood induction procedures' or MIPs. There are a number of mood induction procedures and these have been described by Goodwin and Williams (1982). The most commonly used MIP consists of getting the subject to read aloud a large number of negative statements referring to himself (e.g. 'I feel discouraged and unhappy about myself'). Other MIPs include such things as getting the subject to recall things that made them feel low or rejected and listening to an audiotaped depressive story which asks the subject to imagine a close friend becoming ill, being diagnosed as having an incurable illness, etc. MIPs have been proved to be able to lower mood in subjects and to produce other features associated with depression such as biasing the nature of material recalled from memory (e.g. Teasdale and Fogarty, 1979; Teasdale and Russell, 1983). Coleman (1975) has even shown that observers blind to the experimental procedure could distinguish subjects who had just undergone an MIP to depress mood and those who had not.

As Williams (1984a) points out, it is hardly surprising that unhappy thoughts can lower mood. However, not all low mood can be considered to be depression in the sense that it is generally being considered in this book (i.e. as a psychopathological state). In fact these are analogue studies and run into the same kinds of problems that were referred to in the earlier discussion of the use of analogue experiments in learned helplessness research. It is also possible that lowered mood can lead to depressive forms of thinking although this is a possibility that has not been so extensively researched.

Even though it may be difficult to maintain that cognitive theories provide a convincing model for the production of the depression, they can still be of value for other reasons. They do offer an attempt to describe important features of depression. In this regard there have been some interesting attempts to devise experiments that would test other aspects of Beck's model such as his ideas about depressive schemata.

Derry and Kuiper (1981) attempted to get at the notion of self-schemata in depression by using an experimental technique derived from research into the level of processing models of memory. Subjects were shown words that could be used to refer to the person (adjectives such as 'happy' or 'dejected') and which had either a depressive or a non-depressive content in their meaning. Subjects were required to make three different types of decision about the words relating to their structure (written in upper case or lower case letters), semantic features (means the same as . . .) or self-referent features (does it describe the subject?). All experimental groups showed better recall of words for which a rating about self-reference had been made as opposed to the other two kinds of judgement. Normal and non-depressed psychiatric controls had superior recall for the words subject to judgement of self-reference only when these were non-depressed in tone. Depressed patients had enhanced recall for depression-related adjectives. This result is consistent with the notion that depressed subjects have negative self-schemata, given the further assumption that they recall best those words they see as referring to themselves.

Another attempt to get experimental evidence of self-schemata is reported by Davis and Unruh (1981). When subjects are asked to give an immediate recall of lists of words and this is done several times with the same words appearing in a different random order on each trial, there is a marked tendency for subjects to organize the words in recall as the procedure goes on. This is shown by a tendency for certain words to be clustered together in recall despite their particular position in the order of presentation. Various mathematical formulae have been devised to measure the degree of organization. Davis and Unruh (1981) based their experiment on this general principle, using adjectives that could refer to the self as the words forming the lists.

They had three groups of subjects which consisted of non-depressed controls, a group of short-term depressives and one of long-term depressives (i.e. people who had been depressed for a long time). As the results turned out, both the non-depressed controls and the long-term depressives showed better organization in free recall than the subjects whose depression had only been short-term. The authors suggest that non-depressed subjects have well-developed schemata for organizing terms used in self-description. This is broken down in the more acute stages of depression but after subjects have been depressed for some time a reorganization of self-schemata occurs.

There are problems with this experiment. It seems unlikely that the long- and short-term depressed subjects would differ only in the length of time that they had been depressed and in fact the short-term depressives were significantly older. It is quite possible that the latter group were more likely to consist of cases that could be classified as having endogenous depression. In addition the report says little about the nature of the self-schemata allegedly revealed by organization in free recall. It is of course negative self-schemata that are crucial for Beck's theory.

Whilst both the above experiments are open to criticism and neither could be regarded as a particular crucial test of Beck's theory, or even that aspect of it relating to self-schemata, they do illustrate the point that techniques from experimental cognitive psychology can be used to examine the nature of depressive cognitions. Further possible directions for this work to go in are described by Williams (1984a).

Although this chapter is not concerned with the treatment of depression, it is worth mentioning in passing that Beck's theory has been much more fruitful than the other psychological theories in suggesting ways of treating depressed patients. In a way this is not surprising since Beck is a clinician, rather than an experimental psychologist like Seligman, and is therefore much more directly concerned with therapeutic applications. Cognitive behaviour therapy, much of which can be linked with Beck's ideas, has proved to be effective in the treatment of depressed patients in a number of trials (see Williams, 1984a; 1984b for a discussion of many of these). There is also some indication that cognitive behaviour therapy can be combined very effectively with antidepressant medication (Blackburn *et al.*, 1981). Rarely are psychological treatments so closely tied to the underlying theory that proof of therapeutic effectiveness can be used as strong evidence of the validity of the theory itself. Cognitive therapy for depression is certainly no exception to this rule. Nevertheless, the evidence for therapeutic effectiveness does give some encouragement to the notion that cognitive models might play a useful role in explaining depression.

General comment on psychological theories

As the foregoing discussion has shown, psychological theories of depression have a number of different pedigrees. Psychoanalytical thought was a powerful early influence and has been quite heuristic in terms of inspiring a range of empirical studies. Research on conditioning and learning in animals has provided another source of theoretical ideas. There have been several models based around the notion of disturbed reinforcement characteristics (e.g. reduction in reinforcement or loss of reinforcer effectiveness) which have been based on ideas derived from the field of operant conditioning. The learned helplessness model also derived from animal research, albeit of a rather different kind than the simple operant procedures that inspired the more strictly behavioural models. The learned helplessness model has of course now moved away from its origins. The last of the major theories of depression is that of Beck and this has its background in a clinician's attempts to understand and deal with the phenomena encountered in everyday practice. What this all illustrates is that interesting theoretical ideas can be derived from a large number of sources including some that could not be described in the main part of this chapter. An example of the latter group is Rehm's (1977) 'self-control' model of depression which derives from work in human experimental psychology (see also Kanfer and Hagarman, 1981). The crucial question is not where the theory has originated, but how well it explains the phenomena of interest.

In conclusion, it is worth setting out a small number of points that relate to psychological explanations in general. Although the models discussed are generally intended to show how depression arises in the first place, research to establish the causal influence of psychological factors in depression has not been conspicuously successful in generating positive results. This does not mean that psychological factors play no part at all in producing depression. It could merely be a reflection of the inadequacy of the psychological theories put forward so far or of the experimental tests themselves. In fact it could be argued that it would be rather surprising if psychological factors could ever be shown to play no role at all in precipitating or causing depression. This is especially so in view of the work to be described in the next chapter which suggests that life events and other social influences play a part in causing depression.

One source of difficulty in establishing the possible aetiological role of psychological factors has already been mentioned in discussing the ideas derived from psychoanalysis but it also arises in the other major theories. Just as it is very hard to disentangle the notion of inwardly directed aggression from the statements about worthlessness, the need to be punished and so on that form a part of the syndrome of depression, so it is similarly difficult to disentangle the kinds of attribution or cognitive features posited by other theories from the basic phenomena of depression. This means that it is almost impossible to establish measures of these theoretically important features that are independent of depression. The only potentially satisfactory way around this is to show that subjects exhibit such things as repressed or inwardly directed aggression or a certain kind of attributional style some time before they develop the other features of depression and that none of the other core features are currently present. This demands a prospective study of allegedly normal subjects who are then followed up until a subsample become depressed. Such studies are difficult and expensive to carry out well. In any case, if the key feature (e.g. attributional style) only appears quite close to the onset of depression it is then possible to argue that this feature is nothing more than the first sign of depression to appear. Really convincing proof of causality may therefore be very difficult to obtain.

It is also worth noting that this kind of problem can arise in relation to non-psychological theories as well. If it is considered that depressed patients have a particular biochemical disturbance, such as is implied by the amine hypothesis mentioned at the end of Chapter 4, then the same difficulties in relation to causation also arise. It is possible that biochemical factors might cause depression but it could also be the case that they are part and parcel of a general process that is set in train by some other cause. The success of antidepressant medication in relieving depression does not prove that the basic cause is biochemical just as the success of cognitive therapy does not prove that cognitive processes must provide the cause. It can thus be seen that establishing the causal chain is not a difficulty that just arises in relation to psychological theories.

If the presently available psychological models do not emerge as being of proven value as causal explanations of depression, then how useful are they in explaining what is going on in depression? This question is difficult to answer and the particular stand that is taken will depend upon how impressive some of the supporting evidence for various theories is thought to be. One general criticism that might be put forward is that the theories do not extend much beyond the phenomena that are to be explained. This is basically the same point that has been made above when it was argued that the key features of the theories, whether they be inwardly directed aggression or some cognitive process, are difficult to disentangle from the basic features of depression.

Although this criticism does have some foundation, it would be an exaggeration to claim that the theories do nothing more than describe the standard features of depression in other words. The cognitive theories have certainly taken thinking beyond the classical descriptions of depression. They have pointed to the importance of cognitive processes in depression. Whether depressive cognitions produce depressed mood (as the theories suggest), or the reverse is true, or if both cognitions and mood are the end result of some entirely different aetiological factor, the fact remains that thought processes in depression do seem to be distorted and this is something that needs to be taken into account. Until these theories came along the role of cognition in depression was almost entirely ignored. The idea that cognitive processes in depression are of significance is considerably reinforced by the fact that cognitive therapies designed to influence these depressive cognitive processes do appear to produce appreciable therapeutic benefits. Finally, the derivation of these successful therapies also illustrates that functional theories which aim to describe what is going on are not necessarily a second best to causal models.

7 The Role of Life Events

There is a general assumption based on common sense reasoning that psychological disturbances can be produced as a reaction to environmental stresses. Popular arguments have sometimes had it that the increase in the rate of psychiatric consultation that has taken place in recent decades is a consequence of the stresses and strains of modern living. This latter argument is based on two assumptions, both of which are open to question. The first of these is that the increase in psychiatric consultation reflects a true gain in morbidity as opposed to a greater willingness amongst those afflicted to come forward and seek help. The second assumption is that such things as the potential horrors of nuclear war and worldwide devastation make life today more stressful than it was decades or centuries ago despite the fact that modern life also cushions people against other sources of stress that operated in the past.

It is not the purpose of this chapter to analyse the reasons for the change in consultation rates over time. The present concern is with whether psychological distress or disorder can result from stress brought about by adverse circumstances. In fact with the example of bereavement and its consequent grief in mind it would be very hard to argue that distress could not result from adverse life events. The question at issue is therefore more properly whether psychological distress or disorder of the kinds that could be considered to constitute psychiatric conditions can result from social and environmental occurrences. In line with the previous chapters this question will be discussed with particular reference to depression.

As with most of the other issues that have been dealt with previously, the basic question is by no means as straightforward as it seems. In addition it has not proved easy to obtain evidence that will clearly or unequivocally answer the question in any of the forms in which it might be put. Again it is necessary to begin by looking at the nature of the question and the means by which it might be answered.

Logical and methodological issues

In looking at some of the problems involved it is useful to have a particular example in mind. Holmes and Rahe (1967) were amongst the first to make a determined attempt to look at the impact of life events on morbidity. To do this they developed a social readjustment rating scale (often known as the SRE) based on a list of forty-three life events including such things as death of a spouse, marriage, losing a job, retirement and committing a minor violation of the law. A large sample of subjects was asked to rate each of these items in terms of the readjustment needed to accommodate to them. Marriage was used as the anchor point and given an arbitrary value of what in the final version was 50 points. All the other items were scaled in relation to marriage. Thus death of a spouse counted as 100 and a minor violation of the law as 11. This scale has been used by many authors (see Craig and Brown, 1984 for a review) to demonstrate an apparently higher rate of life events in the months preceding the onset of a number of different types of pathology (including different forms of physical disease).

A little thought reveals a number of problems with the SRE that need to be overcome in any satisfactory study of the impact of life events. A good review of these is provided by Brown and Harris (1978) and Brown et al. (1973). In the first place the SRE assumes that the disruptive effect of the listed events is the same for all people and this seems highly unlikely. Being caught in a minor violation of the law may be a trivial occurrence for individuals in some sections of society and very stressful for others. Of possibly greater importance is the fact that the SRE takes no account of the meaning or significance of the events. Getting married is something that is generally looked forward to by those most directly involved whereas the death of a spouse is a highly aversive occurrence for the new widow or widower. As far as producing depression is concerned it is likely to be the adverse events that are of most significance. The major study by Brown and Harris (1978) which is described in detail later attempts to get round these problems by concentrating on adverse events and especially those that almost everyone would regard as being of real significance (e.g. bereavement or the loss of a job).

Psychiatric disorders can develop insidiously making it impossible to identify a specific date of onset as opposed to a date of identification. This means that if there is a relationship between life events and depression then the direction of influence may not be clear. If a man loses his job and is then diagnosed as being depressed a few weeks later it could be that the depression emerged as a consequence of the job loss. On the other hand, it could be that the depression was developing for some considerable time before it was actually identified and that one of the first consequences was a fall-off in work efficiency. The loss of job could then be a consequence of depression rather than its cause. The SRE cannot cope with this possibility but Brown and Harris (1978) decided only to rely on events where there was a high probability that they were independent of any psychiatric disorder. In the case of an event like losing a job this was only counted in circumstances such as where the individual was one of many losing a job at the same time in a redundancy programme. In this case it is rather unlikely that the job loss was the consequence of an insidiously developing psychiatric disorder.

A further complicating factor is that there is a tendency with some major problems, such as the onset of depression, to indulge in what has sometimes been described as a 'search for meaning'. In other words, the individual searches his memory for things that might explain why he has arrived in his present state. Stott (1958) interviewed mothers with recently born children with Down's Syndrome (mongolism). These mothers reported having experienced more shocks and upsets during pregnancy than mothers whose babies were normal. Since it is now well established that what goes wrong must take place more or less at the time of conception because Down's Syndrome is due to a chromosomal abnormality, the most likely explanation of Stott's finding is not that the mothers of the Down's babies actually experienced any excess of upsetting events. They were either more likely to recall such events that did occur or to reinterpret neutral events in a negative way. This kind of mechanism could occur as well in depression and be exaggerated by the tendency for subjects with depression to recall material with a negative connotation much more readily (see Chapter 5). Where items are vaguely defined as are many of these in the SRE, it gives scope for the depressed individual to redefine them for himself in an idiosyncratic way so as to overidentify events. More recent investigations, like those of Brown and Harris (1978), have countered this possibility by only accepting events which have some independent verification and which would be almost certainly stressful for everybody.

Quite another kind of difficulty can arise in interpreting the significance of particular events. To take a relatively straightforward example, some theorists of a psychoanalytic bent have suggested that depression in adults might be linked to the loss of a parent (by death, divorce etc.) during childhood. Even if an excess of early parental losses can be shown to occur in those who later develop depression this does not mean that early parental loss *per se* is related to depression. It could be that the early loss of a parent leads to other things (e.g. loss of father could produce a reduction in family income and cause some degree of deprivation) and that it is these other things that are the key factors. This possible complication is most readily apparent where the key event is something like early parental loss which precedes the onset of depression by some considerable time. However, the same kinds of arguments can apply to much more recent events. It could be that it is not the loss of a job as such which helps to precipitate depression but something that tends to follow from this. Complications of this kind make the interpretation of positive findings more difficult.

The discussion so far has presumed a situation where retrospective studies are being carried out. This is where cases of depression are identified and then an instrument like the SRE of Holmes and Rahe (1967) or the much more sophisticated techniques of Brown and Harris (1978) is used to examine life events that preceded the onset of depression. The alternative strategy is the prospective study where the investigator identifies individuals who have suffered a particular stressful life event and then follows them to see if they have a rate of disorder in excess of controls that have not suffered the same misfortune. This latter strategy, which has been used less frequently, shares some of the problems of the retrospective studies whilst creating a few methodological difficulties of its own.

Prospective studies are based on an adverse event that most people would regard as being unequivocally stressful. The most commonly used event is bereavement, especially being widowed, the death of a spouse being rated as demanding the most readjustment of all the items used in the development of the SRE (Holmes and Rahe, 1967). The methodological problems will therefore be considered in relation to widowhood as the anchor event although the same general principles would arise regardless of the actual event chosen.

It is easy to identify those who have recently become widows (or widowers, although the latter are less common). This can be done from records of hospital deaths and a sample of widows can be followed for a set period (e.g. six months) to determine the rates and types of psychiatric disorder that occur. A control group of women matched for other likely confounding variables but who have not been widowed can also be followed for a similar period. In general the prospective study enables the investigator to control the kind of life event that he is interested in but he has no control over the kinds of disorder that might be detected during the follow-up period. This situation is reversed in the retrospective study where the kind of disorder being studied is controlled but a large number of possibly relevant life events may be identified.

In the prospective study it is assumed that the selected life event is likely to be sufficient in itself to act as a causal or precipitating factor. It could be that something like widowhood, no matter how distressful, is generally not sufficient to precipitate depression on its own. Hence very large groups of subjects may be required to show any effect and to consider a subset of those who have been widowed and also experienced some other adverse event in the recent past complicates matters considerably.

Being widowed will produce certain psychological reactions such as grief. Space does not permit the discussion of the consequences of being widowed in any detail but Parkes (1972) deals with the topic at length. In order to look at the impact of this event on psychiatric morbidity it is also necessary to be able to distinguish between what might be regarded as a normal grief reaction and a pathological reaction and indeed there may be no clear distinction between the two. Even if a satisfactory distinction between normal and pathological reactions can be made in principle, it may get confounded in practice. Moreover, doctors and mental health professionals in general may believe that the recently widowed are especially prone to psychiatric disorder and so may be more ready to diagnose depression and refer patients to psychiatrists if they know that the person concerned has been recently widowed.

Whilst relying on a single life event, such as being widowed, may tend to attenuate any relationship between life events and disorders like depression, the kind of factors mentioned immediately above are likely to exaggerate any relationship. It seems inherently unlikely that the possible biasing factors will balance one another out and it is difficult to predict in any given context which will predominate.

Even if some sort of relationship can be satisfactorily demonstrated between the occurrence of adverse life events and the consequent development of psychiatric disorder, some problems still remain. Psychiatric disorders are very varied and the role of life events may vary considerably depending upon the nature of the particular disorder under consideration. Thus the conclusions that might seem to follow from a consideration of the evidence to be described later in relation to depression might not be appropriate for schizophrenia or obsessional neurosis (see also Chapter 13). It is also the case that environmental events might influence psychological disorder in a number of different ways. These events might act wholly or partially as causal agents in that they are actually responsible for the production of the disorder (i.e. act as 'formative' agents in the terminology of Brown and Harris, 1978). Alternatively they could precipitate or trigger a disorder whose ultimate cause lies in factors of a quite different kind. The relationship between life events and other factors that might also act to produce disorder is another aspect that needs to be considered. There can thus be no single, simple answer to the role of life events in psychological disorder.

Brown and Harris (1978) have tried to develop a means of distinguishing between formative and triggering effects of life events. This is based on the concept of 'brought forward time'. This concept is a little tricky and difficult to grasp at first presentation. Given a study done on a large community sample, a proportion of which will possess the characteristic of interest (e.g. depression) and for whom the occurrence of significant life events can be ascertained, it is possible to make certain numerical estimates. Assuming that any subject could become depressed, given enough time, it is possible to estimate the likely time between a significant life event and the onset of depression. It is also possible to derive the average length of time between an event and the onset of depression in that subsample of the population studied that actually develops depression. The difference between these two time periods is the 'brought forward time'. For example, if the estimated likely time between the occurrence of an event and the onset of depression is thirty months for the sample as a whole and the mean time between a significant event and the actual appearance of depression in those who actually are depressed is six months then the brought forward time is twenty-four months.

Brown and Harris (1978) then argue that if the brought forward time is large, as in the hypothetical example given immediately above (i.e. twenty-four months), then the influence of life events on depression is likely to be formative (i.e. causal). If the brought forward time is short this does not rule out a formative relationship but it is also quite consistent with the notion that life events merely have a triggering effect thus precipitating the onset of a disorder whose main causation lies elsewhere.

The reasoning used to back up the concept of brought forward time is elegant and appealing. To discuss the matter satisfactorily would involve a long technical diversion which would be slightly beside the point as far as the main thrust of this chapter is concerned. Suffice it to say that, in the present writers' opinion, brought forward time is an interesting pointer with regard to whether events might be considered formative or triggering. It is probably unwise to regard this index as anything like clear and unequivocal proof as to the actual mechanism by which life events exert their effect. To mention but two of the potential problems (chosen for ease of description rather than their relative seriousness as objections), it is not obvious just how long brought forward time has to be in order to indicate causality rather than triggering. It is also possible to have a very long brought forward time and yet still have an appreciable lapse of time between the occurrence of an event and the onset of depression in those subjects who become depressed. If this latter interval were six months or longer (as in the case of the hypothetical example given above) then it is a little surprising that depression directly caused by bereavement, the loss of a job, etc. should actually take such a long time to become apparent. It would then be of interest to look at what had gone on between the noted event and the onset of the disorder.

The Brown and Harris (1978) investigation

Some reference has already been made to the work of Brown and Harris (1978). This is undoubtedly the most significant study in the field both in terms of the sophistication of its methodology and in the interest that it has generated. In many ways these investigators have set the standard for everyone else to live up to. For these reasons it merits separate and much more detailed consideration than the rest of the literature in this area of work.

This particular study involved female subjects only. This was because, firstly, epidemiological evidence suggests a higher rate of depression in women and, where large community samples are required, a reasonable number of depressed subjects from a smaller overall sample can be more easily obtained. Secondly, women are more likely to be at home during the day and are therefore more easily available to interviewers. Another possible consideration not apparently taken into account by Brown and Harris but which emerges more strongly in retrospect is that some of the variables may show sex differences. A mixed sample would then introduce additional complications. This is not to suggest that the basic mechanisms producing depression are different in men and women but the kind of social factors identified by Brown and Harris as making individuals more vulnerable to depression-inducing influences could quite well involve sex differences.

All subjects came from the Camberwell area of London. This is a rather decaying inner-city area whose residents are predominantly of lower socioeconomic status. Three groups were studied. The first consisted of 114 depressed psychiatric patients (either in- or out-patients) together with two separate community surveys of women living in Camberwell. When combined the community surveys gave a total of 458 women. Subjects were between 18 and 65 years of age and all were assessed psychiatrically by means of the Present State Examination (Wing *et al.*, 1974) to establish a diagnosis as appropriate. In addition to the depressed women in the psychiatric sample a proportion of those in the community sample also met the criteria for a diagnosis of depression. All subjects were also interviewed at considerable depth about what had happened to them in the previous year and their reactions to these events. Interviews were tape recorded and ratings derived by independent raters on the basis of these recorded interviews, with the whole procedure trying to take into account the methodological points discussed earlier. Inter-rater reliabilities were generally more than adequate.

It was found that events rated as severe were approximately four times more common in women with depression than those who had not suffered depression. In this context severe events were those that represented a long-term threat either to the woman herself or jointly to the woman and someone else. The excess of severe life events in the depressed women was particularly apparent in the last three months or so prior to the onset of depression. The common characteristic that was noted about the kind of events that were rated as severe was that they involved disturbing events such as bereavement, a life-threatening illness to someone close, a major material loss, enforced change of residence, etc. The evidence also suggested that the effects of these severe events were additive (where they were unrelated) in that experiencing more than one of them increased the likelihood that a woman could be depressed.

Estimates of brought forward time were calculated as a means of looking at the mechanisms by which severe events exerted their effects. For the depressed hospital patients the brought forward time was 1.95 years whereas for those in the community sample who became depressed in such a way as to meet the Present State Examination criteria for the diagnosis, the brought forward time was 2.18 years. Brown and Harris (1978) argue that such lengths of brought forward time are only compatible with formative effects. Also relevant to this claim is the fact that it only appears to be life events that occur within nine to twelve weeks of onset of depression that are significant. In earlier work Brown's group had suggested that life events could produce depression a year, or even longer, after they had occurred and this earlier claim seems rather unlikely. The results on depression do contrast with the same author's findings for schizophrenia where the brought forward time is only ten weeks, and it is therefore argued that in schizophrenia events just act to trigger or precipitate onset.

Whilst almost all the women in the study who had developed depression had experienced a severe life event or major difficulty within the year covered by the investigation there were still a large number who had suffered such experiences and yet who did not become depressed. One possibility is that there may be other factors operating that can make individuals more or less sensitive to the effects of provoking agents. In operational terms a factor that increases vulnerability should not significantly increase the likelihood of depression when it occurs on its own. However, where provoking events occur their potency should be increased if the vulnerability factor is also present. From Brown and Harris's data social class appears as being related to vulnerability in that lower social class subjects were more likely to develop depression in the presence of provoking agents.

A number of specific vulnerability factors emerged. One was the absence of a close, confiding relationship with another person. Usually such a relationship is provided within marriage but such a relationship could be provided by a boyfriend or a friendship with another woman. In addition not all married women have a relationship with their husbands that could be described as 'close and confiding'. Other factors that could make the women more vulnerable appeared to be having three or more children younger than 14 living at home, loss of the woman's own mother early in life, and lack of employment. Of all the vulnerability factors the absence of a close, confiding relationship was the most significant since the presence of such a relationship tended to neutralize the effects of the other three vulnerability factors. The evidence showed a trend towards social class differences in the presence of vulnerability factors and this could at least partially explain the social class differences in the rate of depression.

This account by no means exhausts the rich analysis provided by Brown and Harris (1978) although it does describe the most important features as well as those that have attracted the most attention. The really contentious feature of the study is that it purports to demonstrate that life events do have a substantial causal role in producing depression. Even if Brown and Harris's data and interpretations are taken at face value, they certainly cannot prove that depression is caused solely by social factors. Genetic, bio-chemical and psychological factors were not taken into account and their contribution cannot be excluded. By the same token, investigations of possible biological and psychological mechanisms do not take social factors into account and so cannot exclude the possibility that the latter might also be of some significance. This point is worth making because a few critics of this work, especially some of those with a more biological bias to their thinking about depression, have reacted as if it represents an utter negation of their outlook. This is just not so.

One prominent line of criticism is well represented in a paper by Tennant *et al.* (1981). These authors raise a large number of criticisms of life events research in general though they only attribute some of them to the Brown and Harris (1978) work. In particular they claim some contamination of measures in Brown and Harris's study. For example, things like employment status and the nature of the relationship with a spouse or lover are used to define the degree of threat in an event as well as serving as vulnerability factors. It is also claimed that where indices of stress (or threat in the case of Brown and Harris) are used there is no external criterion against which this can be validated. It is also alleged that very little of the variance in depression is explained by life events in the studies that have been done. At first sight this last point is a very important one but Craig and Brown (1984) argue quite convincingly that conventional estimates of the variance explained are quite misleading in this context and can considerably underestimate the true importance of life events.

Whilst the criticisms offered by Tennant *et al.* (1981) and others of a similar mind do have some validity and, in consequence, suggest further methodological refinements for future research, it is debateable whether taking them into account would make very much difference to Brown and Harris's results or conclusions. When all is considered this study is very impressive and must be regarded as very much strengthening the case that life events can appreciably contribute to the production of depression. If it is rightly claimed that this study does not provide absolutely irrefutable proof then, in the absence of equally well derived contrary evidence, it should also be remembered that in fields like psychology and psychiatry it is extremely rare for any single investigation to provide irrefutable proof of anything. This is so no matter how flawlessly executed an investigation may be.

There are reports of a number of studies that have extended or partially replicated Brown and Harris (1978). Costello (1982) in Calgarry and Solomon and Bromet (1982) in Pennsylvania have both carried out similar studies which have examined vulnerability factors. Solomon and Bromet (1982) found no evidence that being unemployed or having three or more children at home increased the risk of having a depressive disorder in Pennsylvanian women. Similarly Costello (1982) showed no effects attributable to social class, number of children at home, or loss of subject's own mother before 11 years of age. On the other hand, lack of intimacy with a spouse or person in an equivalent relationship did result in an increased risk of depression in Costello's study. It was just this particular vulnerability factor that Brown and Harris (1978) found to be the most potent.

At best this is only partial confirmation of Brown and Harris's work. This difficulty in replication is not necessarily because any of these studies have produced incorrect results. It would not be very surprising if there were marked cultural differences in the kinds of factor that might enhance vulnerability. Brown and Harris (1978) have hinted that they suspected that this might be the case since Brown and his colleagues had already started to extend their work by studying a sample of women on the remote island of North Uist in the Outer Hebrides. This section on the work of Brown and his colleagues will therefore conclude with a brief description of these later studies.

It is difficult to imagine a bigger contrast between communities within Britain than that of the Outer Hebrides and Camberwell. Whereas Camberwell is a decaying inner-city area of London and densely populated the Outer Hebrides are about as isolated and predominantly rural a community as it would be possible to find within the UK. Crofting and fishing are two of the main occupations. The extension of the work to this Scottish community therefore represents about as extreme a test of Brown's general model as could be obtained.

Brown and Prudo (1981) provide an outline of this Hebridean study and of some of the more important findings. The details of the methodology will not be given because these are similar to the Brown and Harris (1978) Camberwell study. The results again confirmed the importance of life events in the genesis of depression. One of the most interesting differences between the Hebrides and Camberwell lies in the vulnerability factors. In the Hebrides it was found that women who could be described as being well integrated into the traditional way of life had a reduced chance of developing depression and, unlike Camberwell, having middle-class status did not offer any protection. By 'integrated into the traditional way of life' Brown and Prudo mean being involved in traditional occupations, having traditional living arrangements (e.g. in crofts) and being participating members of the church. Again this backs up reports like those of Costello (1982) and Solomon and Bromet (1982) which have found that the Camberwell vulnerability factors do not apply in other contexts. As suggested earlier this is not very surprising and it could be that being well integrated into a small and closely knit community in the Hebrides could provide the kind of protection or support that would have to come from a close, confiding relationship for another individual in somewhere like Camberwell.

Other work on life events and depression

The work of Brown and his colleagues has been given considerable prominence because it is the most extensive and sophisticated. In this section some other lines of research will be described although it should be remembered that this other work is generally less adequate from a methodological point of view. A number of useful reviews also exist (e.g. Clayton, 1982; Lloyd, 1980a; 1980b; Paykel, 1982; Tennant, 1983), each tending to cover a different aspect of the literature. This section can only pick up a number of illustrative examples of the kind of work that has been done.

One area that has received considerable attention is that of bereavement, especially being widowed. A number of studies have shown that samples of depressed patients typically contain subjects with an increased incidence of childhood bereavement. This is most typically the loss of a parent before the time of puberty (see Lloyd,

1980a). This work will not be considered further because it is difficult to decide whether it is the identified event itself (i.e. the childhood bereavement) or other things that follow from this event that are significant. For example, loss of a father (by far the most common form of childhood bereavement) can result in the child being raised in altered and more straitened circumstances.

An early study of the effects of bereavement during adult life is that of Parkes (1964). He looked at a large number of psychiatric hospital admissions of all types (in a total sample of over three thousand) and found that 2.9 per cent had experienced a recent bereavement. This figure is around six times more than would have been expected on the basis of demographic data. Bereaved subjects were particularly prone to depression.

In a similar study Frost and Clayton (1977) looked at 249 psychiatric in-patients with a range of diagnoses and a similar number of controls (orthopaedic patients). The overall level of recent bereavement was low. There was also no difference between the two groups with regard to the death of a first-degree relative in the period prior to admission. However, within the group of psychiatric patients who had suffered such a loss there was a strong tendency for the diagnosis to be depression.

Recent bereavement therefore does seem to have some relationship with depression and many other studies confirm this (see Clayton, 1982). This relationship appears to be between recent bereavement and depression rather than with psychiatric disorder in general. In most cases this bereavement consists of being widowed. With regard to loss of a partner there are indications that divorce does not have the same impact as bereavement. Briscoe and Smith (1975) compared three sets of depressed patients. One group had been recently bereaved, another contained subjects with a recent divorce, and the third was a control group that had suffered no comparable recent upset. When the dependent variables were examined the divorced and control groups were very similar. The bereaved group had experienced fewer previous episodes of depression and had fewer family members with a history of depression or other psychiatric disorder. This is indirect evidence that bereavement has a bigger impact than divorce. In some ways this might be expected since in divorce there is usually a mutual desire to end the relationship. On the other hand, divorce can be a very disturbing experience. If the conclusion suggested by this study is correct, then the effect of being bereaved or widowed is not just the consequence of a general upset that might be produced by any negative experience. The finding is then in line with that of those workers interested in the effects of life events who have particularly implicated events involving a loss.

A final point with regard to studies of the effects of being bereaved or widowed is whether the consequences are really the same as depression as it is normally encountered in clinical populations. No one can seriously doubt that bereavement can cause grief and unhappiness but it is a moot point as to whether these emotions constitute the psychiatrist's concept of depression. Clayton (1982) has discussed much of the relevant evidence. In one study (Clayton and Darvish, 1979) it was found that a high proportion of those recently widowed experienced symptoms commonly associated with depression. A month after bereavement a number of somatic symptoms linked to depression can be detected but these have diminished considerably by the time that a year has elapsed. In contrast the more psychological symptoms show a stronger tendency to persist.

Clayton et al. (1972) looked at a sample of a little more than a hundred people who had been widowed recently. Using the Feighner criteria, twenty-two were definitely depressed and a further sixteen were probably depressed. Comparing these thirty-eight with the rest revealed relatively few differences. They did not differ on variables such as the length of the spouse's terminal illness or a previous history of depression. The differences that did emerge were in certain features of mental state (e.g. feeling hopeless or feeling a burden) and fewer of those considered to be depressed were closely supported by their children.

There is, therefore, quite an appreciable overlap between the clinical features of depression and the consequences of bereavement. Despite this overlap some quite consistent differences do emerge. Clayton (1982) comments that in her extensive series of studies of those who have been bereaved or widowed retardation is extremely rare and that she has never encountered a subject who could be described as having a 'retarded depression'. Suicidal thoughts are also very unusual in the bereaved whilst they are quite commonplace in samples of depressed patients. Whilst feelings of guilt can be present after bereavement they differ in quality from those encountered in depression. After bereavement guilt relates to things that were not done for the deceased during the time leading up to death. What is not found is the pervasive sense of guilt which can involve almost anything and everything that occurs in clinical depression. The exact relationship between grief after bereavement and clinical depression is not clear. The importance that is placed on the differences between the two will determine just how significant the evidence from bereavement is considered with regard to questions about the relationship between life events and depression.

Both Lloyd (1980b) and Tennant (1983) have pointed to the undoubted problems inherent in retrospective studies and have stressed the need to examine prospective studies where samples are followed for appreciable lengths of time. Studies of this kind were then reviewed by Tennant (1983). Although Tennant considers these studies as better indicators of the impact of life events the investigations reported so far tend to be concerned with psychological symptoms in general rather than with a specific disorder such as depression. This is unfortunate because many of the leading authorities have suggested that the role of life events is particularly marked in depression. If life events play little or no part in the creation of other types of disorder then any effect on depression may be difficult to distinguish against the noise produced by including all the other signs and symptoms.

Two illustrative studies will be described. Grant *et al.* (1982) studied a large number of male subjects almost half of which were psychiatric out-patients with various diagnoses and the rest being psychiatrically normal. Every two months subjects filled in two scales, one to report significant life events and the other to record symptomatology. The resulting data was subjected to a complex mathematical procedure (Fourier analysis) and this suggested five different types of event-symptom relationship. Only one of these types of relationship corresponded to a possible causal relationship between events and symptoms and this accounted for only 9 per cent of the total sample. Whether this 9 per cent were depressed is not reported.

Andrews (1981) had 407 subjects who were attending a family practice in Sydney. These completed the General Health Questionnaire (GHQ) at the start of the study. The GHQ is a general screening instrument often used to indicate psychiatric morbidity in psychiatric studies of this kind. At four, eight and twelve months later the GHQ was repeated and a scale to record life events was also completed. There was a relationship between life events and symptoms but this was considerably attenuated when life events were related to symptoms that persisted from one testing to the next. Andrews concludes that in people already reasonably well symptoms do emerge after life events but are of short duration.

Symptoms that persist are more determined by other factors. An alternative explanation that might also fit the data is that life events do lead to the creation of symptoms, but, once symptoms have occurred, their duration is governed by other things and not the life events that caused them.

In his review Tennant (1983) draws attention to another point. Although life events may emerge as having some effect the magnitude of this effect is small. As was described earlier this may depend on how the size of the relationship is measured and Craig and Brown (1984) have argued that the usual measures of variance explained may be misleading in this context. In addition there are other reasons why research of life events may give a misleadingly low estimate of their importance. In the prospective studies that are particularly favoured by Tennant (1983) the concern has been with all kinds of psychological symptoms. Restricting consideration to depression might yield stronger results since there is evidence that the role of life events and social circumstances is not the same in depression as in schizophrenia (Brown and Harris, 1978) or possibly even in neurosis in general (Henderson et al., 1981).

Another feature that will reduce the size of any observed relationship is the dependence of empirical studies on events like bereavement and being made redundant which can be established projectively and which would be universally regarded as adverse. Something like the death of a pet, which would be an event that most people could take in their stride but which might be a major upset for a few, generally would not get counted as a potentially significant life event by workers like Brown and Harris (1978). To some extent events whose impact might vary from person to person can be taken into account by looking at the contextual threat that they pose (e.g. if the subject is blind and the pet is also his guide dog then this has different implications than if the subject is sighted and the pet has no obvious functional role in the person's life). Nevertheless, even this added sophistication means that many events of possible importance, but whose exact role in relation to the individual remains ambiguous, have to be left out of consideration in the service of methodological rigour. To put the whole thing the other way round, the reported investigations can set the minimum size of the relationship between life events and depression; they do not reveal what the real size is unless other assumptions can be made.

Comment

The idea that adverse life events can lead to psychological disorder, especially depression, makes intuitive sense. To some degree this notion is enshrined in the belief systems and experience of most people. Demonstrating that this simple proposition is true is fraught with difficulties and it is unlikely that a final answer has yet emerged.

On balance the evidence seems to support the common sense view that adverse life events can help to produce clinically significant depression. Despite Brown and Harris's (1978) sophisticated statistical arguments it is far from finally established whether the effects of life events are formative (i.e. causal) or if they just precipitate or trigger something whose fundamental cause lies elsewhere. Brown and Harris are about the only major investigators to address this question squarely and the indications are that life events do have a formative role.

This chapter has looked at life events as they relate to depression. The role of these events, and the social factors that enhance vulnerability to them, may vary considerably in other psychiatric disorders. As has already been mentioned Brown and Harris (1978) found that their brought forward time measure suggested that events only had a triggering effect in schizophrenia. Others have looked at the role of social factors in neurosis in general. Henderson *et al.* (1981) identified social relationships as being a key factor in neurosis. However, it is not the availability of social relationships that was significant but the adequacy of these relationships as viewed through the eyes of the neurotic subject. Unlike the depressed women in Camberwell, where it was the absence of close relationships that enhanced vulnerability to the influence of life events, Henderson *et al.*'s neurotic subjects seemed unable to make good use of the relationships open to them.

Findings like Brown and Harris's (1978) and Costello's (1982), indicating the importance of a close confiding relationship, and that of Brown and Prudo (1981), indicating the desirability of being well integrated into the local community, suggest possible lines of intervention to help those prone to psychiatric disorder. Enhancing the social support available or, in the case of neurotic patients of the kind studied by Henderson *et al.* (1981), training them in the skills necessary to elicit the support potentially available in their environment, may have beneficial effects (see Winefield, 1984). Space does not permit this issue to be followed here but a related topic, that of the impact of family relationships on schizophrenics, will be discussed in Chapter 13.

8 Treatment: 'Relationship' Therapies

Unlike most other branches of psychology, a major concern of abnormal psychology is the modification and amelioration of the phenomena under study. Not only is treatment an issue of extreme practical importance but the successful modification of abnormal behaviour can often provide insights into fundamental mechanisms which determine and control the behaviour. This chapter and those that immediately follow will describe some of the major methods of treatment and discuss a number of important issues that arise in attempting to evaluate their effectiveness as well as the processes by which they are purported to work. The focus will be almost entirely on psychological treatments but a brief account of biological treatments is also included for comprehensiveness and because these will be referred to at a later point.

There are a large number of different types of psychological treatment with each based on its own rationale no matter how bizarre it may appear to non-initiates (Corsini, 1981). The present descriptions will be confined to four highly influential therapeutic schools. Two of these, psychoanalytic therapy and humanistic psychotherapy, to be discussed in this chapter, focus on the relationship formed during therapy whilst the other two, systematic desensitization and cognitive therapy, the subject of the next chapter, place the emphasis on providing the client with explicit treatment prescriptions and tend to regard the therapeutic relationship as being somewhat incidental. These two classes of therapy will be referred to here as relationship and action therapies.

In considering the descriptions of the four different schools of therapy it should be kept in mind that the major schools tend to evolve in their underlying thinking and to diversify, throwing off variants or even actually splintering into separate subgroups. The following discussion will aim to deal with the basic features of the schools in question rather than covering all the different manifestations or the differences in emphasis that may exist between people espousing the same basic principles.

Psychoanalytic therapy

Psychoanalytic ideas are by now so much a part of Western culture that it is difficult to appreciate their impact on thinking related to psychotherapy. Freud, the prime mover in psychoanalysis, was a prodigious writer on a wide range of topics. These varied from issues in neurology, in his early days, to biographical analyses of literary and historical figures. His major writings are concerned with an account of mind and behaviour, with special reference to their abnormal manifestations, and are set within a developmental framework. His theory of psychological development and his work on the treatment of abnormal behaviour are closely interwoven and it is beyond the scope of this book to deal with them in anything but the most perfunctory manner. All that is offered is an outline of the main features of psychoanalytic treatment. This will be done mainly by examining Freud's early psychoanalytic writings in which many of his later ideas are available in embryonic form. (Extended accounts of Freudian theory can be found in Farrell, 1981 and Wollheim, 1971.) It should also be noted that 'psychoanalysis' refers to a form of treatment that is avowedly Freudian. The terms 'psychodynamic therapy' or 'psychoanalytic therapy' are used to imply that the general methods and ideas from psychoanalysis are in use in treatments which are not strictly Freudian.

Studies in Hysteria is Freud's earliest book, which he produced in conjunction with the neurologist Breuer, in 1895. In this book they reported a number of case studies of hysterical patients who were apparently more or less cured by psychological methods. Hysterical disorders are characterized by complaints of physical discomfort, pain or malfunctioning for which no organic cause can be found. Freud and Breuer's patients complained of pains in their limbs and paralysis, amongst other things.

In the nineteenth century physicians had made considerable inroads into explaining psychological phenomena by physical events. A rudimentary understanding of states such as stupor and confusion was widely established (Berrios, 1981; Ellenberger, 1970). In contrast to these, there were two phenomena of great interest to the medical world that remained untouched and these were hysteria and multiple personality. Charcot had demonstrated that he could produce symptoms which resembled hysteria using hypnotic suggestion. By making post-hypnotic suggestions he could induce the prescribed behaviour when the subject came into contact with a 'trigger' while in full consciousness. For example a subject could be hypnotized and told that when he was next touched on the back, his left arm would become paralysed. He was of course also later told to forget this instruction given in hypnosis. These demonstrations were primary evidence for the view that overt behaviour might be 'caused' by cognitive and emotional factors of which the person was unaware. This view was not particularly new and it was commonly held in the early nineteenth century that hysteria was produced by chronic sexual craving and frustration. By the time that Freud began to practise, this view had been modified by Briquet who declared that any violent unfulfilled emotion could induce hysteria. It was Freud who was responsible for taking this basic idea and elaborating it to provide an apparently comprehensive account of the genesis and control of emotion and its causal influences on behaviour and feelings.

Freud's interest in treating hysteria was stimulated by an account of Breuer's treatment of 'Anna O' between 1880 and 1882. Breuer recounted how he had managed to remove Anna O's various hysterical symptoms by getting her to recall under hypnosis events of an emotional nature that had occurred at the onset of the symptom. Freud and Breuer noted that mere recollection of the original event was insufficient to provide a cure. They held that it was necessary for the patient to describe the event in detail and to arouse and experience the accompanying affect. The aim of therapy was therefore to discover and bring into consciousness painful and forgotten memories.

This aim is still one of the basic goals of the psychodynamic therapies although what has to be recovered and brought into consciousness has extended beyond a single traumatic memory. Indeed in Freud's own early therapy with hysterics recorded in *Studies in Hysteria* he began to note that very often the crucial unconscious event was not a memory of the situation surrounding the onset of the symptoms, but was often an unacceptable idea or impulse to do something and for which the person had strong feelings of revulsion or disgust. From these clinical observations Freud came to formulate his theory of infantile sexuality in which infants are credited with strong sexual and aggressive feelings towards their parents. These feelings cannot be shown for fear of punishment or disapproval so the infant learns to repress them to prevent him feeling what the psychodynamic therapists call psychological pain. The methods of repression were described and classified by Freud.

A further early observation of Freud's was the importance of symbolism in the symptoms of his patients. For example, 'Katharina' suffered from bouts of vomiting which Freud interpreted as being a substitute for feelings of moral and physical disgust. In Katharina's case the disgust was focused on memories of having seen a couple in the act of sexual intercourse and of a time when an uncle had got into bed with her with the apparent intention of seducing her. In fact Freud later revealed that the 'uncle' was actually Katharina's father.

Symbolism has become one of the major features of psychodynamic therapy and its major role is seen in the analysis of dreams. The Freudian theory of dreams hinges on the proposition that dreams are a disguised fulfilment of a suppressed or repressed wish. The wishes themselves are determined by the unconscious conflicts produced by strong impulses faced with the requirement that they should not be acted upon. Because these impulses are so psychologically dangerous they are rendered relatively harmless by what Freud terms 'dream work'. What actually appears in the dream and all that the person can recall on waking is the manifest content of the dream which has been transformed from its latent content. The therapist's main job is to discover what the latent content of the dream is and thereby gain access to the patient's hidden conflicts.

There are other ways of discovering hidden conflicts. Initially Freud used hypnotic methods to get at forgotten memories but in his early cases he noticed that it was very difficult to induce hypnosis in some patients. Furthermore, others flatly refused to be hypnotized. He tried a technique of suggestion whereby he placed his hand on the patient's forehead and told them that when he pressed down they would experience a recollection. This too failed to give consistent results. Eventually he began to employ the now standard technique in which the patient is merely instructed to say whatever comes into his mind. This is the method of 'free association'.

As this latter method was evolving Freud noticed that patients seemed to show a reluctance to speak, although to him they were obviously emotionally distressed. In the first cases Freud seems to have dealt with this problem in an authoritarian way by reminding the patient that they were under an obligation to tell him what they were thinking. It soon became apparent that this reaction could be counter-productive and the patient could show tremendous resistance to therapeutic endeavours. The eventual solution was not to regard resistance as a therapeutic nuisance but to turn it on its head and use it as a therapeutic tool. It now became something for the patient and therapist to examine because it could give information about the underlying conflicts. The notion of resistance has remained central to psychodynamic psychotherapy.

The information obtained from such things as the patient's dreams and free association is sifted, sorted and ordered by the analyst to produce hypotheses about the original cause of the symptoms. Analysts will have to produce many such hypotheses to retrace the supposed causal route from the original impulses to the symptoms. They aim to trace and uncover the defences and resistances which the patient has erected over what may be many years. These obstacles are overcome by interpreting the patient's behaviour to him. Lay persons often have a vision of the analyst remaining silent until the time is ripe for the delivering of a single momentous interpretation which solves everything. This is then thought to be followed by the patient instantly acknowledging the therapist's wisdom with relief, whereupon the symptom disappears and the patient is cured.

In real life things are far from this easy. Firstly, the therapist may remain unsure about the links between the patient's symptoms and the information which he gleans from free association and other methods. He will often begin by making tentative suggestions which are refined as he gains new information including that derived from the response to the original interpretation. Secondly, there is rarely a single interpretation to account for all the person's symptoms. Freud also noted that patients often failed to relinquish a symptom even though they had accepted an interpretation as valid. He concluded that symptoms were overdetermined by which he means that a single symptom might have its origin bound up in many separate memories and impulses. Each of these has to be worked through by the analyst carefully tracking them, developing hypotheses, and interpreting the connections.

Transference

Perhaps the most important discovery made by Freud in his early cases was the nature of the relationship between the patient and the therapist. The fact that patients become emotionally attached to their therapists was not of course new to Freud or to medicine in general. Indeed this relationship had been exploited for generations

(Ellenberger, 1970; Frank, 1973). At the end of *Studies in Hysteria*
Freud used the term 'transference' to refer to the feeling which the
patient might place on to the therapist because of his unconscious
problems. This can be illustrated by Freud's own example:

> In one of my patients the origin of a particular hysterical symptom lay in a
> wish, which she had had many years earlier, and had at once relegated to
> the unconscious, that the man she was talking to at the time might boldly
> take the initiative and give her a kiss. On one occasion, at the end of a
> session, a similar wish came up in her about me. She was horrified at it,
> spent a sleepless night, and at the next session, though she did not refuse
> to be treated, was quite useless for work. After I had discovered the
> obstacle and removed it, the work proceeded further. [p.390]

Although transference is often used loosely to refer to any
feelings which the patient may have for the therapist it should more
properly be reserved for the feelings arising from fundamental
unconscious conflicts. Psychoanalysts propose that during therapy
the patient's behaviour and feelings towards the analyst are in some
way a recreation of earlier patterns of behaviour which were present
at the time that the conflicts were formed. During the critical period
when a child is learning to control and suppress its impulses the
parents are the most prominent figures in its life. Psychoanalytic
theory holds that during therapy the therapist comes to represent,
and to be treated like, the parent. Therapy also aims to exploit this
process. By interpreting the relationship between therapist and
patient, known as the transference-parent link (Malan, 1976), the
therapist and patient can arrive at an understanding of the original
cause of the conflict and understand the conditions under which the
original impulses were repressed. The interpretation of the transference is a long process and subject to resistance.

The therapeutic relationship

Why should the patient treat the therapist as if he were a parent?
Why is the therapist not treated like any other person to whom
strong emotional attachments may not necessarily be made? The
analysts' answers to these questions are twofold. Firstly, patients
may relate to others in ways which reflect their relationships with
their parents. Frequently these relationships with others are
unsatisfactory because they may be destructive and riddled with
guilt, hate, intense love, jealousy or other feelings. Feelings present
in the original conflict become a basis for a habitual way of
responding to others. People may avoid these feelings by changing

their relationships with others or by avoiding any close relationship at all. More often they will erect 'defences' by adopting such patterns of behaviour as being jokey and comical which will serve to prevent them feeling the full force of the relationship.

The second reply is that there are features of the interaction between patient and therapist which prevent the patient from establishing his normal pattern of behaviour. The patient is required to stick to the basic rule of therapy by saying whatever comes into his mind. The therapist may or may not respond to any particular statement. He is relatively passive and does not act as if he were entering into a conversation in which he takes equal responsibility for maintaining the flow of communication. In classical analysis the patient and therapist do not face each other; the patient is recumbent and the therapist sits out of sight. In this way the normal non-verbal cues used to control and maintain interactions are eliminated. Where patient and therapist do face each other the therapist may adopt a 'dead pan' expression with the same intent of removing non-verbal cues. Therapists will rarely give a direct answer to a patient's questions. Instead they might reflect about why the patient thinks that the question is important. Therapists will also not probe issues by direct questioning.

These features do not allow the patient to discover what the therapist thinks about him or what his views are on any particular issue. The patient is therefore prevented from adapting his behaviour in the way that he might normally do in order to maintain social interaction and intercommunication. Farrell (1981) describes the equity of the interaction as being governed by two rules. The first of these is indeterminateness, whereby the patient is unable to discover the therapist's attitudes or values, and the second is non-contradiction, in which the therapist will not respond to criticism or challenges to his authority or behaviour.

This type of interaction is of course subjectively uncomfortable and potentially anxiety-producing for the patient. In consequence he is forced to adopt a strategy in which he reverts to his own fundamental attitudes as a framework for understanding his current experience. These efforts are likely to be what the analyst would call psychologically primitive. They represent the patient's earlier attitudes towards the parents and significant others. When this is coupled with uncertainty and anxiety it facilitates the patient's recall and reconstruction of his basic anxiety and other emotions. The patient will also tend to seek reassurance and guidance from the therapist that he is behaving appropriately as well as seeking the analyst's approval for his behaviour. It is not surprising that under these conditions the patient becomes emotionally attached to the therapist. It is this relationship that the analyst will focus on and interpret with the aim of letting his patient rediscover and rework the basic underlying conflict.

Negative and Counter-transference

There are two other notable features of the interpersonal relationship in psychoanalysis and psychodynamic therapies. One concerns the feelings that arise in the patient towards the end of treatment. These feelings are often characterized by anger and hostility towards the therapist because of impending loss. This part of the relationship is known as negative transference and is dealt with by the usual procedures of interpretation. At this point in therapy the aim is to allow the patient to separate from the therapist in a way that leaves the patient psychologically intact and able to stand alone. The analogy is drawn with previous experiences of separating from other people, usually parents, under unfavourable conditions such as those produced by unresolved conflicts. The therapist can then use the material which the patient brings up in the sessions to help the patient resolve these remaining problems.

The second feature, counter-transference, is of significance because it has practical implications for the training of therapists. Psychoanalytic treatment makes an emotional and intellectual demand on the therapist, as do all other therapies. But because the treatment relies so heavily on the relationship between the patient and the therapist there is a risk that the therapist's own personality and feelings will interfere with his clinical judgement and involvement with the patient. This is the counter-transference of the therapist. In order that the therapist should become aware of his own blind spots he is usually required to undergo a prolonged period of training in which he himself is analysed. This can be an expensive and time-consuming enterprise. In practice it means that few analysts can be trained. Many psychoanalytically derived therapies have similar training requirements but these are often not equivalent to a full analysis.

Summary

The basic assumptions made by psychoanalysis about psychological symptoms and their treatment are:

(a) Symptoms are adopted to protect the patient from a more disturbing aspect of his personality.

(b) The cause of this disturbance is usually a conflict between an unexpressed impulse or idea and the need for the person to express it.

(c) The conflict arises early in the person's life and is usually formed in relationships with parents or significant others. It is also often concerned with repressed sexual impulses.

(d) The goal of therapy is to discover the nature of this basic conflict and to allow the patient to re-experience and re-work the emotions which it induces.

(e) The therapist's task is made difficult because the patient is resistant to revealing the origins of the conflict because of the psychological discomfort associated with it.

(f) To overcome this problem the therapist employs three basic tactics which are free association, interpretation and transference.

Research in psychoanalysis

As psychoanalysis was developed the course of treatment became longer and longer. Whereas early cases were treated in a matter of weeks or months it now requires many sessions, at a rate of four or five per week over a period of three to four years, for a complete analysis. Historically the type of patient treated has also shifted from hysterics to patients with general neurotic and interpersonal problems. Thus in its full form psychoanalytic treatment is extremely expensive and limited in both the number of people and the range of problems to which it can be applied. Some attempts have been made to overcome these limitations. It is clear that psychoanalysis has little to offer those suffering from major psychoses and most analytically oriented therapists will not consider such problems for treatment. An interesting exception to this is a psychoanalytically based model of paranoia developed by Colby. This model has been translated into a computer 'game' which has successfully passed a weak form of Turing's test (Colby *et al.*, 1979; Heiser *et al.*, 1979). Thus far there is little evidence that psychoanalytic treatment based on Colby's theory of paranoia is effective. Colby himself has suggested that some variant of the cognitive-behavioural treatment model (see pages 153–60) might be appropriate.

Generally speaking psychoanalytic therapists have eschewed

research into both the *process* of therapy and its effectiveness or outcome. Process research is concerned with investigating the factors in treatment that are putative causes of its effectiveness. Outcome research deals with the relative effectiveness of different types of therapy. (These points will be taken up in greater detail in Chapters 11 and 12.) Research into psychoanalysis has also been hampered in a number of ways. Freud himself seems to have been sceptical about the possibility and value of research of any sort. He believed that it was impossible to aggregate people with different problems. He also drew attention to the difficulty of measuring outcome from within a psychoanalytic framework. There are also problems of duration and permanence of treatment effects with the possibility of superficial cures in dissembling patients (Freud, 1922).

There are other problems that make research difficult. Firstly, psychoanalysis is a very long treatment and it would be difficult to contemplate establishing and maintaining control groups over the time period required. Secondly, it is difficult to know what are the necessary and sufficient conditions for the effectiveness of treatment. In addition crucial events like interpretations, transference or resistance are not encapsulated occurrences taking place in one session. They are cumulative and dependent upon the judgement of the therapist. Thus it is difficult to standardize the course and content of therapy. Experimental manipulation of the content of the therapist's activities in such a way that it would be acceptable to the practitioners and retain the feel and characteristics of analysis is virtually impossible.

Finally, there is a technical problem in handling the vast amount of raw data arising from treatment sessions. At a very basic level of investigation transcripts of each session must be made and the content coded in a reliable way by two or more judges. In simple economic terms the cost of such a venture would be enormous. It would take many man-years of research time to collect what could be regarded as a statistically reasonable sample of patients. Although there are now a number of data pools of sessional transcripts of patients in psychoanalytic treatment (Luborksy and Spence, 1978), most research on psychoanalytic treatment has focused on shorter-term treatment. It has rarely involved direct observation of patient therapist interactions or, where this has been undertaken, only a few sessions or patients have been monitored.

Most of our knowledge of the process of analytic therapy comes therefore from the first-hand reports of the therapists themselves. These reports could offer reliable and accurate accounts of the content of treatment but it is more plausible to regard them as reflecting the reconstructions of the therapist using his memory codes and schema which are, of course, analytic in nature. This makes it very difficult for a researcher from another theoretical persuasion to retrieve the actual content of sessions and to reconsider them in the light of another theory. The comparative investigation of the process of psychoanalytical psychotherapy is therefore an extremely rare event.

Malan's brief psychotherapy

Despite the problems of investigating psychoanalytic therapy some researcher clinicians have persisted and begun to try to test the validity of psychoanalytic hypotheses. David Malan has reported two series of cases in which he and his colleagues attempted to answer a number of questions (Malan, 1963; 1976). The main practical issue was whether it is possible to conduct a form of brief psychoanalytic therapy which would be successful. Malan noted that therapy had tended to become longer as successive 'facts' such as resistance, transference and so on had been discovered. He also observed that previous attempts to shorten therapy had ended in failure with the innovators gradually 'rediscovering in the end the technique of psychoanalysis itself' (Malan, 1963). Malan investigated which patients were most suitable for brief treatment, which techniques should be used, and what kind of therapeutic outcome might be expected.

The basic findings were that it is possible for brief psychoanalytic therapy to give a successful outcome but that certain patients are unsuitable. Two sets of criteria were used to determine suitability. One came from the corpus of wisdom of colleagues and involved the absolute rejection of people with certain psychiatric diagnoses and clinical histories, e.g. chronic alcoholism, chronic phobic and obsessional symptoms, long-term hospitalization and more than one course of electroconvulsive therapy (ECT). (This list actually excludes a significant number of people in psychological distress who might seek therapy.) The second set of criteria were derived by more empirical means. When patients had been selected for treatment their final outcome scores were related to their characteristics on admission to treatment. Suitable patients were those with a focal problem and who were willing and able to work in a psychological way. By this is meant that they think of their problems as being psychologically produced and can cope with the emotional consequences of therapy such as handling interpretations.

A key feature of Malan's work was a very thorough psychiatric and psychodynamic assessment period of three sessions. During this time, projective tests were administered. At the end of the assessment period the research team constructed individual psychodynamic hypotheses. These hypotheses attempted to relate the patient's symptoms, what was known of the life history, especially those portions concerning parents and early upbringing, and the material obtained from the projective tests. The hypotheses also led to a set of outcome criteria which had two basic features. These were, firstly, that the patient's symptoms should be removed and, secondly, that the underlying conflict, or purported disturbance between the patient and his parents, should be resolved.

Malan's descriptions of what would qualify for successful treatment makes interesting reading because he includes quite specific information. For example, it was predicted that one patient should be able to 'tolerate all kinds of strong emotion without feeling it as a weakness. He should be able to express his own needs particularly with his wife. This should include warmth, tenderness and sexual feeling, with evidence that she is happier and more satisfied. At the same time he should be able to retain and make use of the strength and determination he has developed' (Malan, 1976, pp. 167-8).

At the completion and follow-up of treatment, ratings of outcome were made by different investigators. The agreement between the raters was reasonably high. The relationship between various types of interpretation and outcome was examined. In both of the series the presence of a successful interpretation of the connection between the transference and the patient's feeling for his parents was positively correlated with successful outcome. Unfortunately these ratings of the transference/parent link seem to have been made by one investigator only (Malan himself) and there is no evidence on the reliability of his judgements. It is also the case that only one or two correlations emerged as statistically significant although many were computed. It must be expected that one out of every twenty correlations will be 'significant' at the 5 per cent level by chance alone.

Malan's work is a good example of research into psychoanalytic psychotherapy. His books give a wealth of clinical detail and convey the richness and complexity of the psychoanalytic approach. He also makes a serious attempt to deal with the measurement of outcome from a psychodynamic point of view. Despite this the work is methodologically weak. Few of the scales used have been systematically evaluated. Judgements are based on the therapists' reports of sessions and not on recordings. The research design is correlational with no attempt to manipulate theoretically important variables in a systematic manner. This reflects a dilemma for any practising clinician researching the effects of his treatment in that he is justifiably reluctant to withhold what he regards as a therapeutically beneficial intervention from his patient. In terms of deciding whether the brief psychotherapy offered by Malan and his colleagues really is effective there is no satisfactory evidence provided on the basis of which a decision could be made. In the absence of control groups who were not treated or given an alternative treatment it is not possible to decide whether Malan's patients improved because they were treated or if they would have improved anyway with the passage of time. This particular question will be taken up in greater detail in Chapters 10 and 12.

Humanistic psychotherapy

In contrast to the deterministic view espoused by psychoanalytic theory the humanistic schools of psychotherapy propose that people are potentially rational and have the freedom to make choices which will lead to an improvement in their psychological wellbeing. The purpose of therapy is to help people to appreciate the responsibility which they hold for their own behaviour. Therapy aims to get them to look at the alternatives that face them, and to improve their self-reliance. Implicit in this view of man is a rejection of the immutable power of the unconscious and of the emphasis on people necessarily being slaves to their past. There is also an explicit attempt to dissuade people from invoking special help from other sources such as a deity.

Many exponents of humanistic forms of psychotherapy also propose that the activities of people can be construed as being governed by a single motive to 'self-actualize'. This is a rather nebulous concept and not easily defined. Basically it refers to a tendency for the individual to act to preserve and maintain himself. At the simplest level this is expressed in the active seeking of food and drink. At a more complex level people strive to gain and maintain the love or affection of others. The developmental aspect of self-actualization is crucial to its understanding. It is suggested that an individual constantly strives to order his activities by a variety of means to achieve self-government, regulation and autonomy. Theorists point to the progressive autonomy of children as an example of this motivation.

A number of authorities have put forward different forms of humanistic therapy, e.g. Frankl (1962), Maslow (1962), May (1960) and Perls *et al*. (1951). Although these may differ quite widely in their particular prescriptions for therapy they do tend to share a number of features. To some extent they all concentrate on 'the here and now' (their jargon). That is, they encourage the client to concentrate on what is happening in his life at the time rather than considering the possible historical origins of any symptom. In this sense the therapies are decidedly ahistorical. The purpose of a session is to encourage the client to engage his feelings, to experience them more fully, and to consider their implications for his present and future behaviour. This must be contrasted with the insight orientation of psychoanalytic therapy where the patient is helped to link his present behaviour to historically derived conflicts between 'primitive wishes' and the need to control them.

A further feature of these therapies is that many adhere to a phenomenological view of man. They insist that the client must be understood within his own frame of reference rather than one imposed by the therapist's preconceived theoretical notions. Again in contrast to psychoanalytic treatments, the therapist may take a more active part in eliciting, encouraging and guiding the client during sessions. He may also deliberately try to suspend normal social conventions during therapy in order to force the client to focus on his own resources and thereby produce material which he would not normally be aware of or wish to consider.

It will have been noticed that the terminology used has switched from discussing the 'patient' to considering the 'client'. This is because humanistic therapists typically use this term and it reflects their interest in positive mental health rather than psycho-pathology. In fact many of the clients dealt with by humanistic therapists have been people who have not had contact with psychiatric services and who would not fit into any formal diagnostic category. However, there are notable exceptions to this. For example, one of the best known of this group of therapists, Carl Rogers, investigated the effects of his non-directive therapy on schizophrenics (Rogers *et al*., 1967).

The client-centred therapy of Carl Rogers

In order to look at humanistic therapy in greater detail it has been decided to concentrate on the work of Carl Rogers. This is not because his type of therapy is necessarily better or more effective than the others, but because Rogers was the first theorist to specify a set of conditions which he thought were necessary and sufficient for individual change. He suggested that in as far as certain conditions were present in a therapy (warmth, empathy and genuineness), then that therapy would be effective. He and his colleagues were also the first to investigate what went on in therapy by making audio recordings of sessions and correlating their content with outcome (Kirschenbaum, 1979). Before looking at warmth, empathy and genuineness and the way in which these might relate to change it is necessary to take a step backwards and look at Rogers's theory of personality.

Rogers's view of personality can be set out as a series of propositions (Rogers, 1951). He subscribes to the basic phenomen-ological tenets of the humanistic approach and to a single unifying self-actualizing motive. His concept of emotion is tied to the self-actualizing activity of the individual. In general, emotion facilitates goal-directed activity. The intensity of the emotion is proportional to the perceived importance of its related behaviour in maintaining and enhancing the individual's existence. To take a simple example, the emotion felt when avoiding a fast car will be of greater intensity than that experienced when watching a film showing an identical situation.

In Rogers's theory people come to differentiate part of their total experience as being uniquely them. They come to have a concept of 'self'. The values and attitudes which are subscribed to as part of the self, and which determine the ways in which experiences are perceived and categorized, come from interaction with the world. Some of these attitudes are derived directly from experience. Others are introjected from other people. The usually important sources of introjected values are parents and close associates. These introjected ideas may be accepted without much qualm until such times as contradictory experiences are encountered. New ex-periences can be dealt with in three ways. Firstly, they may be accepted because they are consonant with the self-concept. Secondly, they can be ignored as irrelevant because they have no apparent relationship to the self. Thirdly, the experience can be distorted to fit in with the self-concept because it would otherwise challenge or threaten the individual's integrity. In all these instances the individual is striving to 'self-actualize'.

Consider as an example a person who is paid a compliment. If they have reasonably high self-esteem they will probably accept the compliment for what it is. On the other hand, a person with low self-esteem may well distort the compliment by constructing an alternative explanation. This could be along the lines of 'he only said that because he doesn't really want to tell me that I am a mess'.

Rogers proposes that people are maladjusted when they deny awareness or experiences which are significant for their self-constructs. The experience can arise from the individual's own behaviour or from what others tell him about himself. In most circumstances people behave in a way that is consistent with their self-constructs. The occasional lapse can be written off as of no significance and this is especially true if the behaviour is committed when under pressure from another more powerful person. It is when such behaviour occurs persistently that there is pressure to re-evaluate the view of the self. For example, a person recently separated from his spouse may still think of himself as being married. The more that he does on his own the more that he is forced to face up to the fact that to all intents and purposes he is single. This discrepancy between real experience and what is believed about the self produces a state of tension (Rogers's term). This leads the person to re-evaluate his concept of 'self'. It is of course possible to deny experience completely thus avoiding the sense of threat and the consequent anxiety. A common source of threat to people is the realization that they are doing things not because they want to do them for themselves but because they are following the introjected attitudes and values of other people. Most of Rogers's early clinical work was with young people and college students who are particularly prone to this source of anxiety as they leave home and no longer have to conform to their parents' attitudes.

The necessary therapeutic conditions

Rogers considered that there were certain situations under which people would be more likely to face up to the inconsistencies in their thoughts, feelings and actions and consider the origins of their values and attitudes. They can then decide which values they wish to acknowledge as their own. These conditions are met when the individual is under no threat from anybody else and he can consider his experiences without the fear that someone might admonish or criticize him. In such situations the individual will feel safe to disclose and discover potentially uncomfortable material relating to himself. He can then choose those things concerning himself that he wishes to accept or reject and begin to formulate new ways of perceiving and behaving. When he does this he can replace the present value system, based largely on the introjected values of others, with one of his own within which he can decide his own priorities.

Rogers described three conditions relating to the therapist that he considered necessary for effective psychotherapy. The first of these is *warmth* (otherwise described as non-possessive warmth or unconditional positive regard). This is defined by Rogers as the therapist experiencing a warm acceptance of the client's experience as part of the client and communicating the warmth in such a way that it is unconditionally applied. The therapist does not express his dislike or disapproval or his warmth in an evaluative or selective way.

The second dimension, *accurate empathy*, exists when the therapist is able to sense the client's experience as if it were his own and to convey this to the client in a way that is attuned to the client's current feelings. Rogers is at pains to emphasize that the therapist does not actually have to experience the client's grief, sadness or joy, but should act as if he were experiencing the feelings and be able to communicate his understanding of the impact and importance of these feelings. When a therapist is operating at a high level of accurate empathy he should be able to sense feelings that are only covertly implied. He must therefore have enough understanding of the structure of human emotions to sense the probable emotional consequence of anything that the client describes. It is important to note that at these higher levels of accurate empathy the therapist is not interpreting the client's experience for him, or offering him a way of constructing his experience, and a client is free to express his dissent from the therapist's reflection. Indeed the therapist will probably communicate his empathy in a tentative manner. However, Truax and Carkhuff (1967), who developed scales for rating accurate empathy, imply that at very high levels of empathy something akin to an interpretation is taking place. They describe the therapist as being unerringly accurate and unhesitant towards deep feelings with regard to both their content and intensity. The difficulty is that the criteria by which judges are to decide if such empathy is present remain unspecified.

The final characteristic is *genuineness* (or congruence) and requires the therapist to 'be himself'. In this sense 'being himself' means that the therapist does not present a professional facade.

Although the therapist may be actively reflecting the client's feelings about himself he should also remain aware of his own feelings. In Rogers's phrase, the therapist should be 'freely and deeply himself, with his actual experience accurately represented by his awareness of himself'. This should not be seen as a requirement for the therapist to disclose his feelings or state of mind. The therapist's primary aim is to facilitate the self-exploration of the client and within the constraints imposed by this aim he must be able to judge when it is appropriate to disclose his own feelings. D. A. Shapiro (1969) has pointed out that the concept of genuineness seems rather strained especially when considered against the effects of professional training on the therapist's behaviour. Judgements of genuineness could also be very difficult without the presence of other information about the therapist as a person.

Rogers argued that the presence of these three conditions was necessary for effective psychotherapy. They act by facilitating the crucial variable of self-exploration in the client. Self-exploration occurs when the client is able to recount, elaborate and discover emotionally tinged experiences, feelings or events which are significant to the self. This activity includes examining relationships with others and the client disclosing his own evaluation of his roles and values in life as well as revealing his feelings.

Client-centred therapy research – fundamental problems

Rogers's clear exposition of the necessary and sufficient conditions for psychotherapeutic effectiveness has given rise to many empirical investigations. There are now many hundreds of studies of various aspects of Rogerian psychotherapy. All that can be offered here are a few comments about certain aspects of this work with particular emphasis on those that illustrate difficulties that arise in the investigation of psychological treatments in general. No attempt is being made to offer a 'balanced' description of research within Rogerian tradition in the sense of covering all possible points of view or all the aspects that a committed Rogerian therapist might consider of great importance.

With regard to the effects of therapy it is clear that the basic hypothesis advanced by Rogers as to the role of warmth, accurate empathy and genuineness is difficult to substantiate. The initial favourable reviews (Truax and Mitchell, 1971) have been followed by reanalysis and reconsideration of the evidence. This now supports only a very modest relationship between the warmth, empathy and genuineness dimensions and outcome (Lambert *et al.*, 1978; Mitchell *et al.*, 1977). The general question of outcome will not be followed in detail because it is a major issue in evaluating all forms of therapy which will be taken up later (see Chapter 12).

One more specific question that has been posed is whether Rogerian therapists really are non-directive in the way that they are alleged to be. In particular communications from the therapist indicating warmth, empathy or genuineness should not be directly dependent upon the content of the client's speech. Truax (1966a) reported a study of Rogers's own behaviour during therapy based on an audiotape of sessions. In his analysis Truax found that Rogers's statements were not indiscriminately applied. They tended to be delivered at points where the client was showing signs of reflecting on his own behaviour and feelings (i.e. engaging in self-exploration). At these points it was usual for Rogers to reflect back to the client what he had just said by paraphrasing it and perhaps slightly extending the content of the client's thoughts. For example, after the client has talked about the events surrounding the separation and divorce of his parents the therapist might reflect that the client has said that he has strong feelings of both love and hate for his parents. In addition to this it might also be suggested that the client is having difficulty in accommodating both sets of feelings. The therapist may have noticed the uncertainty with which the client spoke of both sets of emotions and focused on this. In this way it is assumed that the client will be guided towards considering the paradox of the contemporaneous presence of opposite feelings. This may then be followed by an examination of the consequences of the conflict which this situation engenders in the client. The eventual hope is that he will recognize the valid issues behind the evaluation of his parents' behaviour in such a way as to enable him to resolve the conflict.

Truax (1968) conducted a further study to look at the hypothesis that therapists selectively reinforce client behaviour. Clients who received therapist responses indicating warmth, empathy and genuineness contingent on the production of self-exploration showed greater amounts of self-exploration and therapeutic improvement as compared to those where these therapist responses were independent of client behaviour. This is despite the fact that the overall amounts of the relevant therapist responses were the same for both groups. This therefore offers a test of the alternative hypothesis that changes occur because of the reinforcement of selected behaviour rather than by the considered judgement of the client, and the results are consistent with this alternative hypothesis. It must also be remembered that the therapeutic situation is complex and studies of this kind only look at a small proportion of the potentially relevant variables and had additional variables been examined then the results might then require a different interpretation. Although the results obtained are consistent with a reinforcement effect it would also be premature to assume that this effect, even if it were to hold in further and more extensive studies, is mediated by the kind of reinforcement mechanisms which occur in simple operant conditioning experiments.

Investigations like the one by Truax (1968) presuppose that it is possible to measure therapeutic conditions in a reliable and valid manner. This has proved to be rather more difficult than might be supposed. Many investigators have used the scales developed by Truax and Carkhuff (1967). These are five-point measures of warmth and genuineness and a nine-point scale of empathy. Each point on these scales is defined by a description of the therapist's behaviour. Superficially they seem to have high face validity (i.e. they look as if they are measuring what they claim to measure). A content analysis of these scales suggests that the constructs that they try to measure are far from the single dimensions that they are assumed to be. For example, M. B. Shapiro (1977) examined the content of the Accurate Empathy Scale and found that it covered several different aspects of therapist behaviour. It covers sympathetic voice quality, tentativeness in the way in which the therapist offers reflections, awareness in accuracy in reflecting the clients' overt or covert feelings, and the ability to detect new content in the client's talk and to offer an explanation for this. The ability to reflect covert or hidden feelings raises the question as to whether the therapist engages in some form of interpretation. If he does how can the accuracy of these interpretations be validated?

With such complex scales it is not surprising that it has proved difficult to obtain consistently high inter-rater reliability. Although some investigators have been able to ensure reliabilities which fall in the generally acceptable range ($r = 0.8$ or better), others have obtained coefficients that are much less satisfactory. Truax and Carkhuff (1967) and Mitchell et al. (1977) give details of a number of reliability studies. Lambert et al. (1978) note that there is a lack of detail about how the raters in many of these studies were trained. This makes it impossible to replicate procedures across investigations. One way of trying to improve the reliability of ratings might be to begin by making frequency counts of the therapist's behaviour in the therapy session. This might improve consensus agreement between the raters and would increase the specificity of what is actually being rated. With a multidimensional scale, such as the one to measure accurate empathy, it is difficult to be sure, even if two raters agree, that they are actually agreeing about the same thing. Even when high reliability is reached, what is being rated, and does it make sense to call it empathy (Lambert *et al.*, 1978)?

The problem of measuring empathy is not made any easier by attempting to use several measures purporting to measure this variable and seeing if they converge or intercorrelate. Kurtz and Grummon (1972) conducted a study to look at five measures of empathy applied to sessions conducted in a college counselling centre. Their data showed no evidence that these measures intercorrelated. Out of a total of eleven similar studies reviewed by Lambert *et al.* (1978) only three reported significant associations between one or more of the measures. There are other findings which also point to the difficulty in measuring empathy. For example, J. G. Shapiro *et al.* (1968) demonstrated that judges could agree reasonably well about the level of accurate empathy if they were shown videotapes without the verbal exchanges between client and therapist. J. G. Shapiro (1968) found that when he compared 'audio only' with 'video but no sound' and a full video recording of sessions then the single sensory modality ratings correlated moderately with the full video rating but failed to correlate with each other. Furthermore a study by Truax (1966b) showed that raters could estimate levels of empathy just as well when they were presented with the sound track of the therapists' response alone. In other words there was no contextual basis for their judgements.

The question of who should rate the presence and quality of the therapeutic conditions has also been raised. This has usually been in the context of looking at different sources of rating in relation to outcome criteria. Rogers clearly states that accurate empathy should be as judged by the client. However, much of the outcome research has been carried out with the scales developed by Truax and his colleagues which require independent trained raters.

Final comment

Rogers's conjectures about the necessary and sufficient conditions for therapeutic change have been enormously productive and influential. The present discussion has necessarily been brief but it illustrates a number of essential points in the study of psycho-therapy and behaviour change. Firstly there is the focus on the public observation of therapy rather than just the therapist's or client's account of what has happened. This not only allows the process of therapy to be documented but alternative hypotheses can be put to the test. Secondly, it appears that measuring the theoretical constructs of Rogerian therapy is a hazardous exercise. It has proved extremely difficult to realize these constructs un-ambiguously although many potential sources of error have been discovered. Inability to measure these crucial features accurately severely limits the degree to which the theory can be tested in an empirical way. Another problem that emerges in Rogerian therapy is that it is not possible to routinely add and subtract critical components of treatment in the furtherance of experimental investigations (e.g. by getting the therapist not to empathize but to be warm and genuine). In this regard the behaviour therapies are relatively easier to investigate and these are taken up in the next chapter.

9 Treatment: 'Action' Therapies

Behaviour therapy has its roots in nineteenth-century experimental physiology and there are accounts of behavioural treatments in the first half of the twentieth century. Despite this, behaviour therapy as it is known today did not get under way until about 1960. The publication of Wolpe's book *Psychotherapy by Reciprocal Inhibition* in 1958 was probably the major stimulus. Unlike many other therapies behaviour therapy has not been dominated by the thoughts of any one individual. It has been the product of a general approach to psychology which dominated academic psychology for a period. The growth of behaviour therapy has been quite explosive both in terms of the number of papers published (Hoon and Lindsley, 1974) and in the range of problems that have been broached. To date these include phobias and obsessions, children's behavioural and developmental disorders, facets of the rehabilitation of long-stay psychiatric patients and the treatment of problems in mental handicap. In the past ten years the field of behavioural medicine has developed in which psychological approaches to traditional medical problems like headache (see Chapter 14) and hypertension have been initiated. Attention has been given to issues such as compliance with drug regimens.

Systematic desensitization and methods for reducing fear and avoidance

One of the first developments in behaviour therapy was the development of a treatment for phobias. Wolpe (1958) described a technique called systematic desensitization. Not only did Wolpe provide a clear account of how to use the technique but he also expressed a theory as to how it worked that could be tested experimentally. He proposed that fear could be reduced by pairing the fearful object with another stimulus which would inhibit fear.

During successive pairings of these two stimuli the fear response would gradually become deconditioned.

In practical terms the fear could be presented in a hierarchical way with the event producing least fear being presented first. Moreover the feared stimulus could be presented in imagination rather than in reality. (Thus the spider phobic would be initially asked to imagine looking at a picture of a spider, then seeing a very small spider a long way off, and so on). The usual counter-conditioning stimulus was a state of relaxation in which the client was trained at the beginning of therapy. An important feature of the technique is that feared stimuli are presented for very short periods, between five and ten seconds, so that the client does not experience more than a very small amount of fear. As each item becomes unable to evoke fear so the client progresses up the hierarchy. Wolpe reported a high success rate for this method in his monograph and within a few years of its publication controlled trials of its efficacy were being reported (Lang *et al.*, 1966). Its effectiveness as a treatment is established although the mechanism of the effect is still the subject of debate (Kazdin and Wilcoxon, 1976; see Chapter 11).

Shortly after desensitization became established a number of reports appeared to the effect that almost the exact opposite of desensitization could also reduce fear. In this case clients were exposed to fearful stimuli for a protracted period, up to two or three hours if necessary. Attempts to deliberately enhance the fear might be made during this time. This procedure is known as 'implosion' and curiously has its roots in psychoanalytic theory as well as Pavlovian theory (Stampfl and Levis, 1967).

In this treatment there is an emphasis on discovering events which occurred at the time of the original acquisition of the fear. These events may often relate to intense feelings of aggression, sexuality or rejection. As it is not possible to verify that these events actually did happen they are known as 'hypothesized sequential cues' (Levis and Hare, 1977). The therapist will instruct the client to imagine these in conjunction with other cues that are more directly related to the fear. These cues, called 'symptom contingent cues', are those cues that reliably precipitate the feeling of anxiety. For example, in the case of a spider phobic these would be the spider itself, the way it moves and where it is usually found.

'Flooding' is a treatment with many similarities to implosion and was developed at about the same time. The terms are sometimes used interchangeably but there are two clear differences. Firstly, in flooding the therapist only presents the equivalent of the symptom-contingent cues and there is no attempt to discover or present cues of a more 'psychodynamic' nature. The second difference is that in flooding there is no attempt to maximize the anxiety felt by the client during exposure to the fearful stimuli. The differences between the two have been examined experimentally. There is no clear evidence that one is superior to the other but it is apparent that it is not necessary for people to experience intense anxiety during a prolonged exposure for a therapeutic effect to occur (Boudewyns and Shipley, 1983).

Contemporary behaviour therapists tend to make less distinction between these techniques in their clinical practice but work on the premise that exposure to the feared event is a necessary condition for the reduction of anxiety. The duration and level of anxiety experienced in exposure are said to be important in so far as the therapist will aim to let the client have a successful encounter with a feared situation. This means that he will engineer the treatment so that each exposure is finished with the client in a relatively calm state. This can be brought about in a number of ways which correspond to the classical distinctions of desensitization and implosion/flooding. A hybrid treatment in which the client is exposed to successively more fearful events and with no attempt to control the anxiety but where the client is allowed to experience its successive waxing and waning is often used. In other versions there may be an attempt to get the person to employ coping skills to manage the anxiety.

A further development occurred relatively early in the history of behavioural treatments for fear. Whereas the original techniques presented the phobic stimulus in imagination it was soon realized that real life, or *in vivo*, presentation was just as effective. Indeed it had advantages in that the client was also able to learn new ways of approaching and interacting with the feared situation as well as reducing his anxiety. The fearful behaviour could be directly observed, monitored and changed. It should be remembered that at the outset of behaviour therapy the prevailing model of emotion was of the nature of a drive. The behaviour was held to be determined by the individual's subjective and physiological experience. From this perspective it made sense to attempt to reduce the drive state by means of desensitization or flooding. It followed that the behavioural component would change in line with the reduced drive level. Observations have shown that this is not necessarily so.

Modelling and social learning theory

Another major influence on behaviour therapy came from the work of Albert Bandura who, with his colleagues, investigated the phenomenon of learning by observation and vicarious experience, otherwise known as modelling. His work with children demonstrated that they could acquire a variety of emotional behaviours including fear, avoidance and aggressive responses, by watching other children model the behaviour. Similarly he demonstrated that these behaviour patterns could be reduced by observational learning. Bandura's findings prompted other therapists and researchers to investigate the same phenomena in adults with pathological fear. It was quickly appreciated that there was considerable power and generality in modelling as a treatment (Rachman, 1976; Rosenthal and Bandura, 1978).

Bandura's approach offered a fresh perspective prompting researchers to examine events other than reinforcement that might control behaviour. Attention was now paid to the cognitive factors which underpin learning by imitation. The way in which individuals attended to and encoded modelled behaviour was systematically explored. The effects of different sorts of models and their mode of presentation via film, verbal instruction and imagery became potentially important therapeutic questions. Bandura's approach, known as 'social learning theory', emphasizes the interplay between cognitive factors and environmental events, especially of a social nature, as reciprocal determinants of behaviour. Both cognitive and environmental events determine the behavioural output of a person. Beliefs and attitudes about the environment determine the way in which the individual chooses to interact. The interaction reinforces the individual's belief.

Consider a spider phobic who believes that he is frightened of spiders and unable to cope with one found in the bath by killing it or removing it. He will take evasive action to avoid confrontation. Non-engagement with the spider will confirm his own predictions as to his disability and ensure that he will not get the opportunity to learn more appropriate behaviour that would disconfirm his expectancies. On the other hand, if the therapist models successful ways of dealing with the spider and gives the phobic the chance to imitate he will discover that there are ways in which spiders can be removed from baths that are both effective and speedy.

Although the vicarious experience of watching a model does result in some reduction of behavioural avoidance and fear, participant modelling in which the client copies the therapist is known to be more effective (Rosenthal and Bandura, 1978). There is also evidence that certain types of models are more effective. Providing that they do not display undue distress, 'coping models' who cope despite a performance that is not perfectly smooth and accomplished are more effective than models exhibiting a perfect performance. Amongst other things such coping models provide more detailed information about how to retrieve the situation after an error has been committed and this information is not available from a model showing mastery. A similar increase in effectiveness is found if the person has an opportunity to watch multiple models and this again increases the range of coping skills to which the client is exposed. Experimental analyses suggest that the treatment of phobias is more effective when a modelling procedure is combined with systematic desensitization. Not surprisingly the amount of change in the client's behaviour is greater following exposure to a participant modelling programme (e.g. Bandura *et al.*, 1969).

Social performance

Modelling is also a central component of social skills training although many of the ideas about social skills are derived from research on training in motor skills. Many psychiatric patients have poor social skills and social skills training aims to help remedy this by teaching patients to make eye contact when talking to people, how to initiate and maintain simple conversations, etc. The social skills literature has traditionally placed less emphasis on concepts like reinforcement and stimulus control but has derived its concepts from engineering and the design of machines. Central to this are the notions of programmes and feedback (Argyle, 1969).

Despite this difference in emphasis the social skills literature is generally regarded as falling within the purview of behaviour therapy. Many of the methods used are common to both such as the graded presentation of more difficult items, the use of modelling with guidance and corrective feedback by the therapist, and opportunity for rehearsal under non-anxiety-provoking conditions. Social skills training has been applied to many different problems and client groups ranging from institutionalized psychiatric patients to children with social difficulties and sex offenders (Spence and Shepherd, 1983).

Applied behaviour analysis

Yet another contribution to behaviour therapy emanates from the work of Skinner and his colleagues on operant learning in animals. Skinner's central formulation is that behaviour is a function of its consequences and the stimulus conditions that inform the individual as to which consequences are likely to be contingent at a given time. His laboratory work which showed that the type and frequency of delivery of consequences had highly predictable effects on the rate at which animals produced simple responses, is well known.

Four basic types of consequences were defined by the effect which they had on behaviour. A positive reinforcer is an event which increases the frequency of behaviour which it follows. This latter is often known as the target response. Similarly increases in the frequency of a target response can also be produced by negative reinforcement. In this case the presence of the reinforcer is terminated when the individual produces the target response. From a subjective point of view positive reinforcers often have a pleasant quality whereas negative reinforcers are experienced as unpleasant and aversive.

The frequency of a given behaviour can also be reduced by two consequences. An event is punishing if it reduces the frequency of the response on which it is contingent. As with negative reinforcement, punishers are often aversive in nature. (It should be noted that there is sometimes a confusion in terminology with some people incorrectly using the term 'negative reinforcement' to refer to what is here described as a punisher.) Extinction occurs when the withdrawal of a reinforcer results in a decrease in the frequency of the target behaviour.

It is clear from this set of definitions that the type of reinforcement is defined empirically by its consequences. From this perspective there is no way of knowing a priori which event will prove to be reinforcing. In practice clinicians can often make very good guesses as to what will act as a reinforcer for particular individuals but there are some surprises. For example, in a rare metabolic disorder often associated with mental handicap (Lesch-Nyhan's disease) sufferers typically mutilate themselves with repetitive and stereotype actions. Obviously it is humane to try to stop this self-destruction. In this case it is found that mild electric shock, often a potent punisher, is ineffective. In contrast a procedure known as 'time out', in which the child is removed from sources of reinforcement by the therapist ignoring him, has been shown to be much more effective (Anderson *et al.*, 1978).

The application of operant principles to human behaviour is otherwise known as 'applied behaviour analysis'. This approach is typified by careful analyses of individual patients which attempt to discover the stimuli preceding the target behaviour and the reinforcement consequences. Once this analysis has been achieved the therapist will systematically vary these conditions in order to determine their functional control of the target behaviour. Having discovered the most potent combination of events that will control the behaviour these are applied for therapeutic purposes. Applied behaviour analysis has developed a method for investigating behaviour experimentally which relies on the intensive investigation of single cases. In general its practitioners have not favoured experimental investigations which rely on comparing groups of subjects with different therapeutic conditions. This has undoubtedly been an important contribution to the evaluation of therapy and the general issue of single case investigations will be taken up in the next chapter.

Because of the requirements of careful observation and control of stimuli and reinforcement, applied behaviour analysis has figured most prominently in the treatment and amelioration of problems occurring in institutionalized patients. Early applications were in controlling disruptive and bizarre behaviour in long-stay psychiatric patients. Operant methods are also widely used in training mentally handicapped people to increase their levels of self-care and independence. Its use in controlling self-destructive behaviour has already been alluded to. Wider applications have included improving educational skills in retarded and conduct-disordered children. There has also been considerable emphasis on teaching non-professional psychologists such as teachers, nurses and parents to apply the techniques in their own contexts. Applied behaviour analysis differs from many other forms of treatment in maintaining that the individual's behaviour is determined by the immediate environmental conditions. Thus the focus of treatment is in changing the environment and the contingencies operating in that environment.

The token economy is a treatment programme based on the principles of operant conditioning, particularly conditioned reinforcement. Studies with laboratory animals had shown that seemingly innocuous events, such as lights coming on, which have few reinforcing properties of their own, could come to function as reinforcers if they reliably signalled the availability of primary reinforcers like food and water.

This principle was extended in a systematic way to human behaviour by Ayllon and his colleagues in the 1960s. In an attempt to increase the quality of self-care and participation of institutionalized psychotic patients in everyday activities a system was developed in which patients could earn tokens for completing a wide range of prosocial behaviours (see Ayllon and Azrin, 1968). The target behaviours included self-care items like brushing teeth and taking a bath, as well as activities such as cleaning the ward, keeping their bed and linen clean, acting as guide for visitors to the ward, and participating in social activities on the ward. For every target behaviour the patient could earn a token or tokens (the exact number being graded according to the nature of the behaviour). These tokens could then be exchanged for various reinforcers which ranged from extra consumable items (coffee, cigarettes, etc.) to the opportunity to sleep in a single room. All these items were in addition to the basic care provided by the usual hospital routine.

This token economy was successful in achieving its objectives in terms of altering the frequency with which target behaviours occurred. Numerous other programmes have been put into operation with aims such as training patients for eventual discharge from long-term institutional care. One of the best-known and apparently most sucessful applications of the token economy has been in providing non-custodial care and treatment for delinquent adolescents (Braukman and Fixen, 1975). Token economies can also be used successfully with individual cases. Tokens have a number of advantages over direct reinforcers. They are easy to administer and can be delivered more frequently than many primary reinforcers because the patient does not become satiated (even children tire of eating sweets after a while). Because they cannot be immediately consumed like sweets or cigarettes they do not interrupt the sequence of training whilst they are being consumed. It is interesting that token economies do pose a number of practical problems in that they mimic other economies with such things as inflation and theft. These can be controlled in carefully run token economies (Kazdin, 1977).

The main features of behaviour therapy

A number of aspects of behaviour therapy have been described briefly. It has not been possible to cover all the many different techniques that have been derived from these prototypes, and there is no single underlying theme for behaviour therapy, but it does involve a number of basic characteristics.

(a) In contrast to both analytic and humanistic psychotherapies behaviour therapy places little emphasis on the personal qualities of the therapist and the form of the relationship that he establishes with the client/patient. At its most extreme the relationship might be regarded as having no therapeutic properties of its own. The therapist is merely a means of conveying information to the patient. In fact there are studies of desensitization in which the whole procedure is deliverd in a tape-slide format (Lang *et al.*, 1970). These experiments show that for some problems and populations a therapeutic relationship is not necessary. However, most behaviour therapists would feel that their relationship with the client is of some significance. In using modelling the client actually learns through a form of relationship and certain therapist characteristics are important, especially where the therapist is the model. For example, the more similar the therapist is to the client in age and status the more effective the treatment. The way the model behaves is also important in that coping models are better than those showing mastery. In techniques like flooding, where the client has to undergo potentially fearful and stressful experiences, the therapist needs to be able to induce trust and confidence in the client. Finally, the behaviour therapist, like any other therapist, needs to be able to elicit information from the patient who is only likely to disclose potentially intimate or embarrassing information about himself in the context of an appropriate therapeutic relationship. It follows that the relationship between therapist and patient is important in behaviour therapy but its importance lies in helping to create a situation where therapy can go on. Unlike the psychoanalyst or the humanistic psychotherapist, the behaviour therapist does not regard the relationship with the patient as being the central focus of the therapy itself. In general the therapeutic relationship has attracted little attention from behaviour therapists (Wilson and Evans, 1977).

(b) A second feature of behaviour therapy is that it concentrates on discovering and altering the current determinants of the client's problems. Although speculations may arise as to the likely origins of a problem these are regarded as conjectures and not open to experimental verification. The treatment procedures are ahistorical unlike those of the psychoanalytic school. The therapist will focus on antecedent and consequent events in relation to the problem behaviour and on features that may modify their effects such as mood or the presence of others. This description then becomes the basis for developing treatment plans.

(c) The behaviour therapist is directly concerned with the symptom or problem behaviour rather than the 'personality' of the client. Therapy aims to modify the symptoms and not to change the client's personality. Underpinning this is a general adherence to a view of personality that is different from that espoused by analytic or humanistic therapists. This view is clearly seen in the work of Mischel (1968; 1977). It emphasizes the variability of behaviour over situations and the critical role of environmental events in determining behaviour. This position is not entirely universal and one well-known promulgator of behaviour therapy also supports a trait theory of personality (Eysenck, 1980).

(d) This view of behaviour and personality also determines the kinds of measure behaviour therapists use to evaluate their work. They emphasize direct measures of behaviour like role play tests, psychophysiological recordings, and subjective measures of mood or feelings carried out *in situ* whilst the person is faced with the situation that leads to the problem behaviour. The ideal measure is based on observing the patient in the natural environment and this is most often seen in reports of operant treatments. Behaviour therapists tend to reject measures of personality, especially when derived from projective techniques, and this has implications for comparing the effects of different types of treatment as will be seen in the next chapter.

(e) Behaviour therapy has laid great emphasis on the experimental investigation of single cases and in determining therapeutic effectiveness by experiment. It is generally aligned with a positivist-empirical approach. This has rarely been true of other schools of therapy. In line with this behaviour therapists have developed a set of reasonably well defined procedures where the goals of treatment and the operations for assessing outcome are fairly specific. These features make it relatively easy to replicate the methods using different therapists and client groups and in different settings.

(f) A related characteristic of behaviour therapy is that the development of techniques has been stimulated by findings in experimental psychology and from the study of learning in particular.

(g) Many behaviour therapists would also reject the notion that behavioural disorders should be construed as diseases except where they are associated with known organic syndromes.

Cognitive therapy

It is only relatively recently that cognitive approaches to therapy have become part of the mainstream of therapeutic activity. Some of the methods have much in common with behaviour therapy and it is difficult to say where the border lies between the two types of therapy. Indeed, there is a widespread use of the term 'cognitive behaviour therapy' to describe many of the techniques used in cognitive therapy. It is evident from the preceding account of behaviour therapy that systematic desensitization, flooding, implosion and modelling make use of cognitive events and processes. However, in behaviour therapy cognitive events like imagery in desensitization are used without recourse to any cognitive theory. Marzillier (1980) points out that for the most part behaviour therapists have merely regarded these events as weak substitutes for overt behaviour. In other techniques, like covert conditioning where the client is asked to imagine stimulus-response pairings together with their consequences, the imagery sequence involved is regarded as isomorphic with the corresponding overt conditioning paradigm. Marzillier also notes that there have been few attempts from within behaviour therapy to subject the images and thoughts of clients to detailed assessment and analysis. A notable exception to this is Lang's work on emotional imagery (Lang, 1979).

At another level behaviour therapy techniques have been formulated in terms of cognitive processes which might underpin them. As already described, Bandura's account of modelling is essentially cognitive in nature and invokes processes like selective attention, retention, encoding and recall. These are acknowledged as potentially powerful explanations of how modelling works. Experiments which deliberately manipulate these cognitive processes do affect what is learned by subjects and how they behave

(Rosenthal and Zimmerman, 1978). Generally speaking behaviour therapists have made few attempts to alter cognitive events and processes directly.

Cognitive therapists and theorists make strong assumptions about the relevance of cognitive activity in controlling behaviour. They back these assumptions with interventions which are specifically aimed at the reconstruction of the person's cognitive activity. The main contemporary exponents of cognitive therapy all share the following assumptions to some degree (Marzillier, 1980; Morley *et al.*, 1983).

(a) A person's feelings and behaviour can only be understood if one takes into account their cognitive activities. These cognitive activities mediate between the events in the person's environment and the response which the person makes to these events. For example, Ellis (1979) has a simple mnemonic which characterizes this basic assumption. His ABC model proposes that the emotional and behavioural consequences (C) of an activating event (A) are determined by the person's mediating beliefs (B) about the event.

(b) Cognitive therapists assume that people with behavioural and emotional disorders have essentially faulty cognitive activities. The processes by which they extract and assimilate information from their environments are either distorted or malfunctioning. How some theorists actually describe these cognitive dysfunctions will be set out below.

(c) For most purposes it is assumed that the faulty cognitive activities can be revealed in the individual's verbal reports about himself. The task of the therapist is to help the individual discover his faulty cognitions by showing him that they have predictive validity for his behaviour and emotional state.

(d) It is also considered necessary to change the person's faulty cognitions to obtain a therapeutic outcome. Moreover it is held that changes in cognitive activities can best be brought about by explicitly focusing on the faulty cognitions and modifying them directly. This is mainly done in two ways. One is by actively challenging the logical and psychological adequacy of the belief. The second is by setting up tests of a behavioural nature that will challenge the faulty belief and set it in opposition to an alternative and non-dysfunctional belief. The person is thus asked to conduct experiments on his own behaviour, feelings and thoughts.

In practice cognitive therapy techniques share many of the characteristics of behaviour therapy. The therapist is mainly concerned with the current determinants of behaviour and sets explicit goals for the client to work on. He will also set up a monitoring system to track the progress of therapy and he is likely to use 'homework' assignments as a prominent part of the therapy.

Meichenbaum's stress inoculation or self-instruction procedures

Cognitive therapy is dominated by three approaches. These are the rational emotive therapy of Albert Ellis (RET), Aaron Beck's cognitive therapy and Donald Meichenbaum's self-instructional training (SIT). Ellis and Beck both originally started from within the psychoanalytic school and developed their therapies after becoming disenchanted with psychoanalysis. Meichenbaum's work comes from a more conventional psychological background. To some extent these therapies have all been developed independently.

In one way Meichenbaum offers the least radical of these therapies because his procedures do not directly challenge the faulty cognitions. His approach has been applied to people with intense feelings of anxiety although others have extended it to help in the management of pain and anger (Novaco, 1978; Turk, 1978). Self-instructional training is based on the principle that language, in the form of self-instructions, can be used to guide and prompt behaviour. Meichenbaum's original experiments (see Meichenbaum, 1977) showed that schizophrenics could be taught to talk to themselves in a productive manner. They were taught a series of self-statements to be applied when confronted with tasks which demanded their attention and concentration.

When applied to the management of anxiety and other acute emotions SIT has a number of steps. Firstly, the client is taught to discover the situations which precipitate the feelings of anxiety. The client keeps a diary in which he records the thoughts that occur in these situations. He is then presented with a model of emotion along the lines of that put forward by Schacter and Singer (1962) in which the prominence of thoughts as determinants of emotions is emphasized. He is then instructed that it would be more adaptive for him to use the anxiety-provoking thoughts as 'cues for coping'. In other words when they occur he must set about deliberately engaging thoughts which lead him to cope. These coping thoughts are developed by the client in conjunction with the therapist. They usually take the form of instructions to do several things, including instructions to engage in strategies to reduce physiological arousal such as relaxation techniques and regulated breathing. The client will also be told to focus his attention on the task in hand and not on his feelings of fear and this can involve specific advice as to what to do. For example, the socially anxious client may be asked to maintain eye contact and not avoid the gaze of another person. How to manage the feelings of being overwhelmed by the emotion will also be dealt with. The client will be given instructions about the expected time course of the experience with the implication that the intensity of the emotion will eventually reduce. Finally, the person is asked to evaluate his actual coping in the situation so that he can gain accurate feedback about his progress.

These self-instruction messages are not just delivered to the client. The therapist will spend time modelling the procedure. At first he will speak the instructions and demonstrate the coping strategies. The client then joins in as in participant modelling. Finally, they arrange a series of graded exercises in which the client can practise his new skills under conditions which increasingly approximate the real-life stressor. Imagery is often used in this phase. This gradual approximation is analogous to biological inoculation by exposure to weak doses of pathogen. It was for this reason that Meichenbaum also called the procedure 'stress inoculation training'. The expectation is that at the end of training the client will have replaced his earlier maladaptive thoughts with an alternative series of positive coping thoughts.

Rational emotive therapy of Ellis

Both Beck and Ellis also attempt to eliminate prior dysfunctional thinking. Ellis (1980) is quite explicit that the destruction of maladaptive thoughts should be a prime goal for his 'rational emotive therapy' (RET). He argues that although symptom removal is obviously appropriate and beneficial, 'deep seated emotional and behavioural change can only be brought about by ensuring fundamental changes in the client's belief systems. A consequence of this is that only a radically revised outlook to all *new*, present and future situations . . . will semi-automatically help them to stop disturbing themselves in the first place, or to quickly undisturb themselves, in the second place' (Ellis, 1980, p. 327).

As the above quotation implies, Ellis proposes that emotional and behavioural disturbances are mediated by faulty thinking (beliefs), and that people largely create their own emotional disturbances by holding these beliefs. He is adamant that people can choose to change or to hold on to these beliefs. However, they will have to work actively in order to change them and the methods of RET can enable this to be done. Ellis characterizes the disturbing beliefs as being 'absolutistic' and 'mustabatory'. People have the belief that something absolutely must happen (or not happen) for them to remain emotionally undisturbed. For example, a person might hold the belief that he must be loved by everyone for everything that he does. Having such a belief will naturally lead to discomfort when others do not give the approval which the individual feels should occur. Through his experience with clients Ellis originally proposed that there were twelve basic irrational beliefs that could be detected. This figure has been considerably increased with experience to over twenty.

A distinctive feature of RET is the way in which it sets about destroying these beliefs. RET actively engages the client in open debate about the absolute and 'mustabatory' quality of his thoughts. The therapist will dispute and deny the 'must' and examine the implications of holding the belief together with the consequences of relinquishing it. He will do this by breaking the belief down into constituent components each of which will emphasize its irrationality. During the course of this debate the therapist will be prompting the client to take over the role of actively disputing his own beliefs. The aim of this is to ensure that the client internalizes the polemical method. RET stresses the importance of the active participation of the client in order to avoid the idea that the therapist is indoctrinating the client. This also helps the client to use the method in the future and assists in generalization beyond the therapy session.

RET is not entirely a verbal method. Ellis does incorporate a number of behavioural methods to assist therapy including desensitization, a form of flooding/implosion, social skills and assertion training, and operant principles of reward and punishment. These procedures are definitely viewed as adjuncts to the central cognitive component based on changing the client's beliefs. RET also uses extensive homework assignments during which the client is required to practise the application of his newly acquired rational thinking. Finally, it should be noted that Ellis has been consistent in declaring that RET is aligned to ethical humanism. Indeed, one of the key irrational beliefs focused on by RET is the notion that the individual needs something stronger or greater than himself on which to rely. Ellis suggests that a devout faith in a deity almost always leads to poor emotional adjustment.

Beck's cognitive therapy

Some reference to Beck's thinking about depression has already been made in Chapter 6. The present discussion will concentrate on the related therapeutic procedures. Like Ellis, Beck proposes that a person's mood and behaviour are largely determined by the way in which he perceives the world around him. Beck suggests that people have habitual or semi-permanent ways of construing the world that he refers to as schema. The therapeutic tactic espoused by Beck is to try to discover the client's idiosyncratic schema and then to help him to evaluate the evidence that he has for holding them. The examination includes overt behavioural exercises aimed at helping the client to test the reality of his conceptions and to provide experience of changing in an adaptive way.

Beck notes that people are mostly unaware of their particular interpretative biases. For the most part reactions to events are fast and seemingly unthinking. The first problem is to detect these 'automatic' thoughts. This can be achieved by a variety of methods including direct interviewing about specific problem situations, imagery-based recall of difficult events, and having the client keep a diary. In the latter the client is explicitly instructed to 'keep an eye out' for the thoughts which occur in known situations. Thoughts are not just the verbal ideas which come into a person's mind, but also include images and memory flashbacks. Once these are identified the therapist will carefully negotiate with the client to make sure that he understands exactly what the client means.

In exactly the same way as Rogers (described in the preceding chapter), Beck is insistent that therapists understand the phenomenological frame of reference of their clients. In this regard Beck is somewhat different from Ellis who has formulated a set of common irrational beliefs. Beck's therapy focuses on clients' idiosyncratic thoughts and images. However, Beck does recognize some commonality between people's thoughts but these are at a more abstract level as types of cognitive error. For example, a common error is that of 'selective abstracting' in which people recall only one particular type of event that happens. A depressed person may recall only those instances where he has apparently been snubbed or rejected by colleagues at work and not take note of occasions on which the same colleagues behaved towards him in a very different way. The individual might then conclude that nobody likes him. This inference is an example of a second type of error, 'overgeneralizing', in which a person assumes that what is true in one instance must necessarily be true in all others that remotely resemble it.

Once Beck has established the presence of a cognitive error he engages the client in a dialogue in which he issues challenges to the faulty thoughts. For each type of cognitive error there are appropriate alternatives. Thus in the case of selective abstraction the client will be asked to think of those instances when good things have happened to him. In the example given above the client will be encouraged to recall occasions when his colleagues were pleasant to him.

There are a number of techniques to assist the client to discover alternative constructions of his world. These include distancing in which the client describes events and situations which cause him distress in the third person. This reduces the emotional involvement and helps the client to take a rational view of his predicament. Another approach is for the therapist to ask the client to distinguish between fact and hypothesis and to make guesses about the likely consequences were his assumptions actually to turn out to be valid. The therapist will also be working with the client to set up a series of behavioural tests of alternative hypotheses. The client is then urged to carry out these tests as homework exercises. The exercises are arranged in a graded manner so that the client experiences repeated success over more and more difficult situations.

Beck has developed his approach for a variety of emotional disorders but the most prominent clinical group with which his treatment is associated is depression. Although cognitive therapy has been practised in different forms for many years it is only recently that it has been subject to any detailed evaluation. There is now evidence from controlled trials that it is effective (Rachman and Wilson, 1980; Williams, 1984b). What is more difficult is to establish whether it actually works in the manner that is purported. There are problems in doing this. For example, cognitive therapists have relied almost exclusively on the verbal statements of their clients as evidence for cognitive events, processes and schemas. Yet it is almost a truism in psychology to say that what a person states about himself is not necessarily accurate. Self-statements are easily influenced by the conditions under which they are assessed and the ways in which they are assessed. Fortunately it seems that the general methodology of experimental cognitive psychology might be applied with benefit to the issues raised by cognitive therapy (Kendall, 1983).

Summary

This completes the present survey of the main schools of psychological treatment. This survey has attempted to describe the main features and basic assumptions of each school and to indicate to which kinds of disorder the treatment methods are usually applied. In general the psychological therapies described are directed at problems corresponding to the traditional psychiatric category of neurosis. This includes problems of anxiety, fear, obsessional behaviour, and the habit disorders such as excessive alcohol and tobacco use. In children the main problems approached by these methods include emotional maladjustment, conduct disorders and developmental problems which impinge upon education. The psychological treatment of individuals with predominantly psychotic symptoms, such as hallucinations or delusions, has not been extensively examined here. Nevertheless the previous chapter mentioned Rogers's largely unsuccessful trial of client-centred therapy with schizophrenics and, as described above, there has been more successful application of operant behavioural techniques to the management of chronic psychotic institutional residents.

For the sake of brevity these treatments have been discussed as applied to single individuals but many treatments are applied to groups. Sometimes group treatment is merely a more economical way of delivering therapy as when behaviour therapists treat agoraphobics in groups. However, in this case it does also appear that the group can have an extra, beneficial effect in facilitating treatment and improving long-term outcome. Patients can support and reinforce one another. In other cases the emergent psychological properties of the group are used as the major mode of psychological treatment. This is seen in the so-called 'therapeutic community' and many short-term psychoanalytically oriented treatments. Naturally occurring groups, marital dyads and families may also be the subject of psychological intervention. Usually group processes are understood and interpreted within the general framework of one of the therapeutic approaches that has been described (see Bloch, 1982).

Addendum – physical treatments

It is the psychological therapies that are the focus of interest in this book and it is therefore these that have been described in some detail. This emphasis on psychological forms of treatment should not be taken as indicating that they are the most commonly used forms of treatment for psychiatric disorders or that other forms of treatment are necessarily less effective or less appropriate in given circumstances. In fact most people presenting to the health services with psychiatric disorders are likely to be treated mainly by physical means. In order to balance the picture it is necessary to give a brief account of physical treatments in psychiatry.

The most commonly used treatments are undoubtedly pharmacological. There is a vast number of different drugs available for prescription but these generally fall into three main groups. These are the minor tranquillizers (or anxiolytics), the major tranquillizers (or neuroleptics) and the antidepressants. A brief comment on the pharmacological treatment of depression was given at the end of Chapter 4 and it will be recalled that there are two main types of antidepressant, the tricyclics and the monoamine oxidase inhibitors. Both these take some time (usually ten days or more) to produce a therapeutic effect and they are each thought to be maximally effective in cases of depression with slightly different associated features. All other things being equal the tricyclics are preferred because the monoamine oxidase inhibitors can produce toxic side effects in combination with certain foods especially those containing high levels of the amino acid tyramine (e.g. cheese, chianti and caviare). Lithium, in the form of lithium carbonate, appears to be an effective prophylactic for those with bipolar affective disorders but its administration needs to be carefully monitored because it can produce serious side effects such as renal damage if the dosage rises above the therapeutic range.

As the name suggests, the minor tranquillizers are predominantly used for the control of the less severe symptoms of anxiety which are encountered in the general practitioner's surgery or the psychiatric out-patient clinic. Benzodiazapines are now the most commonly used family of drugs in this category and the best known of these is Valium. The benzodiazapines are more effective than placebo medication in reducing the physical and subjective symptoms of anxiety. Their great advantage over the earlier anxiolytics of the barbiturate group is that they are very much less likely to prove lethal when taken in overdose. They also have fewer side effects and are less likely to induce dependence although it is now known that this can be a problem in some people who have been injudiciously kept on them for long periods.

The final group of drugs employed in psychiatric practice is the major tranquillizers or neuroleptics. These drugs have an effect on major symptoms such as delusions and hallucinations but they also sedate the patient. They act rapidly to abort the most distressing symptoms of acute schizophrenia and manic attacks and it has been considered that their continued administration can offer some protection against relapse. Neuroleptics fall into two chemical types, the phenothiazines and the butyrophenones. The former were discovered accidentally when researchers were looking for drugs to sedate autonomic nervous activity. The latter were the product of a systematic search for more effective compounds. The butyrophenones are particularly effective in reducing hypermotor behaviour and so are useful in the management of acute mania. The main side effect of the major tranquillizers is that they can produce Parkinsonian-like effects, with a tremor in skeletal muscles somewhat similar to that occurring in Parkinson's disease. Chronic use of these drugs can sometimes produce irreversible motor disorders (tardive dyskinesia). Because of the tendency to produce Parkinsonian side effects they are often given in conjunction with anti-Parkinsonian medication.

The other main physical treatment in general use is electro-convulsive therapy (ECT). It was first introduced as a treatment for schizophrenia but was found to be ineffective. It is now almost entirely used for the treatment of severe depression and for this reason it was described in Chapter 4. It has been a very controversial treatment but the weight of evidence now points to it being very much safer than is sometimes supposed and to it having a definite antidepressive effect.

As indicated, this is a very brief survey of physical treatments which has avoided going into any detail. More extensive accounts of physical treatments can be found in most textbooks on psychiatry. Berrios and Dowson (1983) and Lader (1980) offer much more detailed information.

Before leaving the topic of biological treatments a further point can usefully be made. The use of drugs and ECT can involve the assumption that the only way to have a therapeutic effect is to change something within the patient. This assumption can equally be shared by the users of most forms of psychological treatment with the exception of operant behaviour therapy. Obviously the psychological and pharmacological approaches will differ in their implications with regard to what aspect of the individual needs to be changed but it is still something within the patient that is being manipulated. It follows from this assumption that if treatment appears to be ineffective the therapist has two responses available. He can either give more of the same thing (increase the dose in the case of drugs) or he can decide that he is not trying to change quite the right thing and change the drug or alter the therapeutic procedure. What this assumption does not do is to alert the therapist to the possibility that social and environmental effects may exert powerful moderating influences and so contribute to long-term recovery or adaptation. This is an issue that will come up again in Chapter 13.

10 Evaluating Treatments: Curious Clinicians

The previous two chapters have described the main approaches to psychological treatment together with their underlying assumptions and rationales. The question that follows most naturally from these descriptions is concerned with how well the therapies work. Experience has shown that this question is nothing like as simple as it sounds. In evaluating treatments a number of more specific questions can be asked. Are treatments effective in reducing the distress reported by individuals and do the benefits of treatment outweigh the costs? (Here 'costs' is being used in a much wider sense than the purely financial and to refer to the time and effort put into treatment and any negative consequences or 'side effects' that may also result from the treatment.) If a treatment works, why does it work? Is it because there are specific therapeutic ingredients or are there powerful non-specific or 'placebo' factors that exert a therapeutic effect? Once specific factors can be identified, how can these be explained in psychological terms? In other words, are the rationales given by the various schools of therapy in order to derive their particular forms of treatment substantially correct? Do some kinds of treatment work better than others, given that all other features that could influence outcome are held constant?

These are the broad questions that a person with a critical mind might want to ask about treatment. Given the large number of therapeutic techniques and rationales set out in the previous chapters, it would be a gargantuan task to attempt to answer these questions comprehensively. In this and the following two chapters, discussion concentrates on dealing with the range of options open to investigators in trying to pursue questions relating to the effectiveness of particular treatments. The examples chosen will come largely from the vast literature on behaviour therapy because this generally offers the most extensively developed field in the experimental evaluation of treatments. Nevertheless some attention will be given later (in Chapter 12) to the important question of comparing the effectiveness of different kinds of treatment. This is an issue that has provoked particularly acrimonious debate as well as much constructive thought but which perforce involves some consideration of non-behavioural treatments.

The problem of measuring change

When a clinician is faced with a single client there is a need to take account of at least the most basic of questions concerned with the effectiveness of interventions. This relates to whether the patient can be considered to have improved or got better. In normal practice the clinician will most likely rely on his judgement based on what the client tells him, what he looks like, and how he presents himself in order to form a global impression of progress. This information may also be augmented by the reports of others such as ward staff (if the patient is in hospital) or members of the patient's family. This global impression is obviously the result of a complicated cognitive calculus which is likely to be highly idiosyncratic. In any case this judgemental process is not publicly observable, although its end results may be, and the criteria on which the judgement is based are unknown. It might also be suspected that there are sources of bias which would distort judgement especially in the direction of favouring a positive outcome and overestimating improvement. The clinician's judgement is essentially an un-validated measure with no known reliability. As such it is highly difficult, if not impossible, to compare any one clinician's 'results' with those of any other, or perhaps even the outcomes of different clients treated by the same clinician.

A first step in rectifying this position is therefore the adoption of some form of standardized measure which, at the very least, can be administered before and after treatment. In clinical work such measures might be symptom checklists, inventory measures of depression or anxiety, a projective test of personality, or an observer-based rating scale of behaviour in a given setting. If after treatment there was a marked improvement in the client's scores on whatever measure or measures were chosen, would it be legitimate to conclude that the client had indeed improved?

In general terms it would seem sensible to place greater confidence in the measures because they are more open to public scrutiny and important features such as their reliability can be established. There is a complication in that there are a number of alternative explanations for any change in the observed scores (Campbell and Stanley, 1966; Cook and Campbell, 1979). It may be that any changes are due to the effects of repeated *testing* alone. It is possible that a patient is 'faking good'. On encountering the items for the second time he is now motivated to dissimulate his true mental state. He may fear that if he admits to certain types of symptom (e.g. hallucinations or delusions) then he is less likely to be discharged from hospital or have treatment terminated. The reverse can also occur where clients choose to 'fake bad' in order to avoid discharge from hospital or to maintain the contact with their therapist. As well as motivated changes in scores there can be practice effects. Experience in dealing with the problems presented by a test of cognitive ability (e.g. one of the standard tests of intelligence) may actually help the subject to perform better next time. In the case of rating symptoms the subject may initially be very concerned with these and rate them as being quite intense. With the passage of time the actual symptom level may not change but the patient adapts to the presence of the symptoms and then sees and rates them as being less intense.

A second possibility is that the measuring instrument itself has changed between the two occasions of testing. Campbell and Stanley (1966) refer to this as *instrumentation*. For example, the criteria by which independent judges will rate the severity of a symptom can be affected by the severity of the same symptom in cases that they have rated immediately beforehand.

The phenomenon of observer drift is a well-known example of instrumentation error in studies using direct observation. In these investigations raters are trained to rate behaviour as it occurs. Ratings are made to preordained categories and it is possible for pairs or groups of raters to achieve very high levels of agreement about what they are rating (inter-rater reliability). Despite a high inter-rater reliability it is still possible for observers to depart from the original rating criteria over a period of time. Indeed there is evidence that observers do 'drift' from the original criteria as experiments progress. When pairs of observers work together they may influence each other. Drift can be detected by comparing pairs of observers who have worked with each other with ratings made by newly trained raters. Ways of avoiding drift include recording all the data on videotape and then randomizing the temporal order of the sessions so that drift is not confounded with time. Investigators might also use standardized training tapes throughout the experiment and so periodically check the raters against these.

Kent *et al.* (1974) provided an elegant demonstration of the effect of observer expectancies on the measurement of target behaviour. They trained ten pairs of observers to rate disruptive behaviour in a school classroom (this consisted of such things as the child being out of his place and touching another's property). The observers were then shown twenty-four tapes, the first twelve of which were said by the experimenters to be baseline sessions where no treatment was applied. Five pairs of observers were then told that the class was then given a token economy treatment for the next twelve tapes. This is a form of treatment that had been described and discussed in some detail by the experimenters. The other five pairs were told that the second set of twelve tapes were taken to examine the generalization of treatment and there was the implication that no change in behaviour was to be expected. The raters were then asked to provide estimates of changes occurring in the second set of tapes. Raters told that the token economy was in operation judged that there was less disruptive behaviour in the second phase whereas the remaining raters reported no difference in behaviour. Although the raters' global judgements were affected by their expectation of therapeutic change there were no differences between the groups of raters when their actual ratings of specific behaviours were examined.

This does not mean that ratings of specific behaviour are not an inviolable form of data. Kent and his colleagues went on to demonstrate that when they provided feedback to raters in the form of approval by the experimenter for the rater performing in accordance with his expectancy of therapeutic change, then the rater actually changed his ratings of disruptive behaviour although no change had occurred (O'Leary *et al.*, 1975). The presence of expectations in conjunction with experimenter feedback is probably a critical potential source of bias in studies based on direct observation.

A further problem that might arise in examining pre- and post-treatment measures is that any change in score could be due to the *reactivity* of the test rather than to an improvement produced by the treatment. A reactive measure is one that induces a change in the behaviour that it is trying to measure. There is ample evidence from research in social psychology to the effect that the presence of observers can alter the behavioural characteristics of the people they are trying to observe.

A commonly used type of measure in experimental studies of fear reduction is also known to be highly reactive. 'Behavioural avoidance tests' (BATs) were developed by Lang (see Lang *et al.*, 1966) to measure the change in phobic avoidance behaviour after treatment by systematic desensitization. The tests usually consist of a graded series of behavioural tasks in which the subject has an opportunity to attain closer proximity or greater contact with the phobic object. For example, snake phobics might be given the initial opportunity to enter a room in which is a glass cage containing a harmless snake. At the top end of the test hierarchy the criterion would be to pick up and hold the snake for a specified period of time. Leading up to this there would be a series of twenty or thirty steps arranged as near as possible on an interval scale. The subject's score is the scale point beyond which he cannot proceed. In addition to the behavioural approach score many BATs make provision for the subject to be observed, usually unobtrusively, by raters who record overt signs of anxiety such as trembling, hesitation and so on.

It is known that the scores obtained from this type of test can be readily influenced by the type of instructions given and the conditions under which the person is tested. For example, subjects given a 'one-shot' presentation where they are told to go as far as they can up the hierarchy in a single attempt do not perform as well as those subjects given a graded introduction to the hierarchy. Better performance levels are also obtained when subjects are told that it is essential that they complete a certain level in order for the experimenter to obtain other measures, usually psychophysiological indices such as heart rate. These 'demand characteristics' are well documented with regard to BATs (Bernstein and Neitzel, 1977) and they are important sources of variance in many studies, especially analogue experiments (see the next chapter).

The improvements that occur after BATs are not entirely attributable to artifacts related to the test procedure. BATs can have high levels of reactivity in that the very exposure to the phobic stimulus that is entailed in the BAT can itself be therapeutic. By way of an illustration of this Rowland and Canavan (1983) describe how a single exposure to a BAT presented in a graded series resulted in dramatic and clinically significant reductions in self-ratings of anxiety. Their patient was severely afraid of spiders to the extent that

she avoided places where spiders might be found, she searched for traces of spiders when visiting anywhere new, she would not remove her shoes in the house, she could not sleep in a bed if the bedclothes had touched the floor, and she would shout and scream if she saw a spider; physically/somatically: she vomited, shook, felt dizzy, her palms sweated, her mouth was dry, she could feel her heart racing and thumping, and she experienced feelings of weakness in her legs. [Rowland and Canavan, 1983, p. 140]

In addition to these symptoms she was unable to go into the country and would leave any room in which a spider had been seen. On her homecoming each evening she would check the house and especially the bathroom for spiders. This is a very good description of a severely phobic person with intense subjective and physical symptoms and a wide range of socially debilitating avoidance behaviours.

Rowland and Canavan (1983) constructed a twenty-item hierarchy which they initially presented to their subject and asked her to rate how upset (anxious) she would feel if she were in the situation corresponding to each stage in the hierarchy. This was then repeated after a short interval and no significant change was observed. The patient was then presented with the hierarchy items one at a time, starting at the bottom and asked if she could perform each item. If she said 'yes' she was then given the opportunity to actually carry out what was involved in that item. Otherwise the item was just passed over with no attempt to exhort the patient to achieve it. From the description given in the report this was definitely a low-demand procedure. At the end of this BAT the subject rated the items for their anxiety-provoking powers yet again as in the original procedure. There was a large reduction of about 50 per cent in her ratings of the degree to which she was 'upset'. The inference that this reduction was caused by the BAT is strengthened by the fact that two subsequent sessions in which she was treated by cognitive methods and a discussion of coping strategies resulted in no change in her ratings. Despite this the patient reported that she had found the therapy sessions useful and that she thought that she had made some improvement. It therefore seems unlikely that the change following the initial BAT was a result of demand characteristics or any therapeutic expectations engendered by the BAT itself.

In passing it is worth noting that BATs were developed at a time when the prevailing theory of avoidance behaviour was that it was determined by a drive (fear). The rationale behind treatment by systematic desensitization, which was then the standard treatment, was that it would reduce this drive. Reduction of drive would then reduce the avoidance behaviour. Since BATs deal with the avoidance behaviour itself, and not the underlying drive, it was not anticipated that the reactivity of the measure would be a major problem. The later development of treatment by direct exposure brings the BAT procedure much closer to what actually goes on in therapy and thus points to why BATs have high levels of reactivity.

Many tests used by psychologists have less than perfect test-retest reliability. This means that when people are tested twice on the same test on different occasions their scores will not necessarily be identical despite the absence of any real change in the variable that is being measured. Some of the reasons for this have already been expounded and in addition it is quite probable that simple errors will occur which will affect the test scores. Temporally unreliable tests pose a particular problem when investigating abnormal behaviour and experience. Abnormal phenomena are partly by definition statistical rarities. On scales and tests devised to measure such behaviour and its deviation from normality people with abnormal behaviour will be located at the extremes of the scale. Because of the unreliability they will tend to produce scores that are nearer to the mean of the scale on retesting simply because they have less opportunity to become more deviant. This effect is known as *statistical regression to the mean* and it affects all sorts of measures based on extreme groups. Thus if the clinician is to employ a battery of tests on his patients before and after treatment then they would tend to show improvements in their scores irrespective of how they were treated. One way round this is to employ measures devised and standardized on abnormal groups and where the subjects start in the middle of the range.

The issue of test-retest reliability also leads to a paradox. If the clinician is to detect small changes in patients with before and after testing it is useful to have a test with high reliability and so reduce the size of the change in score that could be attributed to error of measurement. On the other hand, increasing test-retest reliability usually increases test *stability* over time and thus actually makes the test less sensitive to small changes in the underlying variable that is being measured. This results in a situation where high reliability is a good thing but only up to a certain point. Beyond this it can be counter-productive. In these circumstances a test which has high reliability on each occasion of measurement but which has low test-retest reliability and is sensitive to change is needed.

The single case experiment

Suppose that the problems of measurement caused by reactivity, statistical regression, instrumentation, etc. can be overcome to a satisfactory degree and that measures taken before and after treatment still showed that the client had improved to a significant extent. Is it now possible to claim that it is the treatment *per se* that is responsible for the change? Although this inference would be attractive, especially to the clinician who not unreasonably wants to confirm his efficacy, there are at least two alternative explanations that need to be eliminated.

Firstly, it could be the case that the period of therapy coincides with fortuitous changes in the patient's life circumstances. For example, one of the authors recalls an obsessional-compulsive patient who repeatedly checked her food to ensure that there were no traces of ground glass present. The standard treatment of response prevention had only the most modest success until her husband left her for another woman whereupon a dramatic improvement in the key symptom was noted. It then transpired that at one point in their marriage the husband had apparently tried to harm his wife by placing ground glass in her food! For some unknown reason the patient had not felt able to disclose this fact earlier in treatment. Admittedly this is an unusually extreme example of an 'accident' of history affecting the outcome of treatment but it does illustrate the point that people who present for treatment lead complex lives outside of the treatment sessions about which even the most skilful therapists have little knowledge. What goes on outside may be highly influential in determining the course of psychological disturbances and thus distort treatment effects.

A second factor which might explain change in the patient is known as *maturation*. Whereas history refers to the influence of external events on the crucial measures of outcome, maturation denotes the possibility that naturally occurring, internally gener- ated processes may influence the course of dysfunction. This is most obviously seen in disorders that occur in children, especially where there is a known natural improvement in performance such as in speech or motor ability. Maturation is also a major alternative hypothesis in any research programme in which educational factors are being evaluated in children. Related changes can occur in adults where there is a well-recognized tendency in people with psycho- logical disturbances to get better with time despite the absence of any therapeutic intervention or the occurrence of any external event that might plausibly explain the change. This is commonly referred to as *spontaneous remission*. Tennant *et al.* (1981) found that most people presenting to their general practitioners with psychological problems were likely to recover spontaneously within a few weeks or months.

In order to eliminate these explanations it is necessary to achieve some degree of experimental control. In clinical research this has been greatly helped by the development of single case experimental designs notably by those working within an operant framework (Hersen and Barlow, 1984; Kazdin, 1982a; Morley, 1986). Single case designs are not only of value to the clinician who is concerned with demonstrating the impact of his work with individual clients. In more fundamental research in abnormal psychology it not infrequently happens that conditions of great theoretical interest only appear very rarely. An outstanding example is the famous Montreal case HM, originally described by Scoville and Milner (1957), who showed one of the most severe memory disorders ever recorded after undergoing bilateral removals of parts of his temporal lobes for the relief of epilepsy. These severe memory impairments are one reason why the operation has not been repeated on other patients and therefore HM is virtually unique. Investigations into the nature of HM's memory impairment (e.g. Corkin, 1968; Wickelgren, 1968) are only possible by basing the experiments on a single subject. Elegant arguments for the adoption of single investigations as a central strategy for neuropsychology can be found in Shallice (1979).

The simplest single case design is one in which a series of observations are taken before and after the treatment is implemented. There are thus two phases, A and B, of the experiment. Figure 1 shows data from such an experiment reported by Morley *et al.* (1983). The subject suffered from agoraphobia with repeated panic attacks which kept her relatively housebound. During the course of the initial assessment and later treatment she was asked to keep a record of the occurrence of panic attacks, and their severity was rated on a simple three-point scale. During the assessment (baseline) phase it was discovered that the attacks were precipitated by social situations in which the patient felt trapped. She felt that she was unable to leave these situations because of more pressing reasons such as wanting to prepare dinner, without giving people offence. She was anxious that her behaviour might result in the loss of friends and social pleasure. Before the main treatment was introduced she was instructed in relaxation skills, with the rationale that the panic attacks were manifestations of an overactive nervous system which could be calmed down by regular practice of relaxation. The patient apparently believed this dubious rationale and according to both her own and her husband's reports she practised the techniques regularly. From an empirical point of view it was expected that the relaxation would only have a marginal effect and it was introduced as a placebo treatment or active baseline.

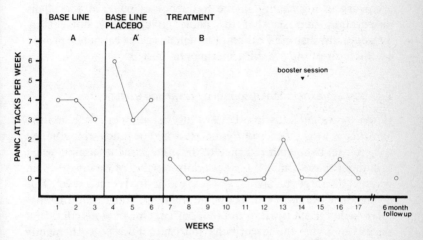

Figure 1. Results of a simple AB single case experiment on the therapeutic reduction of panic attacks. In the baseline (A), the patient kept a log of her panic attacks. In the second phase of the baseline (A'), she was taught muscle relaxation as a placebo. Finally in the treatment period (B) she was taught a version of Meichenbaum's stress inoculation training.

The real treatment was a combination of Meichenbaum's stress inoculation training and covert modelling (Kazdin, 1980) in which the patient imagined herself leaving social gatherings in a variety of socially competent ways. She was also instructed to gradually expose herself to successively more difficult social situations. Figure 1 indicates that when the treatment proper was introduced, there was a notable reduction in the number of panic attacks. It was also clear from her account that she began to go out more often and by the end of treatment she had begun visiting places that she had avoided for a number of years. The relatively stable frequency of panic attacks in the baseline phase (A and A') suggests that the alternative explanations of testing, instrumentation, reactivity and statistical regression can be tentatively excluded. If these factors had been in operation there would have been a marked reduction in the frequency of the attacks over the first few observations. If a maturation factor were operating this would also result in a slow change in the frequency of attacks over the course of the baseline. What cannot be excluded is history since a single event temporarily coincident with the introduction of treatment might produce such a pattern of scores. As it happened no event was noticed at the time of treatment. In addition, during both baseline and treatment phases events of some emotional importance occurred without there being a corresponding change in the frequency of panic attacks. This observation suggests that the panic attacks were not readily influenced by historical events although this claim cannot be proved on the basis of the present experimental design.

Establishing experimental control by reversing treatments

In the treatment situation that has just been under discussion the evidence for the efficacy of treatment would be much strengthened if the target behaviour returned to the pretreatment baseline when treatment ceased and if a further reintroduction of treatment again brought the target behaviour down to the desired clinical level. This sequence of events in which baseline and treatment are alternated is often called the ABAB or operant design. One obvious constraint on its use is that the target behaviour should not be permanently affected by the treatment, at least in the short term. In the previous case the patient rapidly learned new and more adaptive ways of coping with potentially threatening social situations and it would not have been practical to reverse the therapeutic conditions. In some instances behaviour is under the control of powerful and manipulable environmental contingencies and the presence or absence of the environmental event determines the presence or absence of the behaviour. The therapeutic effect of manipulating these contingencies can be readily demonstrated by an ABAB design thus eliminating the possible effect of any historical events as a plausible explanation for the observed changes.

E. S. Shapiro *et al.* (1980) tried to establish whether the simple use of a short-term physical restraint would be effective in reducing the frequency of stereotyped movements in mentally handicapped children. Stereotypic behaviour is common in the severely mentally handicapped and consists of regularly repeated motor sequences. Sitting and rocking the upper part of the body to and fro for long periods is a common example. Sometimes these movements can result in self-injury as when the child repeatedly scratches himself and disfigures his appearance. Even mild stereotypic movements

can be dysfunctional because they interfere with the child's ability
to do other things and so make him even slower in learning adaptive
and useful skills.

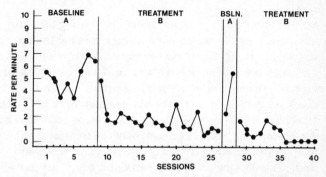

Figure 2. An example of an ABAB single case experiment, in which the
experimenters checked for the effect of the treatment by withdrawing and then
reinstituting the treatment. In this example the investigators (Shapiro *et al.*, 1980)
treated a mentally handicapped girl, Ruth, for stereotyped movements which
resulted in self-mutilation. During baseline conditions (A), the number of times
Ruth touched her face was counted. In the treatment phases (B), a form of
response prevention where her hands were restrained was instituted.
(Reproduced with permission of the Association for Advancement of Behavior
Therapy and the authors, from *Behavior Therapy*, 1980, *11*, 227–33.)

Figure 2 shows some data from an 8-year-old girl, Ruth, whose
stereotyped movements took the form of placing her hands in her
mouth for a few seconds at a time. This repetitive behaviour had
resulted in a dermatological condition which necessitated medical
treatment. In order to be treated, Ruth's arms had to be placed in
restraints. During the experiment Ruth spent fifteen-minute
sessions in a small classroom seated at a desk on which there were
three visuomotor tasks at which she could play. Her activity on
these tasks was continually monitored in order to ascertain whether
the successful treatment of her stereotyped behaviour would lead
her to spend more time in constructive play.

In the baseline phase (A) the rate at which Ruth touched her face
was counted. Treatment (B) consisted of the therapist saying 'No,
Ruth, take your hands out of your mouth', and physically holding
her hands down on the table for thirty seconds. As Figure 2 shows,
the introduction of treatment produced a relatively quick and
significant reduction in the frequency of hand movements. Hand
movements promptly returned to baseline levels when the treat-

ment was withdrawn. It is unlikely that accidental events un-connected with the treatment would occur so as to produce the same changes in behaviour coincident with the alterations in treatment. In any case, if doubt remains further AB combinations could be introduced.

As already indicated, the major limitation in using this design is that it can be affected by 'carry-over' effects from the treatment to baseline conditions. This is where the impact of treatment does not disappear when the treatment is withdrawn. This is a problem often encountered in examining the effects of drug treatments since it may take several days for a drug to become metabolically inactive after it has been withdrawn. Sometimes this can be accommodated by simply having long baseline periods between treatment phases in order to allow for the effects of the previous treatment session to be dissipated. This strategy will not work for many psychological treatments which specifically aim to provide the patient with a means of coping with problem situations which are intended to be used by the patient after treatment is discontinued.

More than one problem: the multiple baseline design

When the treatments are irreversible for practical or ethical reasons it may be possible to control for the effects of history and maturation by using a design known as the 'multiple baseline'. This is especially appropriate where it is necessary to tackle more than one clinical problem or it is necessary to examine the same problem in a number of settings. The fundamental idea behind this design, as in all other single case designs, is that the individual is used as his own control. In a multiple baseline study, therapeutic interventions are made on each target problem in a sequential way holding the conditions relating to the other problems constant. The essential argument is that if the treatments have a specific effect then changes will occur in the target problems only when the treatment is introduced. On the other hand, if there is an event coincidental with the introduction of treatment then its effects will also register on the 'control' problems. Obviously there is an assumption in this argument to the effect that treatments are supposed to influence each key aspect of behaviour independently whereas maturation factors and the accidents of history will have changes that have an impact on all behaviours. This is an unproven assumption and leads to the consequence that the value of investigations relying on multiple baseline designs depends upon their outcome. (Kazdin and

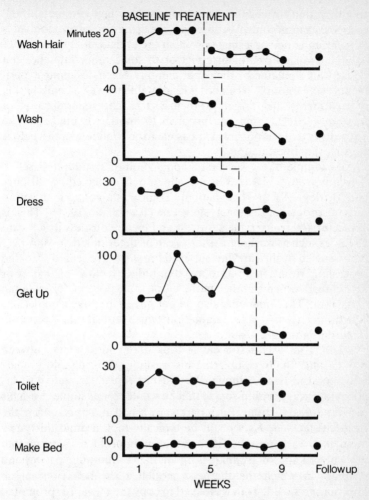

Figure 3. An example of a multiple baseline single case experiment. In this study a young man, Tom, who was excessively slow in completing his morning routine was helped to speed up to more normal levels. The therapists introduced the treatments in a progressive sequence across a number of separate behaviours. As each treatment was introduced so the target behaviour changed and the other untreated behaviours remained constant. The pattern of results indicates that the treatment rather than other factors was responsible for Tom's improvement. (Taken from C. Bilsbury and S. Morley, *Behaviour Research and Therapy*, 1979, *17*, 405–8, reproduced with permission of Pergamon Press.)

Kopel (1975) discuss the issues in some detail.) If the target behaviours change in the appropriate direction and only when the relevant treatment is introduced then it is possible to be moderately confident that the changes were produced by the treatments. If the changes occur in control problems at the same time as a treatment is introduced aimed at a single problem then this could be due either to a generalized treatment effect or to some other influence not directly manipulated by the experimenter. When designing experiments using multiple baselines it is advisable to seek a combination of treatments and target problems such that generalization of treatment effects from one problem to another is unlikely. The difficulty is that it is not always possible to be confident of this before starting the investigation.

An example of the successful application of a multiple baseline design is seen in Figure 3, which shows data collected by Bilsbury and Morley (1979). Their patient, Tom, was a young man with a rare disorder, obsessional slowness (Rachman, 1974). This is characterized by extreme slowness and meticulousness in self-care activities such as washing. As far as can be determined this slowness is not caused by the carrying out of elaborate and repeated checking or washing rituals in order to avoid or reduce feelings of anxiety or discomfort which is the more usual function of obsessional behaviour. These patients also do not have repetitive ruminations concerning harm or contamination which are another common feature in obsessional states.

When Tom was first seen he took about four hours between waking and finally completing his washing, dressing and preparation for the day. Although he did not repeat his activities his behaviour was very unusual in that he would, for example, wash his face in several sections. Each part was washed and dried before the next was tackled. As a result he typically took around thirty-five minutes to wash himself. This and four other problems were treated with a package of techniques involving 'prompting, pacing and shaping' in which the therapist modelled the behaviour at an appropriate speed. Tom was asked to copy the therapist, prompted to hurry up when he lagged behind and instructed what to do next if he started to perform unnecessary movements. Where it was impossible to model behaviour Tom was set target times to achieve and his routine was discussed by the therapist. Figure 3 clearly shows that as each behaviour was treated there was a noticeable reduction in the time taken to complete that part of the routine but no appreciable change in the other aspects of his behaviour that were being recorded. This offers good support for the notion that the therapeutic gains can be attributed to the treatment programme and it would be relatively difficult to account for this data in terms of other factors.

Conclusions

Carefully conducted single case investigations can help the clinician to investigate the effects of therapy in an experimental way. They may also be the only practicable way of investigating the effects of treatment where it is very difficult to get comparable groups of subjects to put into the more conventional form of a clinical trial which compares a treated group with an untreated control group or a control group given some other form of intervention. One criticism that has sometimes been raised with regard to single case experiments relates to the problem of generalization. No matter how unambiguously a single case experiment may demonstrate that the treatment was effective for that patient, to what extent is the finding also likely to be true of other cases? A little thought reveals that this criticism is not as serious as it might appear at first sight. Suppose Bilsbury and Morley (1979) had been able to obtain a large number of patients with obsessional slowness like Tom and compared the results of their treatment package applied to one group with the outcome in an untreated control group. The key assumption behind the experiment is that the subjects within the groups are relatively homogeneous both with regard to the nature of their problems and in response to treatment. It is just this same assumption that lies behind any attempt to generalize from Tom to other patients with apparently similar problems. In any case generalization can also be tested by repeating the same investigation when the next patient with the same kind of problem comes along.

This is not to say that single case experimentation is not without its limitations. The single case approach is best where the interventions are easily controlled by the clinician and when they act rapidly and unambiguously. It is easiest to conduct these experiments when there is relatively tight control over the treatment environment so that there is little opportunity for external events to influence the course or outcome. It is also necessary to use measures that generally have low levels of reactivity and which can be repeated on many occasions without artifacts occurring. Such circumstances are not always easy to arrange. Not surprisingly single case methodology has been most commonly used to investigate treatments coming within the fields of applied behaviour analysis and behaviour therapy. It would be extremely difficult to formulate psychodynamic treatments to fit in with this sort of experimental method.

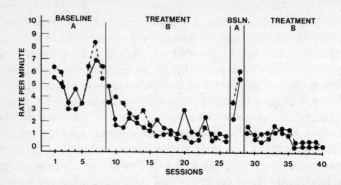

Figure 4. The use of an 'alternating treatments design' to investigate the impact of two treatments within the same subject. This figure is an elaboration of Figure 2. In the study by Shapiro *et al.*, Ruth was treated with positive practice during half of the treatment sessions. In positive practice her hands were systematically guided over the correct task for the treatment session. This additional data is shown by the dashed line. (Reproduced with permission of the Association for Advancement of Behavior Therapy and the authors, from *Behavior Therapy*, 1980, *11*, 227–33.)

Single case methods can be adapted to the investigation of the relative effectiveness of two types of treatment or used for investigating the relative effects of different components in a complex treatment package. In fact the experiment reported by E. S. Shapiro and his colleagues (1980) a little earlier in this chapter was an investigation into the relative effectiveness of two types of treatment. In addition to the programme of physical restraint described earlier Ruth was also exposed to a programme of positive practice. In the positive practice sessions she was given the same verbal warning but instead of being restrained for thirty seconds the therapist took her hands and guided her over the task which she was supposed to be doing. The sessions of physical restraint and positive practice were presented in a counterbalanced manner in what is known as an 'alternating treatments design' to ensure that there were no effects of treatment which could be attributed to the time of day or other factors which might be confounded with treatment. The full results of this experiment are shown in Figure 4 and it is apparent in this case that there were no differences between treatments. Although we might be reasonably confident that Shapiro controlled for many factors by using this approach, there is one overriding problem which can never be totally ruled out when two or more treatments are compared within one subject. This problem is known as multiple treatment interference. That is, one can never finally exclude the possibility that the effects of one treatment might carry over or interact with the effects of the other. The second treatment might be potentiated or inhibited by the first. What is then required to disentangle this situation is an experiment in which treatments or components of treatments can be presented in isolation from each other so that their effects are not confounded. This can only be done in the context of an experiment using matched groups of subjects. Where groups of patients cannot be obtained in sufficiently large numbers or are difficult to obtain at all, investigators have resorted to the use of 'analogue' experiments and this is an issue which will be taken up in the next chapter.

11 Why Do Treatments Work?: Process Research

Proving that a treatment has some therapeutic benefit is quite a different thing from showing why it works. A treatment like systematic desensitization may be effective in reducing fears but its real mechanism of action may be quite different from that implied by the rationale on which the treatment was originally based. Process research is concerned with discovering the mechanisms underlying treatment effects. This is interesting for two reasons. One is that identifying the effective ingredients in treatment is likely to lead to the development of more efficient methods of treatment. The second lies in the fact that understanding the processes that are effective in modifying abnormal behaviour is also likely to help towards the goal of getting a better understanding of such behaviour.

Process research typically involves examining the effects of different components of a treatment package either singly or in different combinations with one another. As such it generally requires the use of large groups of subjects and elaborate between-groups experimental designs. To fulfil these requirements researchers have often used analogue subjects and it is therefore appropriate to begin by looking at the use of analogue research.

Analogues in treatment research

Because of the difficulty of getting large numbers of subjects from patient samples there has been a tendency to use people from the general population who have some psychological characteristics in common with patients having the disorders of interest. For example, the researcher interested in the treatment of phobias may make use of the fact that many people within the general population will report having fears of small animals such as snakes and spiders. Such individuals can be easily detected using inexpensive questionnaires. Those with extreme scores can then be recruited to serve as experimental subjects. In practice this has led to a large number of investigations being carried out on university students who tend to be the most available potential subjects for many researchers (especially in the USA where acting as a subject for university staff may well be a course requirement for the vast numbers who do elementary psychology courses). Not only can such subjects be much more easy to come by than patient populations but they yield relatively homogeneous groups with low drop-out rates.

Not surprisingly, analogue studies have found considerable favour with psychologists. Borkovec and Rachman (1979) argue persuasively for their use and take as an example research on the reduction of fear conducted by Lang and his associates (e.g. Lang *et al.*, 1966). They claim that this research has led to four effects. Firstly, it has answered specific questions about treatments by demonstrating that systematic desensitization is an effective technique for reducing fear and avoidance. It should also be noted that these studies have also tried to investigate what it is about systematic desensitization which makes it effective. Borkovec and Rachman's second claim is that analogue studies have been able to defeat mistaken ideas. In particular they note that psychoanalytic theory predicts that a symptomatic treatment like systematic desensitization can only be partially successful. It may dispose of the avoidance and fear of an event or situation in a particular subject. Because it does not attempt to resolve the presumed underlying conflict a phenomenon known as symptom substitution should occur after treatment. Analytic theory predicts that the unresolved conflict will be expressed itself in the form of another symptom. Early researchers in systematic desensitization took care to try to observe this phenomenon but obtained no real evidence for this particular prediction.

The third alleged benefit of analogue research has been to uncover new information about the relationship between various indices of fear. Specifically, Lang and his colleagues (e.g. Lang *et al.*, 1970) have investigated the relationship between heart rate, imagery, subjective fear responses and the outcome from treatment. Their results led Lang to investigate the physiological concomitants of imagery. This in turn has resulted in a more precise formulation of the therapeutic mechanisms. Finally, the careful examination of various measures used in analogue experiments has led to the realization that these measures are partially independent. This has resulted in an alternative and predominantly psychological analysis of phobias (Hugdahl, 1981; Hodgson and Rachman, 1974).

The main concern with regard to the use of analogue experiments to investigate the effects of treatments lies in the degree to which it is possible to extrapolate the findings to clinical populations and treatments. In this respect it is possible to look at analogue subjects in terms of three sets of characteristics:

A. Features that analogue subjects share with the clinical population.
B. Features that they clearly do not share with the clinical population.
C. Features that they may or may not share with the clinical population.

The features that fall into category A are such things as irrational fears of spiders or snakes or high scores on measures such as the Beck Depression Inventory. There must be some factors in category B otherwise subjects would be regarded not as analogues but as identical, or at least potentially identical, with the clinical samples. In the case of the typical student analogue subjects they will differ from clinical samples in many ways. They have not approached a doctor or clinic to complain about their fear or low mood, or about whatever other problem is of interest. Student samples are likely to be younger, from a more homogeneous social background, of higher intellectual levels, not to be on prescribed medication for their problems and to differ in the level of available social support. Analogue subjects with fears are also likely to differ from phobic patients in the intensity of the fear and possibly also in the ways that they have open to them to cope with the fears.

The features manipulated in any experiment will relate to those in category C. The experiment with analogue subjects is carried out because it is not known which treatment or component of a treatment is effective in patient samples and the answer to this question must also be unknown for analogue subjects or else there would be no need to carry out the experiment at all. It can thus never be known a priori whether the results of the experiment will describe features that by rights ought to belong in category A or B (i.e. those features that the two types of subject have in common or those that divide them). Just how representative the results of analogue experiments are for clinical samples is likely to depend upon the relative potency of variables in categories A and B.

Alternatively, as Borkovec and Rachman (1979) suggest, if subjects are similar to patients on critical dimensions, then generalizing from one group to the next is likely to be successful in many cases (p. 255).

What then are the critical features that are likely to determine whether the findings from analogue studies will also apply to clinical populations? Using phobias as the example one potentially import- ant dimension is the intensity of fear. Although many people in the general population might report being afraid of spiders, very few indeed exhibit the extreme signs of Rowland and Canavan's (1983) patient as described in the previous chapter. In a survey of 499 women selected at random from ten separate communities, Costello (1982) could locate only three with phobias that were incapacitating to any significant degree. On the other hand, he found a prevalence rate of 244 per 1000 for mild fears, which were defined as the mid-point on a three-point scale of intensity with or without any evidence of avoidance. Defining phobias as fears with some evidence of avoidance gave a prevalence rate of 190 per 1000 in the population. So although there is a very low rate of people with handicapping fear, there is a significant proportion in the popu- lation with some degree of fear together with some avoidance behaviour. It is from this latter group that analogue subjects are likely to be drawn.

There is evidence that subjects with mild and moderate ratings of fear differ from those with more severe ratings in the extent to which they are influenced by the demand characteristics and instructions in the experimental situation (Bernstein and Neitzel, 1977). A typical demonstration of this is provided by Trudel (1979). He selected female college students who had reported that they felt 'much fear, very much fear, or terror' on a questionnaire about harmless snakes. This group was then divided into moderately and very afraid subjects. Some of the subjects were given high-demand instructions telling them that they had to try to complete the assigned tasks for the experiment to be carried out successfully. Others were merely told to try to do as much as they could. The experimental task was a standard thirty-item graded BAT. Trudel examined the responses of subjects at two critical points on the BAT. These were touching the snake for the first time and manipulating it. As might be expected, more moderately afraid than highly afraid subjects both touched and manipulated the snake. Also, subjects under high-demand conditions were more likely to touch the snake. However, the interaction between demand and the level of fear was such that highly fearful subjects were less likely to be influenced by the demand effect of instructions at the point at which they had to manipulate the snake.

As a consequence of this and similar findings it is appropriate to err on the side of caution when interpreting the results of analogue experiments in relation to what might happen with clinical populations. Nevertheless some things can be done which might increase the likelihood of satisfactory generalization. One thing is to ensure that in studies of fear only analogue subjects with intense fears are used and that the results cannot be adequately explained on the basis of the demand characteristics inherent in the experiment. Some experimenters have selected subjects on the basis of their physiological responses to phobic stimuli and use only those who show unambiguous signs of arousal to the stimuli. There is evidence that these measures are less influenced by demand characteristics but the relationship between physiological and behavioural measures of fear is not perfect. Thus Borkovec (1974) showed that while physiological measures of arousal were not influenced by instructions, the amount of approach behaviour was affected.

One possible solution to the problem of demand characteristics is to search for common fears other than small animal phobias which are more robust and similar to clinical fears. Borkovec has argued that social anxiety in a number of its manifestations provides suitable analogues, e.g. anxiety about heterosexual relations and public speaking (Borkovec and O'Brien, 1976; Borkovec and Sides, 1979). These fears are reasonably common with people complaining of high-intensity subjective anxiety and also exhibiting much greater physiological arousal than that shown in small animal fears. Social anxieties also seem less susceptible to influence by instruction, suggestion and demand. People with social anxiety also show anticipatory physiological responses such as cardiac acceleration when threatened with encountering the feared situations. Anticipatory anxiety is usually a pronounced feature of clinical phobias.

Borkovec and Rachman (1979) suggest that the conditions eliciting the fear are likely to be an important determinant of the ability to generalize from analogue to clinical populations. While this makes good common sense, it would seem that in practice some of the more frequently encountered clinical phobias just do not have an analogue equivalent. One of these is agoraphobia and Mathews (1978) suggests that agoraphobia is qualitatively different from other fears. This is notably because of the presence of panic attacks which do not appear to be precipitated by any identifiable stimulus complex. Agoraphobia also exemplifies a major problem in using diagnostic categories. Although these categories can be reliably identified by trained clinicians and often have appreciable prognostic validity, they do not necessarily reflect unitary psychological processes or even a homogeneous set of such processes. There is, therefore, little evidence that a diagnostic category, such as phobias, represents a psychologically sensible way of understanding these disorders (Hallam, 1978; 1983).

Not only is it difficult to find analogues for some phobias but it is even more difficult to imagine how analogues could be found for many other types of disorder. For example, Rachman and De Silva (1978) have shown that obsessional thoughts, images and impulses are quite common in normal populations but they are much reduced in their subjective emotional intensity, duration, frequency and the degree to which they produce urges to carry out neutralizing rituals. Normal subjects seem much more ready to respond to habituation training (the controlled repetition of the thought) than do clinical obsessionals. One difference between these groups that may be highly significant is the presence of a mood disturbance which is very often a feature of clinical obsessionals but absent in normal people with obsessional thoughts. Looking at a wider range of psychiatric phenomena there are clearly no corresponding analogue groups for such things as psychotic depression, hypomania and schizophrenia. There is then no alternative to working with the criterion groups.

A final problem with analogue research is that its generalization to clinical populations may actually lead to conclusions about treatment that are misleading or offer no evidence on important questions. Mathews (1978) cites some evidence relevant to this point. Imaginal flooding is a treatment with variable effectiveness in analogue studies but which appears to be much more potent and successful when used with clinical populations. Analogue research has also failed to identify potentially important treatment components or effects. It has failed to provide a reliable guide to the optimum duration of exposure to the phobic stimulus that is required for fear reduction. Neither does it provide information on the importance of inter-session practice and the effects of treatment in facilitating this. There is also little information from analogue research on the role of social reinforcement and general social and family processes which can be important in facilitating treatment adherence and effectiveness (Colletti and Brownwell, 1982). Finally many clinical patients, and even those with relatively mild anxiety-based disorders, are on medication and this may have important facilitative inhibiting effects on the impact of psychological treatments (Gray, 1982). This is a factor that is less easy to take into account in analogue experiments.

The role of analogue research

Analogue research has certainly had a useful part to play in developing and refining psychological treatments. As the foregoing discussion has amply indicated, it also has important limitations. In some areas analogue research has gathered a momentum of its own and it almost seems that in some instances the study of problems relating to either treatment or theories of disorder has been carried on in analogue almost for their own sake with the clinical populations almost forgotten. Analogue research is probably at its best where it forms part of a programme of investigations using both analogue subjects and clinical subjects. A good example of this is shown in the work of Ley and his colleagues (for a good review see Ley, 1977). Ley has been concerned with the factors that help patients to remember the information given to them by their doctors. He started with studies on clinical samples, tested out possible hypotheses in analogue experiments, and then went back to the clinical setting to show that the resulting conclusions about the way the information should be given did actually enhance the recall of that information by real patients in the actual clinical setting.

The key issue is not whether analogue research is good or bad, right or wrong. At its best, when directed at the right kind of question in an appropriate context, it can provide very useful information with a bearing on specific questions. At its worst it can be irrelevant or possibly even misleading. Despite the advantages that can accrue from analogue research when sensibly employed, it also has to be remembered that the crucial questions are concerned with what happens in the case of clinical populations. At the end of the day it is only possible to be sure about what is happening in clinical populations by actually studying those populations and not some substitute, no matter how close that substitute might be to the real thing.

Why does a treatment work?

As we mentioned at the beginning of this chapter, it is relatively simple to demonstrate that a particular treatment works. The appropriate experiment compares the treatment with a control group using measures of important clinical or social features which are applied pre- and post-treatment to the treated group and at comparable times to the control group. The results will give little indication about why the treatment works. Apart from intellectual curiosity there are sound practical reasons for wanting to discover the method of therapeutic effect. If the effective components can be isolated, it may well be possible to increase the value of the treatment by presenting the effective component more efficiently and by deleting the irrelevant aspects. Where pharmacological treatments are involved there is the added incentive that it might be possible to eliminate the components responsible for unwanted side effects. Side effects may also occur in psychological treatments but seem rather rare (e.g. Shipley and Boudewyns, 1980).

The process of discovering how a treatment works can be rather complicated. In dealing with this issue, Wolpe's systematic desensitization will be used as the example because it is known to be a clinically effective procedure for a relatively circumscribed set of disorders, the phobias. It is considerably less effective as a treatment for other disorders with a fear component such as obsessional behaviour and it is ineffective as a treatment for depression and the psychoses. It should also be noted that direct *in vivo* exposure to feared situations has replaced systematic desensitization as the treatment of choice for some phobic problems, and it must now be regarded as one of a number of treatment strategies based upon exposure to the phobic stimulus. Nevertheless, and despite its reduced clinical importance, systematic desensitization does have a number of advantages in the present context because it has been so extensively investigated. In spite of this there is still no clear comprehensive account of its mode of action.

There have been three major theoretical approaches to explaining the action of systematic desensitization. The first is based on learning theory. The second emphasizes the therapeutic relationship and is based in psychodynamic theories. Finally, there are explanations based on social influence particularly in relation to such concepts as expectation and credibility. These will be looked at in turn.

Learning theory explanations

Wolpe's (1958) account of systematic desensitization (SD) is not at all clear as to the mechanism (Watts, 1979) but the fundamental notion is that a fearful response could be reciprocally inhibited if it was evoked in a situation when the individual was in a state antagonistic to fear. This is usually a state of muscular-skeletal relaxation but could also be sexual arousal, aggression or a number of other things. Wolpe stipulated that for the treatment to be effective three conditions should be met: (1) fear-evoking stimuli should be presented by ascending a graded hierarchy; (2) responses neutralizing anxiety-induced arousal were necessary; and (3) the first two conditions should be presented contiguously. He argued that by presenting weak phobic stimuli the state of relaxation (if that is the neutralizing response) will not be disrupted and no anxiety is experienced. To account for the permanent effects of this contiguous pairing Wolpe proposed that associating the anxiety-producing stimulus with no anxiety was reinforced by the Hullian principle of drive reduction. As each item in the hierarchy is desensitized so the next items lost some of their capacity to evoke fear through the process of generalization decrement. It will be recalled that at the time that SD was proposed as a treatment the overt behaviour was construed as being under the control of specific drives which 'pushed it along'. In the case of fear-motivated behaviour it followed that once the fear drive was reduced by SD so overt manifestations of fearful behaviour should dissipate. It is now known that this is not necessarily the case (Rachman, 1976b).

Wolpe's account is inadequate in several ways. At a practical level it is clear that it is not necessary to present fearful stimuli in a graded manner, nor is it necessary to present them in conjunction with a deliberately induced counter-response. If stimuli that evoke intense fear are presented for long enough and often enough, fear responses will be reduced, assuming that they are not followed by negative (aversive) consequences (Boudewyns and Shipley, 1983). This indicates that Wolpe's proposed requirements for the reduction of fear are misleading.

A second problem with Wolpe's formulation is that his theoretical propositions are far from clear. Watts (1975) has noted that Wolpe implies that he views anxiety both as a drive state and as a particular response. In this case reciprocal inhibition could occur at both peripheral and central levels. The fundamental problem is that there are too many theoretical constructs and too few measures of these constructs. Furthermore, it is not readily apparent how the theoretical constructs are to be tied to observables.

Evans (1973) has argued in a similar vein that an adequate

account of SD must fulfil the usual criteria for developing a theory. The procedural elements must be specified as must the way in which they relate to theoretical constructs. The temporal relationships between the variables should be set out and the boundary conditions as to what the theory is explaining need to be delineated. Evans notes that most of these conditions have not been met by Wolpe's (1958) explanations or indeed any other explanation of SD. Evans also considered some of the particular accounts of SD. He dismissed counter-conditioning as an explanation on the grounds that there is no correspondence between the procedures involved in SD and the usual laboratory counter-conditioning procedure where there is explicit reinforcement of an alternative response. This objection tends to confuse procedure with process unless it is further assumed that the process is specifically dependent upon following the details of the laboratory paradigm.

Another explanation has been drawn from an analogy between SD and extinction procedures. Extinction is merely the presentation of a conditioned stimulus without subsequent reinforcement. Evans points out that a number of parameters involved in the presentation of conditioned stimuli are known to affect extinction. It would be relatively easy to replicate these conditions in SD. If the results emerge as being congruent with what is already known about extinction this would lend support to the analogy. Unfortunately invoking extinction as an explanation of SD appears to be inadequate. While there is reasonable correspondence at a procedural level there are immense problems at the level of theory. Extinction is not a theory as such; indeed there are a number of theories of extinction (Mackintosh, 1974). Each of these theories of extinction makes differential predictions about the course of response decrement under varying conditions and empirical support can be found for each theory. As yet there appears to be no consensus on what extinction is even in relatively simple laboratory situations.

The idea that SD might be considered as analogous to habituation was put forward by Lader and Wing (1966) and Lader and Mathews (1968). At a procedural level habituation is identical to extinction and involves the repetition of a stimulus with no reinforcement and the subsequent decrement in responding. Evans dismissed this as a potential explanation for SD on the grounds that in most studies of habituation the response decrement is transient whereas in SD it seems to be permanent. However there is some evidence that habituation is not always a transient event (for a review see Watts, 1979). Others have protested that habituation applies only to unconditioned stimuli whereas SD is concerned with fear that is conditioned. In fact this is an assumption that does not fit too well with the known facts concerning phobias. There are considerable problems for a conditioning theory of phobia acquisition (Rachman, 1977) and Gray (1982) presents a powerful argument for considering fear stimuli as sensitized unconditioned stimuli.

The original proposal by Lader and his colleagues was the maximal habituation theory. This states that fear stimuli would habituate under repeated presentation and that this rate of habituation would be maximized by factors which lowered the amount of physiological arousal. Arousal can be manipulated by relaxation as well as pharmacological means and is also a function of individual differences. Subsequent evidence for this proposition was not entirely convincing (Watts, 1979).

Table 4 *Contrast between the hypothetical processes of habituation and sensitization.*

Habituation	Sensitization
Purely decremental	Decremental at first, then incremental
Specific to one stimulus	Affects general responsiveness
Independent of stimulus intensity	Proportional to stimulus intensity
Decays spontaneously	Decays spontaneously but is more transient than habituation

In a series of stimuli there is progressively more habituation and less sensitization

An alternative theory of habituation has been developed by Groves and Thompson (1970) and applied to SD by Watts (1979). The 'dual process theory' proposes that the observed response is the consequence of the summation of two inferred processes, habituation and sensitization. Habituation and sensitization can be differentiated in a number of ways which are set out in Table 4. This theory is capable of predicting a number of new findings which could not be derived from the maximal habituation or reciprocal inhibition theories. For example, it proposes that low-intensity items will habituate more rapidly if they are presented for short durations whilst the reverse will be true for high-intensity items. The crucial difference between the conditions is the amount of sensitization which is allowed to occur. The theory also predicts that there will be interactions between the stimulus intensity and the presence or absence of relaxation in determining the amount of anxiety reduction. A further implication of the theory is that there will be differences between the amount of short- and long-term reduction in anxiety under different procedures. More importantly, it is not restrictive in its explanation of effective fear reduction to the relatively brief exposures generally associated with SD. It can account for the fact that prolonged exposure can be effective and indicates what variables might be related to outcome. As far as learning theory approaches are concerned the dual process theory seems to be the most fruitful heuristically as well as being able to account for many of the basic findings.

Personal relationship and psychodynamic explanations

When SD was initially proposed psychoanalysis was the predominant theory of behaviour change and as such dominated the practice of psychological treatments. It will be recalled that psychoanalytic thought in relation to therapy has two central features concerning both the aims of treatment and how it should be conducted. It is argued that treatment has to aim at the resolution of underlying conflicts and that this can only be achieved through the engaging of the client in an intense transference relationship with the therapist. Psychoanalytic theory allows that SD, a treatment specifically directed at symptom removal, might be successful in removing the symptoms. However, it also leads to the expectation that the underlying conflict would remain unresolved and the person could therefore show further evidence of disturbance by developing one or more other symptoms ('symptom substitution'). This is a general prediction but psychoanalytic theory does not specify exactly what these new symptoms will be or when they will occur.

Although the generality of the prediction of symptom substitution makes it difficult to test, a number of experiments on SD, especially the early ones (e.g. Davison, 1968; Lang *et al.*, 1966; Paul, 1966), took considerable care to try to identify new symptoms after successful treatment by SD. These analogue studies gave no evidence of symptom substitution. Many other investigations have consistently failed to record this phenomenon including many carried out with 'real' psychiatric patients (e.g. Sloane *et al.*, 1975). It should however be appreciated that as far as psychoanalytic theory is concerned sympton substitution should occur just as readily in analogue populations. Despite the overwhelming contrary evidence concerning symptom substitution most clinicians have experienced the situation where a client develops further problems after an initial success. This is certainly not prima facie evidence for symptom substitution and there are many ways to account for the occasional as opposed to the regular occurrence of this phenomenon (e.g. Kazdin, 1982b). For example, theories of fear acquisition would generally not predict that having one phobic symptom would protect the individual against developing others and in a few cases this could obviously happen during or shortly after treatment of the first.

There seem to be no investigations in which the therapeutic relationship has been manipulated along psychodynamic lines to ensure the development of a transference relationship. Neither do the transference components of behaviour therapy appear to have been systematically measured. The former manipulations are alien to the process of psychoanalytic psychotherapy and would probably not be regarded as a reasonable test of the theory should they be attempted. As far as measuring transference is concerned, it is obviously a complex construct which is far from static. Quantification of the processes alleged to underly it is fraught with difficulties. There have been very few attempts to measure transference from a psychoanalytic perspective.

The nearest that empirical research has got to looking at the possible role of transference is in studies of SD with a control group which has had a high degree of interpersonal contact with the therapist. Some of these experiments have been devised to encourage control subjects to explore their feelings of fear via the free associations which occur when they reflect on their fear. For example, Davison (1968) had his control subjects imagine scenes from their childhood which were related to conflict but unconnected with their target fear of snakes. Gelder *et al.* (1973) in a study of out-patient phobic subjects had one group explore their feelings elicited by the presentation of the anxiety-evoking stimulus. In neither of these studies (one with analogue and one with clinical subjects), nor in many others employing similar manipulations, has this type of control procedure given outcomes as good as those produced in the SD group.

It should already be evident that a proper test of the psycho-dynamic account of the client-therapist relationship as a necessary component for effective therapy is virtually impossible. Also it will be realized that the claim about the status of this relationship is a general one which can be applied to all psychological therapies and not just SD. What could be tested in relation to SD is the hypothesis that it is the interpersonal contact between client and therapist that is the main agent of change and not the specific procedures involved in SD. This can be tested by comparing a therapy that involves the same amount and quality of client-therapist interaction but with none of SD's specific ingredients (relaxation, exposure via a graded hierarchy, etc.) with SD itself. This is more or less what the study by Gelder *et al.* (1973), described above, attempted to do and this does not support the hypothesis.

A different theory of interpersonal relationship has been proposed by Frank (1973) to account for both psychotherapeutic changes and the omnipresent placebo response found in psycho-logical and medical research. Frank suggests that there are six factors which are necessary but not sufficient for therapy to be effective. Firstly, there must be an intense, emotionally charged relationship between the therapist and the patient in which the patient can confide and disclose his worries and anxiety. Secondly, the therapist and patient must have a shared rationale in their formulation of the problem and an agreement as to what constitutes the appropriate form of therapy. For Frank the precise nature of this rationale would seem to be unimportant and thus his theory can take account of cross-cultural observations of healing in non-Western societies. Thirdly, the therapist must provide new information to the client about the causes of his distress and the steps which he must necessarily take to overcome it. In this regard the therapist has a didactic role to play. As a fourth constituent the therapist must arouse hope in the client that his distress can be relieved. This component has been thoroughly investigated by Frank and his associates in a set of experiments in which hope has been deliberately manipulated. This appears to confirm the import-ance of hope (Frank, 1973; 1974). The fifth factor is the arousal and facilitation of emotion. The precise nature of the emotion is not specified. It could be intense feelings of guilt, anger, anxiety or any other emotion which the client perceives as being relevant to his problem and which will help him to restructure his experiences in some way. The sixth and last point is that the therapist gives the client opportunities for success experiences. These allow him to develop a sense of mastery over what had appeared to be problematic influences exerting unwanted control over his behaviour and feelings.

Returning to SD, it can be seen that Wolpe's procedures probably involve all but the fifth factor. This is the one stressing the arousal of emotion and the procedure used in SD explicitly tries to ensure that the client does not experience intense emotion. The extent to which there is an intense, emotionally charged relationship in SD could also be queried although the client does disclose important information which is the other half of Frank's first requirement. However, once this information has been disclosed adequately enough for the therapist to make his initial assessment of the client's problems and to construct the hierarchy, there is no reason to suppose that therapy sessions will necessarily continue in this vein. If an intense relationship involving disclosure were a necessary aspect of treatment then improvement as a result of SD should occur in the early sessions involved with assessment and the construction of the hierarchy. The rest of the sessions would then be largely irrelevant. Whilst improvement can be noted over the preliminary sessions there is little evidence that the major change takes place during this time.

A better test as to whether factors of this kind are the main cause of change in SD comes from experiments in which the elements of SD are provided automatically via computer-controlled displays of phobic stimuli. The only contact with a human 'therapist' is with research assistants who prepare the subjects, administer self-report scales and conduct the relevant behavioural avoidance tests. In experiments comparing this sort of procedure with standard SD there is typically no difference between the two conditions (e.g. Lang *et al.*, 1970). It must therefore be concluded that a close relationship with a therapist is not a necessary condition for therapeutic gain in systematic desensitization and that this type of theory will not account for anything like all the response that is found to this form of treatment.

Social influence: credibility and expectation

More recently the outcome literature with respect to psychotherapy in general and to SD in particular has come under critical examination from a particular point of view. The basic argument has been well set out by D. A. Shapiro (1981, p. 112) in the following words:

In simple terms the expectancy-arousal hypothesis states that treatments differ in their effectiveness only to the extent that they arouse in clients differing degrees of expectation of benefit. According to this hypothesis, arousal of such expectancies is the necessary and sufficient precondition of treatment effectiveness. Differential treatment outcomes unaccompanied by correspondingly differential credibility are of especial interest because they disconfirm this hypothesis. Such findings suggest that there are indeed specific mechanisms mediating the differential effectiveness of treatments.

This hypothesis is analogous to Frank's fourth condition specifying the arousal of hope in the client, but it can equally well be applied to forms of therapy in which Frank's other five conditions are absent. Thus on the credibility hypothesis Lang *et al.*'s (1970) finding that automated SD and clinician-delivered SD have equivalent therapeutic effects can be explained on the grounds that both of these generate equivalent expectations for improvement in the client. It is therefore quite reasonable to treat the question of credibility quite separately from that of the importance of the therapeutic relationship.

The basic argument that SD has yet to be demonstrated to be more effective than an equally credible control manipulation has been supported by two extensive reviews of the literature (Kazdin and Wilcoxon, 1976; Lick and Bootzin, 1975). It is important to note that both of these reviews refrained from claiming that SD was no better than an equally credible control procedure. They merely concluded that there was no good evidence to the contrary. Lick and Bootzin (1975) made three criticisms of the then available data. In the first place experimenters had generally failed to carry out independent checks on the credibility of their control procedures. In most cases control conditions had been developed and utilized without any attempt to examine their credibility. A number of studies using students as subjects have demonstrated that SD procedures were rated as being more credible than a variety of control 'treatments' recorded in the literature. This is no substitute for data collected at the time the experiments were conducted and from the subjects actually used in those experiments but it reinforces Lick and Bootzin's second point to the effect that unconvincing placebo manipulations had been employed. Their third point was that many experiments had been conducted on mildly fearful and poorly motivated 'analogue' subjects. It will be remembered that these subjects are easily influenced by instructions and testing conditions and it has been suggested that, in consequence, they will be the most susceptible to placebo manipulations. Kazdin and Wilcoxon (1976) identified ninety-two experiments on SD that had been published between 1965 and 1974 in leading journals. They report that in only five of these had there been an independent demonstration that the control procedure was of equal credibility to the SD treatment. Furthermore only one of this group of five (Gelder *et al.*, 1973) had found that the group given SD had a better outcome than the control group.

A question that immediately comes to mind is why this critical alternative explanation had not been much more thoroughly examined? Lick and Bootzin (1975) suggest that in part it is due to the fact that the early investigators did not believe that cognitive factors, such as the expectations induced by treatment, could have any significant effect on fear reduction. This belief could arise from the fact that the predominant theories of learning on which the treatment was based were avowedly non-cognitive. This belief could also be backed up by clinical experience which shows that people with simple but severe phobias cannot be influenced by cognitive attempts (e.g. persuasion) to moderate their fear (see Rowland and Canavan, 1983). Of course the apparent absence of any effect due to persuasion and similar devices does not rule out the possibility that cognitive changes are important in the reduction of fear and avoidance behaviour. Indeed one contemporary theory of therapy proposes that treatments work by producing cognitive changes pertaining to the person's beliefs as to his self-efficacy (Bandura, 1977) and this will be taken up later.

A problem with the credibility-expectancy hypothesis is that it is unable to explain certain data without recourse to additional *post hoc* arguments. There are a number of examples of this. The evidence reviewed by Watts (1979) of the differential impact of variations in the parameters of item presentation are difficult to accommodate. D. A. Shapiro (1981) has also reported some interesting findings. In his experiments undergraduate subjects were presented with descriptions and rationales of treatments used in published studies. In general SD was rated as more credible than other treatments such as client-centred therapy, rational emotive therapy and an attention placebo condition. These differences in credibility matched the actual outcome differences obtained in the source experiments. However, Shapiro's own subjects could not mimic the more detailed results found in the source experiments. For example, in one source experiment (Di Loreto, 1971) the effectiveness of the treatments was dependent upon the personality characteristics of the patient. To explain this the credibility-expectancy hypothesis would have to postulate that different expectancies for change are aroused in people with different personalities. Shapiro measured the critical personality traits in his subjects and could find no evidence for this proposition.

A more fundamental difficulty with the credibility-expectation hypothesis is that the relationship between the credibility of the treatment and the expectation of improvement are not precisely stated. In general these two constructs are treated as if they were clearly interrelated with a more or less perfect correlation. In fact the operations used to measure them are variable and they may not intercorrelate at a level sufficient to be confident that the same constructs are being measured across experiments. The most common way of measuring credibility is a variant of a short questionnaire originally devised by Borkovec and Nau (1972). Each of the questions is accompanied by a simple visual analogue scale upon which the subject indicates his response. The usual questions are:

(1) How logical does the treatment seem to you?
(2) How confident are you that this treatment will be successful in dealing with . . . ?
(3) How confident would you be in recommending this treatment to a friend with the same problem?
(4) How easy do you think the treatment will be?
(5) How successful do you think the treatment will be?

It will be observed that all these are rather global indications and they are incapable of providing any but the grossest measure of expectancy or credibility. Kirsch and his colleagues have explored this issue in some depth (Kirsch et al., 1983). They compared SD with a placebo condition which had been devised so as to have a similar level of credibility. The placebo, systematic ventilation, required subjects to relive in fantasy, and free associate to, a series of childhood events which subjects were told research had been established as being related to their target fear. As well as measuring the credibility of the treatments subjects were asked to provide estimates of their expected performance on a behavioural avoidance test (BAT) at the end of treatment. In fact they estimated how far up the hierarchy they thought they would progress and how much anxiety they thought they would experience at each stage. The two treatments, SD and SV, were shown to be equally credible and they were equally more effective than a waiting list control. However, the credibility ratings were not able to predict individual variations on the outcome measures. Outcome was predicted by expectancy ratings obtained before treatment was begun.

An alternative explanation of these results is that the subjects differed in suggestibility and that the pretreatment statement of what they thought they could achieve made them act accordingly. The authors partly ruled this out by measuring suggestibility. Whilst they found that credibility was correlated with suggestibility there was no relationship between suggestibility and the expectation estimates.

There are also a number of methodological problems associated with the credibility-expectation hypothesis (Kazdin, 1979). Not least of these is the problem that treatments which are initially perceived as equally credible may induce changes in the subjects' estimates of credibility once the subjects actually experience them. How these dynamic fluctuations in credibility are to be accommodated within the framework of the hypothesis is difficult to see.

Despite these difficulties with the credibility-expectancy hypothesis it is clear that in investigating why a treatment works there are important general changes at work and which need to be taken into account. As yet there is little information as to how they work. Lick and Bootzin (1975) made a number of suggestions all of which are plausible and remain to be explored in detail. The first is that it is intuitively likely that treatments with high credibility will induce subjects to comply with treatment instructions. In so far as the treatment contains potent specific elements this will enhance progress. Secondly, people who believe that they are being successfully treated will tend to test reality. If the treatment is for a phobia this will mean that the subject will be more ready to expose himself to fear-evoking stimuli and this in itself will lead to further fear reduction since this exposure is equivalent to a purported active treatment component in SD.

Lick and Bootzin's (1975) third possibility is that credible treatments might be regarded as an alternative version of the demand characteristic hypothesis. Thus more credible treatments will lead to greater compliance with the posttreatment measurement requirements. These subjects may therefore be seen to have improved. As was noted in the previous chapter a measure like a BAT may be therapeutic in its own right because it contains the important ingredient of exposure to the feared stimuli. Finally, there is the suggestion that credibility-expectancy manipulations might directly alter important cognitive processes which mediate changes in behaviour or affective state.

Bandura (1977) has put forward a cognitive theory of behaviour change which is more explicitly stated than the general credibility-expectancy hypothesis. This theory is a more detailed version of Frank's sixth condition (Frank, 1973). This is the necessity to develop a sense of mastery. Like Frank's theory Bandura's is a general theory of behaviour change and is not specific to SD. Unlike other general theories in this field it is clearly formulated and Bandura has suggested ways in which the central constructs should be measured. In recent years this theory has begun to exert an influence on research into psychological treatments.

The central concept in Bandura's theory is 'self-efficacy'. This is defined as the 'conviction that one can successfully execute a behaviour to produce a specified outcome'. Thus someone who is sure that he can hold a snake would be said to have great self-efficacy in comparison with the phobic person who would refuse to enter the room in which the snake is housed. Efficacy expectations can also be assessed along dimensions of strength and generality. Strong expectations of efficacy are those which are resistant to extinction despite the occurrence of disconfirming episodes. Thus people with strong efficacy expectations will show persistence in coping with difficult behavioural tasks. In contrast to this weak efficacy expectations are easily diminished by unsuccessful attempts at coping. The generality dimension refers to the extent to which efficacy expectations extend beyond circumscribed situations. Thus an agoraphobic may have an appreciable belief in her ability to get to the corner shop but a virtually minimal expectation about her ability to get to the supermarket in the town centre.

Bandura differentiates between self-efficacy and outcome expectations and defines the latter as the person's estimate that a particular course of action will lead to a given outcome. In this way an individual can believe that a certain behaviour will produce a desirable outcome but have grave doubts about his ability to perform that behaviour.

According to Bandura, self-efficacy is the common cognitive event that underpins all successful psychological interventions. The extent to which a particular treatment is successful is determined by the degree to which it alters the individual's sense of self-efficacy. Thus self-efficacy theory is proposed to account for the effects of diverse forms of treatment and also for the effects of placebo manipulations. Bandura suggests that all the person's experiences in therapy and between therapy sessions are weighed in a cognitive calculus to determine the level of self-efficacy, its strength and generality. He proposes that therapies which give the person direct interactions with their problem, such as participant modelling, will be more efficacious than those in which the person receives less information about his ability to interact with the target problem: mere verbal persuasion for example.

This theory has been tested in experiments which have exposed phobic subjects to a variety of treatments of known differential effectiveness. Following treatment subjects are required to make ratings of the level, strength and generality of their efficacy pertaining to a series of test items structured like a BAT. Typical findings from these experiments (e.g. Bandura *et al.*, 1980) are that the subjects' rating of the level of their efficacy correlate highly with their actual performance. Moreover Bandura's theory suggests that these ratings will be the best predictors of a person's performance. It is a common observation that subjects equivalent in their level of avoidance often do not change by the same amount when exposed to the same treatment regimen. Bandura's theory explains this by arguing that the observed behaviour change will be a function of the change in the level of self-efficacy. The available data support this high correlation between efficacy ratings and behavioural performance.

Despite the seeming elegance of the predictions that can be derived, Bandura's theory has not escaped criticism (Rachman, 1978). Borkovec (1978) suggests that self-efficacy may not be the prime cause of behaviour change. Rather self-efficacy changes as a consequence of treatment and in temporal conjunction with the other changes that take place. Thus Bandura proposes the following sequence:

Therapy → change in self- → changes in behaviour,
efficacy   physiological activity
and subjective wellbeing

whilst Borkovec suggests:

Therapy → concurrent changes in { self-efficacy,
behaviour,
physiological activity,
subjective wellbeing

The main issue is therefore to establish the temporal priority of the hypothesized change in self-efficacy and to see if it actually precedes the other changes rather than just accompanies them. Borkovec and others (e.g. Kirsch, 1982) have argued that ratings of self-efficacy can also be construed as statements about the subject's response intentions. They thus correspond to the literature on attitude change which persistently reports high correlations between what the subject says he will do in a given situation and what he actually does when he is immediately faced with that situation. Much lower concordance is found when subjects make general predictions about their behaviour and when the prediction and test are separated in time.

In the experiment by Kirsch *et al.* (1983) described earlier, ratings of self-efficacy were taken as were ratings of expected anxiety and a measure of the subject's actual behaviour. The results showed that the two ratings correlated equally well with the actual behaviour and, more importantly, they correlated very highly with each other (approximately 0.9). It seems that measures of self-efficacy and expected anxiety predict behaviour equally well and there is no way of separating their temporal priority. From this data Kirsch argues that the two measures can be treated as one and the same thing. Hence there is no need to attribute any special explanatory status to the self-efficacy construct. Indeed this finding is quite damaging to self-efficacy theory because it challenges the construct validity of the central component. However, the theory is relatively new and may well be developed further because of its breadth of appeal.

Comment

It has proved extraordinarily difficult to work out just why a relatively simple psychological treatment like systematic desensitization has a therapeutic effect. This is at least partly due to the fact that treatments that appear simple at first sight can prove to be very much more complex on further analysis. Even the application of simple procedures can involve forming some sort of a relationship with the patient, induce expectations and so on. In many ways it remains easier to state some things that treatments are not. For example, intensive interpersonal contact between therapist and client does not seem to be a necessary ingredient of some treatments such as systematic desensitization.

12 Comparing Different Treatments

Given that there are psychological treatments that appear to be effective, at least to some degree and by mechanisms that are ill-understood, the next question that can be asked is whether some treatments are more effective than others. This can otherwise be referred to as the question of comparative outcome. It is a question that has generated more discussion and research than any other single issue in the study of psychological treatments. Since the early 1950s there has been an intense debate about whether treatments based within the tradition of psychoanalysis, often lumped together under the rubric of verbal psychotherapy, are effective at all and about whether behavioural psychotherapy is more effective than other forms of psychological treatment.

The initial debate was stimulated by H. J. Eysenck, who in 1952 published a review paper based on the then existing literature relating to outcome studies. Eysenck concluded that neurotic disorders showed considerable evidence of spontaneous remission without the benefit of any systematic psychological treatment. He calculated that in a two-year period about 70 per cent of those afflicted with neurotic disorders would show appreciable signs of recovery. He also argued that the addition of psychotherapy, at that time almost entirely verbal and psychodynamically oriented, did not enhance the recovery rate beyond that achieved by spontaneous remission. The implication was that psychotherapy is ineffective. Since then there has been a good deal of debate about whether Eysenck's estimate of 70 per cent for spontaneous recovery was accurate but this does not need to be expanded upon here (see Bergin and Lambert, 1978; Rachman and Wilson, 1980 for relevant reviews and discussions). Suffice it to say that there is at least agreement that spontaneous remission does occur although there may still be controversy about how much occurs, under what set of circumstances and why.

The most obvious way of discovering whether psychotherapy

works and if behavioural treatments are more effective is to conduct a controlled outcome study. This involves randomly allocating a set of suitable subjects to two treatment groups and comparing them with an untreated control group. Since this kind of study is not concerned with why the treatments work there is no need to invent a plausible placebo condition for the control group. The untreated control group will enable various alternative explanations of change such as regression to the mean and the effects of retesting to be ruled out. The change scores observed in this group will be the consequence of such factors together with the effects of any spontaneous remission. Although this type of experiment is very simple in conception there have been very few studies of this kind conducted using 'real' patients as subjects. This is because considerable administrative and methodological problems arise. These can be illustrated by examining one relatively good study in detail.

The Temple University study

The study carried out at Temple University (Sloane *et al.*, 1975) is generally regarded as the most complete outcome study to date by both psychoanalytic and behaviourally oriented commentators. Sloane and his colleagues set out to investigate four questions:

(1) To examine the comparative effectiveness of behaviour therapy and analytically oriented psychotherapy. The therapists were free to use any technique that they would normally employ in clinical practice. To ensure that there was no problem in deciding what constituted the two types of therapy the researchers drew up sets of criteria defining each type as shown in Table 5. It will be evident that these criteria correspond to the descriptions of the forms of treatment given in Chapter 8. The treatments were carried out on a sample of mixed neurotic out-patients with various diagnoses. The study is therefore a test of the generality of treatment effectiveness.
(2) The second aim was to examine the similarities and differences between the two forms of therapy. In the previous chapter it was seen that Frank (1973) has proposed that therapies share many common aspects as well as having specific components. The Temple study actually monitored the content of the therapy sessions to ensure that the treatments were different and to identify the commonalities.

Table 5 *Summary of the stipulative definitions of behaviour therapy and psychotherapy (after Sloane et al., 1975).*

Behaviour therapy	Psychotherapy
Resistance not interpreted	Resistance interpretation used
Specific advice	Advice infrequent
Relaxation taught	Encourage report of dreams, may or may not use this in sessions
Desensitization used explicitly	Desensitization not explicit but may occur through congenial interview with therapist
Practical retraining undertaken	Retraining not emphasized
Encourage report of symptoms to be explained biologically	Symptoms interpreted symbolically if they are reported at all
No emphasis on childhood memories	Memories are of interest: their recall is encouraged
Deliberate attempt to curb behaviour which results in anxiety	Behaviour control is rarely tried
Assertive training undertaken (social skills)	Only indirect encouragement of assertive behaviour in everyday life

(3) The effect of various therapist variables (e.g. warmth, empathy and genuineness as well as therapist experience and age) were to be examined because these are often purported to determine outcome.

(4) To examine whether personality, diagnosis or any other characteristic of the patient was influential in determining whether a particular treatment was effective.

The main concern in the present discussion is with the aspects of the study relevant to the first two questions.

In brief the design of the experiment involved randomly assigning ninety patients attending the University Hospital psychiatric clinic into three groups. Subjects in two groups were offered treatment and those in the third were placed on a waiting list. The patients, aged between 18 and 45, were not seriously disturbed, did not require an in-patient admission and were considered suitable for some form of psychological treatment. Two-thirds were diagnosed as being neurotic and the remainder were described as being personality-disordered. All but four had had their problem for more than one year prior to entering the study and 64 per cent had experienced previous psychotherapeutic treatment. All were around average on intelligence tests. Various measures were taken at the time of intake, four months later when treatment was terminated and again at one year after their initial assessment. The waiting list control group obviously received no formal treatment but were reassessed at the same intervals as the treated groups.

For the initial assessment the subject met an assessor (a psychiatrist) who was blind to the treatment to which the subject had been allocated. After a period of discussion the patient and assessor agreed on three main target symptoms, an example of which might be something like anxiety about social interactions at work. The assessor rated these on a five-point scale of severity (severe, moderate, mild, trivial, absent). These points do not give the impression of being equally scaled and seem weighted towards the lower end. The assessor also completed a standardized interview to assess general adjustment (the Structured and Scaled Interview to Assess Maladjustment – SSIAM). This general assessment was made because any symptomatic change might not be reflected in more widespread beneficial changes that could also result from therapy. The authors point out that it is possible for the patient to lose his symptoms but remain generally distressed and vice versa. Actually what researchers decide to assess is determined by their general theory of therapy as will be seen below. The assumptions that the Temple workers adhered to in their measurements seem to be those of a general medical and psychodynamic approach. Information about symptoms and the points covered by the SSIAM was also obtained from an informant with close knowledge of the subject by a research assistant.

At both the four- and twelve-month reassessments the assessor rated the severity of the target symptoms and administered the SSIAM without consulting his previous records. He also rated the amount of change since the original assessment on a thirteen-point scale ranging from 'very much worse' through 'no change' to 'completely recovered'. Subjects, therapists and informants also completed some of these ratings. Because anxiety is such a central component in most neurotic disorders it was rated for all subjects with the five-point scale used for target symptoms.

The main results

The results at four months showed that the assessors ratings of the target problems had changed by equal amounts for the two treatment groups. They had moved from a pretreatment mean of 'moderate' to a posttreatment mean midway between 'mild' and 'trivial'. The reliability of these estimates was not examined by using another judge. Both the treatment groups showed significantly more improvement than the waiting list controls. When the thirteen-point improvement scale was used and the data aggregated over symptoms about 80 per cent of both therapy groups were judged to have improved or recovered compared with only 48 per cent of the control group. When a single measure of overall improvement was derived from the assessors then 93 per cent of the behaviour therapy patients were considered improved compared with 77 per cent in each of the psychotherapy and control group. This is the only reported measure on which the two treated groups were substantially different.

According to the SSIAM, behaviour therapy subjects showed significant improvements in both work and social adjustment. Those receiving psychotherapy had no change in social adjustment and only a small improvement in work adjustment. Nevertheless there were no significant differences between these two groups and the controls on any of these measures.

Examination of the ratings obtained from the therapists, subjects and informants revealed some interesting information. Subjects' estimates of their improvement on target symptoms and overall gains reflected the observations of the blind assessors. Members of the two treatment groups thought that they were improved to approximately the same degree. The proportions in the behaviour therapy and psychotherapy groups were 74 per cent and 81 per cent respectively. In contrast only 44 per cent of the control group considered that they were improved or recovered. Those considering that they had gained some overall benefit consisted of 93 per cent of the behaviour therapy group and 80 per cent of the psychotherapy group as opposed to 55 per cent of the controls. This latter figure was the only one for which there was a significant disagreement between the assessors and the patients. Other comparisons using therapist ratings suggested that behaviour therapists tended to overestimate improvements made in sexual symptoms whereas psychotherapists underestimated these gains. When compound scores of overall improvement were derived for

each of the patients, assessor, therapist and informant, the correlations between the various raters were found to be far from
perfect. These correlations are shown in Table 6.

Table 6   *Correlations between different sources of outcome ratings in the
Temple outcome study (after Sloane et al., 1975).*

	Patient	Informant	Assessor
Therapist	0.21	−0.04	0.13
Patient		0.25	0.65
Informant			0.40

The twelve-month follow-up was also reported in some detail.
Ideally it would have been best if the control group had received no
treatment at all until the end of the twelve-month follow-up and if
the treated subjects had experienced no further treatment between
four and twelve months. Neither of these conditions were met and
the twelve-month follow-up data is confounded by other things. No
firm conclusions can be drawn but it is interesting to note that the
improvements found at four months were maintained and there was
no evidence of symptom substitution.

Recordings of therapy sessions were examined and the analysis
revealed that the therapists did have different styles of interacting
with their patients which were in accord with the specified criteria.
Behaviour therapists tended to give more advice, information and
instructions to the patient. They also made more value judgements
and controlled the content of the interactions as well as speaking
more. Briefly, it might be concluded that they were more active and
directive. The authors also note that, much to their surprise, the
behaviour therapists were rated as being significantly more
emphatic and genuine than the psychotherapists. Early accounts of
behaviour therapy had stressed an apparent lack of personal contact
between therapist and patient as being a hallmark of this therapy.
The therapists' own accounts of their aims in therapy also matched
the criteria. Thus the psychotherapists put their emphasis on the
interpersonal relationship. As Sloane *et al.* (1975) put it, 'to our
psychotherapists it does not much overstate the case to say that for
many patients the personal relationship *was* the therapy. In nearly
all cases it was the single most important factor, essential if
psychotherapy was to succeed' (p. 170). On the other hand,
behaviour therapists felt that a positive relationship was all that was

necessary for therapy to progress satisfactorily. A strong emotional attachment was not encouraged and the therapists did not spend much time pursuing this goal.

Problems in interpreting the results

Despite the general acceptance of this study as an excellent attempt to compare two therapeutic approaches, there have been a number of criticisms directed at it, mainly from prominent behaviour therapists. It would be tempting to dismiss these as sour grapes, given that a much vaunted claim for the superiority of behaviour therapy has been refuted. Whilst such an attitude may have played some part this is not the whole story and the criticisms are instructive because they highlight some of the difficulties inherent in the assessment of any form of treatment. These are, firstly, the nature of the outcome measures and their evaluation. The second is the problem of heterogeneous samples. The third concerns the difficulties of testing a general statement about a therapy and the heterogeneity of the treatments.

(1) *The nature of outcome measures.* The only form of outcome measure used in the Temple study and the predominant form in widespread use is that of sets of ratings. In the Temple study these ratings were made by several people, some trained and some untrained, and across a number of different target behaviours and domains. As Table 6 shows, the agreement between raters was not always very high. Even in studies where there are two independent assessors similar findings occur. Little confidence can be placed in the assumption that the raters are measuring the same thing and there may be many reasons why this is so.

The raters may have different 'filters' through which they observe the behaviour. Consider the 'blind' assessors in relation to the therapists. It might be expected that the assessors would be relatively impartial in their appraisals. In contrast to this the therapists will have spent considerable time and effort in formulating the patients' problems and trying to solve them. Even if they do not deliberately distort their reports clinicians might be highly selective in what they recall about a patient. Their disposition will be to recall the successful parts of therapy as opposed to the trials and failure. It may also be that the therapist has a different view of what a suitable outcome is. For example, in contrast with the patient the therapist might be satisfied if the latter were to lose his symptoms in one or more specified situations. The patient, from his viewpoint, might be expecting not only relief for his symptoms but a general improvement in other areas of his life unconnected to his symptoms in any functional way. The assessor with a different perspective on the patient may have a third opinion on outcome.

This situation could probably be improved if the outcome criteria were clearly specified in advance in a form that was quite precise for each patient. This would involve the setting up of a graded series of goals which the patient and therapist would agree to work towards. There would therefore be no misunderstanding about what therapy was aiming to achieve. There are a number of problems with this approach. Firstly, it might prove to be almost impossible to equate the difficulty of the goals across different patients. Direct comparisons can only be made by a subsequent exercise in goal-scaling (Kiresuk and Sherman, 1968). To date this does not seem to have been used in any comparative outcome trial. A second problem is that the client or therapist may be unwilling to include important aspects for assessment in this contractual method. More importantly different schools of therapy are likely to opt for different outcome measures and this is an issue that will be considered later. A final problem is that even when both client and therapist can agree on goals at the start of treatment these goals may then legitimately change as therapy progresses and the true nature of the client's problems becomes much clearer.

It is highly likely that assessments by therapists and patients will be biased in a number of ways. One answer to this is to use assessors who are blind to the treatments given to the subjects that they rate. This information can be supplemented by getting further information from others. Both of these options have limitations. The assessors see only a very limited sample of the subject's behaviour in an interview. Most of the information gained by the assessor comes from the patient himself, who merely recounts his version of what has happened, and this may well be biased. Patients, as was indicated in the previous chapter, may distort their accounts either towards or against a good outcome. How assessors elicit information may also be important. A general enquiry of the kind 'How are things now?' is likely to yield less information than detailed questioning about the person's activities over the past week. This is especially so with regard to judgements as to how frequently things occur. It is also much easier to quantify outcome for such things as excessive smoking than it is for a problem such as a general fear of going out.

The Temple study has rightly been commended for obtaining

ratings from another person who knew the patient in his everyday life. This procedure was included 'to provide another vantage point from which to view each patient, and also to show whether or not information obtained from people in this relation to a patient would differ from data collected by other raters . . .' (Sloane *et al.*, 1975, p. 73). Clearly this is an attempt to validate one set of ratings against another but the interpretation of the scores made by various raters is open to too many possible rival explanations as to why they differed. With regard to informants it is probable that they only saw the patients in a limited number of situations and there is no guarantee that these were the ones in which the target problems occurred. For example a husband's problems may centre on a work situation that the wife does not see.

An important point to note is that the collection of data from several sources and of different types should not be construed as an attempt to get closer and closer to a single 'true' measure of the patient's state. There is ample evidence that such a view could be highly misleading. Contemporary views about fear conveniently illustrate this. The behavioural, physiological and subjective aspects of phobias do not covary perfectly (Rachman and Hodgson, 1974). Even within the behavioural domain the fear reaction may show considerable situational specificity. Thus the socially anxious patient may behave differently if a spouse is also present. There is thus no one 'correct' measure of outcome and discrepancies between any two measures may reflect the inherent unreliability of either or both of them. On the other hand, the discrepancies could equally well be due to the fact that they deal with different aspects of the patient's problem or its expression under different circumstances and that both are equally valid in their own ways.

One thing that has been stressed in the recent behaviour therapy literature is the idea that assessments should get as close as possible to the patient's real-life behaviour and circumstances. In commenting on the Temple study Kazdin and Wilson (1978) state, 'from a behavioural point of view the assessors' ratings would have been far more informative if they had been based on samples of clinically relevant behaviour' (p. 53). But this might be more easily said than done. As was described in the previous chapter the behavioural avoidance test is an attempt to measure target behaviour directly but it has run into difficulties in that it is reactive and influenced by such things as the form of instructions, demand characteristics and the way in which the hierarchy is presented. Attempts have also been made to measure various aspects of social and assertive behaviour using role play tests. In these subjects act out a range of social situations in which they are presented with opportunities to exhibit key pieces of social behaviour, such as refusing an unreasonable request.

Despite the apparent face validity of the role play test there is considerable doubt as to whether the scores obtained from role play actually predict how the person will perform outside the clinic or the laboratory (Bellack *et al.*, 1978). Attempts should be made to monitor the problem directly in the real-life setting (Shepherd, 1983). In this respect the work of the applied behavioural analysis school is particularly important. These researchers have usually selected problem behaviours which they attempt to modify in the natural setting, and this is particularly true of token economies. There is thus little doubt that the actual behaviour of importance has changed and the problems that arise in generalizing the change to beyond the treatment setting are then expected on theoretical grounds.

An important feature of comparative trials is that the theoretical leanings of the researchers play an important part in determining what sort of outcome measures will be chosen. Those following a line of thinking which assumes the problem to be rather like an infectious disease that the person can have with greater or lesser severity will opt for measures that will intercorrelate highly. These are then treated as if they converge on the basis of the problem. It would also be expected that areas of the patient's life, such as social, occupational and sexual adaptation, would also tend to improve with the successful treatment of the problem. This expectation is predicted on the grounds that the disorder will be likely to interfere with normal activity.

On the other hand, the psychoanalytic school proposes that it is possible to relate symptomatic features with the wider social, occupational and sexual functioning by a single dynamic hypothesis which explains the connections between these various spheres. It follows that the evidence from all these domains should be collated and a single outcome measure derived. This argument is most forcibly presented by Malan (1963; 1976). It is possible that symptoms can improve in the absence of change at a 'deeper' dynamic level. This situation is reflected by the lack of change in other areas and the outcome score for this person would be relatively poor. There is evidence (Mintz, 1981) that symptom changes are important in determining how psychodynamic raters form their judgements about outcome. However, it is not clear how these psychodynamic outcome criteria interrelate with simpler measures of symptomatic and general functioning.

The other major school of therapy, behaviour therapy, has already been discussed in some detail. Behaviour therapists have generally moved away from rating-scale measures and towards attempts to measure chosen target problems in the situation where they are most prominent and disabling. There are problems with this approach which remain to be solved. What is worth noting is that the behavioural school makes one assumption which is not shared to any great extent by the others. This is that there is no reason to expect that treatment-induced changes in a symptom will necessarily be reflected in other areas of a person's life. To give an example, there is no reason why the spider phobic treated by Rowland and Canavan (1983) should show an improvement in her relationships with others or her sexual adjustment. If problems also exist in these areas they could equally well be determined by completely different and unrelated psychological processes. For the behaviour therapist there is an emphasis on the relative specificity of behaviour, feelings and thoughts.

The differences between these schools are not easily resolved. It is easy to see how the behaviour therapist will be satisfied that a treatment is effective if it changes a target symptom. For the therapist from a psychodynamic background, working with entirely different assumptions, this is not necessarily evidence of any change in the 'real' or underlying problem. Disputes about the relative efficacy of different kinds of treatments cannot be resolved in a way satisfactory to everyone until there is agreement on what the appropriate criteria of success would be.

(2) *Heterogeneity of the subjects.* This issue will not be elaborated to the same degree as the discussion of measures. The basic concern is with what can be thought of as the 'apples and oranges' problem. The analogy is with fruit and the extent to which it is possible to deal with all fruit (apples, oranges, bananas, grapes, etc.) as a single category and where it becomes necessary to think of them as being different from one another. All fruits are involved in plant reproduction and most have nutritive value. However, from a culinary point of view there are important differences. To give just one example, apples can be cooked and served in pies whilst it is difficult to conceive of 'orange pies' prepared in the same way as apple pies.

Similarly the mixed sample of neurotic subjects used by Sloane *et al.*, (1975) may have some features in common (e.g. most will have some degree of anxiety). Nevertheless they could also differ in significant ways. It could be that some types of neurotic problem respond well to behaviour therapy, others respond well to verbal psychotherapy and that for some both types of treatment are equally effective (or ineffective). If this situation were to hold exactly then it is easy to see how a study like that of Sloane and his colleagues could end up by apparently showing both forms of treatment to be equally effective and yet mask real and important differential treatment effects within subsections of the subject population. Of course, it would be possible to subdivide the subject groups according to types of problem and reanalyse the data for subgroups with similar problems. The limitation is that the original subject groups would need to have very specific and well-defined problems but samples of an adequate size might then be difficult to obtain.

So far the line of argument has tended to imply that the more homogeneous the samples studied the better the experiment is. A little reflection reveals that, apart from the problem of obtaining adequate samples, the search for homogeneity of subjects can be pushed to undesirable extremes. Behaviour therapists could argue that their forms of treatment may not be clearly better than the verbal psychotherapies when applied to random groups of neurotic patients of all kinds but that behavioural approaches are clearly best when applied to phobias. If an appropriate study were done and still failed to show differential effects then it might be argued that behaviour therapy was best for certain kinds of phobias when manifest in certain kinds of subjects (e.g. those with phobias for small animals or in whom the phobia was acquired before a certain age). At some point this continued dissection will become ridiculous.

A closely related point is that the more homogeneous the subject sample is the less the results will generalize to people encountered in routine clinical practice. If one form of therapy is shown to be more effective than the usual alternatives for agoraphobic patients in a study where the subjects are selected so as to be all female, below a certain age, with prominent panic attacks, and where the problem is particularly manifest when shopping, then how does it apply to a patient with agoraphobia who is male, rather older, without such prominent panic attacks and where the problem centres around deviating from the normal route between home and place of work? In general terms the more homogeneous the samples the easier it is to interpret the results unambiguously but this precision is paid for at the cost of reduced generality. As with the problem of selecting suitable measures, there is no single ideal solution.

(3) *The heterogeneity of treatments.* A third major criticism to be levelled at the Temple study, as well as many other outcome studies, is that the precise nature of the treatments given is not known. The behaviour therapists were allowed to use any technique that they considered to be part of their normal treatment repertoire. It is argued (Kazdin and Wilson, 1978; Rachman and Wilson, 1980) that this makes it impossible to identify what the critical components of treatment were. It is also suggested that because of this the Temple study is an unfair test of behaviour therapy which is usually carried out on the assumption that there are specific treatments for specific disorders. Amalgamating these various treatments will obfuscate real differences between procedures (i.e. the 'apples and oranges' problem described in the previous section but applied to treatments rather than to subjects).

However, it must be kept in mind what the general aims of the Temple study were. Firstly, it was explicitly stated that it was a general comparison between two schools of therapy. As such it may well be a good test of clinical practice in the field as well as a test of Eysenck's (1960) statements about the comparative effectiveness of behavioural treatments. Rachman and Wilson (1980) themselves cite Eysenck thus: 'Neurotic patients treated by means of psychotherapy procedures based on learning theory improve more significantly than do patients treated by means of psychoanalysis or eclective psychotherapy', and, 'with the single exception of psychotherapeutic methods based on learning theory (behavioural therapy), results . . . suggest that the therapeutic effects of psychotherapy are small or non-existent.' These statements are clearly about the generality of treatment effectiveness and should therefore be testable in a general way.

Secondly, the study did not set out to examine the mechanism of therapeutic effectiveness. As has already been argued, determining whether a treatment works, whether one treatment is better than another and the reasons why a particular treatment is effective are quite distinct questions. Although questions about mechanism are important it is just not reasonable to criticize a study because it set out to answer a different kind of question.

Nevertheless Wilson and his co-authors do make an important point about the general strategy for research into psychological treatments. They argue that at the present stage of development it might be wiser to pursue a policy of investigating the specific effectiveness of particular treatments for well-defined problems rather than attempting an omnibus trial of general therapeutic procedures. With hindsight it does seem unfortunate that Eysenck's general claims received so much attention. Despite this there is one important lesson to be gained from the accumulated outcome studies. This is that there is a greater degree of difference between even apparently related disorders, such as phobias, with regard to their psychological composition than was once suspected. This returns discussion to the topic of subject heterogeneity that was dealt with in the previous section.

It should now also be obvious that the three types of objection to the Temple study are interlinked. Treatments may well turn out to be relatively specific with regard to the changes that they will produce and in relation to the particular kinds of problem for which they are effective. It is in testing out these complex relationships inherent in the problem of effectiveness that analogue research and extended series of single case experiments may have an important role to play (Barlow *et al.*, 1984).

Comparing and combining outcome studies

Given the extensive criticisms of the Temple study it might be tempting to conclude that it ought to be disregarded together with other similar experiments on the comparative efficacy of different therapeutic techniques. To do this would be tantamount to throwing out the baby with the bathwater. In addition the criticisms of the Temple study raise issues which are themselves open to empirical investigation. Even if the Temple study is accepted as being methodologically adequate most people would be reluctant to set too great a store by the results of one experiment. It is always useful to have confirmatory evidence and especially so in a field as messy and controversial as the evaluation of psychological treatments.

This raises a general problem in considering psychotherapy outcome research in the light of the enormous variability between the various studies with regard to the measures, subjects and procedures that they may have employed. Because of these variations it is difficult to find studies that are exact replications of one another. Discrepant results can always be explained, *post hoc*, by reference to differences between studies. The traditional way of investigating the generality of any phenomenon is to conduct a review of the relevant literature. Commonalities between studies are sought and general conclusions are drawn by the reviewer. This procedure is open to a number of criticisms (Smith *et al.*, 1980).

In the first place, the data base from which the studies are drawn is rarely specified and inclusion and exclusion criteria are not explicit. There is therefore no way of judging the representativeness of the studies selected for consideration. Secondly, the reviewer is required to make judgements about the methodological adequacy of the studies. These judgements are typically imposed a priori without any attempt being made to determine whether differences in outcomes are really due to the differences in the methodology of the studies. It is therefore possible to exclude unwittingly sections of data which can make meaningful contributions to the debate. For example, it is a relatively common practice to exclude analogue studies and studies reported as doctoral dissertations on the grounds that they employ irrelevant populations and probably inadequate methodology. But there is little attempt to justify these claims apart from the appeal to the prejudices of the scientific community.

One refinement of the literature review is the 'box score' analysis proposed by Luborsky *et al.* (1975). This method follows the usual procedure of the literature review in selecting studies. Its innovation comes in the way that it presents the results from these studies. Instead of giving a verbal summary of the results a score is given a '1' or '0' (although the scoring could, in principle, be made more sophisticated than this), according to whether one type of therapy or another emerges as superior in each particular study. So in a study comparing the effects of systematic desensitization with brief psychoanalytic therapy, if SD is significantly more effective (in terms of the outcome of the reported statistical tests) then it receives a score of 1 and the analytic therapy scores 0. At the end of the review the scores from the individual studies can be totted up. A 'winner' then emerges and the reviewer draws the appropriate conclusion as to which is the more effective therapy.

The box score analysis is open to many of the same general criticisms as the conventional literature review as well as highlighting other difficulties in assimilating results from different studies. The summary of the results in the suggested manner ignores any variations in the sample sizes within the component studies. This could result in biased results if the sample sizes vary greatly. A preponderance of studies with small samples, which are less likely to detect differences between treatments, will unduly weight the survey in the direction of detecting no differences between types of therapy. A second problem is that the frequency of statistically significant results tells us nothing about the size of any effect that may be detected. Thus a survey of 55 outcomes studies comparing treatments 'A' and 'B' could result in the apparent establishment of B's superiority by a margin of 30:25. However, it could also be that in studies where A's superiority is indicated A generally 'wins' by a big margin. Also in studies where B is apparently superior it is generally only marginally so. In these circumstances a conclusion that B is the more effective treatment could be misleading.

A third problem with box score analysis is that it has no way of satisfactorily dealing with the situation where multiple statistical comparisons are carried out within one study. In a treatment trial where eight outcome measures are used one aggregate score (1 or 0) is entered in the box score analysis based on a simple count of the number of measures on which each treatment is superior. Thus if A is superior to B on seven out of the eight measures then this has exactly the same impact on the box score analysis as if A was superior on three measures, B on two measures, and the rest showed no significant difference. This is clearly an inequitable way of accumulating the results and also takes no account of how independent the particular measures are of one another. It will also be noted that this method is not able to detect any differential impact of the treatments on different outcome measures. All measures are treated as if they are representations of a single outcome scale along which the treatments can be ordered. It has already been argued that this assumption is probably wrong and that there may well be a number of separate domains of psychological functioning which require independent assessment. One solution to the problems raised by the conventional literature review and the box score analysis approaches to the comparison of differences between therapeutic techniques is known as meta-analysis.

Meta-analysis

Meta-analysis has two primary objectives. The first is to combine findings from a large number of independent experiments in such a way that general trends in the data can be discerned. It attempts to do this by minimizing the effects of non-explicit judgements by deciding in advance which data shall be entered into the analysis.

The rules for entering the data are explicitly stated to allow replication. The second aim is to allow the investigator to explore the effects of variations in the data base (such as differences in the measures or subject populations) on the conclusions that can be drawn. In contrast to the traditional review the impact of different methodological approaches can be empirically examined rather than merely discussed.

There are three requirements for the execution of a meta-analysis. The first rule is that studies to be entered in the meta-analysis should not be excluded on arbitrary grounds, e.g. just because they are unpublished dissertations. It is necessary to set boundaries for inclusion and exclusion and these must be clearly stated. Thus an investigator looking at the comparative effects of different kinds of treatment for headache might specify that all controlled trials referenced in the Science Citation Index between certain years will be included.

The second requirement is that the data from the various studies to be included be transformed into a common metric so that comparisons between studies can be made. There are a variety of ways of doing this (Straube and Hartman, 1982) but the most favoured by meta-analysts looking at psychotherapy is a statistic known as the effect size (ES). This is an expression of the difference between the therapy and control groups after treatment expressed as a function of the standard deviation of the control group.

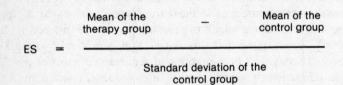

$$ES = \frac{\text{Mean of the therapy group} - \text{Mean of the control group}}{\text{Standard deviation of the control group}}$$

For ease of exposition it will be assumed that the distribution of scores in each group is normal. In this case the effect of treatment can be easily interpreted as the difference between normal distributions expressed as the difference in percentiles on the control group curve. Figure 5 shows that when the experimental (therapy) group's scores are shifted to the right of the control group this is expressed as a positive number indicating that the experimental group have probably obtained some benefit from treatment. In this example the ES is 0.85, i.e. the means of the two groups are separated by 0.85 standard deviation. With reference to the normal distribution curve it can be shown that the average person in the treatment group is at the 80th percentile of the control group. In one sense this average treatment group can be regarded as being better off than 80 per cent of the untreated group (Smith *et al.*, 1980 give a very clear account of the logic of this method).

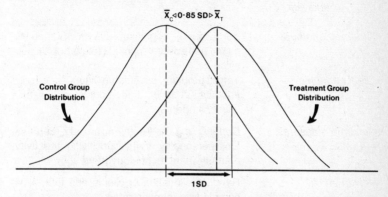

Figure 5. A graphical representation of the effect size statistic. The effect size of 0.85 indicates that the mean of the experimental group is shifted 0.85 standard deviation units from the mean of the untreated control group.

Since the ES is a common metric for each type of measure used in the data base, it becomes possible to average ESs over different experiments. Using the ESs, the meta-analyst can then examine the data to see if the magnitude of the ESs are affected by chosen variables such as the sample sizes of the constituent experiments, the type of client or patient studied, whether the subjects were recruited from clinical populations or from other sources, or whether variations in the type of measure used contribute to the ES.

There are several published meta-analyses dealing with the comparative effectiveness of different kinds of psychological treatment (e.g. Andrews and Harvey, 1981; Smith *et al.*, 1980; D. A. Shapiro and D. Shapiro, 1982). The work of Shapiro and Shapiro (1982) has been chosen for discussion because it has a number of methodological advantages. Although it used a different data base it also broadly replicated the findings of an earlier meta-analysis of Smith *et al.* (1980). Shapiro and Shapiro identified 143 studies published over a five-year period in which two or more experimental groups (therapy groups) were compared with a control group. For each study they calculated ESs for the outcome variables giving them a total of 1828 ESs, about thirteen for each study. They also coded each study on a number of variables and these are set out in Table 7. The impact of these variables on the ESs was then investigated.

Table 7 *Summary of some of the variables studied by Shapiro and Shapiro (1982) for their impact on the effect size in a meta-analysis.*

Treatment methods	Behavioural, cognitive, dynamic-humanistic mixed behavioural, minimal (placebo), unclassified
Client variables	Target problem, psychiatric diagnosis, client's educational level, age, source of subjects (clinic, students)
Outcome measures	Domain (e.g. self-esteem, anxiety, depression, personality trait), specificity, reactivity, measurement technology (hard soft)
Design quality	Random allocation of clients and therapists, sample size, attrition rates

In summary Shapiro and Shapiro (1982) found that treatments, other than those which were minimal (i.e. placebos), resulted in an average ES of 1.03 indicating that treatment by psychological methods is broadly beneficial. Splitting the treatments into five broad categories gave mean ESs of 1.42 for 'mixed behavioural', 1.06 for behavioural, 1.00 for cognitive, 0.71 for minimal or placebo treatments and 0.40 for dynamic and humanistic therapies. There was, therefore, evidence that the more active treatments were more effective than the predominantly relationship-oriented therapies. However, the authors do note the scarcity of studies using dynamic and humanistic therapies. This may reflect the unenthusiastic attitude towards outcome studies typically manifest amongst adherents of these schools (see Chapter 8).

There was no evidence in this meta-analysis that different features of the client such as age, educational level, source (clinic vs. recruitment from the community) had any appreciable effect on ES. There was also no evidence that analogue subjects gave a better response to treatment. On the other hand there was a considerable relationship between the nature of the target problem and ES and this accounted for more than 20 per cent of the variance. Phobias gave a large ES (1.29 on average) whilst at the other end of the spectrum anxiety and depressive disorders had a mean ES of 0.67. Finally, there was a relationship between the type of measurement device used and the ES. Measures which were more specific to a target problem (e.g. a BAT) produced bigger ESs than general tests of personality. As has already been noted the theoretical leanings of the experimenter will determine the kind of measure that is used and it is the behaviour therapists who are most likely to opt for the more specific measures of behaviour change. A second finding was that measures known to be more reactive (e.g. therapist ratings) produced bigger ESs than less reactive measures (e.g. physiological indices such as heart rate), and this is hardly surprising.

Shapiro and Shapiro (1982) also coded the measurement procedures on a scale of measurement technology ranging from soft measures like self-ratings and projective tests to hard indices such as observations of real-life performance. Soft measures were associated with larger ESs. To the extent that different treatments deploy different types of measure the outcomes could be influenced by the measurement device rather than any real difference in therapeutic effectiveness. This shows up a major problem in meta-analysis in that types of therapy can be confounded with other variables.

This problem can be circumvented in two ways. Firstly, it is possible to look for a subset of the data base containing those studies in which two kinds of therapy have been compared using the same measures. Shapiro and Shaprio attempted this but found few examples (only twenty-one) which compared major classes of treatment. The alternative method is to fall back on statistical techniques that can partial out the effect of different kinds of measurement. However, when this was done by Shapiro and Shapiro there was little indication of any change in the relationship between the different types of treatment and ES.

As would be expected meta-analysis has been criticized in relation both to the general approach and to specific meta-analytic studies (e.g. Eysenck, 1978; Rachman and Wilson, 1980; Wilson and Rachman, 1983). The thrust of the various criticisms generally mirrors those applied to the Temple study and described earlier. They concern sample selection, measurement and the uniformity of treatments. Some of these criticisms seem to be based on a misunderstanding of the aims of meta-analysis, blaming it for things that it does not set out to do. The foremost of these aims is the establishment of statements about the general effects of therapeutic interventions. In contrast to this meta-analysis cannot give information as to how therapies work nor can it provide a detailed analysis of the most effective components in therapy. In addition it will not increase psychological understanding of the nature of conditions such as agoraphobia or depression. These issues are best dealt with using smaller research projects in which the alleged critical variables can be experimentally manipulated.

A major criticism of meta-analysis was voiced by Eysenck (1978) who described it as an exercise in 'mega-silliness'. Eysenck argued that the exercise was essentially one of recycling garbage (along the lines of the old maxim about computing, 'garbage in leads to garbage out'). Meta-analysis aggregates studies of widely differing methodological competence. Behind this criticism lies the assumption that there are absolute standards of experimental design and method.

Two points can be made in relation to this argument. Although it cannot be denied that studies do vary in methodological sophistication and the way that they are designed there is no reason why these differences should not be empirically examined in order to ascertain whether they do indeed have a profound impact on the outcomes obtained and their subsequent interpretation. Meta-analysis explicitly includes such considerations. Secondly, if there are absolute canons as to what constitutes scientific research then these are not laid down unambiguously. The history of science suggests that new methods and experimental techniques are constantly being developed as investigators come to appreciate the inadequacies of those presently existing. Unless a method has been shown to produce wrong results it is not just rejected out of hand and as methodology advances so older data is usually reinterpreted rather than just being rejected.

The second type of criticism of meta-analysis is yet another version of the 'apples and oranges' problem. It lumps together dissimilar clients or patients and assumes that they represent some uniformity of abnormality. It is therefore dubious to attempt to draw meaningful conclusions from the aggregation of heterogeneous sets of people and problems. In defence of meta-analysis it should be obvious that the technique does recognize dissimilarities between people and the problems with which they present (Glass and Kliegl, 1983). It makes attempts to discover the contribution of variation along these dimensions to the effect of treatment as measured by ES. A second point made by Glass and Kliegl (1983) is that many of the original studies which have been included in the published meta-analyses fail to make clear-cut distinctions between clients and the types of problem which they present (e.g. the Temple study). Meta-analysis cannot be blamed for the apparent design faults of the original studies which comprise its data base.

This does, however, highlight an important limitation of meta-analysis. It can only take into account features explicitly covered in the studies forming the data base and it cannot deal with any systematic biases that may have been present in those studies. It has been argued earlier that control of 'placebo' treatments may need to take into account the credibility of the main treatment or the expectancy for change that it induces in the patient. Very few studies have done this. In consequence it could be that the relative impact of different forms of treatment established by Shapiro and Shapiro (1982) simply reflects their differential credibilities. There is no means of telling this from the meta-analysis unless enough studies that have taken credibility into account are available for the data base.

A third major criticism of meta-analysis has already been alluded to. This pertains to the problem of equating different measurements over different studies. This is referred to as the incommensurability problem by Glass and Kliegl (1983). Given that different approaches to treatment lead to different measures because their conception as to what constitutes therapeutic change is different, there is no possibility that treatments can be compared unless the one set of measurements can be successfully translated into the other. It has already been shown that psychodynamic theory prescribes the use of certain types of outcome measure and proscribes the use of others. The same applies to behaviour therapy and the two show little overlap in what they might regard as adequate measures of response to treatment. In the absence of rules that will enable the theoretical constructs of one school to be adequately translated into those of another there is little chance of a comparison between them on a theoretical level. At the practical level it is still possible to be undeterred in evaluating therapies that tend towards different measurement strategies as the meta-analysis of Shapiro and Shapiro (1982) has shown.

There are other more technical problems of measurement in meta-analysis. The technique depends upon all outcome comparisons being expressed in the form of a common metric, the effect size. There is a legitimate argument, too complicated to be outlined here, as to the adequacy of the commonly used measure of effect size (e.g. Hedges, 1982; Mitchell and Hartman, 1981). Alternatives, including non-parametric measures of effect size, have been proposed. Meta-analysts generally assume that their chosen measure of effect size is acceptable but it has yet to be demonstrated that any of the suggested alternatives is adequate for the purpose.

In trying to make sense of the accumulation of a vast amount of information relating to the effects of different kinds of treatments there seem to be two major alternatives. Either the outcome data can be fed into a meta-analysis (or something akin to it) which will enable the potentially relevant variables to be explored in so far as they have been taken into account in the original studies. This involves accepting all the limitations of the meta-analytic method. The alternative is to make a priori judgements about the methodological adequacy of the original studies and to reject those that fail to live up to very stringent standards (in practice most of the published studies). Not only does this lead to the possibility of subjective bias in determining which studies are acceptable and which not but the ultimate consequence of the search for methodological purity means that it becomes impossible to compare different types of treatment at all. This is because what is required to demonstrate that one kind of treatment works is different from what is required for another. An experiment to compare behavioural and psychodynamic forms of therapy that is to be equally fair to both and entirely pure methodologically is impossible to design.

Summary

In this and the previous two chapters an attempt has been made to examine some of the issues surrounding the evaluation of treatments. What appear to be simple questions about the effectiveness of treatments and the mechanisms by which they work turn out to be much more complex. Their attempted resolution has sometimes led to acrimonious debate. What should be clear from the discussion is that simple conclusions such as 'behaviour therapy works and psychotherapy does not' are usually also simple-minded. Possibly the best way forward lies not in trying to verify or refute assertions of this kind but in taking treatments that are known to work, exploring the limits of their effectiveness and the reasons why they work. In particular, identifying the key components in treatments may allow new, and even more effective therapeutic methods to be devised. In addition enhancing understanding of why treatments work is the one aspect of treatment evaluation research that is likely to improve understanding of the nature of the problems that need to be treated.

13 Beyond Therapy to Changing the Environment: The Example of Schizophrenia

In the discussion of treatment so far the concern has essentially been with methods that are directed, in some way or other, at 'internal change'. The basic assumption has usually been that some kind of change in the internal state of the individual needs to be achieved in order that there may be a therapeutic effect. The effect may involve the resolution of historical conflicts (psychoanalysis), the restructuring of faulty cognitions (cognitive therapy), changes in stimulus-response expectations (behaviour therapy), self actualising (humanistic therapy) or some readjustments of neurochemical functioning (drug treatment). Environmental influences are assigned to a secondary position and only rarely explicitly considered, measured or manipulated. Indeed in Malan's work on short-term psychotherapy (see Chapter 8 and Malan, 1963; 1976) changes in psychological functioning which could have been brought about by concurrent changes in the individual's living conditions are regarded as spurious. Although the patient might feel better and his functioning improve, he would be regarded as having made little real improvement in terms of psychodynamic criteria. The only therapy outlined in Chapters 8 and 9 that explicitly recognizes the impact of environmental variables in controlling abnormal behaviour and maintaining therapeutic gains is Skinnerian (or operant-based) behaviour modification.

Against this must be set the fact that much abnormal behaviour is not immutably fixed. It is well recognized that neurotic symptoms fluctuate and tend to improve. This so-called 'spontaneous remission' has been the subject of much debate often in a relatively futile attempt to establish the 'true' rate of remission. It will be recalled that the control group in the Temple study (Sloane *et al.*, 1975), described in Chapter 12, showed an overall improvement of about 40 per cent on crude outcome measures. This level of improvement is fairly typical of untreated control groups in therapy trials. The improvement could be due to some of the artifacts discussed at the beginning of Chapter 10 such as regression to the mean, instrumentation effects, the consequences of repeated testing, etc. These are unlikely to account for the whole of the effect and it could be that some genuine improvement has occurred as well. The sources of this improvement are largely unknown. It has been speculated that phobics may become accidentally exposed to phobic stimuli under propitious conditions so that, in effect, they are treated by exposure produced by random environmental variations. This is quite possible but as yet there is little corroborative evidence.

It has also been suggested that the social environment of neurotic patients is an important determinant of recovery (Beiser, 1976). People with more supportive, accessible social contacts are hypothesized to recover sooner from minor neurotic symptoms (anxiety/depression, irritability, sleep disturbances, etc.). There is also evidence that the perceived adequacy of social support can protect people from the effects of adverse circumstances (Henderson *et al.*, 1981). On the other hand, evidence that support can speed recovery is still awaited (Henderson and Moran, 1983). Surtees (1980) has shown that women recovering from a depressive episode do not relapse as readily if they have a confiding relationship with another person. Apart from a few studies of this nature there is very little detailed knowledge about what factors produce spontaneous remission.

Traditional psychiatric research has examined a variety of indicators of outcome for the different disorders. Variations in symptoms, gross socioeconomic indicators like age, sex, marital status and income, as well as family history of psychiatric illness, have been investigated. Very often these variables produce weak correlations with psychiatric outcome and do not predict whether patients will relapse in the future (Strauss and Carpenter, 1981). Even when such correlations are found it is difficult to understand what they mean in relation to specific psychiatric symptoms. Conversely, attempts to correlate symptoms with a variety of outcome measures like employment and social independence have also given very modest results. This approach is based on the assumption that symptoms are the central determining feature of the patient's adjustment and that other factors are of much less significance.

It is increasingly evident that attempting to understand recovery in this kind of way is too simple-minded. There is no necessary correlation between functioning in one domain of a person's life and his wellbeing in another. For example, Watt *et al.* (1983) examined the natural history of a cohort of people treated for schizophrenia. In a follow-up five years after initial treatment they measured social and psychological functioning. There was no clear relationship between the two. It was possible for an individual to remain symptomatic and yet be reasonably well adapted in other areas of his life. Thus one man who still retained extensive paranoid delusions still functioned adequately in a teaching post in a medical school.

This chapter will attempt to look at the way in which the environment and biological treatments interact to determine recovery from a serious psychological disturbance, schizophrenia. Before doing so it is necessary to outline the features of schizophrenia. A fuller discussion of this disorder can be found in Neale and Oltmanns's (1980) excellent text.

Schizophrenia: the clinical features

Approximately 1 per cent of the population will be diagnosed as schizophrenic at some point in their lives. Schizophrenia is the term used to describe one of the most severe forms of psychiatric disturbances as judged in terms of the disruption of normal life, the deviance of the symptoms from normal experience, the risk of long-term hospitalization and the secondary handicaps that can accrue from having the disorder. Until recent years the diagnosis of schizophrenia was held to have a very poor prognosis. It was thought that sufferers progressively lost their intellectual, emotional and social capacities to such an extent that they were likely to require permanent asylum. Indeed the initial formulation of schizophrenia as a distinct psychiatric category emphasized the loss of these abilities by using the term '*dementia praecox*'.

Since the mid-1950s the treatment of schizophrenia has changed remarkably so that it is now more and more unlikely that those so diagnosed will end up as long-term residents in psychiatric hospitals. The change in prognosis is due to a number of factors.

These are advances in pharmacological treatment, changes in social and political attitudes to mental health and the care of the mentally ill, and an increased understanding of the psychological impairments associated with schizophrenia. Before looking at these approaches to treatment it is necessary to describe the nature of the disorder itself and to discuss some of the problems encountered in studying its attributes.

The usual psychiatric description of acute schizophrenia delineates disorders in thought, perception, affect and motor behaviour. Not all the patients described as schizophrenic will have all of these features. Changes in the same modalities can also occur in patients with certain organic brain diseases such as those induced by viral infections (e.g. meningitis). However, the main differentiating point is that schizophrenics show no disturbance or 'clouding' of consciousness. In other words they are not confused and 'out of touch' in the sense that they remain oriented within their environment, knowing where they are, the time of day and so on. (Consciousness has a technical meaning in neurology and psychiatry that does not entirely correspond with its everyday meaning.)

Thought disorder in schizophrenia is one of the least reliably diagnosed features and, at least in terms of its most florid manifestations, is fairly rare. Hamilton (1974) describes it as 'the production of false concepts by the blending together of incongruous elements'. The most obvious feature of formal thought disorder is that it makes it very difficult to understand what the person is saying. Although the form of utterance complies with the normal rules of spoken language the semantic content has a bizarre quality about it. The flow of thought can appear to jump from one thing to another with little in the way of logical association. There may be a sudden break in the flow of speech, known as 'thought blocking', and novel words may be coined. The latter are called 'neologisms' and an example of a neologism is where a patient with delusional ideas causing him to worry about whether he was truly male or female and to doubt his sexual potency described himself as in need of a 'hermaphrodisiac'.

More common features linked to the thinking of schizophrenics are found in a cluster of symptoms in which the patient believes that things are happening to his mental processes. Thought insertion is where the patient claims that thoughts are being put into his mind by persons or things over which he has no control. The reverse of this, thought broadcast, can also occur and the claim is that the patient's thoughts are being transmitted to the minds of other people. Schizophrenics also experience thought withdrawal in which they report that their minds are suddenly emptied of all thoughts. Alternatively they may describe their thoughts as being echoed immediately after coming to mind or feel that their thoughts are audible and can be heard by others.

Schizophrenics commonly experience frightening delusional ideas. The most common of these are delusions of control and paranoid delusions. Delusions of control involve the idea that some outside force is determining the patient's actions and that the patient himself is not in control of his own actions and feelings. The patient may state that he is being forced to commit some heinous act against his will. Paranoid delusions are where some person or persons are alleged to be expressing malevolent thoughts, feelings or acts against the person. For example the patient may believe that he is being continually followed and spied upon by the secret police of some sinister organization. The central feature of delusions is that the patient accepts palpably false, or at least very highly improbable ideas as being entirely true. Textbooks typically define delusions as 'false beliefs' although there are inadequacies in this definition. Normally when people say that they believe something there is the implicit acceptance that what is believed might not in fact turn out to be the case. Delusions can carry absolute conviction and thus might more accurately be described in some ways as 'false knowledge'.

Perceptual disturbances take the form of hallucinations or perceptual experiences without the presence of a corresponding external stimulus. Although hallucinations can occur in any sensory modality schizophrenic hallucinations are most typically auditory in nature. Hallucinatory experiences can vary quite widely. Some patients report that they hear other people commenting on their actions or thoughts. The comments may be quite trivial and concern the things that the patient is doing at that time. On the other hand they may be emotionally laden and abusive or threatening. Hallucinatory voices may also tell the patient to do things.

Hallucinations in which the content is clear and verbal are not the only kind. Patients may also experience sounds of events happening. Thus a paranoid man may report hearing the sound of a drill on the other side of the wall which is then interpreted as being due to the efforts of his persecutors who are trying to get at him. If there really was a drill but it was being used by workmen in the road outside, the patient's report would then be designated a delusional perception.

Affective changes are not the most prominent feature of acute schizophrenia although they can be quite marked in chronic cases. People with paranoid ideas can become frightened and agitated but the most obvious feature of affect is its apparent incongruity. There is a lack of correspondence between the overt signs of emotion and the current situation. A schizophrenic may suddenly burst into laughter when there is no apparent reason for hilarity or he may weep inexplicably. It is possible that the emotional reaction corresponds with covert events, such as the patient's thoughts or hallucinatory experiences, but reasons are typically not communicated to the interviewer who finds it very hard to understand the patient's reactions. In a small number of schizophrenics the picture is mainly one of incongruity of affect and it may be hard to elicit other features such as delusions, hallucinations or thought disorder.

Motor activity is the final domain of disturbance in schizophrenia. A now rather rare feature of schizophrenia is catatonia in which the patient may be frozen into bizarre postures for long periods. It may be that the patient's limbs can be moved by the examiner and will then stay in whatever position that they are left. This feature is rather poetically known as 'waxy flexibility'. Much more common motor features are stereotyped movements of the patient's hand or head which might be related to delusions or hallucinations. A patient might lean forward to listen to his 'voices'. Alternatively a patient may usually stand with his hands in a rather unusual and stereotyped position.

It will be noticed that many of the features of schizophrenia can also occur in other psychiatric disorders. For example, patients with affective psychoses may have delusions and hallucinations. In this case the content is congruent with the patient's low mood and the severely depressed individual will have delusions about such things as having committed dreadful sins for which he is being justly punished. In contrast the schizophrenic with paranoid delusions does not have the marked affective features of depression and is not being persecuted for any good reason that would cause him to merit this persecution. It is therefore not just the nature of the symptoms that determines whether they are schizophrenic in nature but also their flavour and the context in which they occur.

Subtypes and diagnostic reliability

Not all schizophrenics display all of these symptoms in the acute phase of their problem. Kraepelin, the first modern investigator of schizophrenia, recognized this and developed a subclassification of schizophrenic disorders based on the apparent coherence of clinical symptoms and the presence of the most salient features. Kraepelin's original scheme delineated three subtypes; catatonic, paranoid and hebephrenic. In the first two of these the most prominent features were catatonic states and paranoid delusions respectively. Hebephrenic schizophrenia was more marked by emotional incongruity. After being influenced by the writings of Bleuler, Kraepelin introduced the fourth category of simple schizophrenia in which no single symptom predominated. Kraepelin's approach was basically descriptive and he did not search for causes for the features of schizophrenia.

Bleuler, a near contemporary of Kraepelin, took a very different approach to the problem of variability in schizophrenic symptomatology. Bleuler tried to formulate schizophrenia in such a way that the different features could all be understood as the consequences of a common psychological mechanism. He suggested that the key feature was a disturbance in the associative capacities of the mind. Bleuler's own phrase was a 'breaking of the associative threads'. For Bleuler the associative capacities of the mind were central to its integrity. He sought to demonstrate how an impairment of this fundamental mechanism could result in disturbances of speech and thought and the problems in concentration and attention that are so noticeable in schizophrenics. Bleuler was also influenced by Freud and he hoped that the use of Freudian ideas would give an understanding of the specific content of individual schizophrenics' symptoms.

Although Kraepelin was influenced by Bleuler he does not appear to have taken up Bleuler's causal hypothesis. However, this became very influential in the USA whereas Europe, and particularly Britain, remained more with the Kraepelinian mould. It has been argued that this is what produced the markedly different diagnostic practices on the two sides of the Atlantic. Bleuler's formulation of schizophrenia led to the situation in which schizophrenia was diagnosed if the clinician *inferred* that the patient was exhibiting a loosening of associative capacities. The basis for the diagnosis then shifted from a set of relatively clearly described and potentially publicly observable symptoms to inferences made about the individual's mental processes. Not surprisingly these inferences are made less reliably than overt symptoms which can be identified. Furthermore evidence of loosened associative capacity can be found in symptom complexes other than schizophrenia. The end result of all this is that schizophrenia became much more frequently identified by American psychiatrists than their European counterparts.

This phenomenon was studied by a collaborative research project involving researchers in New York and London (Cooper *et al.*, 1972). A series of admissions to hospitals in both cities was examined. Each subject was diagnosed by the psychiatrist providing the local service and by research psychiatrists who used predetermined criteria for the various disorders. These criteria were constructed so as to rely on the presence of overt symptoms. The results of the study showed that clinical psychiatrists in London were likely to diagnose schizophrenia and affective disorders in roughly equal numbers and these diagnoses agreed reasonably well with those of the research psychiatrists. On the other hand the New York psychiatrists made many more diagnoses of schizophrenia but relatively few of affective psychosis. This was not because schizophrenics were more common in New York, because the independent research diagnoses showed affective disorders to be just as frequent as in London. Psychiatrists in New York tended to diagnose people with affective disorders as schizophrenics because their criteria for making diagnoses were different from the established research criteria.

One implication of these findings is that it is necessary to be very careful in comparing data obtained from different countries on apparently similar subject populations. In particular this is so when looking at research from the USA and Britain on schizophrenia that was published in the 1950s and 1960s. Since that time there has been a considerable improvement in diagnostic practices and standardized interview schedules have come into common use for research purposes. These schedules set out consistent diagnostic criteria and have been shown to have good reliability. In addition, general diagnostic practices in North America have moved much closer to those in use in Europe with a greater emphasis on the observation of overt symptomatology as opposed to inferred causal factors.

Chronic symptoms

The description offered so far has concentrated on the symptoms of the acute stages of schizophrenia. Many schizophrenics recover more or less from their first acute episode. In fact about 25 per cent seem to have one episode only (Watt *et al.*, 1983; Wing, 1982). A small proportion (5 to 10 per cent) will have unremitting acute symptoms whilst the rest will run a variable course in which there are periods when the symptoms are relatively quiescent but these are interspersed with acute exacerbations. As time passes there is an increasing chance that the schizophrenic patient will come to display chronic symptoms which differ from those found in the acute state, but these chronic symptoms may occur very early on during the disorder's history.

The chronic symptoms are sometimes known collectively as a 'defect state' or the 'clinical poverty syndrome'. The characterizing feature is a relative lack of behaviour rather than the presence of florid symptoms. For this reason the acute and chronic symptoms are also referred to as 'positive' and 'negative' symptoms. According to Leff (1982) there are several negative symptoms. There is a *lack of initiative* in which the patient appears unable to instigate activities of his own volition, which may go so far as a state of being totally inert. Related to this is a *lack of energy* with slowness of movement and complaints that everything takes great effort. Patients also have a *lack of alertness* in that their mental processes seem slowed and they are difficult to arouse by external stimulation. Whilst schizophrenic patients typically show great difficulty in concentrating and sustaining attention they may remain quite preoccupied by their hallucinations, delusions and other abnormal experiences and this may make them less alert in general. Leff noted that one prominent feature of the defect state is a *lack of interest*, and chronic schizophrenics seem to have few interests outside their normal routine.

Other features of the defect state include a *lack of emotional responsiveness* (or 'flattened affect') in which emotional responses are reduced both in range and intensity, a marked tendency to *social withdrawal* where they may go to extreme lengths to avoid being in the company of other people, and a *loss of social graces* resulting in a slovenly appearance and a boorish manner with no regard to the sensibilities of others. The schizophrenic family member spends much time alone in his room and may even reverse his sleep pattern so as to be active at night when the rest of the family wish to sleep (Creer and Wing, 1974). Not surprisingly the failure to observe the usual social conventions and to take the possible reactions of others into account can be upsetting for the rest of the family. Neighbours and members of the public with no knowledge of schizophrenia may be put off or even frightened by the patient's appearance and behaviour and this will also contribute to the family's problems as well as confirming the stigmatization of mental illness and all that goes with it.

Outcome and management

A number of attempts have been made to discover which features of schizophrenia or the premorbid history will predict outcome in a person at the time of the first breakdown. Historically it is true that the outcome of a schizophrenic disorder has been regarded as rather poor. Thus the diagnosis of schizophrenia conveyed the expectation of an inevitable progression into a chronic state with the pattern being relatively uninfluenced by the social and psychological environment. Strauss and Carpenter (1981) likened this to the diagnosis of a known physical disease such as measles which, when made, tells the clinician what to expect. It is possible to anticipate the course of the symptoms and offer a reasonable prediction as to when the patient will get better. The other feature of this kind of diagnosis is the relatively unitary nature of the disease. The patient either has it or he does not and having the disease does not affect social role functioning except in the short term during confinement to bed. Potentially there is a single outcome measure in the presence or absence of an active virus. (In fact this is too simplistic a view of even a well-known physical disease like measles but it provides a useful contrast with schizophrenia.)

In comparison, it has already been shown (see Chapter 12) that even simple psychological disorders can be 'unpacked' into component parts which may not be closely tied to each other. In a more complex problem, such as schizophrenia, this is even more likely to be the case. Outcome can be looked at in terms of a number of domains other than the presence of symptoms. The obvious domains affected by schizophrenia are the occupational, social and personal adjustments made by the individual. The term 'domains' is used deliberately to emphasize the point that these aspects of behaviour can be relatively independent of one another and so the situation is not easily summarized by one single measure. Even a domain like the social domain can encompass a number of different activities such as forming and maintaining relationships with others, maintaining independent social existence, and so on.

The early formulations of schizophrenia simply assumed that the occurrence of the disorder indicated a poor outcome in all aspects of behaviour in line with the symptomatic picture. That this is not necessarily the case is well illustrated by an individual resident in a neighbouring village to one of the authors. This person continually displays and updates a set of notices outside his house which proclaim the nefarious activities of various organizations which allegedly continually torment and persecute him and his brother. The nature of these communications is such that most clinical opinion would have little hesitation in describing them as the manifestation of paranoid delusions. Yet the individual responsible has lived independently in the community for a considerable length of time and even supports and looks after a severely mentally handicapped and deaf brother.

The only sensible approach to looking at outcome in schizophrenia must be to regard it as a highly complex phenomenon which influences many different domains of behaviour in addition to symptomatology and where outcome in these domains may not be predicted by symptom levels. Additional information about premorbid adjustment and the individual's response to his disorder is also required in order to make any kind of reasonable attempt at predicting non-symptomatic outcome. What is apparent from recent research are the very varied outcomes in those diagnosed as schizophrenic. Some can be rather like the example given above and achieve more or less adequate performance in some areas of life despite the presence of acute symptoms. Others can be the reverse and have very few symptoms but be very impaired in terms of their ability to live independently and interact with other people.

A second consequence of this view of outcome is that it becomes possible to conceive that performance in some domains may be influenced by factors other than those responsible for the occurrence of symptoms. Even if symptom production and control were well understood, and this is certainly a long way off, this would not guarantee the same understanding and control of non-symptom domains.

There is good evidence that this more complex view of schizophrenia can provide better prediction about prognosis. In a series of studies Strauss and Carpenter (1972; 1974; 1977) have looked at various outcome domains and the predictive relationships both within and between domains. The five domains selected were symptom type, symptom duration, hospital status (in-patient vs. out-patient), social functioning and work performance. The fundamental finding was that each domain was the best predictor of itself. Thus the best predictor of time spent out of hospital between the index admission and the next admission was the time between the previous and index admissions. Measures of symptomatology contributed very little to predictions of hospitalization. In fact hospitalization was very poorly related to all the other domains. Similar results also emerged for the other domains with, for example, the best predictor of employment being the time spent in employment prior to the initial admission to hospital.

Findings of this type have also been obtained by other investigators. In one instance Watts and Bennett (1977) showed that a patient's previous employment record predicted whether he would return to open employment again after a psychiatric admission. In contrast symptomatology was of no value in predicting return to work. Results like these offer yet more evidence of a considerable degree of specificity in psychological and behavioural variables, even under the circumstances of as severe a disruption of normal mental functioning as is produced by schizophrenia.

There is one fairly consistent finding in research on outcome in schizophrenia. This is that people with a rapid onset of florid symptoms are likely to do considerably better than those who have a slowly developing incipient disorder. Judging whether an acute episode has been precipitated by some stressor is notoriously difficult and the methodological problems have been discussed in Chapter 7. However, most research into schizophrenia that has looked at this issue has revealed that the presence of an apparent precipitating event is associated with a good outcome (Neale and Oltmanns, 1980; Strauss and Carpenter, 1981; Wing, 1982).

It would also appear that those with a rapid onset of symptoms are more likely to have a good premorbid adjustment in other areas of their lives. They are likely to have good records of social integration, interpersonal relationships and employment. In comparison those with a slow onset never seem to have achieved a reasonable adjustment in non-symptomatic domains of their lives. They may give a history suggestive of poor social integration from childhood or puberty and sometimes of a steady deterioration in their intellectual performance at school and college. It has been supposed that some of the central features of the disorder, including the disruption of fundamental cognitive processes, are already developing in the years prior to clinical presentation and that they prevent the person from developing normal functioning in the various non-symptomatic domains. In any case the evidence of better outcome after a rapid onset of symptoms can be reformulated as further evidence that adjustment (social, interpersonal, etc.)

prior to initial onset is associated with later adjustment.

The treatment of acute episodes

Until the 1950s there was no reliable treatment for the acute episode of schizophrenia although this was not for want of trying. A number of things had been tried including ECT, insulin-induced coma, and a variety of other 'shock' treatments (Brandon, 1981). For the most part patients in the most disturbed states were confined to locked wards. Pharmacological treatment was generally directed at sedating the patient as much as possible.

It was with the accidental discovery of chlorpromazine that a specifically antipsychotic drug became available in the 1950s. This drug has the property of selectively reducing the major symptoms of schizophrenic psychosis, such as hallucinations, delusions and thought disorder, without grossly impairing the patient's consciousness. Since its discovery a number of other drugs belonging to the same chemical family (the phenothiazines) have been developed. These neuroleptics (a term that includes a wider range of drugs than just the phenothiazines like chlorpromazine) all have a similar effect in that they tend to reduce acute symptoms but have little, if any, effect on the so-called negative symptoms. Their use has led to consideration of the mechanisms by which they might exert their effect and so to hypotheses about underlying neurochemical dysfunctions in the central nervous system which might cause schizophrenia.

In brief, a major proposal is that the neuroleptics work because they block the dopaminergic system. Evidence for this hypothesis comes from two sources (Mackay, 1983; Rodnight, 1982). One is that it has been observed that psychoses very similar to the acute forms of schizophrenia can be induced by amphetamines. Pharmacological research showed that amphetamine produces its behavioural effect by stimulating the release of dopamine and that neuroleptics can block such release. Secondly, it has been found that about 30 per cent of patients treated with neuroleptics suffer side effects similar to the symptoms seen in Parkinson's disease. These are known as extrapyramidal side effects because they are associated with the extrapyramidal motor system and this system is involved in Parkinsonism. The symptoms include rigidity of the limbs, slowed movements (bradykinesia), a coarse 'Parkinsonian' type of tremor, and accompanying changes in posture and gait. Patients may also complain of having a dry mouth and difficulty in swallowing and speaking. In addition to this their facial expression can be mask-like or frozen. These symptoms can be relieved quite well by anticholinergic drugs. More to the point it has been shown that Parkinson's disease involves a degeneration of dopamine-releasing synapses. It therefore seems that neuroleptics can mimic this degenerative process. However, it should also be remembered that whilst the side effects of neuroleptics are very similar to the symptoms of Parkinson's disease, they are not absolutely identical.

From these two sets of observations it is only a short step to the proposal that schizophrenia is caused by excessive dopamine transmission or by the relative supersensitivity of the receptor neurones. Unfortunately this hypothesis has not stood up well under experimental test and there has been a general failure to find evidence of excessive dopaminergic activity or heightened sensitivity in receptors (Neale and Oltmanns, 1980; Rodnight, 1982). In passing, it can be noted that biochemical research in this field is no less likely than psychological research to develop apparently promising lines of enquiry which end up in dead ends or contradictory findings.

It can be asked whether neuroleptic medication cures schizophrenia in the sense that penicillin or some other antibiotic can cure a bacterial infection by killing off the cause of the disease process. The answer to this is relatively clear-cut and in the negative. In all but about 7 per cent of patients there is a fairly quick reduction in acute symptoms (i.e. less than five weeks) and about 25 per cent of those treated will never have another episode. As has been discussed already (page 238), there are some guidelines as to which features are associated with a good outcome but the correlations are far from perfect. Thus even people with an apparently good prognosis can relapse and have further attacks of acute symptoms. The indication is, therefore, that whilst neuroleptics may correct a malfunctioning system involved in the production of symptoms they do not correct the primary cause (unless we suppose the schizophrenic becomes reinfected!).

One way of getting round the problem of relapse has been to place patients on maintenance doses of medication. This is not usually tried until the patient has had two or more acute episodes. This tactic is well researched and there is substantial evidence that it offers some protection against relapse. Davis (1975) reviewed twenty-four double-blind trials which had compared maintenance neuroleptic medication against placebo on a total of over 3000 patients. There was convincing evidence that relapse rate was halved by medication but even so about 30 per cent of those on medication still relapsed. The next step is to see if there is anything that might reduce relapse even further.

Hogarty and his colleages (Hogarty *et al.*, 1973; 1974a; 1974b) conducted a large controlled trial looking at the effects of continuing medication and what they called major role therapy (MRT). MRT is a complex and rather general form of social work and psychological counselling given during the follow-up of patients from hospital. It was used on the grounds that it might have a relatively specific effect on patients' social adjustment just as pharmacological treatment produces alterations in symptoms. One of the aims of the study was in fact to see if MRT had an effect on symptomatology as well. A total of 374 schizophrenics discharged from hospital after an admission period of less than two years (so as to prevent the inclusion of more institutionalized subjects) were allocated to one of four groups in a 2 × 2 factorial design so as to be able to look at drug vs. placebo and MRT vs. non-MRT. Measures relating to a number of domains were used and the areas covered included such things as symptoms, time spent out of hospital, interpersonal relationships, use of (and satisfaction with) spare time activities, and disruption to family life. Subjects were assessed on several occasions between one month and two years after discharge.

One aspect of the data was very clear-cut. At the end of the two year follow-up period 80 per cent of the placebo group had relapsed as opposed to only 48 per cent in the drug group. Since Hogarty and his colleagues had regular contact with their subjects, and could measure the level of symptoms, they were able to assess symptomatic relapse independently of readmission to hospital (an important point since exacerbation or recurrence of symptoms does not necessarily lead to readmission). MRT had no real effect for the first six months of the study but by the end of the first year there was a small effect and the MRT lessened the probability of relapse irrespective of whether it was given in conjunction with placebo or drug treatment. However, considered over the whole two-year period there was no significant effect for MRT on its own. Indeed at the end of the study there was a trend to higher levels of relapse in those given placebo and MRT as opposed to just placebo alone. On the other hand, those receiving both active drug treatment and MRT did rather better than those receiving drugs alone. There was also some evidence that for those in the drug treatment groups MRT did have a specific effect on social adjustment as judged by ratings of social performance away from home and a global measure of their overall functioning. In the absence of drugs (i.e. placebo conditions) MRT appeared actually to increase the level of psychopathology as measured by a number of rating scales.

It is interesting that these results suggest that any effect of the psychosocial treatment is deferred until a year after the inception of the programme. One implication of this is that long-term active treatment may be necessary to prevent relapse and maintain adjustment in non-symptomatic domains. There is evidence from other research to be considered later that this may be an appropriate therapeutic strategy.

One problem in considering the Hogarty study is that there is very little information to indicate why MRT should be beneficial in one group and yet be ineffective or even harmful in another. MRT itself is a blunderbuss treatment with the general aim of improving the social performance and adjustment of schizophrenics. It is possible that the treatment could be refined if the critical social variables affecting relapse were known. Treatment could then be more specifically directed at the critical factors. Life events and a certain form of family interaction described as 'expressed emotion' both seem to be significant determinants of relapse. They will be examined separately although both are closely tied in with the work of George Brown and his associates.

Life events and symptomatic relapse

Although general social conditions have been thought to contribute to psychiatric morbidity for a long time the causal relationship between general social factors (indicated by such things as social class and demographic variables) and mental disorder has proved difficult to demonstrate conclusively (e.g. Goldstein and Caton, 1983). However, there is evidence that discrete transient events can precipitate the onset of an initial episode or provoke a relapse. Evidence for this comes from two reports by Brown and Birley (Birley and Brown, 1970; Brown and Birley, 1968; Brown, Birley and Wing, 1972).

These reports were concerned with interviews of schizophrenic patients and their relatives after admission to a psychiatric unit. Those patients used as subjects were selected because of their acute onset of symptoms thus enabling a relatively precise onset date to be determined. The interviews were designed to collect data relating to such things as changes in the subject's relationships with others, loss or death of a close relative or friend, change of job or illness in the family preceding the onset of the disorder. The general focus of enquiry was to determine whether the patient had experienced a change in any of his social roles. In many ways this investigation can be seen as a precursor to the Brown and Harris (1978) study described in Chapter 7, and some of the same methodological points were taken into account. For example, events were classified as independent if they could not possibly be due to the patient's psychiatric state (e.g. death of a brother) or as possibly independent if there was some possibility that the incipient onset of the disorder could have helped to precipitate the event (e.g. separation from spouse).

The temporal relationship of these events to onset was examined by looking at their distribution in blocks of three weeks for a total period of twelve weeks prior to the recorded onset of symptoms. This data was compared with similar data derived from non-psychiatric controls matched for age with the experimental sample. From the initial analysis it was clear that the schizophrenics did experience an increase in the total number of life events (see page 111) just prior to the onset of symptoms. In the three weeks just prior to onset, 60 per cent of the schizophrenics had experienced one or more life event compared with only 19 per cent of controls. There was no difference between groups over the earlier three-week blocks.

Brown and Birley concluded that schizophrenic symptoms could be precipitated by life events and that these life events were most likely to cluster around the period of just prior to the onset of symptoms. They were able to discount the possibility that the results were an artifact due to the insidious onset of the disorder because the same temporal relationship between onset and events occurred when clearly independent events were compared with the rest. Subsequent work by Brown and Harris (1978) and discussed in Chapter 7 indicates some differences between the role of events in the onset of schizophrenic symptoms and depression. Not only do life events appear to have a more 'causal' role in depression than they do in schizophrenia but there seem to be differences in the kinds of event that are of significance. Unlike depressives, schizophrenics appear to be susceptible to more or less any kind of event that might produce a strong emotional reaction. Events in Brown and Birley's work which preceded schizophrenic breakdown included such apparently positive things as having a baby or moving from an overcrowded house. In contrast, the events that are important in the onset of depression are predominantly those which would be expected to induce a depressive affect and have as a central feature the loss of something valued. Furthermore events appear to be able to influence depression over a much longer period (six months as opposed to three weeks).

At present there is no good account as to why events should precipitate symptoms in schizophrenia. There is no theory of emotion in schizophrenia that would permit even a tentative guess as to how a schizophrenic processes emotional information or the nature of the cognitive mechanisms which mediate between the event and the apparent emotion. This stands in contrast to the cognitive models of depression (see Chapter 6) which seem able to accommodate at least some of the findings on life events and depression. In consequence there is little chance at present of devising an intervention to ameliorate the impact of life events on relapse. It is also extremely difficult to control the actual occurrence of the life events themselves. In contrast, certain findings relating to the nature and quality of the schizophrenic's interaction with his close relatives do offer hope that successful intervention can be devised.

Expressed emotion and relapse

In an early study of the consequences of discharging long-term psychiatric patients from hospital it was noted that the chance of the individual patient being readmitted was related to whether he returned to his family. Somewhat surprisingly those discharged to the care of their families were more likely to be readmitted. It was then suspected that the emotional atmosphere of the home into which the patient returned was of significance. Brown *et al.* (1962) interviewed schizophrenics and members of their families just prior to and shortly after discharge to the family home. The content of the interview was rated on scales of hostility, dominance and general emotion. They found that those discharged to homes rated as having a high emotional involvement were more likely to relapse in the following year and so be readmitted to hospital. It could be that the more disturbed patients are both more likely to relapse and induce greater involvement and concern in their relatives. The indications are that this was not the case since controlling for the amount of behavioural disturbance in the patient at the time of discharge still left the basic finding intact. It thus seems that it is the family's high emotional involvement that contributes to relapse.

Subsequent research has developed the concept and measurement of emotional involvement and excluded a number of other factors that might be responsible for the association between the emotional atmosphere of the home and relapse in the afflicted family member. It has also demonstrated an interaction between drug treatment and certain family and social conditions. The initial findings of Brown *et al.* (1962) were replicated by Brown *et al.* (1972) and were taken into account in the carrying out of a seminal study by Vaughn and Leff (1976a) which merits discussing in some detail.

Vaughn and Leff identified potential schizophrenic subjects on admission to hospital. Shortly after admission the spouse or both parents were interviewed separately (depending upon with whom the patient lived). This interview was carefully structured to cover information about the various activities and events that go on in every family. For example, the interview determined who did particular domestic tasks. The emotional circumstances prevailing in the house were also investigated together with the frequency of quarrelling and the various interpersonal likes and dislikes of family members. As well as scoring the content of the interview it was possible to get reliable ratings of the emotional quality of the informant by observing the apparent warmth and intensity of their replies. A standardized assessment of the patient's mental state was made just after admission to hospital and again if they were readmitted after discharge or at nine months after discharge, whichever was the sooner. This enabled relapse to be determined by the patient's mental state and not just in terms of hospital readmission. At the later interview the psychiatrist collected information about medication and the patient's compliance with taking medication. This data was cross-checked with hospital records wherever possible.

The data analysis was designed to look for reliable predictors of relapse. The family interview protocols were rated to produce measures of hostility, emotional overinvolvement, number of critical comments made about the patient, and a total 'expressed emotion' score. The composite 'expressed emotion' score (EE) was found to discriminate between those patients who relapsed and those who remained well. High EE relatives were those who made six or more critical comments and/or showed marked emotional overinvolvement. This latter component can include positive feelings of concern by the relatives for this affected relation and might include expressions of concern about such things as the patient's physical health or nutritional state. There is some indication that this quality is mainly observed in the parents of schizophrenics but not in their spouses (Vaughn and Leff, 1976b).

High EE in the family was clearly associated with an increased likelihood that the patient would relapse within the nine-month follow-up period (48 per cent relapsed). As opposed to this, low EE as defined by less than six critical comments and no marked emotional overinvolvement showed only a 6 per cent relapse rate. This does not necessarily mean a cause and effect relationship between level of EE and relapse. A plausible alternative hypothesis is that patients likely to relapse exhibit more disturbed behaviour and this results in relatives becoming overconcerned or more critical and so increasing their level of EE. As with the earlier Brown *et al.* (1972) study, controlling for the level of disturbed behaviour by statistical means did not affect the relationship between EE and relapse. This lends weight to the notion that EE is at least one causal factor in determining relapse.

The association between EE and relapse is by no means perfect. In fact about a half of those with high EE relatives do not relapse. It therefore follows that other factors need to be taken into account. An obvious possibility is the amount of time that the patient spends in contact with his relatives. It would be surprising if high EE relatives could have much effect without being in contact with the patient. In the interviews with relatives it was possible to obtain an estimate of the way in which time was spent at home. This revealed that the amount of time spent in face-to-face contact between relatives and patient was related to relapse but only in the high EE group, as might be expected if the hypothesis is correct. Within the high EE group the chance of relapse was reduced by more than a factor of two if the patient spent less than thirty-five hours per week in face-to-face contact with his relatives. Another significant factor was medication. Again this was only the case for the high EE group but within this group taking medication offered protection from relapse. A patient from a high EE home who was both maintained on medication and had a low level of contact with other family members had a relapse risk very similar to a patient from a low EE home. The effect of these factors can be seen in Figure 6, which is taken from the paper by Vaughn and Leff (1976a) and is based on combining their data with those of Brown *et al.* (1972).

Before examining the treatment implications of these findings, some further comment on the nature of the results is required. Family factors have been implicated in the aetiology of schizo-phrenia for many years and a number of theories have proposed

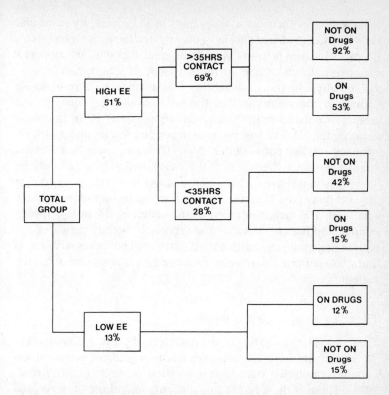

Figure 6. Graphical representation of the effects of high and low EE family environments, the amount of contact time and medication on relapse rate of schizophrenic patients. (Taken from C. E. Vaughn and J. P. Leff, 1976, *British Journal of Psychiatry, 129*, 125–37, and reproduced with permission of the authors and the Royal College of Psychiatrists.)

that there is an abnormal mode of communication which can be found in the families of schizophrenics and which plays a causal role in the development of schizophrenia. Despite a considerable amount of work it has been difficult to translate the theoretical variables into well-defined measures. Even where this has apparently been achieved the results are often inconclusive or contradictory (Leff, 1978; Neale and Oltmanns, 1980). In any case, where distortions of communication between schizophrenics and their relatives have been identified there is the perennial problem of inferring causality. That having a disturbed member should produce distortions in communication within the family is also a very plausible hypothesis.

The results obtained by Brown, Leff and their colleagues are remarkable for their consistency but it is made clear by them that the data offer evidence only as to the effect of family interactions on the probability of relapse. No claim is made that the data support a sociopsychological model of the aetiology of schizophrenia (nor, incidentally, do the data refute such a model). A remarkable feature of the results is that the relationship between EE and relapse is derived only from observations made in an interview between the relative and the researcher and not by direct observations of relative-patient interactions. It is surprising that such an indirect measure, from which the crucial behaviour can only be inferred, should have such predictive power. From the point of view of developing possible interventions it would be important to know what high EE means in terms of the actual interactions between relative and patient. Because the relative is directly critical of the patient in an interview with a third party does not necessarily mean that this criticism is overtly expressed in interaction with the patient.

The construct of expressed emotion

There is evidence relating to the construct of expressed emotion to the effect that high EE relatives do have a direct effect on the patient's emotional state merely by their presence (Tarrier *et al*, 1979). These authors re-examined twenty-one of the subjects used by Vaughn and Leff (1976a) about two years after their discharge. They took psychophysiological measures under two conditions. One of these was a standardized laboratory test situation involving such things as measures of orientation to simple auditory stimuli (tones). This showed no difference between subjects with high and low EE relatives. All patients were also seen three times at home under constant conditions. On each occasion the experimenter connected the transducers and then spent fifteen minutes talking to the patient about his illness, experiences of hospital and psychiatry. At the end of this time the key relative entered the room and joined in the conversation.

The results of the home recordings were very clear. The number of spontaneous fluctuations in skin conductance (a valid measure of emotionally induced sweating) were examined. All patients showed more fluctuations in the presence of the experimenter than did age- and sex-matched non-psychiatric controls. This was to be expected on the basis of previous research on the psychophysiology of schizophrenia (Lader, 1975). However, the introduction of the key relative had a marked effect on the skin conductance activity of the low EE patients such that their rate of spontaneous fluctuations decreased in the following fifteen minutes. In contrast high EE relatives had no effect on spontaneous fluctuations. The inference is that low EE relatives offer a protective effect to their afflicted family member against the stress of the interview with the relatively unknown person. Since these effects appeared in only the first interview this corroborates the interpretation if it is assumed that the experimenter becomes known to the patients and so is less emotionally arousing on the second and third occasions. Further supportive evidence comes from an elaboration of the design whereby Tarrier *et al.* recorded life events in the three weeks prior to each interview. It was found that the introduction of the relative into the interview session increased the rate of spontaneous fluctuations when there had been recorded life events in the preceding three weeks as opposed to occasions when life events had been absent. Unfortunately there were too few subjects to analyse the effect of EE in relation to life events.

Sturgeon *et al.* (1981) were able to replicate the main findings of Tarrier *et al.* by using a similar experimental format with a fresh sample of patients. In this study, however, patients were seen soon after their admission to hospital with an acute schizophrenic episode. As Sturgeon *et al.* note, their replication strengthens the hypothesis that it is the social interaction between the patient and his relative that determines relapse rather than any correlation between other features in the home environment and the dependent variable. In looking a little further Sturgeon *et al.* could find no direct effect on fluctuations in skin conductance of specific critical comments. This means that there is no evidence so far that patients of high EE relatives are responding to particular critical comments with increased emotional arousal. It seems that the presence of the relative is enough to maintain high electrodermal activity. It is also possible that this background activity in the presence of a high EE relative is in fact so high that an increased emotional response to any particular comment just cannot register. (Tarrier and Barrowclough (1984) have further shown in a single subject that spontaneous fluctuations in skin conductance are raised in the presence of a high EE parent but not in the presence of a low EE parent.)

In a second report based on the same experiment (Kuipers *et al.*, 1983), communication patterns between patient and relative were analysed for the period when they were both with an experimenter. They found that high EE relatives spent more time talking and were less tolerant of uncomfortable silences than low EE relatives. They suggest that this finding is consistent with the hypothesis that high EE relatives have a more socially intrusive style. They note that high EE relatives tended to express their own anxiety and to answer for the patient rather than waiting for him to reply to questions. In contrast to this low EE relatives were more likely to pause before replying. They were also more likely to consider and answer the patient's responses or questions.

Further support and extension of this work has come from North American studies. Vaughn *et al*. (1984) have replicated the crucial Vaughn and Leff (1976) findings on a sample of Californian schizophrenics, thus demonstrating that the EE construct is quite robust across cultures. Minklowitz *et al*. (1984) looked at schizophrenic patients (selected according to the same criteria employed in the UK studies of EE) in their family setting. The patient and his family were asked to discuss together a real problem concerning their family relationship. They were encouraged to express their feelings about the problem and to try to resolve it. Records of the conversations were scored along three categories. These were benign criticisms (defined as circumscribed judgements about the patient's behaviour), harsh criticisms (involving personal, vilifying, character-assassinating or guilt-inducing statements), and neutral-intrusive comments. The latter were comments in which the parent claimed to have special knowledge about their offspring's behaviour, attitudes or feelings. It was argued that whilst such comments are not overtly critical they could be experienced as intrusive and stressful by the patient.

The results did show that, as expected, the high EE parents were generally more critical when the two types of criticism were summed. The high EE parents were subdivided on the basis of their initial interview scores into those who were predominantly critical and those who were more biased to overinvolvement. As might be predicted the high EE critical parents tended to make more critical statements during the discussion with their offspring. Conversely, the overinvolved parents used more neutral-intrusive statements. Miklowitz *et al*. also showed that the type of EE was not associated with the clinical symptoms or premorbid adjustment of the patient. Thus the level and content of EE is unlikely to be determined by the specific features of the patient's illness. Whether there is a relationship with other patterns of family interaction or personality differences in the other members of the family is as yet unknown. This study also raises the question as to whether the two types of EE are independent and if they might be modifiable by different means.

In summary there is evidence for the construct validity of the concept of expressed emotion but as yet this is fragmentary. The causal mechanism which acts between relatives' EE as expressed in an interview with a researcher on the one hand, and patient's relapse on the other, is unknown. It is not even absolutely certain that the relationship is causal. Brown, Leff and their colleagues have attempted to rule out some of the alternative hypotheses which might explain the relationship but their evidence comes from the statistical control of what is essentially correlational inform- ation. The case for a causal relationship would be considerably strengthened if it could be shown that an intervention specifically directed at reducing high EE in relatives acted to prevent relapse. The above discussion has shown that such an intervention is hazardous because the precise nature of the critical interactions between the parties is far from fully understood. The intervention therefore has to be based on common sense and intuition. If the intervention then produces no effect it can always be argued with some plausibility that the intervention had failed to get at a critical variable. Also it would still be possible that EE is not causally related to relapse or that a third and yet undetected variable accounts for the relationship. Fortunately the available research along these lines has so far managed to produce positive findings for the effects of interventions aimed at the family on relapse.

Therapeutic reduction of EE

Leff *et al*. (1982) randomly assigned twenty-four high EE families to either a package of social-family interventions or to routine out- patient care. All of the patients were kept on long-acting neuro- leptics. The first part of the social-family intervention was given whilst the patients were still in hospital. The families were visited at home and given factual information on the aetiology, symptoms, course and treatment of schizophrenia. Thereafter the intervention became more flexible and less standardized. Groups were set up whereby the high EE relatives could meet with those of low EE families. The rationale for this was the assumption that low EE relatives had developed ways of coping with the daily problems encountered in living with a schizophrenic person. It was thought that the low EE relatives had two tactics. They avoided distressing the patient and they provided him with emotional support. It was hoped that the low EE relatives would teach the high EE relatives the 'tricks of the trade'. The researchers acted as facilitators and tried to keep discussion oriented towards practical details of how to deal with day-to-day incidents rather than acting as therapists who might interpret the relatives' behaviour.

The intervention in this study can thus be seen as one that is aimed at fostering self-help by trying to make explicit and public the knowledge of those who seem to know how to manage difficult problems successfully. This sort of intervention is very different from the therapeutic stance discussed in previous chapters where the therapist is usually acting on the basis of a well-formed theory which prescribes what action he and the patient should take. The design of this study can of course be criticized along the lines of poor specification and control of the independent variable (i.e. the intervention). The defence is that it is a reasonable course to take given the state of knowledge and which should have heuristic value if careful observations of naturally occurring variations are made.

The third component of the intervention was the availability of sessions in which the particular family, including the schizophrenic member, could meet with a psychiatrist and a psychologist. Every family was seen in this way on at least one occasion and thereafter by negotiation up to a maximum of twenty-five sessions. In these sessions the therapists were guided by two principles derived from their previous research. These were to reduce the amount of social contact time in high-contact families and to try to alter the quality of the interaction between relatives and patient such that it was of a low EE type. The therapists were free to use any technique they felt might help to achieve these objectives and to derive these from any therapeutic model they wished.

Despite the variation in the therapeutic regimen the results were clear-cut in terms of prevention of relapse. In the nine months after discharge half (six out of twelve) of the control group had relapsed as opposed to only one of the experimental group. As in the previous research relapse was defined by recurrence of symptoms and not by hospital readmission. At the end of the nine months the family interview to assess EE was repeated as was the time budget measure of the amount of face-to-face contact. The compliance with medication was also assessed and found to be good in all but one member of each group. Analysis of the family interviews showed a reduction from a pretreatment mean of 15.8 to a final mean of 6.8 in the experimental group. The posttreatment mean is just above the putative critical threshold. Five of the twelve relatives reduced their critical comments to below the threshold.

The effect of treatment on overinvolvement was less obvious but the results ran in the predicted direction. Contact time was reduced to below the thirty-five-hour threshold for six relatives (two belonging to one patient). Contact time also reduced in three of the control group. These findings suggest that the social-family intervention package used was a valid manipulation of the EE construct. They also support the notion that relapse is causally related to EE. This is also buttressed by the fact that the one relapse that did emerge in the experimental group happened in a patient with high contact with a parent who was both critical and overinvolved and where the relationship was relatively unaffected by the intervention.

Supporting evidence for the importance of working with the families of schizophrenic patients comes from a second trial by Falloon *et al.* (1982). This had considerable similarities with the Leff *et al.* (1982) investigation with the exception that the intervention employed was much more rigidly defined and controlled. In this case families were given instructions in 'problem-solving' family difficulties. A behavioural programme with a social skills format was used to teach family members to improve their interactions with each other. They were also shown how to define and solve family problems including those which focused on the schizophrenic family member. These included such things as managing medicine compliance and intrusive symptoms. All the sessions were carried out in the family home to help circumvent problems in generalization.

The control group was given clinic-based, individual supportive psychotherapy in an attempt to provide care that was equivalent to the best available routine community treatment. That this goal was achieved was indicated by the control group spending 50 per cent less time in hospital over the nine months of the study than they had in the equivalent period prior to the inception of the study. Despite this the control group was still inferior to the experimental group with regard to clinical status and time spent in hospital during the period of the study. This result confirms that of Leff *et al.* (1982).

One notable consequence of family intervention was to increase compliance with pharmacological treatment and this itself might have therapeutic benefits. However, it should also be recalled that Vaughn and Leff (1976a) showed that relapse still occurs even when total compliance is obtained.

Summary

This chapter has used the example of schizophrenia to illustrate the argument that changing the environment can be an important way of ameliorating the impact that a mental disorder can have on a person's life. There is no doubt that avoiding admission to hospital is something that is desired by both prospective patients and their families (Shepherd, 1984). It has only been possible to look at the issue in relation to a small group of patients but the reader might like to note the burgeoning literature on the importance of 'partial hospitalization' including day hospitals, sheltered work places and special hostel units in helping to prevent relapse of severe psychiatric disorders (for reviews of this work see Shepherd, 1984; Watts and Bennett, 1984). These facilities can each provide an environment with the support needed to sustain patients at their best level of functioning and autonomy and without the overwhelming blanket support of psychiatric hospital admission.

The literature on relapse in schizophrenia also illustrates other points. Firstly, it is reasonably clear now that more than one approach to the management of the disorder is required if those afflicted are to achieve the best possible outcome. Neither the pharmacological nor the social-family interventions are entirely adequate on their own. There is prima facie evidence of a beneficial interaction between these two kinds of treatment in the management of schizophrenia. The second point is that despite the good evidence of the efficacy of these approaches to management there is still uncertainty as to how or why they work. This state of affairs is not uncommon in the treatment of psychological disorders and the problems inherent in determining how treatments work have been discussed in Chapter 11.

14 Headache: Psychological Approaches to a 'Medical' Problem

The relationship between psychological processes and physical disorders has always been subject to debate within psychology and medicine. Intuitively it seems that psychological and physical states interact in a reciprocal manner. However, turning these intuitions into clear accounts of causal mechanisms has always been an exercise fraught with difficulty.

This area of investigation, psychosomatic medicine, was dominated until about fifteen years ago by attempts to identify the relationship between specific psychological states and physical pathology. The main impetus came from the psychoanalytic school and particularly from workers in North America. It was proposed on the basis of clinical experience that distinct pathological processes were associated with particular types of personality. Crudely put, it was considered that the physical symptoms were a manifestation of psychological processes. One example is constipation which was interpreted as a symbolic withholding of a person's acts. The individual believes that he cannot expect anything from anybody and so decides not to give anything away: 'what I have I hold' (Alexander, 1950; see Graham, 1972).In a similar way it was suggested that Parkinson's disease resulted from an inability to express anger. The patient with Parkinson's disease has a tremor because he is, in effect, shaking with the rage that he cannot express.

There were a number of attempts to put conjectures of this kind on to an empirical level. These were partially successful (Graham, 1972) but a number of problems limited the impact of this research. Firstly, there was considerably less specificity in the relationships between psychological types and specific illnesses than had been supposed. Then there was the perennial logical problem of trying to infer causality from experiments on selected clinical groups. It is always possible to argue that any differences between the groups in their response to independent variables is a result of the factors differentiating between the group rather than a cause of them. A third problem is that the direct measurement of the physical processes and responses involved had proved a technical problem although this has now been at least partially resolved with the advent of more sophisticated psychophysiological techniques. Finally, the putative causal variables, unconscious conflicts, are difficult to define and manipulate experimentally. Another possible reason for the failure of this kind of research to thrive was that its treatment implications were very limited. The discovery of a causal connection between some psychological state and a physical disorder would not readily lead to a viable form of treatment for this disorder nor would it necessarily suggest a preventive programme.

A revival of interest in psychosomatic research was generated by the advent of biofeedback. Work on biofeedback itself arose out of two concerns. One of these was an interest in altered states of consciousness in humans. The second concern lay in the fact that it had been held that autonomic nervous system responses were only influenced by classical conditioning and not by operant procedures (N. E. Miller, 1969). A result of this work was the attempt to treat certain physical disorders by attacking the focal symptom by conditioning procedures.

The procedure is essentially very simple. Activity relating to the target physical symptom is recorded and a prescribed component of this signal is fed back to the person (as a display on a TV screen for example). He is then asked to increase or decrease the amount of activity in the target response by using information about how successful he has been obtained from observing changes in the display. For example, a patient with hypertension (blood pressure chronically raised above clinically desirable levels) can observe changes in his blood pressure on the display within a fraction of a second of their occurrence. Any changes induced in blood pressure are easily observable and can be highlighted by the experimenter arranging that responses above a set criterion are reinforced or given extra emphasis in the display. From the point of view of understanding the disorder this treatment is entirely atheoretical and no assumptions need to be made about possible psychological precursors or about psychological events which maintain the physical problem. Despite this the arrival of biofeedback has stimulated renewed interest in traditional 'psychosomatic' disorders and raised a number of interesting problems in the area as well as increasing the understanding of some disorders.

In looking at this general area it has been decided to focus on headache because it represents a problem where there is an apparently clear medical/physiological account of the relationship between bodily events and pain. It has been well researched and besides making contributions to the treatment of head pain psychological approaches have in part initiated a further refinement in understanding of the phenomena. The reader with a particular interest in biofeedback should note that headache is not the best example of the inventiveness of work on biofeedback (Yates, 1980).

Headache

Headache is an extremely common complaint. If randomly selected members of the general population are asked if they have had a headache in the last six months about 77 per cent will respond positively. Slightly more women (80 per cent) than men (74 per cent) say that they experience headaches. Of greater interest is the fact that 21 per cent of the population claim to have a headache more than once a week and 28 per cent say they have experienced headaches for more than twenty years. When asked to rate the severity of their headaches 15 per cent categorize them as being severe or extremely severe where these two categories are the most extreme on a seven-point rating scale of severity (Philips, 1977).

Most headaches are benign despite the discomfort and disruption that they cause. A small proportion of headaches are acute and these can be symptoms of serious neurological disorders such as brain tumours or cerebral haemorrhage. Headache can also be a sympton of other metabolic and vascular diseases such as essential hypertension. Clearly these potential causes need to be excluded when investigating the more common forms of headache, and medical screening is therefore necessary. When these causes of headache are eliminated, received medical wisdom delineates two main categories of benign headache. These are migraine, with all its varied subforms, and tension headache. The present discussion is concerned with the more common forms of benign headache, and not with headache as a symptom of some other physical disease. In addition the rarer and more exotic forms of migraine such as cluster headache and basilar artery migraine will be ignored. Lance (1982)

Table 8 *Essential components of the definition of migraine and tension headaches as stated by the Ad Hoc Committee (Friedman et al., 1962).*

Migraine	Tension
Phenomenology	
Widely varied in intensity, duration and frequency; commonly unilateral onset; some preceded or associated with sensory, motor or mood disturbances; associated with anorexia, nausea/vomiting	Widely varied in intensity, duration and frequency; commonly sub-occipital; aching sensation of tightness, pressure or constriction; may be long-lasting, 48 hours +
Putative physiological basis	
Cranial arterial dilation and distension are implicated in the painful phase; there is no permanent structural change to the vessels	Associated with the sustained contraction of muscles in the absence of structural change
Trigger factors	
Related to environmental, menstrual, occupational or other variables	Usually as part of the individual's reaction to life stress
Personality types and headache types	
Ambitious, perfectionist, orderly-compulsive, rigid, inflexible, unable to express aggressive feelings	Worrisome, depressed, anxious and chronically tense, hostile dependent and psycho-sexually conflicted

provides a discussion of these.

Contemporary definitions and classification of headache are based on a mixture of uncontrolled clinical observations and quasi-experimentation. The distillation of this knowledge can be seen in the most influential classification proposed by the American Neurological Association's Ad Hoc Committee (Friedman *et al.*, 1962). The main basis of their definitions of migraine and tension headache can be seen in Table 8. It will be evident that these types of headache should be distinguishable on the basis of phenomenological report and there are apparently different physiological mechanisms which underlie the production of pain. There are also alleged to be psychological precipitants of the headache attacks. Other early observations led to the proposal that migraineurs and tension headache sufferers had different personality features which were responsible for their headache (Friedman *et al.*, 1953; Wolff, 1937). These are also indicated in Table 8 and arise out of the kinds of psychodynamic thinking about psychosomatic disorders described above.

Treatment of migraine

In migraine headache the proposed sequence of physical changes leading to pain is set out in Figure 7. The crucial changes are supposed to be in the internal and external cranial artery supply. In classical migraine the attack is thought to begin with a phase of arterial constriction. This reduces the blood supply to the cortex thus producing the neurological prodromal symptoms (visual disturbances, such as scotomas or loss of vision in parts of the visual field, and even more alarming symptoms such as aphasia and paraesthesiae in some individuals). For unknown reasons this period of constriction is followed by excessive 'rebound' dilation. During this phase the arterial walls are assumed to be hypotonic and subject to greater than usual distension during each cardiac cycle. Pain arises as a consequence of excessive distension produced by the pulsatile blood flow. It is proposed that only the external arteries are pain-sensitive and although the internal ones are

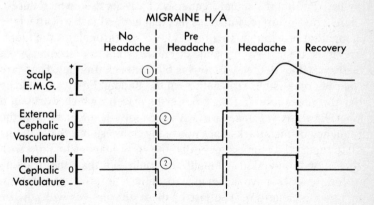

Figure 7. A diagrammatic representation of the sequence of changes occurring in scalp EMG and the internal and external cephalic vasculature during a migraine attack. These systems are shown occupying one of three states: 0 = normal; + = increased activity/dilation; − = decreased activity/constriction.

equally dilated no pain from them is experienced. Changes in the scalp muscles are thought to be a secondary consequence of the pain produced by arterial dilations. As such they might be viewed as part of the emotional expression of pain in which the victim screws up his face, hunches his shoulders and so on. A series of biochemical changes is also said to occur but these have not played any part in developing psychological approaches. The interested reader is referred to Lance (1982).

On the basis of this account it is relatively easy to develop a treatment. Pain relief could be achieved by constricting the artery artificially during the period of rebound dilation. The primary pharmacological treatment is based on this principle. Ergotamine and its derivatives are potent vasoconstrictors and have some success in reducing headache pain. Unfortunately these drugs have other effects and can, if used extensively, induce headaches themselves or cause serious side effects. The worst of these is a form of gangrene. An alternative possibility is to use biofeedback to teach the person to control his vasodilation voluntarily. A number of experiments have shown that this is a strategy that has had some modest success (Friar and Beatty, 1976; Gauthier *et al.*, 1983).

There is one puzzling feature of the results with biofeedback, which is that the premise on which the treatment is based predicts that training people to control their own vasodilation should enable them to either abort the attacks when they detect them coming on or to reduce the pain experienced during the attacks. What is not predicted is that the actual frequency of attacks should be reduced. There is no a priori reason to suspect that biofeedback will affect the factors that precipitate an attack. However, throughout the literature it is clear that patients do report that the frequency of headaches does decrease following biofeedback training. There are a number of possible explanations of this finding. Firstly, it could be that the procedure is a very powerful placebo which works in a generalized, as yet unknown way. Secondly, it might be that the frequency of the attacks does not really decrease but that patients fail to report the minor attacks that they now manage to abort with their new-found skills. Finally it could be that the training procedure does have a genuine prophylactic effect through an unknown mechanism. The last of these alternatives will now be examined.

In relation to prophylaxis there is a biofeedback procedure which is based on another theory of the aetiology of migraine attacks. This is the proposition that migraineurs suffer from a generalized vascular instability caused by excessive autonomic nervous system activity (Appenzeller *et al.*, 1963; Morley, 1977). In addition it is held that certain events may act so as to provoke this instability into the sequence of constriction and dilation. In accord with this theory there are pharmacological agents which aim to induce stability and these should also act prophylactically. These drugs have been partly successful but it is by no means guaranteed that they will succeed in every case and it is impossible to predict who will respond. One noted medical authority (Lance, 1982) has commented, 'The extraordinary variety of drugs which have been employed in migraine testify to the fact that none is so remarkably effective that the frantic polypharmacy can be abandoned. . . . Why some patients respond to one particular agent and not to another remains a mystery.'

Thermal biofeedback is an attempt to teach patients to control their excessive sympathetic activity. The blood supply to the fingers is under the exclusive control of the sympathetic nervous system (SNS) and it is argued that the SNS can be trained in a general way by providing the patient with information about the temperature of his fingers (temperature being a function of blood supply). More specifically patients should be taught to increase their peripheral temperature because this is a sign of reduced SNS activity. The controlled trials of thermal biofeedback show that it can reduce the frequency of headache attacks (Blanchard *et al.*, 1978). Unfortunately experiments which teach subjects to decrease the temperature (i.e. increase SNS activity) produce the same therapeutic effect (Kewman and Roberts, 1980). Moreover those studies that include relaxation as an active but supposedly non-specific treatment find that it is just as effective as the purportedly therapeutically effective treatments.

In summary, there is a series of biofeedback/psychological treatments which work more or less equally effectively and certainly better than a placebo of either a medical or a psychological nature (Blanchard *et al.*, 1982). Each of the treatments is based on different models of migraine headache. This concentration on treatment and its effectiveness may have had some pay-off for sufferers but it has meant that two areas of research have been relatively neglected. In the first place treatment trials have typically not collected data of a sort that would allow researchers to examine the underlying assumptions on which the treatments are based. For example, research into the biofeedback-mediated control of cephalic vascular activity should collect information about changes in vascular responses in locations which are not the focus of training, e.g. from the contralateral side of the head. Such data would help to distinguish between the alternative models of the causation of headache.

A second neglected area is the investigation of basic psycho-physiological activity in migraine patients outside the treatment context. One possibility is that migraine is not a homogeneous disorder but that there are different causal mechanisms in operation. In this case it would be necessary to explore the variation across individuals in an attempt to isolate subgroups and the correlates of such variation. There is some evidence (to be discussed later in this chapter) that migraine may not be such a distinct category as is presupposed by the usual medical classification of headache.

Tension headache and its treatment

The causal chain thought to be responsible for the production of pain in tension headache is set out in Figure 8. The relationship between increased muscle activity and pain was thought to be clear and in this case there was said to be no link between pain and vascular changes. Some early experiments (Wolff, 1962) did report that there was reduced blood flow during the painful phase but this

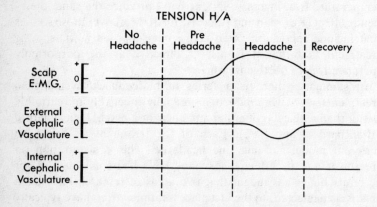

Figure 8.
A diagrammatic representation of changes occurring in scalp EMG and the internal and external cephalic vasculature during a tension headache attack. Key as for Figure 7.

was interpreted as being a secondary consequence of muscle contraction. The chronically contracted muscle is presumed to squeeze the embedded artery and thus produce ischaemia. The more recent psychophysiological investigations have not looked at vascular changes in any depth and so their significance remains obscure.

This account of tension headache predicts that if patients can be taught to reduce the excessive muscular activity there should be a corresponding reduction in the frequency and intensity of pain. Budzynski *et al.* (1973) showed that biofeedback treatment directed at this goal did have beneficial effects and subsequent studies have almost always confirmed this (e.g. Blanchard *et al.*, 1980; Blanchard and Andrasik, 1982). However, biofeedback is in general no more effective than the simpler, less time-consuming procedure of training in muscle relaxation without biofeedback. The use of relaxation training is of course also consistent with the muscle tension account of tension headache.

An alternative test of the muscle tension hypothesis can be made if an experimental group is taught to increase muscle tension or just trained to maintain muscular activity at the level of the pre-treatment baseline. If the hypothesis is correct, these procedures should result in either an increase or no change in the amount of pain experienced. Studies that have included these experimental manipulations show that they are just as effective in reducing complaints of pain as treatment directed at reducing muscle activity (Holroyd and Andrasik, 1982; Philips and Hunter, 1981a). The crucial question is why this should be so, and Holroyd has proposed an essentially psychological account of treatment effectiveness for which there is some evidence.

Holroyd and Penzien (1983) propose that what is important in the treatment of headache is not the direct training of physiological responses but the psychological changes that occur in biofeedback (and it is not difficult to extend his ideas to relaxation treatments). He suggests that people see biofeedback as a credible treatment. If they then perceive themselves as being effective and successful in the learning experience that goes with treatment, this will lead to two changes. Firstly, they will begin to view their headaches as having an internal locus of control. They will come to think that their headaches are influenced by their own psychological state rather than being imposed upon them by contingencies over which they have no control. The second change is that they will come to believe in their own self-efficacy in controlling headache. Holroyd also suggests that biofeedback teaches people to focus on the somatic sensations associated with the onset of headache, thus leading to them being able to identify the headache at an earlier stage in the attack. They can then begin to initiate active coping strategies at this point rather than wait for the full impact of the pain.

Another consequence of earlier identification is that the person will begin to gain more precise information about the possible physical and psychological precursors of an attack. He can then develop strategies to deal with these precipitants. Thus Holroyd clearly proposes that the physiological changes involved in remediating headache are a consequence of psychological changes involving what the person believes about his headaches and his ability to control them rather than the direct control of the physiological causes themselves.

A crucial test of this hypothesis is the direct manipulation of the subject's belief about his success in controlling his responses via biofeedback. Holroyd and Penzien (1983) reported an experiment which made just such a test of the hypothesis. A group of tension headache sufferers were informed that they would be treated by biofeedback by which they would learn to reduce muscle tension in the scalp. The rationale offered for the treatment was the traditional model of tension headache. Half the subjects received feedback for decreases in muscle activity and the rest for increases in activity. Within each of these groups one half were led to believe that they were highly successful in controlling the target response, whereas the other half had the feedback adjusted to indicate that they had only been moderately successful. Holroyd also took measures of the subject's belief in their own success, pre and post measures of their belief as to the locus of control of their headaches, and ratings of their perceived self-efficacy.

The results of this experiment were quite unambiguous. The feedback did lead to subjects either increasing or decreasing their muscle tension within sessions in the appropriate direction but there was no effect of this manipulation on reports of headache. This of course runs contrary to the physiological model of treatment of tension headache. On the other hand, manipulating how successful the subjects thought they were in controlling their response did influence reports of headache in the predicted direction. Those patients who believed that they were successful showed significantly more improvement and there were significant correlations between the measures of internal control, self-efficacy and outcome.

Holroyd's model was proposed in the context of tension headache but it would not be difficult to extend it to migraine. As yet there has been no direct test of it with migraineurs. The model does bear a striking resemblance to the credibility-expectancy model of general psychotherapeutic change discussed in Chapter 11 and is susceptible to the same methodological problems in investigating it. There are also two issues related to the ideas proposed by Holroyd which have been the subject of some research on headache. Firstly, there are doubts about the adequacy of the physiological model, and secondly, the relation between stress and headache is assumed to be in line with the 'Ad Hoc' definition given at the beginning of the chapter.

Physiological studies of headache

As far as tension headache is concerned there are a number of embarrassing findings for a thoroughgoing physiological model. These have been discussed in some detail by Philips (1978; 1980). An immediate problem is that there is no consistent evidence that muscle activity is raised during a headache attack. This is so either when headache sufferers are compared with non-headache controls or with their own state when not suffering a headache. There is also no consistent evidence that tension headache sufferers have generally elevated levels of muscle tension when not in pain as might be implied by the Ad Hoc Committee's definition. It is also interesting that when experimenters have included migraineurs as a comparison group there have been some indications that the latter have levels of muscle activity either equal to, or even greater than, those observed in subjects with tension headaches (Andrasik *et al.*, 1982).

All of these investigations are essentially correlational. That is, they do not attempt to manipulate the crucial variable of scalp muscle activity. Inferences are made on the basis of correlations in the form of between-group differences. There also do not appear to be any observations of longitudinal changes in relevant physiological measures and the complaint of pain. Most studies are cross-sectional and subjects are observed for relatively brief periods of time.

There is one relatively direct test of the muscle contraction hypothesis of tension headache in which headache subjects who were not in pain raised their scalp muscle activity in a controlled manner using biofeedback (Pearce and Morley, 1981). Both migraine and tension headache sufferers were used as subjects. The results showed that despite raising muscle tension considerably above initial levels, or any level reported in the literature, no significant report of pain could be induced. Such pain as was produced was regarded by the subjects as being trivial and very unlike that experienced in a headache attack. Moreover there were no differences between the two headache groups.

With regard to migraine there is good evidence that the sequence of changes to the internal cranial blood supply does follow that proposed by the physiological theory (Marshall, 1978) and that such changes do not occur in tension headache sufferers. It has also been shown that reducing dilation of the external cranial arteries by pharmacological means is accompanied by a corresponding reduction in the experience of pain (Graham and Wolff, 1938). This of course is not equivalent to showing that the arteries of migraineurs are excessively dilated during an attack. It might be that they are merely more sensitive to pulsatile dilation during a pain episode.

Here there is a problem in measuring the activity of the cranial arteries. Most measures are based on non-invasive procedures in which transducers are attached directly over the artery on the surface of the skin. This procedure can only give a relative measure and, strictly speaking, it is only possible to interpret changes occurring within an individual on a single occasion of measurement. This is because slightly different placements of the transducer will produce different readings and absolutely identical placements cannot be guaranteed either between subjects or between individuals at different times. Furthermore other factors, like skin pigmentation, can affect the size of the obtained response.

In so far as can be judged, there is good reason to believe that during pain attacks the external cranial vasculature is dilated. There is also some evidence that migraineurs display unusual variability in the artery at the site where pain onset is most frequent and this is not seen with tension headache (Morley, 1985; Morley and Hunter, 1983). These observations suggest that there is something distinctly different about the state of migraineurs' vasculature even when they are not in pain.

Research has also attempted to test the hypothesis that migraineurs have unstable vascular responses usually by examining peripheral vascular responses to innocuous stimulation. As with many other data in this field, the results are equivocal and it is very difficult to make direct comparisons across laboratories. These tend to use different procedures for selecting subjects as well as different experimental techniques and measures. There are also problems in controlling for the effects of medication and other conditions that might determine whether differences are detected (Morley, 1977). Nevertheless there is a persistent suggestion in the results that subjects with migraine do show more variable peripheral vascular responses to a variety of stimulus conditions.

In summary, the data from direct muscular recordings do not support the usual physiological model of tension headaches. Moreover the supposed distinction between tension headache and migraine on the basis of muscle activity is difficult to substantiate. As far as migraine is concerned there is some evidence that the alleged vascular changes during a headache do occur. Evidence for other differences between migraineurs and controls or subjects with tension headaches is also difficult to come by. On these grounds it is necessary to treat the usual physiological account of headache with some caution.

'Stress' and headache

Many of the psychophysiological experiments described have attempted to examine possible differences between headache groups in the laboratory using fairly standard psychophysiological techniques and stimuli. The investigations are based on the assumption that between-group differences can be observed at rest or that differences can be made to occur under appropriate stimulation. In the latter case it is thought that differences can be produced by any set of stressful conditions and even sometimes by non-stressful stimuli. To achieve experimental control stimuli are standardized across all subjects and usually tend to be rather innocuous (slides, lights, tones, and so on). These stimuli are also discrete and relatively transient. They have little face validity when compared with peoples' reports of what they themselves presume to be the triggers of their headache attacks. What people describe are things like having an argument, being overtired and having a consistent pressure of work. Such things are difficult to reproduce in the laboratory and it is also difficult to know whether the events that sufferers report are really of significance let alone causal.

It is very difficult to identify triggers. The usual clinical method is to ask patients whether their headaches are preceded by any event. There are a number of checklists that can be used to prod the patient's memory. Unfortunately this method has to rely on an imperfect and possibly selective memory and it is possible that people may also respond to the demand characteristics of the situation. They may then check items that are consistent with their beliefs about what might be the kinds of stressor that would produce headaches. The use of prospective diaries to overcome some of the problems associated with memory bias can give a better indication of possible triggers. Despite this, people may still selectively attend to what they feel might be the causes of their headaches rather than the actual precipitants of pain (Nisbett and Ross, 1980). Nevertheless this method could be used to obtain preliminary information about possible triggers and their predictive validity could then be checked by experimentally exposing subjects to them. This strategy has been tried on a number of occasions but there are still problems that make interpretation difficult. Most of the studies record headache as a verbal complaint of pain and direct measurement of any relevant physiological response has not been made. In addition it is impossible to present the stressful stimulus in a blind manner and there is therefore the possibility of interpreting the results of the experiment as being the consequences of demand characteristics.

A number of studies have attempted to provide a weak test of the hypothesis that stressful events induce headache by using mental imagery as a stessor. This has the advantage that the image can be tailored to the idiosyncratic requirements of the subject. Images are selected from subjects' self-reports of stressful events or reliable precipitants of headache. These can be compared with either non-stressful images or with a generalized stressful image such as a gruesome car accident. Use of the latter scene can test whether headache sufferers are susceptible to particular stressors as opposed to generally unpleasant events (the fact that such a wide variety of stressors are claimed to invoke headache tends to suggest this latter hypothesis). If the stress-response hypothesis is correct, it would be expected that tension headache sufferers would show abnormal responses in the muscles of the scalp, compared with controls, and that migraineurs would show unusual activity in the external cranial vasculature.

There is some evidence that this approach could be successful. For example, Philips and Hunter (1982) found that headache cases showed greater reactivity of their scalp muscles in response to stressful images than did controls. This excessive response appeared to be more persistent in tension headache sufferers than in migraineurs. In contrast to this, no between-groups differences could be found in response to a standard stimulus of a loud noise. It has proved more difficult to find any selective effect of stress on the temporal artery (the one particularly implicated in pain production) in migraineurs (Andrasik *et al.*, 1982; Feuerstein *et al.*, 1982; Morley, 1985; Thompson and Adams, 1984). However, a failure to confirm the hypothesis under test is never very conclusive since it can always be argued that the experiments are not a sensitive enough test of the hypothesis. Possibly the stressors identified by the subjects were not particularly potent for the reasons discussed above.

Most of the stressful events studied in the psychophysiology laboratory are discrete events of a transient nature lasting from a few seconds to several minutes. They are also presented as passive stimuli to which the subject merely attends and they rarely occur more than once or twice. In terms of content validity these stressors are a very poor imitation of the type of event often reported by headache sufferers. These events are often repetitive or continuous stresses, such as working for a very demanding boss, and are not received passively but engage the subject in some active coping behaviour. In the case of the demanding boss this might consist of trying to produce all the work by a given deadline. In addition, many sufferers report that their headaches seem to appear when they have the opportunity to relax, say, at the weekend or on holiday. So far there have been no experimental analogues of this kind of situation.

A further problem arises when it is realized that not all headaches may be precipitated by stressful psychological situations. Subjective reports of a correlation between stress and headache are often not entirely convincing and it must also be remembered that a significant proportion of sufferers can detect no relationship between their headaches and psychological factors (Henryk-Gutt and Rees, 1973). This of course is not to deny that such a relationship does exist for many sufferers, but it certainly complicates the issue when it comes to investigating this relationship.

In conclusion it must be admitted that the stress-reactivity hypothesis with regard to the triggering of headaches does have considerable intuitive appeal. Providing a convincing experimental demonstration of this alleged causal mechanism in action, however, is very difficult.

Pain experience and behaviour

According to the Ad Hoc Committee definitions, the experience of headache pain, its topographical distribution and its association with other symptoms should all differentiate between the two main diagnostic categories. Migraine should be differentiated from tension headache in that it should be located unilaterally, frontally and ocularly as opposed to having a bilateral, occipital location. Also the quality of the pain is allegedly different with migraineurs experiencing a throbbing, pulsating or thumping sensation round the head. These phenomenological features, plus the possible presence of associated symptoms like nausea/vomiting and sensory or motor disturbances, are potentially important since they form the basis for diagnostic classification and subsequent treatment decisions.

With the exception of standard clinical neurological tests carried out to eliminate the possibility of any sinister pathology, there are no direct tests of the supposed physiological components that are normally carried out in the investigation and diagnosis of benign headache. It therefore becomes of considerable interest to know whether the phenomenological accounts given by patients actually correspond to diagnostic categories in the way proposed by the Ad Hoc Committee.

Two strategies have been used to answer this question. The first has been to administer a standard questionnaire about headache symptoms to a pool of subjects. The data obtained is then subjected to some form of multivariate analysis to see if this reveals separate factors or components that correspond to the standard diagnostic categories. Thus it should be possible to derive a migraine factor heavily loaded with such features as unilateral onset, nausea/vomiting and sensory prodromata. Despite considerable variation in the subject samples and questionnaires used, the results of studies based on this strategy have given a reasonable consensus (Diehr et al., 1982; Peck and Attfield, 1981; Zeigler et al., 1972). It has not proved possible to obtain factors corresponding to the main diagnostic categories. Instead single factors tend to emerge which represent a relatively small proportion of the total variances and which correspond to a symptomatic category. Thus Zeigler et al. (1972) found a factor which contained the items of nausea before and during pain and 'spots before the eyes' but not a unilateral distribution or other neurological signs. These were present in two other factors and the number of people who overlapped with high scores on all three factors was rather small.

Waters and O'Connor (1971) looked at the distribution of the common symptoms and their overlap in a large (N = 945), randomly selected population of women. They found that all combinations of symptoms could occur and there was no evidence of clustering into distinct groups. On the other hand, when they examined the way in which the symptoms of headache were diagnosed by a neurologist there was a definite tendency for subjects with the traditional symptoms of migraine to be diagnosed as migrainous. But even this was not perfect, so for the particular neurologist involved there was considerable latitude and variability in his diagnostic application.

The second strategy for approaching the distinction between categories of headache is to take groups previously defined as having tension or migraine headache and collect detailed accounts of their headache symptoms with a standard questionnaire. The preferred method is to ask subjects to record their symptoms at the time or soon after they experience them. Bakal and Kaganov (1977) used this method and found that different diagnostic groups were almost identical with respect to the location of their pain during attacks. Also 40 per cent of subjects from each group reported that their pain had a throbbing kind of quality and 52 per cent of each group had some form of visual disturbance associated with the attack. The diagnostic groups were generally similar with regard to their phenomenology. Similar results have emerged from Kaganov *et al.* (1981) and Philips (1977).

Other studies looking at the quality of pain experience rather than its location have also tended to find that there is less of a difference between the diagnostic groups than might be expected (Hunter, 1983; Hunter and Philips, 1981). Traditionally the assessment of pain has focused on measures of its intensity usually by getting the subject to mark the appropriate descriptive adjective (e.g. mild, moderate or severe) on a simple rating scale. This type of assessment is derived from the reductionist specificity theory of pain in which the amount of pain experienced is assumed to be directly related to the degree of physiological disturbance, and the quality of the pain is determined by the specific pain receptor involved (Melzack and Wall, 1982). Both of these assumptions are now untenable and so alternative methods for assessing pain have now been developed. (In passing it can be noted that the Ad Hoc Committee's definitions tacitly adhere to the reductionist theory and so assessment in terms of the intensity of experienced pain is consistent with this position.)

A prominent contemporary instrument for assessing pain experience is the McGill Pain Questionnaire (MPQ). In this questionnaire, subjects are asked to select adjectives from a number of different sets of adjectives (e.g. tingling, taut, cutting, piercing, pricking) which describe their pain. The final scoring system of the questionnaire is such that three scores are available which represent the sensory, affective and evaluative (i.e. overall intensity) components of the pain (Melzack and Wall, 1982).

Hunter and Philips (1981) administered the MPQ to groups of tension headache and migraine sufferers who were reliably diagnosed according to the Ad Hoc Committee's criteria. Their analysis of the results indicated that these groups were remarkably similar when the scores on the sensory scales were examined. This suggests that certain sensory scales may be chosen more frequently by headache sufferers regardless of their diagnoses. When the particular adjectives chosen were examined there was some evidence that the two groups could be differentiated. Migraineurs chose words like sharp and blinding but tension headache cases were less specific in their choice of descriptors. Words like throbbing and tight which might have been expected to be highly discriminative were chosen with roughly equal frequency by both groups. When the affective scores were examined there was a difference in that migraineurs chose words like sickening and suffocating and tension headache subjects selected words like fearful and punishing. However, there was no difference in the overall affective score.

Subjects in the Hunter and Philips study were selected because they had a high frequency and intensity of headaches. Hunter (1983) compared groups with a much wider range of both frequency and intensity of headache on a scale developed from the MPQ. Comparisons between migraineurs and tension headache sufferers failed to show any gross differences, but there was a between-groups difference with respect to the choice of words on the affective component of the scale. Subjects with migraine described themselves as being more frightened, miserable, exhausted and tired by the pain experience. This group also reported that their headaches were experienced as more intense than those of subjects with tension headaches. In fact the intensity of the headache discriminated between the two groups better than the descriptors chosen to indicate pain quality.

As a result of these findings, as well as those from the psycho-physiological research, there has been a concerted move away from a categorical model of headache. The more recent view is that headache is best construed as lying on a continuum of severity. The precise nature of this continuum has yet to be defined but it is clear that no one feature will suffice. Thus mere reference to the intensity of the headache will be insufficient to predict what other symptoms will be present. Bakal (1982), who has been the most vociferous proponent of the continuum model, suggests that it should be defined in terms of the number of attacks, hours of head pain, and the number (rather than the kind) of symptoms experienced. The data do give some indication that as headaches become more severe so they are accompanied by the increasing involvement of both tension and migraine symptoms.

Bakal's research shows that more severe headaches tend to have more migrainous or vascular symptoms and that when these symptoms are present people are more likely to regard their headache as a problem that interferes with their life. This relationship between migrainous symptoms and interference with daily life is by no means perfect. It is possible that a person with few tension headache symptoms may regard himself as incapacitated by his pain. When all is considered the relationship between pain-motivated behaviour and intensity and that between intensity and physiological measures is not that expected on the basis of the naive reductionist position.

Pain behaviour

Early experiments on treating headache with biofeedback obtained patients' records of their medication rate. It was supposed that as subjects learned to control the physiological substrate of their pain, with a consequent reduction in the frequency, intensity and duration of episodes, so their use of medication would decline. Although the expected relationship between pain reduction and medication did emerge on some occasions, it failed to do so on others. In essence the relationship between pain and medication rate was assumed to be one in which pain reduction was seen as providing the motivation for the use of medication. As such, this model of pain behaviour has clear parallels with the model of fear and avoidance discussed in Chapter 11. There is good evidence that pain-motivated behaviour is not necessarily a direct function of the experienced intensity of pain.

Philips and Hunter (1981b) constructed a checklist of pain-related behaviour of the kinds frequently described by headache sufferers. It included avoidance and complaint as well as the taking of medication. Avoidance items consisted of such things as taking time off work and items relating to complaint covered both verbal complaints and non-verbal indications such as moaning, crying out or grimacing. Their subjects kept a headache diary for two weeks and the relationship between traditional measures of pain (intensity, frequency and duration) as assessed through the diaries and subjects' self-reports of pain behaviour were examined. Scores from the MPQ were also obtained and put into the analysis. With only one exception there was no relationship between traditional measures of pain and pain behaviour. The exception involved medication rate which correlated (at a relatively low level) with the frequency of headache. The lack of any association between intensity and pain behaviour is particularly noteworthy.

In contrast there were persistent relationships betwen MPQ measures of the sensory and affective components of pain and the indices of avoidance, complaint and use of medication. The number of self-reported complaints was correlated with both sensory and affective measures of pain but the extent of avoidance was only related to its affective qualities. On the other hand, medication rate correlated with the sensory components of pain but not its affective quality. The fact that avoidance and complaint were themselves not strongly interrelated provides further indication that it is necessary to develop more sophisticated accounts for the various types of pain behaviour. Knowing one component of pain, whether it be the intensity, sensory quality or the extent to which it induces avoidance of normal activities, gives little indication as to what the other components will be. This is moving quite a way from the simple reductionist-specificity theory inherent in the Ad Hoc Committee's definitions.

Headache and personality

Although personality does not come into the Ad Hoc Committee's definition of headache, the idea that people with distinct personality types might be prone to particular kinds of headache is a theme which runs through much of the literature. The earlier theories of psychosomatic disorders proposed that there was a specific relationship between the physical symptoms and the personality of the sufferer. In accord with Freudian theory the symptom was a symbolic representation of unacceptable unconscious mental processes.

On the basis of a series of eight patients treated by psychoanalysis, Fromm-Reichman (1937) proposed that the 'choice' of migraine symptoms occurred because the patient experiences strong repressed hostility which is in conflict with a wish to solve his problems by more intellectual means. This conflict then allegedly leaves the person in a state in which he feels that he could literally bash his head against a wall. Thus the expression of headache as a symptom. Wolff (1937), who was a neurologist, was led by informal clinical observations to suggest that migraineurs were generally perfectionists, achievement-oriented, tense, driving personalities with a degree of obsessionality, as well as having a welter of repressed hostility.

Professional opinion has been much less forthcoming when it comes to linking a particular personality type with tension headache. Martin *et al.* (1967) wrote: 'there does not seem to be a single psychological determinant of muscle contraction headaches. Multiple conflicts are usually evident . . . poorly repressed hostility . . . unresolved dependency needs and psychosexual conflicts are also frequently present' (p. 203).

Descriptions of this kind were arrived at through uncontrolled clinical observations which are open to two general sources of error. In the first place it is possible that people arriving at clinics are in some way self-selected and not a random selection of headache sufferers. They are the people whose complaint behaviour has led them to seek help and it has already been shown that complaint behaviour is not necessarily related to the intensity or quality of pain. Secondly, it is more than probable that the clinician's judgement is biased. He may select and seek out certain patient characteristics whilst relatively ignoring others. It is difficult to determine just what information he uses to reach his conclusions.

It is possible to control for these biases by selecting headache samples at random from the general population and by using standardized personality tests whose sources of error are relatively well known. Unfortunately when such tests are used the gain in objectivity is bought at the expense of using the personality constructs measured by the test rather than the sorts of personality features described by clinical observations. Reliable personality tests tend to measure more global and less specific constructs such as extraversion and neuroticism. Projective tests which might measure the purported personality characteristics of headache patients have immense problems of reliability and validity (Vernon, 1964) and this makes interpretation of the results hazardous.

When random samples and objective tests are used there is a reasonable consensus between studies. Headache patients tend to score highly on the neuroticism scale within Eysenck's personality system but only if they have been selected from clinic populations. Samples taken from the general population do not differ from subjects with either no headaches or very low levels of headache (Henryk-Gutt and Rees, 1973; Lucas, 1977; Maxwell, 1966; Philips, 1976). This finding adds support to the suggestion that the early reports may have been influenced by selection bias. It also accords with investigation of pain other than headache pain where neuroticism relates to complaint behaviour. Philips and Hunter (1981) in their study of pain behaviour in headache found a correlation between both complaint and avoidance, on the one hand, and neuroticism on the other. These findings suggest that personality in headache may have an important moderating function. The important qualification is that, as with all correlational data, the direction of causality is always open to doubt and so great care is needed in formulating testable hypotheses.

There is very little evidence on the relationship between anger and headache. This is partly because there have been few scales devised to measure anger. Henryk-Gutt and Rees (1973) did find some suggestion that migraineurs scored higher on a scale of hostile behaviour which was a composite of a number of more specific variables such as overt behaviour, indirect hostility, verbal hostility and irritability. Bihldorf *et al.* (1971), using a scale specially developed for their study, found some evidence that migraineurs were more inhibited in expressing anger and felt guilty for longer after they had given vent to their angry feelings. Although these results are suggestive that the personality of headache sufferers might accord with earlier clinically formed hypotheses they are not strong and it remains to be seen whether the differences observed are specific to migraineurs and people with chronic tension headache. One alternative hypothesis to be explored is that any person who becomes afflicted with repetitive severe pain comes to feel resentful, irritable and hostile. Indeed there is some evidence which supports this interpretation (Melzack and Wall, 1982; Sternbach and Timmermans, 1975).

Summary

Although it may appear that we have dealt with one disorder in disproportionate detail in this chapter we have actually only presented a thumbnail sketch of some of the issues current in research on headache. Each of the issues is in fact a reflection of a wide range of work on the same problem which appears in many other disorders. For example the relationship between stress and cardiovascular dysfunction is currently the subject of detailed experimental work, as are the constructs of pain behaviour and experience. Each of these areas presents fascinating problems for a psychologist and their solutions have theoretical and clinical consequences.

15 Learning in the Mentally Handicapped

Although it is a topic that does not have an initial appeal for most students, mental handicap presents fascinating problems for the psychologist. To some degree this is because if anything can be considered to be the central problem of mental handicap it is an inadequate capacity to learn. Learning is a major field for experimental psychology and it would be expected that experimental psychology could make a major contribution to analysing this problem and suggesting ways in which it might be relieved. To some degree this promise has been fulfilled, and a major aim of this chapter is to look at what is known about learning processes in those with severe mental handicap. However, before embarking on this topic it is necessary to give a background coverage of the problem of mental handicap in general.

Background

What is here being called 'mental handicap' is also known by a large number of other terms. These include 'mental deficiency', 'mental retardation', which is the commonly used term in the USA, and 'mental subnormality', which is a term that has been used in British legislation. Depending on the exact definition, this is something that afflicts about 2 per cent of the population. In IQ terms, it corresponds to those with an IQ of around 70 or less. This is not a homogeneous population and within the UK it is common to make distinction between what is described as 'mental handicap' and 'severe mental handicap', with the latter corresponding to an IQ level of less than around 50 to 55. This severe group accounts for about 0.4 per cent of the population.

It should be stressed that the exact definition of mental handicap varies from country to country. For example, in the USA the definition used in practice is much more in terms of IQ levels.

Without going into the exact legal definitions, British practice has been to define mental handicap much more in terms of social and educational competence (or rather the lack of it). Relying heavily on IQ levels has the advantage of applying a standard metric in all cases. Relying on judgements of competence takes into account the fact that, especially in borderline areas, competence has an imperfect correlation with IQ. Thus it is possible to have two people both with an IQ of, say, 68 where one clearly needs to be treated as handicapped whilst the other copes fairly well. The disadvantage of using competence as the criterion is that it is a much vaguer concept than IQ thus leading to greater unreliability in definition.

The causes of mental handicap are multiple and it is not intended to give an account of the various pathological conditions. Such details can be obtained from the standard texts (e.g. Craft, 1979; Crome and Stern, 1967). In general terms the causes can be classified into two, or possibly three major groups. The first major cause (or set of causes) lies in the factors that contribute to normal variation in intellectual ability. Given the alleged normal distribution of intelligence, just as a few will have unusually high ability so there will be some who are quite the reverse. In general the majority of the mildly handicapped can be seen in this light as the lower end of the ability range. Another possible causal factor can come into play in mild mental handicap. This has been described as 'subcultural' causes by A. M. Clarke and A. D. B. Clarke (1976). The notion involved here is that there are children who are naturally at the lower end of the ability range but not to such a degree that would normally warrant classification as mentally handicapped. If such children are reared under exceptionally adverse social circumstances their level of functioning may be depressed so that they become indistinguishable from the mildly mentally handicapped. There is evidence that children whose mental handicap owes something to subcultural factors have a rather better long-term outcome, especially when removed from their adverse circumstances (A. D. B. Clarke et al., 1958).

The final set of causal factors are those resulting in organic brain pathology. There are a very large number of different conditions that can produce either damage to, or maldevelopment of the brain. The specific disorders may be genetically transmitted (e.g.. tuberous sclerosis or epiloia), the consequence of chromosomal abnormalities (of which the best example is Down's syndrome), the outcome of factors that can affect the foetus (e.g. maternal rubella) or diseases that can permanently damage the brain which occur early in childhood (e.g. a severe bout of meningitis). The causes can therefore be anything that can have a serious adverse effect on the brain and which can act at any point from conception through to childhood.

Although a small proportion of those with the milder degree of mental handicap may owe their state to pathological causes, well over 95 per cent of the severely handicapped show pathology of the nervous system (e.g. Birch *et al.*, 1970; Crome, 1960). In practice a specific diagnosis or cause cannot be identified in many cases of severe mental handicap and so the brain pathology has occurred for reasons that cannot be ascertained. Nevertheless the damage can still be demonstrated either by appropriate neurological examination or at autopsy.

The degree of handicap, cause and social class tend to be interlinked. The mildly mentally handicapped, whose handicap results from being at the extreme of the normal ability range, or is due to subcultural factors, have parents who are predominantly within the lower social classes. Where middle- and upper-class parents have a mildly mentally handicapped child the cause is usually pathological. Severely mentally handicapped children where the causes are almost entirely pathological are fairly evenly distributed throughout the social classes, at least in terms of parental social class.

Mild mental handicap

This chapter is basically concerned with the severely mentally handicapped but to make the coverage a little more complete a few comments will be made about those with milder degrees of handicap. As a general rule the mildly mentally handicapped are not much of a 'clinical' problem in that they do not typically come into contact with the health services (either out-patient or in-patient) because of their mental handicap. Of course they suffer exactly the same kinds of health problems as the rest of the population and their main need in terms of special service provision lies in education.

The typical child with mild mental handicap will develop fairly normally but be slow to pass the usual milestones. It is not usually until he comes into contact with the educational system and fails to cope adequately with its demands that any special provision needs to be made. Sooner or later special educational provision will be required. This will be in terms of special remedial or 'opportunity' classes within the ordinary schools or by transfer to what in Britain are known as 'schools for children with learning difficulties'. These schools obviously have a less academic curriculum than the normal schools, although basic academic skills like reading, writing and arithmetic are still taught, and place a greater emphasis on the practical skills needed to get by in life.

Contrary to many people's expectations, the longer-term outcome of the mildly mentally handicapped after leaving school is generally quite good. In one long-term outcome study Baller *et al.* (1967) dealt with over 200 people then middle-aged who had been pupils in the 'opportunity rooms' of schools in Lincoln, Nebraska. All had had a history of educational failure and an IQ of less than 70 whilst in the school system. In terms of their status in middle age there was considerable overlap with control groups within the average intelligence range who had been educated in the ordinary classes of the same school system and at the same time. There were differences but these were by no means large. For example, slightly fewer of the mildly handicapped subjects had married and had children and where they had married their marriages tended to be less stable. The mortality rate was higher. In terms of employment 80 per cent of the males and 77 per cent of the females were described as 'usually employed' whereas the rate for controls was about 15 per cent higher. Where employed most of the key group tended to be in unskilled or semi-skilled work but 13 per cent were engaged in non-manual commercial employment or had their own businesses. As a group their crime rate was raised but the violations tended to be fairly minor with traffic offences and drunkenness being prominent.

There is no reason to consider that Baller *et al.*'s results are atypical. Most authorities agree that the majority of those considered mildly ESN at school do fairly well in adult life. Those that have problems also tend to be those with additional handicaps, whether physical or mental, and in general the mildly handicapped will be a little overrepresented in the clientele of social work departments. It is also probably the case that this group will also suffer most at times of high unemployment.

Also relevant to any discussion of outcome is a point that A. D. B. Clarke and A. M. Clarke (1978) draw attention to. In epidemiological studies of mild mental handicap it has been found that the prevalence levels change with age. In particular the prevalence declines appreciably after a point around the age at which compulsory education ends. Although a few mildly mentally handicapped children will die before reaching the end of their schooling and in the few years afterwards, any excess mortality will not be enough to account for the decline in prevalence. Clarke and Clarke suggest three reasons for this decline in mild mental handicap with age. One of these is 'camouflage'. The time of secondary schooling is likely to be the period of greatest intellectual demands for many people. Children who cannot cope with normal schooling may then be able to manage ordinary life and a job that does not rely on educational skills. A second possible factor is that the process of learning ways of dealing with the demands of living in ordinary society will still go on after leaving school and many will eventually learn what is required. Finally, there may be delayed maturation especially in those whose early circumstances have been most adverse. The operation of processes like these may well explain why the casualties of the educational system are not necessarily the casualties of the adult world.

Severe mental handicap

Severe mental handicap is usually apparent at birth or within the first few months afterwards. Since the cause is almost always organic, with damage to or maldevelopment of the brain, the severely mentally handicapped individual is often multiply handicapped. Many have cerebral palsy (i.e. are 'spastic'), epilepsy or sensory impairments. As already indicated a specific cause or syndrome, such as Down's syndrome (mongolism), hydrocephalus or phenylketonuria, cannot be identified in many cases. Even where a specific condition can be identified it is only in a relatively small proportion of these cases that specific medical treatment can have any impact. The best example of these is phenylketonuria which is due to an inborn error of metabolism which can be identified very shortly after birth and where eating a special phenylalanine-free diet can considerably improve outcome. It is also important that hereditary disorders can be identified so that parents can be given genetic counselling.

   The severely mentally handicapped child will develop slowly and often takes a very long time to acquire the simple skills of everyday living such as dressing himself, feeding himself, urinary and faecal continence, etc. Speech may also remain very limited. The educational system in Britain puts these children in 'schools for children with severe learning difficulties'. In these schools the curriculum is very different from the normal schools and concentrates on sensory awareness and basic living skills. In Britain it is now fortunately the case that the vast majority of severely mentally handicapped children remain at home with their parents. The few who enter any form of long-term residential care are usually those with major additional physical handicaps or severe behaviour disorders.

In Britain schooling is provided for these children up to the age of 19 years. Local authorities then provide 'adult training centres' which ideally provide suitable daytime activities. These include such things as simple industrial work and training in socially useful skills like simple cookery. Since the severely mentally handicapped usually cannot manage to live totally independently a problem comes as their parents age or die and are unable to look after them. In the not-too-distant past a large proportion of the adults would have spent much of their lives in large 'hospitals' for the mentally handicapped. These have by no means disappeared yet but the recent moves to community care have shown that many of the severely mentally handicapped can live at least a semi-independent life in small hostels or group homes where four or five individuals share an ordinary house in an ordinary street with support from social workers, community nurses and other staff who can visit these homes on a regular basis. Of course careful preparation and training is required but what can be achieved with these people given properly designed training programmes vastly exceeds what even the professional workers in the field would have imagined possible only a couple of decades ago.

Analysing the problem

Mental handicap is a complex problem with medical, psychological, social and educational aspects. Medical studies of causation are important since it is only by understanding the causes that preventive measures can be taken and prevention is the only ideal solution to a problem like severe mental handicap. Enough is now known to prevent some mental handicap and there is some evidence that preventive measures have had some impact in incidence (Clarke and Clarke, 1978). It is worth noting in passing that the lowered incidence has not yet had much of an effect on prevalence. If anything prevalence may have increased due to the fact that medical advances have also decreased the mortality of those born with severe mental handicap.

Once severe mental handicap occurs it is only in rare instances, like phenylketonuria, that anything can be done which might negate the central handicap. Most intervention is therefore directed at amelioration or attempting to help the individual to function as well as possible despite being mentally handicapped. For the most part amelioration depends upon being able to counteract the central handicap of inadequate mental functioning. This means that understanding psychological processes in the severely mentally handicapped is extremely important.

It is possible to describe the central psychological problem of mental handicap in a number of ways. The most obvious is in terms of low IQ. Although it is true that the severely handicapped have very low IQs this by itself gives very little indication of what might be done to relieve the problem. Similarly, severe handicap, especially in children, can be seen in terms of a retarded rate of development but again this is not a great deal of help in counter-acting the effects of handicap. The basic deficit can also be seen as a problem in learning. The severely mentally handicapped child is extremely slow to learn the everyday skills that normal young children seem to acquire with such little effort. These are things like dressing, feeding and even talking. In general psychology has a long history of looking at learning and if it is possible to analyse the learning process in the mentally handicapped then it might also be possible to devise training programmes that would use the handi-capped individual's residual learning capacity in the most efficient way.

Because of its central importance the rest of this chapter will concentrate on studies of learning (and memory) in people with severe mental handicap. This does not of course mean that other aspects of psychological functioning are of no concern in dealing with the overall problem of mental handicap. Some analysis of these other problems can be found in A. M. Clark and A. D. B. Clarke (1974a) and Ellis (1979). Concentrating on the problem of learning serves the purpose of illustrating how the methods and techniques of experimental psychology can be used to analyse a clinical problem. However, before looking at this problem directly it is necessary to consider the methodological issues.

Methodological issues

A more extensive discussion of the points raised here is provided by Clarke and Clarke (1974a) who also give reference to a number of important primary sources. Zeaman (1965) has suggested that investigators can approach the problem of mental handicap in two ways. They can strive to delineate the laws, principles or regularities that govern the behaviour of these people. Alternatively they may wish to find the *unique* features of their behaviour. If concern is with the latter then comparison with normal subjects becomes essential and it is the question of normal control groups that has resulted in much of the methodological heart-searching. If the concern is with understanding the behaviour of the mentally handicapped regardless of whether this involves principles that are different from those of normal people then normal control groups can be dispensed with. Zeaman and some others have confined themselves to this lesser aim in order to avoid the methodological problems.

A large amount of the research involves mentally handicapped children who are compared with groups of normal children. It is then necessary to decide which group of normal children will provide the most appropriate control group. There are two major possibilities. The handicapped group can be compared with normal children of the same chronological age (CA). If this is done then the controls inevitably differ from the experimental group in general intellectual ability. Any difference between the two groups could therefore merely reflect differences in intellectual capacity rather than fundamental and permanent differences in their psychological functioning. Thus if the handicapped group had been allowed to develop to the same intellectual level as the CA matched group is now, then the difference might disappear.

The obvious control for this is to match handicapped and control groups for mental age (MA) rather than CA. It can then be argued that intellectual differences are controlled for. There are problems with MA matched controls since in matching for MA other variables then go out of alignment. The control group will necessarily be much younger than the handicapped group with the comparison possibly being contaminated by such things as the extent of background experience. This need not always act in favour of the handicapped group. For example, in a task relying on verbal skills it could be that the handicapped group, having had a long history of failure in acquiring effective language, may have shifted to non-verbal forms of communication or non-verbal forms of mediation in cognitive tasks. The much younger control group has not had this same experience of failure with language and may be more ready to make use of the linguistic skills that they have. Another difficulty with MA matching is that the same MA on the usual intelligence tests like the Stanford Binet scale may be achieved by different routes and the same MA level in the two groups may still conceal important intellectual differences.

There is no really satisfactory way out of this problem and many investigators have used both CA and MA matched controls in an attempt to cover all possibilities. It should be evident from the above discussion that even this is still not an ideal solution.

Ellis (1969) has made a careful analysis of these methodological problems and draws attention to the limitations of MA matching, many of which have already been outlined. In theory MA is matching controls for 'development'. Unfortunately 'development' can be a rather slippery concept and its possible meanings in this context are not usually examined. Ellis himself favours CA matching since this usually has greater theoretical significance for getting at the key features inherent in mental handicap. It certainly gives a clearer and less ambiguous comparison. The limitation is that it confuses the primary characteristics of the mentally handicapped with secondary effects such as the handicapped subjects' more restricted educational experience. MA matching attempts to control for certain possible contaminating factors but it is not clear for which of these, if any, it offers an adequate control.

Another and important limitation of CA matching is that there are typically very large differences in performance between the severely handicapped and their CA matched controls. This means that it is very difficult to design experiments which do not produce either floor or ceiling effects or both. This can be illustrated in the context of another point made by Baumeister (1967). Baumeister has suggested that the most appropriate comparisons between the handicapped and normal are when similar experimental manipulations of task variables are applied to the same situation for both groups. It is easiest to explain this point in the light of a hypothetical example.

Let us assume that handicapped and normal children are being compared on a task requiring the learning of some form of shape discrimination. It is a common observation that young normal children often use verbal cues in such tasks and make statements to themselves of the order 'it is always the one with the square in it'. Handicapped children typically do not make use of verbal mediation in this way despite the fact that their ordinary level of speech appears to be at an appropriate level of sophistication. An experimenter may then hypothesize that normal children learn more rapidly because they also use verbal mediation. To check on this the experiment is designed so that similar learning tasks are carried out in the normal way and with special measures designed to prompt the subjects into using verbal mediation even though they may not do so spontaneously. The prediction is then that forcing subjects to use verbal mediation will produce a much greater improvement in the handicapped group.

Let it further be assumed that results are obtained rather like those given in Figure 9 in graphical form. At first sight these certainly appear to confirm the hypothesis but this is not necessarily so. Especially if the groups are CA matched there will be a large difference in average performance levels. It could be that the normal group fail to show much improvement because of a ceiling effect, i.e. they start off at such a high level of performance that they have less room to improve under conditions that might otherwise enhance performance. If the trend in the result had been the other way with only the normal controls showing a strong effect then it might be argued that there could be a floor effect with the handicapped group not really learning well enough to provide an adequate base for the verbal mediation effect to build on. In any case there is the general point that the effect of a manipulation like forcing verbal mediation may vary as a function of the original starting level regardless of any ceiling or floor effects.

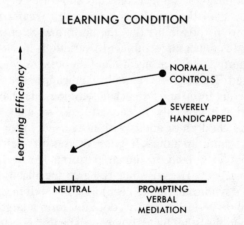

Figure 9. Results of a hypothetical experiment in which normal and severely mentally handicapped children learn shape discrimination under two experimental conditions.

This of course casts doubt on Baumeister's suggestion that the interesting comparisons are of the kind revealed in Figure 9. There is another limitation on comparisons of this kind which involve what statisticians refer to as interactions (i.e. where the effect of one variable is influenced by the state of another as in the hypothetical example being considered). This arises out of the fact that the exact measures that are used in psychological research are often arbitrary. For example, in Figure 9 the measure of learning could be the number of responses correct in a given sequence, number of trials to criterion or some mathematical transformation such as the logarithm of such measures. The data can be expressed as scores of one kind or another under both conditions or the data relating to the forced verbal mediation condition may be plotted as a proportional increase of that in the neutral condition. The apparent interaction may be considerably affected by the nature of the particular way of expressing the results that is used and may even be made to appear and disappear according to how the data is presented. This problem makes interactions of this kind exceedingly difficult to interpret. From this point of view the only interaction that can be interpreted unambiguously is when there is a cross-over in that, say, one group's performance is enhanced by the manipulation and the other is impeded. In this case the way in which the data is presented will not alter the basic picture.

Baumeister (1968) has also pointed to the fact that samples of mentally handicapped subjects typically show greater variability in performance than the normal control groups that are used. He relates this to the possibility that the performance of the mentally handicapped is much more subject to variations in such factors as attention, motivation or arousal. Another possibility also needs to be mentioned. The severely mentally handicapped are certainly not a homogeneous group and the specific aetiology may have a bearing on performance. Usually researchers use samples of severely handicapped children or adults with little concern for the specific cause of the handicap although those with sensory defects or other physical problems likely to impair performance on the task are often screened out. There is some research specifically on children with Down's syndrome (mongolism) and on children with cerebral palsy and hydrocephalus but this does not form a large part of the literature. On the other hand, it may well be that severely mentally handicapped people have more in common with one another regardless of aetiology than any of the subgroups might have with subjects of normal intelligence. Getting sizeable homogeneous groups of subjects with any but the most common syndromes (e.g. Down's syndrome) would be very difficult.

There are no satisfactory answers to those methodological

problems. In general they are avoided if Zeaman's (1965) position is adopted and interest is confined to the behaviour of the handicapped without reference to comparison groups. It is the comparison between the handicapped and the normal that is fraught with difficulty once the methodological issues are examined carefully. In practice the very fact that the differences between the handicapped and the normal are so vast means that in some cases the exact nature of the control group will make little difference.

Experimental Studies of Learning and Memory

Medical texts up to about the 1950s give the impression that the severely mentally handicapped were capable of learning very little and that they would probably have great difficulty in retaining and putting to use any skills that they did manage to learn. The early psychological experiments were directed at refuting these prejudices. The results of this research were then put into practice. At the same time the more fundamental work was extended in an attempt to analyse the exact nature of the impairments.

A not untypical early experiment is that of Tizard and Loos (1954). They used the Minnesota Spatial Relations Test which consists of four boards of more or less equal difficulty into each of which fifty-eight different shapes have to be fitted. Each board contains fifty-eight appropriately shaped holes. Eight severely mentally handicapped adults (IQ range 24 to 42) were used in the experiment and full data were obtained from four of these. Subjects had two trials per day for four days in fitting the shapes into the holes of one board as quickly as they could. They then had another eight trials on the second board, and so on until they had completed eight trials on all four boards. The mean time taken on the first trial of the first board was about twenty-three minutes. By the last trial on the first board, the time had come down to around seven minutes. Good transfer of training was shown from the first board to the second and by the final trial on the last board the mean time had come down to something of the order of four minutes.

The results of this experiment show the extremely poor starting levels of such subjects on the task (twenty-three minutes as opposed to rather less than five minutes for normal subjects on the first trial), a dramatic learning effect with practice and good transfer from one board to the next. In addition, Tizard and Loos retested their subjects one month later in order to look at long-term retention by giving a further single trial on each board. These later trials showed considerable retention, giving a mean time of little less than six and a half minutes. Other early research gave similar results (e.g. Clarke and Hermelin, 1955), thus confirming the suggestions made by Tizard and Loos's study.

Early work of this kind found application in the setting up of industrial workshops in institutions for the mentally handicapped. Just as the severely mentally handicapped could be trained up to fairly normal levels of performance on a rather complex perceptual motor task like the Minnesota Spatial Relations Test, so they could be trained to carry out semi-skilled industrial assembly work. This even included such things as soldering components for TV sets (this was in the days before the extensive use of transistors and integrated circuits made the soldering of relatively large components like valves redundant). Again the severely mentally handicapped had extremely poor starting levels and took a long time to train. Special highly structured training programmes were also needed in which the final task was carefully broken down into simple steps to be taught one at a time. Nevertheless, as in the experimental work, the final level of performance was good and, once learned, the skills were retained quite well.

From the point of view of a more fundamental interest in the processes involved the next question that emerges is, what is the basis for the learning impairment in severe mental handicap? This is difficult to define with any certainty but a number of interesting lines of research have emerged. A classic series of experiments was reported by Zeaman and House (1963). These authors carried out a series of experiments with severely mentally handicapped children using discrimination learning in a modification of the Wisconsin General Test Apparatus originally used by Harlow (1949) and others for similar kinds of research with monkeys. Basically House and Zeaman used two-choice discrimination learning where detection of the correct stimulus was reinforced by the subject obtaining a small sweet (e.g. a 'smartie').

The results of an initial experiment are shown in Figure 10. This suggests that the mentally handicapped subjects start to learn fairly early on in the training sequence but then learn very slowly indeed so that it takes a considerable time for them to reach criterion. This contrasts with the performance of normal children on a similar task. Normal children would show a typical ogival learning curve with very much more rapid learning.

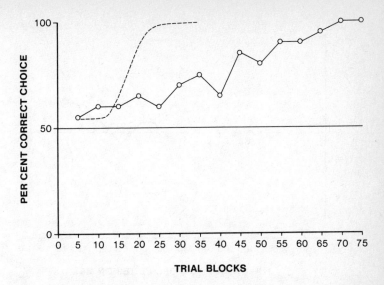

Figure 10. A group average learning curve for learning a two choice discrimination task. The 50 per cent mark is the score which would be expected by chance. The handicapped group are shown with a solid line. The impression gained from the figure is that they learn rather slowly. The dotted line gives some hypothetical results for a group of non-handicapped subjects.

The data in Figure 10 has been averaged in the usual kind of way (i.e. the points on the curve being given by the average number of trials correct in the first block, second block, and so on). Such averaging however can produce a picture that is not at all typical of any individual subject. Hayes (1953) has suggested the use of 'backward learning curves'. Here the anchor point for the curve is the block of trials on which each subject reached criterion. The next point to the left is the average number of correct responses for each subject on the trial preceding the one at which criterion was reached, and so on. To do this with the data under consideration reveals a curve like that shown in Figure 11. This curve is rather dissimilar to that in Figure 10 and is more typical of the performance of individual subjects. What seems to happen is that subjects respond more or less at chance level for a period and then start to learn. Once they start to learn they learn very rapidly, when their learning curve starts to look very much like normal subjects' curve over this later period.

Zeaman and House (1963) developed an attentional model to explain their data. Specifically they propose that learning on a task like this proceeds in two stages. Firstly, the subject has to learn

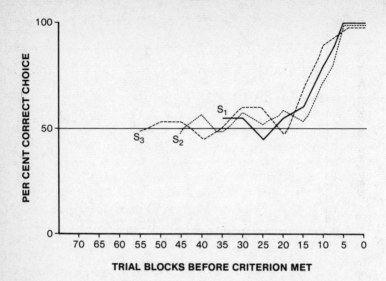

Figure 11. In this figure the data from three hypothetical subjects (S₁, S₂, S₃) are displayed. It can be seen that each subject begins by responding at a chance level and then learns reasonably rapidly. In this figure the data has been plotted backwards from the point where the learning criterion was met. It can be seen that S_1 took fewer trials to learn than S_2 or S_3. Also, it is clear that once a subject begins to learn he learns with relative rapidity.

which stimulus dimension to attend to. If the stimuli to be discriminated vary in shape, size and colour and change randomly from trial to trial, but with the blue stimulus always being rewarded rather than the red, then subjects have to identify that colour is the stimulus dimension which they need to take note of. Once this stage has been reached they then need to learn the correct cue (e.g. blue) within that dimension. Under these circumstances responding will be essentially random until the correct dimension has been identified. Learning will then show up at the stage of learning the correct cue and this progresses very rapidly. Essentially similar backward-learning curves in two-choice discrimination learning with a long period of responding at chance levels followed by rapid learning have been obtained by Ellis *et al.* (1982) for the most profoundly handicapped subjects (with mean measured IQs of below 10). What appears to differentiate subjects is not the speed of learning once learning starts to occur but the length of time spent at chance levels of responding prior to the occurrence of significant levels of a detectable learning. Thus in Zeaman and House's (1963) model it is the first, or attentional stage, that is the source of the learning difficulty in mental handicap.

Zeaman and House (1963) have further elaborated their basic model in a mathematical form which has enabled them to carry out experiments whereby the performance of real mentally handicapped children can be compared with that of computer-based predictions derived from the theory (the performance of so-called 'stat-children'). Many of these experiments were based on transfer designs using both extra- and intradimensional shifts. Space does not permit the further elaboration of the work described in their 1963 paper. One of the suggestions emerging from this work is that mentally handicapped children are only able to attend to one of the many possible stimulus dimensions in the situation or, at best, to very few of them.

More recently Zeaman and House (1979) have updated their model. In this later paper they present a number of lines of evidence that was difficult for their initial attentional theory to cope with. For example, certain of their experimental manipulations appeared to place considerable demands on short-term memory and these revealed signs of additional short-term memory deficits. An important feature of the attentional model as proposed by Zeaman and House (1963) is that attention to particular stimulus dimensions precedes responding to specific cues. Even within a given stimulus dimension (e.g. brightness) the length of the period of chance level responding, which theoretically relates to learning to attend to the right dimension, was influenced by the particular cues that were used (i.e. black and white as opposed to two shades of grey). This finding of Shepp and Zeaman (1966) is not predictable on the basis of the early model.

In consequence Zeaman and House (1979) have chosen to extend their original theory by including such things as some features from Atkinson and Shiffrin's (1969) retention model. They have chosen to refer to this new model as 'attention-retention theory'. Rather than follow this rather complex model with its long chain of argument which only deals with a very restricted range of behaviours (those encompassed by simple discrimination learning), it seems more sensible in this chapter to pick up the newly introduced concept of retention, or memory, to examine in a different context.

One prominent proposal to explain the difficulties of the severely mentally handicapped has been that they have a deficiency in short-term memory (Ellis, 1963). In particular the Ellis model proposed that the stimulus trace was attenuated in amplitude and duration. This particular model has spawned more research than most other models within this field.

One of the most extensive examinations of the Ellis (1963) trace decay model has been provided by Holden (1971). Holden has described a series of experiments which have all been based around the same general experimental procedure. The subject is faced by a two-dimensional array of lights so arranged that he cannot actually see how many lights are available. The subject is just aware of each light as it is lit and is seen on a screen placed in front of the array. The lights can then be lit, one at a time, in a sequence that can trace the outline of a letter 'P', or a triangle, or some such similar kind of shape. The experimenter can also manipulate the time that each individual light is on and the time interval between each light.

In general the results failed to support the notion that the mentally handicapped suffer from a rapid decay of traces in short-term memory. For example, if the hypothesis was correct then increasing the time interval between successive lights should make identification of the shape outlined relatively more difficult for handicapped subjects compared with the situation where this time interval is zero or very short. Such an effect was not found.

On the other hand Ellis (1970) modified his position with regard to the nature of the memory impairment in mental handicap. In another extensive series of experiments reported in the 1970 paper he had an apparatus with a horizontal row of small circular screens on to each of which a visual stimulus (usually a digit) could be projected. The experimental procedure involved projecting a stimulus on to each of these screens in sequence running from left to right with one stimulus being removed before the next was shown. At the end of the sequence a stimulus corresponding to one of those already shown was projected on to a further small screen set above the rest. The subject's task was simply to press the screen that originally showed the stimulus on this further screen. Obviously a large number of parameters can be manipulated within this general experimental procedure. Normal subjects typically show a serial position effect in that it is easiest to identify the stimuli that occurred at either the beginning or the end of the list, with those in the middle causing the least accurate responding.

Ellis (1970) further assumes that two separate memory processes are required to account for the serial position effect. Stimuli presented last are easy to identify because they can be recalled from primary memory. The first few stimuli manage to get processed by a 'rehearsal strategy' and thereby get transferred from primary memory to the rather more stable secondary memory. These can

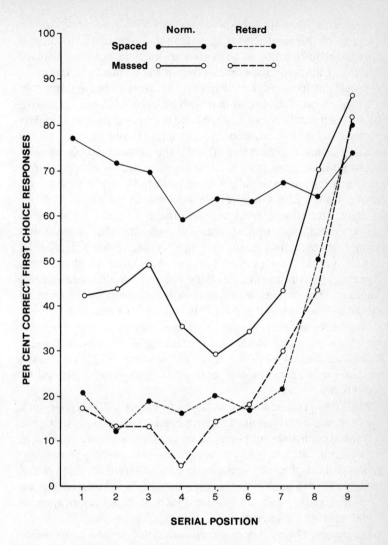

Figure 12. Performance of normals and retardates under massed (0.0-second interitem interval) and spaced (2.0-second interitem interval) conditions on the 9-position task.

then easily be identified from secondary memory. Stimuli in the middle of the sequence presumably get lost because they fade from primary memory before they can be transferred to secondary memory. This model is comparable to that advanced by Glanzer and Cunitz (1966) to account for the free recall of lists of words.

In general the results obtained by Ellis (1970) and interpreted on the basis of this model do suggest that the mentally handicapped have problems relating to secondary memory rather than primary memory. Ellis further speculates that this is because of a failure of rehearsal mechanisms. To cite but one line of evidence in support of this conclusion, Ellis found that with no delay between successive stimuli both mentally handicapped and normal subjects had similarly enhanced identification of the last items in the list (i.e. similar primary memory effects) but only the normal group showed increased identification of the first items, suggesting little information was reaching secondary memory in the handicapped group. On the basis of Ellis's theoretical model it would be expected that if the inter-stimulus interval was increased then this should give subjects additional opportunities to pass the first few stimuli through to secondary memory and so enhance identification of items from the first part of the list. As Figure 12 shows, this happened for the normal controls but not for the handicapped subjects. This implies a problem in transferring information to secondary memory and presumably rehearsal mechanisms.

One problem with this series of experiments is that the basic model of memory on which the whole edifice is built has come under attack (see Baddeley, 1976; Craik and Lockhart, 1972). This makes for caution in accepting the particular interpretations offered by Ellis (1970).

Some more recent work (e.g. Baumeister *et al.*, 1984; Nettelbeck and McLean, 1984) has used experimental techniques involving the very rapid tachistoscopic presentation of material in order to look in more detail at the earliest stages of information-processing. Although both the cited experiments use different techniques and relate their work to different theoretical models, both agree that the mentally handicapped are impaired in their initial registration of stimuli and in the initial processing of this information.

Detterman (1979) has provided a detailed review of evidence relating to memory disturbances in mental handicap. In line with the very small sample of the extensive research in this field that has been described here, Detterman concludes that the best evidence of impairments arises from studies implicating perceptual/attentional processes and rehearsal mechanisms. He does not rule out the possibility of effects relating to other aspects of the overall memory process, including primary and short-term memory. It is just that the evidence with regard to perception/attention and rehearsal is by far the most convincing. As a very general rule it is also true to say that the evidence for impairment in learning and memory is least strong with regard to long-term memory. The basic problem seems to lie in getting information properly established in long-term memory rather than in its rapid loss once so established. Nevertheless an increased rate of forgetting in long-term storage is by no means excluded.

This discussion of learning and memory in the mentally handicapped can be concluded with a further methodological caveat. In discussing the then available evidence on possible memory impairments in mental handicap, Belmont (1966) held that the ideal experiment to test for memory impairments in the handicapped needed to take into account three basic principles. Firstly, the level of learning as assessed by probability of correct performance must be equated for all subjects. This is because retention is influenced by the degree of original learning. Secondly, the highest level of performance attained during acquisition or learning must be below the maximum level of performance. This is to ensure that overlearning does not take place to a greater degree in one group than another, since overlearning can influence later retention without showing any change in level of performance during learning. Finally, Belmont pointed out that there must be a criterion against which later retention can be judged. This criterion consists of an indication of what subjects would have achieved had the retention interval been zero. This permits change in performance over time to be evaluated in a way that is uncontaminated with other possible effects.

Very few studies indeed match up to these criteria. One is that of Klausmeier *et al.* (1959), and this showed no long-term memory deficit in mentally handicapped subjects compared with normals.

Comment

Mental handicap is an area that raises a number of fascinating psychological problems and where the experimental analysis of the impairments can lead to practical application. It is undoubtedly the case that the care of the severely mentally handicapped has improved dramatically since about 1950, and it is now possible to help them to live a far more normal and independent life than was previously conceived possible. As in all social change, the causes of these improvements are multiple. Nevertheless, the study of learning processes in the mentally handicapped and the application of the knowledge gained has been a major factor.

Applied behaviour analysis (ABA or operant learning) has proved to be very effective when applied to mental handicap. The procedures of ABA include many features which from the discussion of learning in the mentally handicapped would be expected to facilitate learning. For example, tasks to be learned are first subjected to analysis to break them into smaller subtasks. This procedure ensures that there is a greater probability that the person will attend to the immediately relevant stimulus dimensions. Another procedure, backward chaining, arranges teaching so that the person starts with a high probability of successfully completing the task and receiving reinforcement. For example, in learning to tie a shoelace the actions required can be broken down into a series of discrete events: the initial crossing of the laces, putting one lace under the other, and so on until the final step consists of passing one loop through a hole and pulling the loops tight. In teaching a mentally handicapped person to do this, one would start with the final step of pulling the loop through. Careful teaching of this nature will enable even quite severely handicapped persons to acquire some measure of autonomy and independence.

Although mental handicap can be regarded as one area of success for applied experimental psychology, there are still many gaps in our understanding of the associated psychological problems. In general, research indicates that the problem lies largely at the input end of the system (i.e. in registration and initial learning) rather than long-term retention and retrieval. However, these latter aspects are less well explored and it could be that there are problems in these aspects of the overall process as well. As has been indicated, resolution of many of the questions will also depend upon a closer attention to the methodological issues surrounding research in this field.

Finally, it can be noted that many of the leading authorities in the field (e.g. A. D. B. Clarke and A. M. Clarke, 1977) are continually pointing out that what has been achieved so far indicates that the potential of the severely mentally handicapped is still in excess of what is commonly achieved in practice even in the better services for this client group. Not only are there gaps in knowledge, but what is known is often not put into practice as quickly as it might be, and sometimes not even at all.

16 Concluding Discussion

This book has attempted to describe the main questions that arise in investigating abnormal behaviour and the ways in which this behaviour might be modified. As was explained at the beginning, the aim was to concentrate on these questions and the ways in which they can be answered or resolved. Certain disorders and approaches to treatment were used as examples in this endeavour. The hope is that the reader will have picked up something in the way of general principles that can be used in answering the same sorts of questions in relation to other disorders and modes of treatment. Anything approaching a comprehensive coverage of either disorders or methods of treatment has not been possible within the space available.

Although certain conceptual and methodological strands run through abnormal psychology, and it is right that these should be pointed out in an introductory text, it is also important to remember that the field has considerable heterogeneity when viewed from other perspectives. Abnormal psychology encompasses a very wide range of phenomena. More than almost any other area of psychology it has been subjected to a vast range of different kinds of approaches and explanatory models. These in turn relate to a number of very different assumptions about the fundamental nature of the basic phenomena. In general there is an assumption that much of what is considered 'abnormal' is also in some way or other undesirable. This makes the direct manipulation or modification of abnormal behaviour an important issue. This issue of manipulation or 'treatment' does not arise in the same way for the experimental psychologist studying behaviour presumed to be 'normal'. An extremely large number of different forms of treatment for behavioural abnormalities have been proposed, many of which are mutually contradictory in terms of their underlying assumptions.

These points are not introduced at this stage with the intention of leaving the reader thoroughly confused. However, they do indicate the need to set the material covered by this book in a wider and more general context. This final and brief chapter is written with this in mind.

The range of phenomena

The phenomena that form the basis of abnormal psychology are extremely diverse. This book has only managed to touch in any detail upon a small sample of the abnormalities that could have been covered. The phenomena associated with depression and schizophrenia have been described in some detail. Other things like headache and mental handicap have been dealt with to some degree. Neurotic disorders, like phobias and obsessional states, have been touched upon in passing but not considered in any systematic way as problems in their own right. Many of the disorders listed in Table 1 and mentioned in the accompanying discussion in Chapter 2 have been more or less ignored.

   Some of these disorders can be quite bizarre and are very difficult to explain satisfactorily. One of these is the condition referred to as 'conversion hysteria'. Here the patient exhibits apparently physical symptoms, such as paralysis or sensory loss, which cannot be adequately understood in terms of any known physical disorder or physiological mechanism. In some instances it is even possible to demonstrate that the allegedly affected bodily system can indeed function normally. For example, Grosz and Zimmerman (1965) studied a subject with hysterical blindness who claimed to be unable to see at all. They asked their subject to participate in what they claimed was a sight retraining exercise. They asked him to 'look at' an array of three stimuli and to press a button to indicate which was the odd one out. Their subject consistently produced scores that were well below chance levels of performance, thus indicating that he must have been using visual information in order to ensure that he did not achieve the third correct responses that would be expected by chance. This finding was repeated by Miller (1968) with another subject 'blind' in one eye as a result of a fairly trivial industrial accident when using only the affected eye. Of course, it can always be claimed that the patient is consciously dissimilating and faking his symptoms. This is difficult to prove conclusively and may well be the case in a good number of instances. Nevertheless, most authorities that have considered the problem in any detail remain convinced that at least some cases they study are not deliberately faking. Merskey (1979) has provided a review of the topic of hysteria.

In addition to the functional disorders are a whole range of abnormalities that can be encountered in people with damage to, or disease of the brain. Focal lesions of the brain can produce some fascinating phenomena. To give but one example, neurological patients with lesions in the posterior parts of the right hemisphere sometimes show 'hemispatial neglect'. They tend to respond less readily to stimuli coming from the contralateral (i.e. left) side and in extreme cases may totally ignore such stimuli. Thus the nurse who approaches from the left side of the patient's bed is ignored whilst the same nurse approaching from the right side is responded to normally.

Because neglect, especially in its more severe forms, is often associated with a left hemianopia (i.e. loss of vision in the left half of the visual fields), it has often been assumed that neglect is simply a consequence of sensory loss for stimulation coming from the affected side. On the other hand, milder forms of neglect can occur in the absence of demonstrable field defects which suggests that the phenomena is not purely sensory. This can be countered by arguing that minimal degrees of sensory loss might not be detected by conventional tests of sensory awareness but still show up as mild neglect. This issue was resolved by a very elegant set of experiments by Bisiach *et al.* (1979). Essentially what these authors did was to demonstrate that subjects with neglect due to right-sided brain lesions did not fully appreciate the variation in pattern on the left sides of standard objects even though the stimuli were not viewed in the left parts of the visual field that might be affected by any minimal sensory loss. Also, they could make accurate judgements about the right sides of these same objects when viewed in the same position in the visual fields. The work of Bisiach and his colleagues indicates that the phenomenon is not purely sensory and must involve a lack of appreciation of the left half of space that operates at a more cognitive level. Just what is involved at this higher level is very difficult to say. Introductory accounts of neuropsychological disorders can be found in Beaumont (1983) and Heilman and Valenstein (1979).

Most other texts on abnormal psychology try to give a much more extensive and even-handed coverage of the various disorders than we have managed in this book even though this means a less detailed discussion of some of the issues that we have dealt with. For the reader who would like to consult an introductory text with a more comprehensive account of the different disorders then the book by Davison and Neale (1982) is recommended.

The range of approaches

If the phenomena encompassed by the field of abnormal psychology are very varied then this heterogeneity is well matched by the wide range of explanatory models that have been employed. As the account of work on depression (Chapters 3 to 7) has indicated, theoretical approaches based at every possible level of explanation between genetics and biochemistry, on the one hand, and social influences on the other, have been utilized. To this can be added the ideas put forward in some circles to the effect that the kinds of approach taken in this book are not only all equally wrong but based on a complete misconception of the nature of the basic phenomena. For adherents to this latter point of view (which presumably could not be applied to people with neuropsychological impairments or severe mental handicap), any concentration on problems that might exist within the individual, at whatever level of explanation, is entirely misplaced. The real problem lies in society and the individual's behaviour is a response to a form of 'pathology' which exists within the structure of the society of which the individual forms a part.

Even if consideration is restricted to psychological models, there is still a degree of heterogeneity that can sometimes be uncomfortable. At one extreme are models derived from psychodynamic principles involving internal psychic processes. At the other are those based on operant conditioning which regard abnormal behaviour as being under the control of reinforcers (or sometimes the lack of reinforcers) just like any laboratory rat's bar-pressing responses. Not only are there very varied psychological models but their exact status is often open to question. The cognitive theories of depression (see Chapter 6) were put forward largely as if they were causal accounts of how and why some people come to be depressed. If our analysis of these models is anything like correct then they do not fare well as causal explanations. They emerge much better when regarded as functional models giving an account of the operation of disturbed cognitive processes in depressed people and leaving aside the question as to how these cognitive processes come to be as they are.

The extreme variety of the basic phenomena coupled with the **heterogeneity** of the possible factors that may need to be taken into account can be very confusing. Some appear to react to this by defending one particular level of analysis, whether it be bio-chemical, behavioural, psychoanalytic or social, to the death and by assuming that their favoured form of analysis will eventually be shown to explain more or less everything. It seems to us not at all unlikely that such varied phenomena may have very varied explanations and that anything from genetics to social pressures or influences might have an impact on at least some aspects of abnormal behaviour. As has been emphasized earlier, to allow that genetic factors might play a part in predisposing some individuals towards developing depression is not to deny that other kinds of factors, psychological, biochemical or social, could operate; nor is it to claim that genetic influences are of significance for all manifest-ations of abnormal behaviour. For example, there is no evidence that hysterical conversion symptoms are genetically transmitted. Being prepared to consider all the possible influences is much more likely to result in a balanced picture than a rigid commitment to one type of explanatory model.

Another possibility, that may not have attracted the attention that it deserves, is that some abnormalities, like depression or paranoid schizophrenia, may not always have the same cause although the behavioural features are very similar. Thus the features that form the common clinical picture could be the final common pathway of a number of different causal mechanisms that can act relatively independently. Thus depression in a few indi-viduals may be the almost inevitable consequence of a heavy genetic predisposition or a biochemical abnormality. In others it might be the response to a series of adverse life events or experiences which bias the individual's cognitive style towards the internal, global and stable attributions postulated by Seligman and his colleagues. This kind of complication has been raised in the past, by Ni Bhrolchain (1979) for example, but has rarely been taken into account in any systematic way in studies of possible causal influences.

The varied types of treatment

If the clinical phenomena are varied and demand a wide range of explanatory models then it hardly seems surprising that the proposed methods of treatment should also be very varied. The main schools of thought with regard to psychological forms of treatment were described in Chapters 8 and 9. These are of course

just the main themes, with each being subject to many developments and adaptations in the hands of different authorities. Even
then the accounts given do not touch upon a multitude of other
treatment methods that have been proposed. It is possible to go
through the literature on psychological treatments and list quite
literally hundreds of names purporting to describe different forms
of psychotherapy. Whether the critical observer is really able to
detect any significant difference between all of them is open to
question, but exotic terms like 'gestalt therapy', 'neurolinguistic
programming' and 'family sculpting' abound.

As Chapters 8 to 12 have shown, the issues surrounding the
development and evaluation of treatments are quite complex. Two
very general conclusions seem to have some justification. One is
that at least some forms of psychological treatment do appear to
yield a degree of therapeutic benefit. The second is that where the
mechanisms by which this effect is obtained have been investigated
these remain more or less obscure. Treatments do not emerge as
being effective for the reasons that inspired their development in
the first place and systematic desensitization is a good example of
this. It still remains very difficult to finally silence the critic who
argues that psychological treatments work by means of 'non-
specific' effects such as by inducing an expectancy of change.
Despite this, it is also true that, from a practical point of view
concerned with treating patients, there is no doubt that considerable strides have been made over the past twenty to thirty years in
the treatment of problems by psychological means.

Final comment

Given this general situation it is not surprising that the field of
abnormal psychology is one in which there is not an overabundance
of certainties and where considerable controversies exist over
almost every significant issue. This may result in some confusion
and difficulty for the student encountering the field for the first time.
On the other hand, it represents a considerable challenge for the
investigator.

The authors of this book hope that the reader who has persevered
so far will not be left in too confused a state and will have acquired a
firm base from which to explore the more controversial aspects. In
fact they go beyond this and anticipate that the reader will not be
satisfied with the far-sightedness, perspicacity and wisdom of the

views expressed in the preceding chapters but will relish the prospect of further controversy.

Bibliography

Abraham, K. (1911) Notes on the psychoanalytic investigation and treatment of manic-depressive insanity and allied conditions. In *Selected Papers on Psycho-Analysis*, 137–56. Hogarth Press: London.

Abraham, K. (1916) The pregenital stage of the libido. In *Selected Papers on Psycho-Analysis*, 248–79. Hogarth Press: London.

Abraham, K. (1924) A short study of the development of the libido, viewed in the light of mental disorders. In *Selected Papers on Psycho-Analysis*, 243–54. Hogarth Press: London.

Abramson, L. Y., Seligman, M. E. P. and Teasdale, J. D. (1978) Learned helplessness in humans: Critique and reformulation. *Journal of Abnormal Psychology*, 87, 49–74.

Alder, M. R. (1974) Self poisoning: what is the future? *Lancet*, 1, 1040–43.

Alexander, F. (1950) *Psychosomatic Medicine: Its Principles and Applications*. New York: Norton.

Altman, J. H. and Wittenborn, J. R. (1980) Depression-prone personality in women. *Journal of Abnormal Psychology*, 89, 303–8.

American Psychiatric Association (1980) *Diagnostic and Statistical Manual of Mental Disorders – DSM III*, 3rd edn, APA: Washington DC.

Anderson, L., Dancis, J. and Alpert, M. (1978) Behavioural contingencies and self-mutilation in Lesch-Nyhan disease. *Journal of Consulting and Clinical Psychology*, 46, 529–36.

Andrasik, F., Blanchard, E. B., Arena, J. G., Saunders, N. L. and Barron, K. D. (1982) Psychophysiology of recurrent headache. The methodological issues and new empirical findings. *Behaviour Therapy*, 13, 407–29.

Andreasen, N. C. (1982) Concepts, diagnosis and classification. In E. S. Paykel (ed.) *Handbook of Affective Disorders*. Churchill Livingstone: Edinburgh.

Andreasen, N. C., Grove, W. and Maurer, R. (1980) Cluster analysis and the definition of depression. *British Journal of Psychiatry*, 137, 256–65.

Andreasen, N. C. and Pfohl, B. (1976) Linguistic analysis of speech in affective disorders. *Archives of General Psychiatry*, 33, 1361–7.

Andreasen, N. C. and Winokur, G. (1979) Newer experimental methods for classification of depression. *Archives of General Psychiatry*, 36, 447–52.

Andrews, G. (1981) A prospective study of life events and psychological symptoms. *Psychological Medicine*, 11, 179–81.

Andrews, J. G. and Harvey, R. (1981) Does psychotherapy benefit neurotic patients? A re-analysis of the Smith, Glass and Miller data. *Archives of General Psychiatry*, *38*, 951–62.

Appenzeller, O., Davison, K. and Marshall, J. (1963) Reflex vasomotor abnormalities in the hands of migrainous subjects. *Journal of Neurology, Neurosurgery and Psychiatry*, *26*, 447–50.

Arfwidsson, L., D'Elia, G., Laurell, B., Ottosson, T. O., Perrig, C. and Persson, G. (1974) Can self rating replace doctors' rating in evaluating antidepressive treatment? *Acta Psychiatric Scandinavia*, *50*, 16–22.

Argyle, M. (1969) *Social Interaction*. Methuen: London.

Atkinson, R. C. and Shiffrin, R. M. (1969) Human memory: a proposed system and its central processes. In K. W. Spence and J. T. Spence (eds) *The Psychology of Learning and Motivation: Advances in Research and Theory*, vol. 2. Academic Press: New York.

Ayllon, T. and Azrin, N. H. (1968) *The token economy: a motivational system for therapy and rehabilitation*. Appleton-Century-Crofts: New York.

Baddeley, A. D. (1976) *The Psychology of Memory*. Harper & Row: New York.

Baddeley, A. D. and Hitch, G. (1974) Working memory. In G. A. Bower (ed.) *The Psychology of Learning and Motivation*, vol. 8. Academic Press: New York.

Bakal, D. A. (1982) *The Psychobiology of Chronic Headache*. Springer: New York.

Bakal, D. A. and Kaganov, J. A. (1977) Muscle contraction and migraine headache: psychophysiologic comparisons. *Headache*, *17*, 285–9.

Baller, W. R., Charles, D. C. and Miller, E. L. (1967) Mid-life attainments of the mentally retarded: a longitudinal study. *Genetic Psychology Monographs*, *75*, 235–329.

Bandura, A. (1977) Self-efficacy: toward a unifying theory of behaviour change. *Psychological Review*, *84*, 191–215.

Bandura, A., Adams, N. E., Hardy, A. B. and Howells, G. N. (1980) Tests of the generality of self-efficacy theory. *Cognitive Therapy and Research*, *4*, 39–66.

Bandura, A., Blanchard, E. B. and Ritter, B. (1969) The relative efficacy of desensitization and modelling approaches for inducing behavioural affective and cognitive changes. *Journal of Personality and Social Psychology*, *13*, 173–99.

Barlow, D. H., Hayes, S. C. and Nelson, R. O. (1984) *The Scientist as Practitioner: Research and Accountability in Clinical and Educational Settings*. Pergamon: New York.

Baumeister, A. A. (1967) Problems in comparative studies of mental retardates and normals. *American Journal of Mental Deficiency*, *71*, 869–75.

Baumeister, A. A. (1968) Behavioural inadequacy and variability of performance. *American Journal of Mental Deficiency*, *73*, 477–83.

Baumeister, A. A., Runcie, D. and Gardepe, J. (1984) Processing of information in iconic memory: differences between non retarded and retarded subjects. *Journal of Abnormal Psychology*, *93*, 433–47.

Beaumont, J. G. (1983) *An Introduction to Neuropsychology*. Blackwell: Oxford.

Beck, A. T. (1961) A systematic investigation of depression. *Comprehensive Psychiatry*, *2*, 163–70.

Beck, A. T. (1967) *Depression: Clinical Experimental and Theoretical Aspects*. Hoeber: New York.

Beck, A. T. (1976) *Cognitive Therapy and the Emotional Disorders*. International Universities Press: New York.

Beck, A. T., Shaw, A. J., Bush, B. F. and Emery, G. (1979) *Cognitive Therapy of Depression*. Wiley: New York.

Beck, A. T., Ward, C. H., Mendelson, M., Mock, J. E. and Erbaugh, J. K. (1962) Reliability of psychiatric diagnosis. *American Journal of Psychiatry*, *119*, 351–7.

Beiser, M. (1976) Personal and social factors associated with the remission of psychiatric symptoms. *Archives of General Psychiatry*, *33*, 941–5.

Bellack, A. S., Hersen, M. and Turner, S. M. (1978) Validity of role play tests. Are they valid? *Behaviour Therapy*, *9*, 448–61.

Belmont, J. M. (1966) Long term memory in mental retardation. In N. R. Ellis (ed.) *International Review of Research in Mental Retardation*, vol. 1. Academic Press: New York.

Bentin, S., Silverbeck, R. and Gordon, H. W. (1981) Asymmetrical cognitive retardation in demented and Parkinsonian patients. *Cortex*, *17*, 533–44.

Bergin, A. E. and Lambert, M. J. (1978) The evaluation of the therapeutic outcome. In S. L. Garfield and A. E. Bergin (eds) *Handbook of Psychotherapy and Behavior Change: An Empirical Analysis*, 2nd edn. New York: Wiley.

Bernstein, D. A. and Neitzel M. T. (1977) Demand characteristics in behaviour modification. The natural history of a nuisance. *Progress in Behaviour Modification*, *4*, 119–62.

Berrios, G. E. (1981) Delirium and confusion in the 19th century. A conceptual history. *British Journal of Psychiatry*, *139*, 439–49.

Berrios, G. E. (1983) The convulsive therapies. In G. E. Berrios and J. H. Dowson (eds) *Treatment and Management in Adult Psychiatry*. Baillière Tindall: London.

Berrios, G. E. and Dowson, J. H. (eds) (1983) *Treatment and Management in Adult Psychiatry*. Baillière Tindall: London.

Bihldorf, J. P., King, S. H. and Parnes, L. R. (1971) Psychological factors in headache. *Headache*, *11*, 117–27.

Bilsbury, C. and Morley, S. (1979) Obsessional slowness: a meticulous replication. *Behaviour Research and Therapy*, *17*, 405–8.

Binney, W. E. and Murphy, D. L. (1973) The behavioral switch process in psychopathology. In J. Mendels (ed.) *Biological Psychiatry*. Wiley: New York.

Birch, H. G., Richardson, S. A., Baird, D., Horobin, G. and Illsley, R. (1970) *Mental Subnormality in the Community: A Clinical and Epidemiological Study*. Williams & Wilkins: Baltimore.

Birley, J. L. T. and Brown, G. N. (1970) Crises and life changes preceding the onset or relapse of acute schizophrenia: clinical aspects. *British Journal of Psychiatry*, *116*, 327–33.

Bisiach, E., Luzatti, C. and Perani, D. (1979) Unilateral neglect, representational schema and consciousness. *Brain*, *102*, 609–18.

Blackburn, I. M. (1974) The pattern of hostility in depressive illness. *British Journal of Psychiatry*, *125*, 141–5.

Blackburn, I. M., Bishop, S., Glen, I. M., Whalley, L. J. and Christie, J. E. (1981) The efficacy of cognitive therapy in depression: a treatment trial using cognitive therapy and pharmacotherapy, each alone and in combination. *British Journal of Psychiatry*, *139*, 181–9.

Blanchard, E. B. and Andrasik, F. (1982) Psychological assessment and treatment of headache: recent developments and emerging issues. *Journal of Consulting and Clinical Psychology*, *50*, 859–79.

Blanchard, E. B., Andrasik, F., Ahles, T. A., Teders, S. J. and O'Keefe, D. (1980) Migraine and tension headache: a meta analytic review. *Behaviour Therapy*, *11*, 613–31.

Blanchard, E. B., Theobald, D. E., Williamson, D. A., Silver, B. V. and Brown, D. A. (1978) Temperature biofeedback in the treatment of migraine headaches. *Archives of General Psychiatry*, *35*, 581–8.

Blaxter, M. (1978) Diagnosis as category and process: the case of alcoholism. *Social Science*, *12*, 9–17.

Bloch, S. (1982) *What is Psychotherapy?* Oxford University Press: Oxford.

Borkovec, T. D. (1973) The role of expectancy and physiological feedback in fear research: a review with special reference to subject characteristics. *Behaviour Therapy*, *4*, 491–505.

Borkovec, T. D. (1974) Heart rate process during systematic desensitization and implosive therapy for analog anxiety. *Behavior Therapy*, *4*, 636–41.

Borkovec, T. D. (1978) Self efficacy: cause or reflection of behavioural change. *Advances in Behaviour Therapy and Research*, *1*, 163–70.

Borkovec, T. D. and Nau, S. D. (1972) Credibility of analogue therapy rationales. *Journal of Behaviour Therapy and Experimental Psychiatry*, *3*, 257–60.

Borkovec, T. D. and O'Brien, G. T. (1976) Methodological and target behavior issues in analogue therapy outcome research. In M. Hersen, R. M. Eisler and P. M. Miller (eds) *Progress in Behavior Modification*, *3*. Academic Press: New York.

Borkovec, T. D. and Rachman, S. (1979) The utility of analogue research. *Behaviour Research and Therapy*, *17*, 253–62.

Borkovec, T. D. and Sides, J. K. (1979) Critical procedure variables related to the physiological effects of progressive relaxation: a review. *Behaviour Research and Therapy*, *17*, 119–26.

Boudewyns, P. A. and Shipley, R. H. (1983) *Flooding and Implosive Therapy: Direct Therapeutic Exposure in Clinical Practice*. Plenum Press: New York.

Boyd, C. J. and Weissman, M. M. (1982) Epidemiology. In E. S. Paykel (ed.) *Handbook of Affective Disorders*. Churchill Livingstone: Edinburgh.

Brandon S. (1981) The history of shock treatment. In R. L. Palmer (ed.) *Electroconvulsive therapy: An appraisal.* Oxford University Press: Oxford.

Braukman, C. J. and Fixen, D. L. (1975) Behavior modification with delinquents. *Progress in Behavior Modification*, *1*, 191–234.

Briscoe, C. W. and Smith, J. B. (1975) Depression in bereavement and divorce. *Archives of General Psychiatry*, *32*, 439–43.

Brown, G. W. and Birley, J. L. T. (1968) Crises and life changes and the onset of schizophrenia. *Journal of Health and Social Behaviour*, *9*, 203–14.

Brown, G. W., Birley, J. L. T. and Wing, J. K. (1972) Influence of family life on the course of schizophrenic disorders: a replication. *British Journal of Psychiatry*, *121*, 241–58.

Brown, G. W. and Harris, T. (1978) *The Social Origins of Depression.* Tavistock: London.

Brown, G. W., Monck, E., Carstairs, G. M. and Wing, J. K. (1962) *British Journal of Preventive and Social Medicine*, *16*, 55–68.

Brown, G. W. and Prudo, R. (1981) Psychiatric disorders in a rural and an urban population: 1. Aetiology of depression. *Psychological Medicine*, *11*, 581–99.

Brown, G. W., Sklair, F., Harris, T. and Birley, J. L. T. (1973) Life events and psychiatric disorder: 2. Some methodological issues. *Psychological Medicine*, *3*, 74–8.

Budzynski, T. H., Stoyva, J. M., Adler, C. S. and Mullaney, D. J. (1973) EMG Biofeedback and tension headache: a controlled outcome study. *Psychosomatic Medicine*, *35*, 484–96.

Buss, A. H. and Lang, P. J. (1965) Psychological deficit in schizophrenia: I. affect, reinforcement and concept attainment. *Journal of Abnormal Psychology*, *70*, 2–24.

Byrne, D. G. (1981) Sex differences in the reporting of symptoms in the general population. *British Journal of Clinical Psychology*, *20*, 83–95.

Cadoret, R. J. (1978) Evidence of genetic inheritance of primary affective disorder in adoptees. *American Journal of Psychiatry*, *135*, 463–6.

Campbell, D. T. and Stanley, J. C. (1966) *Experimental and quasi-experimental designs for research.* Rand McNally: Chicago.

Cantor, N., Smith, E. E., French, R. de S. and Mezzich, J. (1980) Psychiatric diagnosis as prototype categorisation. *Journal of Abnormal Psychology*, *89*, 181–93.

Carney, M. W. P., Roth, M and Garside, R. F. (1965) The diagnosis of depressive syndromes and the prediction of ECT response. *British Journal of Psychiatry*, *111*, 659–74.

Carney, M. W. P. and Sheffield, B. F. (1972) Depression and the Newcastle scales: their relationship to Hamilton's scale. *British Journal of Psychiatry*, *121*, 35–40.

Carroll, B. J. (1982) The dexamethasone suppression test for melancholia. *British Journal of Psychiatry*, *140*, 292–304.

Carroll, B., Curtis, C. G. and Mendells, J. (1976) Neuroendocrine regulation in depression. *Archives of General Psychiatry*, *33*, 1039–44.

Clark, D. M. and Teasdale, J. D. (1982) Diurnal variation in clinical depression and accessibility for positive and negative experiences. *Journal of Abnormal Psychology*, *91*, 87–95.

Clarke, A. D. B. and Clarke, A. M. (1977) Prospects of prevention and amelioration of mental retardation. *American Journal of Mental Deficiency*, *81*, 523–33.

Clarke, A. D. B. and Clarke, A. M. (1978) Prospects for prevention and amelioration of mental subnormality: an overview. In A. M. Clarke and A. D. B. Clarke (eds) *Readings from Mental Deficiency: The Changing Outlook*. Methuen: London.

Clarke, A. D. B., Clarke, A. M. and Reiman, S. (1958) Cognitive and social changes in the feeble minded – three further studies. *British Journal of Psychology*, *49*, 144–57.

Clarke, A. D. B. and Hermelin, B. (1955) Adult imbeciles: their abilities and trainability. *Lancet*, *2*, 337–9.

Clarke, A. M. and Clarke, A. D. B. (1974a) *Mental Deficiency: The Changing Outlook*, 3rd ed. Methuen: London.

Clarke, A. M. and Clarke, A. D. B. (1974b) Experimental studies: an overview. In A. M. Clarke and A. D. B. Clarke (eds) *Mental Deficiency: The Changing Outlook*, 3rd edn. Methuen: London.

Clarke, A. M. and Clarke, A. D. B. (1976) *Early Experience: Myth and Evidence*. Open Books: London.

Clayton, P. J. (1982) Bereavement. In E. S. Paykel (ed.) *Handbook of Affective Disorders*. Churchill Livingstone: Edinburgh.

Clayton, P. J. and Darvish, H. S. (1979) Course of depressive symptoms following the stress of bereavement. In J. D. Barrett (ed.) *Stress and Mental Disorder*. Raven Press: New York.

Clayton, P. J., Halikas, J. A. and Maurice, W. L. (1972) The depression of widowhood. *British Journal of Psychiatry*, *120*, 71–8.

Cochrane, N. and Nielson, M. (1977) Depressive illness: the role of aggression further considered. *Psychological Medicine*, *17*, 283–8.

Cofer, D. H. and Wittenborn, J. R. (1980) Personality characteristics of formerly depressed women. *Journal of Abnormal Psychology*, *89*, 309–14.

Cohen, R. M., Weingartner, H., Smallberg, S. A., Pickar, D. and Murphy, D. L. (1982) Effort and cognition in depression. *Archives of General Psychiatry*, *39*, 593–7.

Colby, K. M., Faught, W. S. and Parkison, R. C. (1979) Cognitive therapy of paranoid conditions: heuristic suggestions based on a computer simulation model. *Cognitive Therapy and Research*, *3*, 55–60.

Coleman, R. E. (1975) Manipulation of self-esteem as a determinant of mood of elated and depressed women. *Journal of Abnormal Psychology*, *84*, 693–700.

Colletti, G. and Brownwell, K. D. (1982) The physical and emotional benefits of social support: applications to obesity, smoking and alcoholism. In M. Hersen, R. M. Eisler and P. M. Miller (eds) *Progress in Behaviour Therapy*, *13*. Academic Press: New York.

Coltheart, M., Patterson, K. and Marshall, J. C. (1980) *Deep Dyslexia*.

Routledge & Kegan Paul: London.

Cook, T. D. and Campbell, D. T. (1979) *Quasi-experimentation: Design and Analysis Issues for Field Settings*. Rand McNally: Chicago.

Cooper, J. E. (1983) Diagnosis and the diagnostic process. In M. Shepherd and O. L. Zangwill (eds) *Handbook of Psychiatry, vol. 1: General Psychopathology*. Cambridge University Press: Cambridge.

Cooper, J. E., Kendell, R. E., Gurland, B. J., Sharpe, L., Copeland, J. R. M. and Simon, R. (1972) *Psychiatric Diagnosis in New York and London*. Oxford University Press: London.

Corkin, S. (1968) Acquisition of motor skill after bilateral medial temporal lobe excision. *Neuropsychologia*, *6*, 255–65.

Corsini, R. J. (1981). *Handbook of Innovative Psychotherapies*. Wiley: New York.

Costello, C. G. (1970) *Symptoms of Psychopathology*. Wiley: New York.

Costello, C. G. (1972) Depression: loss of reinforcement or loss of reinforcer effectiveness. *Behavior Therapy*, *3*, 240–7.

Costello, C. G. (1978) A critical review of Seligman's laboratory experiments in learned helplessness and depression in humans. *Journal of Abnormal Psychology*, *87*, 21–31.

Costello, C. G. (1982a) Social factors associated with depression: a retrospective community study. *Psychological Medicine*, *12*, 329–39.

Costello, C. G. (1982b) Fears and phobias in women: a community study. *Journal of Abnormal Psychology*, *91*, 280–6.

Coyne, J. C. and Gotlib, I. H. (1983) The role of cognition in depression: a critical appraisal. *Psychological Bulletin*, *94*, 472–505.

Craft, M. (1979) *Tredgold's Mental Retardation*, 12th ed. Baillière Tindall: London.

Craig, T. K. J. and Brown, G. W. (1984) Life events, meaning and physical illness: a review. In A. Steptoe and A. Mathews (eds) *Health Care and Human Behaviour*. Academic Press: London.

Craik, F. I. M. and Lockhart, R. S. (1972) Levels of processing: a framework for memory research. *Journal of Verbal Learning and Verbal Behaviour*, *11*, 671–84.

Creer, C. and Wing, J. K. (1974) *Schizophrenia at Home*. National Schizophrenia Fellowship: Surrey.

Crome, L. (1960) The brain and mental retardation. *British Medical Journal*, *1*, 897–904.

Crome, L. and Stern, J. (1972) *Pathology of Mental Retardation*, 2nd edn. Churchill Livingstone: Edinburgh.

Curran, D., Partridge, M. and Storey, P. (1980) *Psychological Medicine*. Churchill Livingstone: Edinburgh.

Davidson, M. (1939) Studies in the application of mental tests to psychotic patients. *British Journal of Medical Psychology*, *18*, 44–52.

Davis, H. and Unruh, W. R. (1981) The development of the self-schema in adult depression. *Journal of Abnormal Psychology*, *90*, 125–33.

Davis, J. M. (1975) Overview: maintenance therapy in psychiatry. I. Schizophrenia. *American Journal of Psychiatry*, *132*, 1237–45.

Davison, G. C. and Neale, J. M. (1982) *Abnormal Psychology*, 2nd edn.

Wiley: New York.

Davison, G. C. (1968) Systematic desensitization as a counterconditioning process. *Journal of Abnormal Psychology*, *73*, 91–9.

Depue, R. A. and Monroe, S. M. (1978a) The unipolar-bipolar distinction in the depressive disorders. *Psychological Bulletin*, *85*, 1001–9.

Depue, R. A. and Monroe, S. M. (1978b) Learned helplessness in the perspective of the depressive disorder: conceptual and definitional issues. *Journal of Abnormal Psychology*, *87*, 3–20.

Derry, P. A. and Kuiper, N. A. (1981) Schematic processing and self-reference in clinical depression. *Journal of Abnormal Psychology*, *90*, 286–97.

Detterman, D. K. (1979) Memory in the mentally retarded. In N. R. Ellis (ed.) *Handbook of Mental Deficiency: Psychological Theory and Research*. Lawrence Erlbaum: Hillsdale, New Jersey.

Detre, T., Himmelhoch, J., Swatzburg, M., Anderson, C. M., Byck, R. and Kupfer, D. J. (1972) Hypersomnia and manic-depressive disease. *American Journal of Psychiatry*, *128*, 1303–5.

Dickinson, A. (1980) *Contemporary Animal Learning Theory*. Cambridge University Press: Cambridge.

Diehr, P., Diehr, G., Loepsell, T., Wood, R., Beach, K., Wolcott, B. and Tompkins, R. K. (1982) Cluster analysis to determine headache types. *Journal of Chronic Diseases*, *35*, 623–33.

Di Loreto, A. O. (1971) *Comparative Psychotherapy: An Experimental Analysis*. Aldine Atherton: Chicago.

Donnelly, E. F., Murphy, D. L., Goodwin, F. K. and Waldman, I. N. (1982) Intellectual function in primary affective disorder. *British Journal of Psychiatry*, *140*, 633–6.

Dunbar, G. C. and Lishman, W. A. (1984) Depression recognition memory and hedonic tone: a signal detectional analysis. *British Journal of Psychiatry*, *144*, 376–82.

Eastman, C. (1976) Behavioural formulation of depression. *Psychological Review*, *83*, 277–91.

Eaves, G. and Rush, A. J. (1984) Cognitive patterns in symptomatic and remitted unipolar depressives. *Journal of Abnormal Psychology*, *93*, 31–40.

Eccleston, D. (1982) The biochemistry of affective disorders. *British Journal of Hospital Medicine*, *27*, 627–30.

Ellenberger, H. F. (1970) *The Discovery of the Unconscious: The History and Evolution of Dynamic Psychiatry*. Basic Books: New York.

Ellis, A. (1977) The basic clinical theory of rational emotive therapy. In A. Ellis and R. Grieger (eds) *Handbook of Rational Emotive Therapy*. Springer: New York.

Ellis, A. (1980) Rational-emotive therapy and cognitive behaviour therapy: similarities and differences. *Cognitive Therapy and Research*, *4*, 325–40.

Ellis, N. R. (1963) The stimulus trace and behavioural inadequacy. In N. R. Ellis (ed.) *Handbook of Mental Deficiency*. McGraw-Hill: New York.

Ellis, N. R. (1969) A behavioural research strategy in mental retardation:

defence and critique. *American Journal of Mental Deficiency*, 73, 557–66.

Ellis, N. R. (1970) Memory processes in retardates and normals. In N.R. Ellis (ed.) *International Review of Research in Mental Retardation*, 4, Academic Press: New York.

Ellis, N. R. (1979) *Handbook of Mental Deficiency: Psychological Theory and Research*. Laurence Erlbaum: Hillsdale, New Jersey.

Ellis, N. R., Deacon, J. R., Harris, L. A., Poor, A., Ankers, D., Diorio, M. S., Watkins, R. S., Boyd, B. D. and Cavalier, A. R. (1982) Learning, memory and transfer in profoundly, severely and moderately mentally retarded persons. *American Journal of Mental Deficiency*, 87, 186–96.

Endicott, J. and Spitzer, R. L. (1978) A diagnostic interview: the schedule for affective disorders and schizophrenia. *Archive of General Psychiatry*, 35, 837–44.

Evans, I. M. (1973) The logical requirement for explanations of systematic desensitization. *Behaviour Therapy*, 4, 506–14.

Everitt, B. S. (1972) Cluster analysis: a brief discussion of some of the problems. *British Journal of Psychiatry*, 120, 143–5.

Eysenck, H. J. (1952) The effects of psychotherapy: an evaluation. *Journal of Consulting Psychology*, 16, 319–24.

Eysenck, H. J. (1960) The effects of psychotherapy. In H. J. Eysenck (ed.) *Handbook of Abnormal Psychology*. Pitman Medical: London.

Eysenck, H. J. (1970) The classification of depressive illness. *British Journal of Psychiatry*, 117, 241–50.

Eysenck, H. J. (1973) *Handbook of Abnormal Psychology*, 2nd edn. Pitman: London.

Eysenck, H. J. (1978) An exercise in mega-silliness. *American Psychologist*, 33, 517.

Eysenck, H. J. (1980) Mischel and the concept of personality. *British Journal of Psychology*, 71, 191–204.

Eysenck, H. J. and Wilson, G. D. (1973) *A Textbook of Human Psychology*. MTP: Lancaster.

Falloon, I., Boyd, J., McGill, C. W., Razini, J., Moss, H. B. and Gilderman, A. M. (1982) Family management in the prevention of exacerbations of schizophrenia: a controlled study. *New England Journal of Medicine*, 306, 1437–40.

Farrell, B. A. (1981) *The Standing of Psychoanalysis*. Oxford University Press: Oxford.

Fava, G. A., Kellner, R., Munari, F. and Pavan, L. (1982) Losses, hostility and depression. *Journal of Nervous and Mental Diseases*, 170, 474–8.

Faverilli, C. and Poli. E. (1982) Stability of the diagnosis of primary affective disorder: a four-year follow-up study. *Journal of Affective Disorders*, 4, 35–9.

Feighner, J. P., Robins, E., Guze, S. B., Woodruff, R A., Winokur, G. and Munoz, R. (1972) Diagnostic criteria for use in psychiatric research. *Archives of General Psychiatry*, 26, 57–63.

Fennell, M. J. V. and Campbell, E. A. (1984) The cognitions questionnaire: specific thinking errors in depression. *British Journal of Clinical*

Psychology, *23*, 81–92.

Ferster, C. B. (1973) A functional analysis of depression. *American Psychologist*, *28*, 857–70.

Feuerstein, M., Bush, C. and Corbisiero, R. (1982) Stress and chronic headache: a psychophysiological investigation. *Journal of Psychosomatic Research*, *26*, 167–82.

Flynn, W. R. (1962) On the psychology of the shaking palsy. *Psychiatry Quarterly*, *36*, 203–21.

Foulds, G. A. (1952) Temperamental differences in maze performance. Part II. The effect of distraction and electroconvulsive therapy on psychiatric retardation. *British Journal of Psychology*, *43*, 33–41.

Foulds, G. A., Caine, T. M. and Creasy, M. A. (1960) Aspects of extra- and intro-punitive expression in mental illness. *Journal of Mental Science*, *106*, 599–610.

Frank, J. D. (1973) *Persuasion and Healing: A Comparative Study of Psychotherapy*, 2nd edn. Johns Hopkins University Press: London.

Frank, J. D. (1974) Therapeutic components of psychotherapy. A 25 year progress report. *Journal of Nervous and Mental Diseases, 159*, 325–42.

Frankl, V. E. (1962) *Man's Search for Meaning*. Beacon Press: Boston.

Freud, S. (1917) Mourning and melancholia. In *Collected Papers*, *4*. Hogarth Press: London.

Freud, S. (1921) Group psychology and the analysis of the ego. In J. Strachey (ed.) *Standard Edition*, *14*. Hogarth Press: London.

Freud, S. (1922), *Introductory Lectures on Psychoanalysis*. Hogarth Press: London.

Freud, S. (1923) *The Ego and the Id*. In J. Strachey (ed.) *Standard Edition*, *19*, 12–66. Hogarth Press: London.

Freud, S. and Breuer, J. (1974) *Studies on Hysteria*. Penguin: Harmondsworth. (First published 1895.)

Friar, L. R. and Beatty, J. (1976) Migraine: management by trained control of vasoconstriction. *Journal of Consulting and Clinical Psychology*, *44*, 46–53.

Friedman, A. P., De Sola Pool, N. and Van Storch, T. J. C. (1953) Tension headache. *Journal of the American Medical Association*, *151*, 174–7.

Friedman, A. P., Finley, K. M., Graham, J. R., Kunkle, E. C., Ostfeld, A. M. and Wolff, H. G. (1962) Classification of headache. The Ad Hoc Committee on the classification of headache. *Journal of the American Medical Association*, *179*, 717–19.

Fromm, D. and Schopflocher, D. (1984) Neuropsychological test performance in depression patients before and after drug therapy. *Biological Psychiatry*, *19*, 55–72.

Fromm-Reichman, F. (1937) Contributions to the psychogenesis of migraine. *Psychoanalytic Review*, *24*, 26–33.

Frost, N. R. and Clayton, P. J. (1977) Bereavement and psychiatric hospitalization. *Archives of General Psychiatry*, *34*, 1172–5.

Gatchel, R. J., Paulus, R. B. and Maples, C. W. (1975) Learned helplessness and self-reported affect. *Journal of Abnormal Psychology*, *84*, 589–620.

Gauthier, J., Doyon, J., Lacroix, R. and Drolet, M. (1983) Blood volume pulse biofeedback in the treatment of migraine headache: a controlled evaluation. *Biofeedback and Self Regulation*, *8*, 427–42.

Gelder, M. G., Bancroft, J. H. H., Gath, D. H., Johnson, D. W., Mathews A. M. and Shaw, P. M. (1973) Specific and non-specific factors in behaviour therapy. *British Journal of Psychiatry*, *123*, 445–62.

Gibbons, J. L. (1968) Biochemistry of the affective illness. *Hospital Medicine*, *2*, 1164–71.

Glanzer, M. and Cunitz, A. R. (1966) Two storage mechanisms in free recall. *Journal of Verbal Learning and Verbal Behaviour*, *5*, 351–60.

Glass, G. V. and Kliegl, R. M. (1983) An apology for research integration in the study of psychotherapy. *Journal of Consulting and Clinical Psychology*, *51*, 28–41.

Goldstein, G. (1984) Neuropsychological assessment of psychotic patients. In G. Goldstein (ed.) *Advances in Clinical Neuropsychology*, vol. 1. Plenum Press: New York.

Goldstein, J. M. and Caton, C. L. M. (1983) The effects of the community environment on chronic psychiatric patients. *Psychological Medicine*, *13*, 193–9.

Goldstein, S. G., Filskov, S. B., Weaver, L. A. and Ives, J. A. (1977) Neuropsychological effects of electroconvulsive therapy. *Journal of Clinical Psychology*, *33*, 798–806.

Goldstein, G. and Shelly, C. (1981) Does the right hemisphere age more rapidly than the left? *Journal of Clinical Neuropsychology*, *3*, 65–78.

Golin, S., Sweeney, P. D. and Shaeffer, D. E. (1981) The causality of causal attributions in depression: a cross-lagged panel correlational analysis. *Journal of Abnormal Psychology*, *90*, 14–22.

Goodwin, A. M. and Williams, J. M. G. (1982) Mood induction research – its implications for clinical depression. *Behaviour Research and Therapy*, *20*, 373–82.

Grad de Alarcon, J., Sainsbury, P. and Costain, W. R. (1975) Incidence of referred mental illness in Chichester and Salisbury. *Psychological Medicine*, *5*, 32–54.

Graham, D. T. (1972) Psychosomatic medicine. In N. S. Greenfield and R. A. Sternbach (eds) *Handbook of Psychophysiology*. Holt, Rinehart & Winston: New York.

Graham, J. R. and Wolff, H. G. (1938) Mechanism of migraine headache and action of ergotamine tartrate. *Archives of Neurology and Psychiatry*, *39*, 737–63.

Grant, I., Yager, J., Sweetwood, H. L. and Olshen, R. (1982) Life events and symptoms. Fourier analysis of three series for a three year prospective inquiry. *Archives of General Psychiatry*, *39*, 598–605.

Gray, J. A. (1982) *The Neuropsychology of Anxiety: An Inquiry into the Functions of the Septo-hippocampal System*. Oxford University Press: Oxford.

Greden, J. F., Azbala, A. A., Smokler, J. A., Gardner, R. and Carroll, B. J. (1981) Speech pause time: a marker of psychomotor retardation amongst endogenous depressives. *Biological Psychiatry*, *16*, 851–9.

Greden, J. F. and Carroll, B. J. (1980) Decrease in speech pause times with treatment of endogenous depression. *Biological Psychiatry*, *15*, 575–87.

Grosz, H. J. and Zimmerman, J. (1965) Experimental analysis of hysterical blindness. *Archives of General Psychiatry*, *13*, 256–60.

Groves, P. M. and Thompson, R. F. (1970) Habituation: a dual process theory. *Psychological Review*, *77*, 419–59.

Hall, K. R. L. and Stride, E. (1954) Some factors affecting reaction times to auditory stimuli in mental patients. *Journal of Mental Science*, *100*, 462–77.

Hallam, R. (1978) Agoraphobia: a critical review of the concept. *British Journal of Psychiatry*, *133*, 314–19.

Hallam, R. (1983) Agoraphobia: deconstructing a clinical syndrome. *Bulletin of the British Psychological Society*, *36*, 337–40.

Hamilton, M. (1960) A rating scale for depression. *Journal of Neurology, Neurosurgery and Psychiatry*, *23*, 56–62.

Hamilton, M. (1974) *Fish's Clinical Psychopathology*. Wright: Bristol.

Hankoff, L. D. (1982) Suicide and attempted suicide. In E. S. Paykel (ed.) *Handbook of Affective Disorders*. Churchill Livingstone: Edinburgh.

Hargreaves, I. R. (1982) 'A Test of the Reformulated Learned Helplessness Model of Depression'. Unpublished dissertation: University of Aberdeen, Scotland.

Harlow, H. F. (1949) The formation of learning sets. *Psychological Review*, *56*, 51–65.

Hayes, K. J. (1953) The backward curve: a method for the study of learning. *Psychological Review*, *60*, 269–75.

Heaton, R. R. and Crowley, C. (1981) Effects of psychiatric disorders and their somatic treatments on neuropsychological test results. In S. B. Filskov and T. J. Boll (eds) *Handbook of Clinical Neuropsychology*. Wiley: New York.

Hedges, L. V. (1982) Estimation of effect size from a series of independent experiments. *Psychological Bulletin*, *92*, 490–9.

Heilman, K. M. and Valenstein, E. (1979) *Clinical Neuropsychology*. Oxford University Press: Oxford.

Heiser, J. F., Colby, K. M., Faught, W. S. and Parkinson, R. C. (1979) Can psychiatrists distinguish a computer simulation of paranoia from the real thing? *Journal of Psychiatric Research*, *15*, 149–62.

Henderson, A. S. and Moran, P. A. P. (1983) Social relationships during the onset and remission of neurotic symptoms. A prospective community study. *British Journal of Psychiatry*, *143*, 467–72.

Henderson, S. (1981) Social relationships, adversity and neurosis: an analysis of prospective observations. *British Journal of Psychiatry*, *138*, 391–8.

Henderson, S., Byrne, D. G. and Duncan-Jones, P. (1981) *Neurosis and the Social Animal*. Academic Press: Sydney.

Henry, G. M., Weingartner, H. and Murphy, D. L. (1973) Influence of affective states and psychoactive drugs on verbal learning and memory. *American Journal of Psychiatry*, *130*, 966–71.

Henryk-Gutt, R. and Rees, W. L. (1973) Psychological aspects of migraine. *Journal of Psychosomatic Research*, *17*, 141–53.

Hersen, M. and Barlow, D. H. (1984) *Single Case Experimental Designs: Strategies for Studying Behaviour Change in the Individual*, 2nd edn. Pergamon Press: Oxford.

Hinchliffe, M. K., Lancashire, M. and Roberts, F. J. (1971) Depression: defence mechanisms in speech. *British Journal of Psychiatry*, *118*, 471–2.

Hodgson, R. J. and Rachman, S. (1974) Desynchrony in measures of fear. *Behaviour Research and Therapy*, *12*, 319–26.

Hogarty, G. E., Goldberg, S. C. and Collaborative Study Group (1973) Drug and sociotherapy in the aftercare of schizophrenic patients. *Archives of General Psychiatry*, *28*, 54–64.

Hogarty, G. E., Goldberg, S. C., Schooler, N. R., Ulrich, R. F. and Collaborative Study Group (1974a) Drug and sociotherapy in the aftercare of schizophrenic patients: II. Two year relapse rates. *Archives of General Psychiatry*, *31*, 603–608.

Hogarty, G. E., Goldberg, S. C., Schooler, N. R. and Collaborative Study Group (1974b) Drug and sociotherapy in the aftercare of schizophrenic patients: III. *Archives of General Psychiatry*, *31*, 609–18.

Holden, E. A. (1971) Sequential dot presentation measures of stimulus trace in retardates and normals. In N. R. Ellis (ed.) *International Review of Research in Mental Retardation*, *5*. Academic Press: New York.

Holmes, T. H. and Rahe, R. H. (1967) The social readjustment rating scale. *Journal of Psychosomatic Research*, *11*, 213–18.

Holroyd, K. A. and Andrasik, F. (1982) A cognitive-behavioural approach to recurrent tension and migraine headache. In P. C. Kendall (ed.) *Advances in Cognitive-Behavioural Research and Therapy*, *1*. Academic Press: New York.

Holroyd, K. A. and Penzien, D. B. (1983) EMG biofeedback and tension headache: therapeutic mechanisms. In K. A. Holroyd, B. Schlote and H. Zenz (eds) *Perspectives in Research on Headache*. Hogrefe: New York.

Hoon, P. and Lindsley, O. (1974) A comparison of behaviour and traditional therapy publication activity. *American Psychologist*, *29*, 694–7.

Hugdahl, K. (1981) The three-systems model of fear and emotion – a critical examination. *Behaviour Research and Therapy*, *19*, 75–85.

Hunter, I. M. L. (1962) An exceptional talent for calculative thinking. *British Journal of Psychology*, *53*, 243–58.

Hunter, M. (1983) The Headache Scale: a new approach to the assessment of headache pain based on pain descriptions. *Pain*, *16*, 361–73.

Hunter, M. and Philips, C. (1981) The experience of headache: an assessment of the qualities of tension headache pain. *Pain*, *10*, 209–19.

Johnson, O. and Crockett, D. (1982) Changes in perceptual asymmetries with clinical improvement of depression and schizophrenia. *Journal of Abnormal Psychology*, *91*, 45–54.

Kaganov, J. A., Bakal, D. A. and Dunn, B. E. (1981) The differential contribution of muscle contraction and migraine symptoms to problem headache in the general population. *Headache*, *21*, 157–63.

Kanfer, F. M. and Hagarman, S. (1981) The role of self-regulation. In Rehm (ed.) *Behaviour Therapy for Depression*. Academic Press: New York.

Kazdin, A. E. (1977) *The Token Economy: A Review and Evaluation*. Plenum Press: London.

Kazdin, A. E. (1979) Therapy outcome questions requiring control of credibility and treatment generated expectancies. *Behaviour Therapy*, *10*, 81–93.

Kazdin, A. E. (1980) Covert and overt rehearsal and elaboration during treatment in the development of assertive behaviour. *Behaviour Research and Therapy*, *18*, 191–202.

Kazdin, A. E. (1982a) *Single case research designs: methods for clinical and applied settings*. Oxford University Press: New York.

Kazdin, A. E. (1982b) Symptom substitution, generalization and response covariation: implications for psychotherapy outcome. *Psychological Bulletin*, *91*, 349–65.

Kazdin, A. E. and Kopel, S. A. (1975) On resolving ambiguities in the multiple baseline design: problems and recommendations. *Behaviour Therapy*, *6*, 601–8.

Kazdin, A. E. and Wilcoxon, L. A. (1976) Systematic desensitization and nonspecific treatment effects: a methodological evaluation. *Psychological Bulletin*, *83*, 729–58.

Kazdin, A. E. and Wilson, G. T. (1978) *Evaluation of Behaviour Therapy*. Ballinger: Massachusetts.

Kearns, N. P., Cruickshank, K. J., McGuigan, K. J., Riley, S. A., Shaw, S. P. and Snaith, R. P. (1982) A comparison of depression rating scales. *British Journal of Psychiatry*, *141*, 45–9.

Kendall, P. C. (1983) Methodology and cognitive-behavioural assessment. *Behavioural Psychotherapy*, *11*, 285–301.

Kendell, R. E. (1968) *The Classification of Depressive Illness*. Oxford University Press: London.

Kendell, R. E. (1975) *The Role of Diagnosis in Psychiatry*. Blackwell: London.

Kendell, R. E. (1976) The classification of depressions: a review of contemporary confusion. *British Journal of Psychiatry*, *129*, 15–28.

Kendell, R. E. (1983) The principles of classification in relation to mental disease. In M. Shepherd and O. L. Zangwill (eds), *Handbook of Psychiatry: 1. General Psychopathology*. Cambridge University Press: Cambridge.

Kendell, R. E. and Gourlay, J. (1970) The clinical distinction between psychotic and neurotic depression. *British Journal of Psychiatry*, *117*, 257–60.

Kendrick, D. C., Parboosingh, R. C. and Post, F. (1965) A synonym learning test for use with elderly psychiatric subjects: a validation study. *British Journal of Social and Clinical Psychology*, *4*, 63–71.

Kent, R. N., O'Leary, K. D., Diamment, C. and Dietz, A. (1974)

Expectation biases in observational evaluation of therapeutic change. *Journal of Consulting and Clinical Psychology*, *42*, 774–80.

Kewman, D. and Roberts, A. H. (1980) Skin temperature biofeedback and migraine headache: a double blind study. *Biofeedback and Self Regulation*, *5*, 327–45.

Kiloh, L. G. (1982) Electroconvulsive therapy. In E. S. Paykel (ed.) *Handbook of Affective Disorders*. Churchill Livingstone: Edinburgh.

Kiloh, L. G., Andrews, G., Neilson, M. and Bianchif, G. N. (1972) The relationship of the syndromes called endogenous and neurotic depression. *British Journal of Psychiatry*, *121*, 183–96.

Kiresuk, T. J. and Sherman, R. E. (1968) Goal attainment scaling: a general method for evaluating comprehensive mental health programs. *Community Mental Health Journal*, *4*, 443–53.

Kirsch, I. (1982) Efficacy expectations or response predictions: the meaning of self efficacy ratings as a function of task characteristics. *Journal of Personality and Social Psychology*, *42*, 132–6.

Kirsch, I., Tennen, H., Wickless, C., Saccone, A. J. and Cody, S. (1983) The role of expectancy in fear reduction. *Behaviour Therapy*, *14*, 520–32.

Kirschenbaum, H. (1979) *On Becoming Carl Rogers*. Delacorte Press: New York.

Klausmeier, H. J., Feldhusen, J. and Check, J. (1959) *An Analysis of Learning Efficiency in Arithmetic of Mentally Retarded Children in Comparison with Children of Average and High Intelligence*. University of Wisconsin Press: Madison.

Kreitman, N. (1961) The reliability of psychiatric diagnosis. *Journal of Mental Science*, *107*, 876–86.

Kuipers, L., Sturgeon, D., Berkowitz, R. and Leff, J. (1983) Characteristics of expressed emotion: its relationship to speech and looking in schizophrenic patients and their relatives. *British Journal of Clinical Psychology*, *22*, 257–64.

Kupfer, D. J., Himmelhoch, J. M., Swartburg, M., Anderson, C., Byck, R. and Detre, T. P. (1972) Hypersomnia in manic depressive disease (a preliminary report). *Diseases of the Nervous System*, *33*, 720–4.

Kupfer, D. J., Weiss, B. L., Foster, F. G., Detre, T. P., Delgado, J. and McPartland, R. (1974) Psychomotor activity in affective states. *Archives of General Psychiatry*, *30*, 765–8.

Kurtz, R. R. and Grummon, D. L. (1972) Differential approaches to the measurement of therapist empathy and their relationship to therapy outcomes. *Journal of Consulting and Clinical Psychology*, *39*, 106–15.

Lader, M. H. (1975) *The Psychophysiology of Mental Illness*. Routledge & Kegan Paul: London.

Lader, M. H. (1980) *Introduction to Psychopharmacology*. Scope Publications, Upjohn: Kalamazoo.

Lader, M. H. and Mathews, A. (1968) A physiological model of phobic anxiety and desensitization. *Behaviour Research and Therapy*, *6*, 411–21.

Lader, M. H. and Wing, L. (1966) *Physiological Measures, Sedative Drugs and Morbid Anxiety*. Oxford University Press: London.

Lambert, M., De Julio, S. and Stein, D. (1978) Therapist interpersonal skills. *Psychological Bulletin*, *83*, 467–89.

Lance, J. W. (1982) *Mechanism and Management of Headache*, 4th edn. Butterworth: London.

Lang, P. J. (1979) A bio-informational theory of emotional imagery. *Psychophysiology*, *16*, 495–511.

Lang, P. J. and Buss, A. H. (1965) Psychological deficit in schizophrenia: II. Interference and activation. *Journal of Abnormal Psychology*, *70*, 77–106.

Lang, P. J. and Lazovik, A. D. (1963) Experimental desensitization of a phobia. *Journal of Abnormal and Social Psychology*, *66*, 519–25.

Lang, P. J., Lazovik, A. and Reynolds, D. (1966) Desensitization, suggestibility and pseudotherapy. *Journal of Abnormal Psychology*, *70*, 395–402.

Lang, P. J., Melamed, B. G. and Hart, J. (1970) A psychophysiological analysis of fear modification using an automated desensitization procedure. *Journal of Abnormal Psychology*, *76*, 220–34.

Lang, R. J. and Frith, C. D. (1981) Learning and reminiscence in the pursuit rotar performance of normal and depressed subjects. *Personality and Individual Differences*, *2*, 207–13.

Lazarus, A. (1968) Learning theory and the treatment of depression. *Behaviour Research and Therapy*, *6*, 83–9.

Leff, J. P. (1978) The social and psychological causes of the acute attack. In J. K. Wing (ed.) *Schizophrenia: Towards a New Synthesis*. Academic Press: London.

Leff, J. P. (1982) Chronic syndromes of schizophrenia. In J. K. Wing and L. Wing (eds) *Handbook of Psychiatry: 3. Psychoses of Uncertain Origin*. Cambridge University Press. Cambridge.

Leff, J., Kuipers, L., Berkowitz, R., Vaughn, C. and Sturgeon, D. (1983) Life events, relatives' expressed emotion and maintenance neuroleptics in schizophrenic relapse. *Psychological Medicine*, *13*, 799–806.

Leff, J., Kuipers, L., Berkowitz, R., Eberlein Vreis, R. and Sturgeon, D. (1982) A controlled trial of social intervention in the families of schizophrenic patients. *British Journal of Psychiatry*, *141*, 121–34.

Levis, D. J. and Hare, N. (1977) A review of the theoretical rationale and empirical support for the extinction approach of implosive (flooding) therapy. *Progress in Behavioural Modification*, *4*, 300–76.

Lewinsohn, P. M., Steinmetz, J. L., Larson, D. W. and Franklin, Y. (1981) Depression related cognitions: antecedents or consequences. *Journal of Abnormal Psychology*, *90*, 213–19.

Lewinsohn, P. M., Weinstein, M. S. and Alper, T. A. (1970) A behavioural approach to the group treatment of depressed persons: a methodological contribution. *Journal of Clinical Psychology*, *26*, 525–32.

Lewis, A. (1938) States of depression: their clinical and aetiological differentiation. *British Medical Journal*. ii, 875–8.

Ley, P. (1972) The reliability of psychiatric diagnosis: some new thoughts. *British Journal of Psychiatry*, *121*, 41–3.

322   Investigating Abnormal Behaviour

Ley, P. (1977) Psychological studies of doctor-patient communication. In S. Rachman (ed.) *Contributions to Medical Psychology*, *1*, Pergamon Press: Oxford.

Lick, J. and Bootzin, R. (1975) Expectancy factors in the treatment of fear: methodological and theoretical issues. *Psychological Bulletin*, *82*, 917–31.

Lindsay, W. R. (1982) The effects of labelling: blind and non-blind ratings of social skills in schizophrenic and non-schizophrenic control subjects. *American Journal of Psychiatry*, *139*, 216–19.

Linford-Rees, W. (1976) *A Short Textbook of Psychiatry*. Hodder & Stoughton: London.

Lishman, W. A. (1972a) Selective factors in memory: Part 1. Age, sex and personality attributes. *Psychological Medicine*, *2*, 121–38.

Lishman, W. A. (1972b) Selective factors in memory: Part 2. Affective disorder. *Psychological Medicine*, *2*, 248–53.

Lloyd, C. (1980a) Life events and depressive disorder reviewed: I. Events as predisposing factors. *Archives of General Psychiatry*, *37*, 529–35.

Lloyd, C. (1980b) Life events and depressive disorder reviewed: II. Events as precipitating factors. *Archives of General Psychiatry*, 37, 541–8.

Luborsky, L., Singer, G. and Luborsky, L. (1975) Comparative studies in psychotherapy: Is it true that 'everyone has won and all must have prizes'? *Archives of General Psychiatry*, *32*, 995–1008.

Luborsky, L. and Spence, D. P. (1978) Quantitative research of psycho-analytic psychotherapy. In S. L. Garfield and A. E. Bergin (eds) *Handbook of Psychotherapy and Behaviour Change*, 2nd edn. Wiley: Chichester.

Lucas, R. N. (1977) Migraine in twins. *Journal of Psychosomatic Research*, *20*, 21–34.

Lyons, H. A. (1972) Depressive illness and aggression in Belfast. *British Medical Journal*, *1*, 342–4.

McAllister, T. W. (1981) Cognitive functioning in the affective disorders. *Comprehensive Psychiatry*, *22*, 527–86.

Mackay, A. V. P. (1983) Antischizophrenic drugs. In G. E. Berrios and J. H. Dowson (eds) *Treatment and Management in Adult Psychiatry*. Baillière Tindall: London.

Mackintosh, N. J. (1974) *The Psychology of Animal Learning*. Academic Press: New York.

Mackintosh, N. J. (1983) *Conditioning and Associative Learning*. Oxford University Press: Oxford.

Malan, D. (1963) *A Study of Brief Psychotherapy*. Tavistock Press: London.

Malan, D. (1976) *The Frontier of Brief Psychotherapy*. Plenum Press: New York.

Marshall, J. (1978) Cerebral blood flow in migraine. In R. Greene (ed.) *Current Concepts in Migraine Research*. Raven Press: New York.

Martin, J. J., Rome, H. P. and Svenson, W. M. (1967) Muscle contraction headache: a psychiatric review. *Research and Clinical Studies in Headache*, *1*, 184–204.

Marzillier, J. S. (1980) Cognitive therapy and behavioural practice. *Behaviour Research and Therapy*, *18*, 249–58.

Maslow, A. H. (1962) *Toward a Psychology of Being*. Van Nostrand: New York.

Mason, C. F. (1956) Pre-illness intelligence of mental hospital patients. *Journal of Consulting Psychology*, *20*, 297–300.

Mathews, A. M. (1978) Fear reduction research and clinical phobias. *Psychological Bulletin*, *85*, 390–404.

Maxwell, A. E. (1971) Multivariate statistical methods and classification problems. *British Journal of Psychiatry*, *119*, 121–7.

Maxwell, H. (1966) *Migraine: Background and Development*. Wright: Bristol.

May, R. (1960) *Existential Psychology*. Random House: New York.

Meichenbaum, D. (1977) *Cognitive-Behaviour Modification: An Integrative Approach*. Plenum Press: New York.

Melzack, R. and Wall, P. D. (1982) *The Challenge of Pain*. Penguin: Harmondsworth.

Mendels, J. (1976) Lithium in the treatment of depression. *American Journal of Psychiatry*, *133*, 373–8.

Mendels, J. and Cochrane, C. (1968) The nosology of depression: the endogenous-reactive concept. *American Journal of Psychiatry*, *124*, 1–11 (supplement).

Mendlewicz, J. and Rainer, J. D. (1977) Adoption study supporting genetic transmission in manic-depressive illness. *Nature*, *268*, 327–9.

Merskey, H. (1979) *The Analysis of Hysteria*. Baillière Tindall: London.

Miller, E. (1968) A note on the visual performance of a subject with unilateral functional blindness. *Behaviour Research and Therapy*, *6*, 115–16.

Miller, E. (1977) *Abnormal Ageing*. Wiley: Chichester.

Miller, E. (1980) Cognitive assessment of the older adult. In J. E. Birren and R. B. Sloane (eds) *Handbook of Mental Health and Ageing*. Prentice Hall: Englewood Cliffs, New Jersey.

Miller, E. (1983) A note on the interpretation of data derived from neuropsychological tests. *Cortex*, *19*, 131–2.

Miller, E. (1984) Neuropsychological assessment. In D. W. K. Kay and G. D. Burrows (eds) *Handbook of Studies on Psychology and Old Age*. Elsevier: Amsterdam.

Miller, E. and Lewis, P. (1977) Recognition memory in elderly patients with depression and dementia. *Journal of Abnormal Psychology*, *86*, 84–6.

Miller, N. E. (1969) Learning of visceral and glandular responses. *Science*, *163*, 434–45.

Miller, W. R. (1975) Psychological deficit in depression. *Psychological Bulletin*, *82*, 238–60.

Miller, W. R. and Seligman, M. E. P. (1975) Depression in humans. *Journal of Abnormal Psychology*, *84*, 228–38.

Minklowitz, D. J., Goldstein, M. J., Falloon, I. R. H. and Doane, J. A. (1984) Interactional correlates of expressed emotion in families of schizophrenics. *British Journal of Psychiatry*, *144*, 482–7.

Mintz, J. (1981) Measuring outcome in psychodynamic psychotherapy. *Archives of General Psychiatry*, *38*, 503–6.

Mitchell, C. and Hartman, D. P. (1981) A cautionary note on the use of omega squared to evaluate the effectiveness of behavioral treatments. *Behavioural Assessment*, *3*, 93–100.

Mitchell, K., Bozarth, J. and Krauft, C. (1977) A reappraisal of the therapeutic effectiveness of accurate empathy, non-possessive warmth and genuineness. In A. Gurman and A. Razin (eds) *Effective Psychotherapy*. Pergamon Press: Oxford.

Mischel, W. (1968) *Personality and Assessment*. Wiley: New York.

Mischel, W. (1977) On the interface of cognition and personality: beyond the person-situation debate. *American Psychologist*, *34*, 740–9.

Montgomery, S. A. and Åsberg, M. (1979) A new depression scale designed to be sensitive to change. *British Journal of Psychiatry*, *134*, 382–9.

Morley, S. (1977) Migraine: a generalized vasomotor dysfunction? A critical review of evidence. *Headache*, *17*, 71–4.

Morley, S. (1985) An experimental investigation of some assumptions underpinning psychological treatments of migraine. *Behaviour Research and Therapy*, *23*, 65–74.

Morley, S. (1986) Single case methodology in behaviour therapy. In S. J. E. Lindsay and G. E. Powell (eds) *A Handbook of Clinical Psychology*. Gower: Aldershot.

Morley, S. and Hunter M. (1983) Temporal artery pulse amplitude wave shapes in migraineurs: a methodological investigation. *Journal of Psychosomatic Research*, *27*, 485–92.

Morley, S., Shepherd, G. and Spence, S. (1983) Cognitive approaches to social skills training. In S. Spence and G. W. Shepherd (eds) *Developments in Social Skills Training*. Academic Press: London.

Mulhall, D. J. (1976) Systematic self-assessment by P.Q.R.S.T. (personal questionnaire of rapid scaling techniques). *Psychological Medicine*, *6*, 591–7.

Murphy, G. E., Woodruff, R. A., Herjanic, M. and Fischer, J. R. (1974) Validity of the diagnosis of primary affective disorder: a prospective study with a five year follow-up. *Archives of General Psychiatry*, *30*, 751–6.

Neale, J. M. and Oltmanns, T. F. (1980) *Schizophrenia*. Wiley: New York.

Nettelbeck, T. and McLean, J. (1984) Mental retardation and inspection time; a two stage model for sensory registration and central processing. *American Journal of Mental Deficiency*, *89*, 83–90.

Ni Bhrolchain, M. (1979) Psychotic and neurotic depression. Part 1 (Some points of method). *British Journal of Psychiatry*, *134*, 87–93.

Ni Bhrolchain, M., Brown, G. W. and Harris, T. D. (1979) Psychotic and neurotic depression. Part 2. (Clinical characteristics). *British Journal of Psychiatry*, *137*, 94–107.

Nisbett, R. E. and Ross, L. (1980) *Human Inference: Strategies and Shortcomings of Social Judgement*. Prentice-Hall: Englewood Cliffs,

New Jersey.

Novaco, R. W. (1978) Anger and coping with stress; cognitive-behavioral interventions. In J. P. Foreyt and D. P. Rathjen (eds) *Cognitive Behavior Therapy: Research and Application*. Plenum Press: New York.

Nurnberger, J. I. and Gershon, E. S. (1982) Genetics. In E. S. Paykel (ed.) *Handbook of Affective Disorders*. Churchill Livingstone: Edinburgh.

O'Leary, K. D., Kent, R. N. and Kanowitz, J. (1975) Shaping data congruent with experimental hypotheses. *Journal of Applied Behavior Analysis*, *8*, 43–51.

Osgood, C. E., Suci, G. J. and Tannenbaum, P. H. (1957) *The Measurement of Meaning*. University of Illinois Press; Urbana, Illinois.

Parkes, C. M. (1964) Recent bereavement as a cause of mental illness. *British Journal of Psychiatry*, *110*, 198–204.

Parkes, C. M. (1972) *Bereavement: Studies of Grief in Adult Life*. Tavistock: London.

Paul, G. L. (1966) *Insight vs desensitization in psychotherapy*. Stanford University Press: Stanford, California.

Paykel, E. S. (1971) Classification of depressed patients: a cluster analysis clinical grouping. *British Journal of Psychiatry*, *118*, 275–88.

Paykel, E. S. (1972) Cluster analysis. *British Journal of Psychiatry*, *120*, 695–6.

Paykel, E. S. (1982) *Handbook of Affective Disorders*. Churchill Livingstone: Edinburgh.

Paykel, E. S., Kierman, G. L. and Prusoff, B. A. (1974) Prognosis of depression and the endogenous-neurotic distinction. *Psychological Medicine*, *4*, 57–64.

Payne, R. W. (1973) Cognitive abnormalities. In H. J. Eysenck (ed.) *Handbook of Abnormal Psychology*, 2nd edn. Pitman: London.

Pearce, S. and Morley, S. (1981) An experimental investigation of pain production in tension headache. *British Journal of Clinical Psychology*, *20*, 275–81.

Peck, D. F. and Attfield, M. E. (1981) Migraine symptoms on the Waters headache questionnaire: a statistical analysis. *Journal of Psychosomatic Research*, *25*, 281–8.

Perls, F., Hefferline, R. F. and Goodman, P. (1951) *Gestalt Therapy*. Penguin: Harmondsworth.

Perris, C. (1966) A study of bipolar (manic depressive) and unipolar recurrent depressive psychoses. *Acta Psychiatrica Scandinavica Supplement*, *194*, 9–42.

Perris, C. (1982) The distinction between bipolar and unipolar affective disorders. In E. S. Paykel (ed.) *Handbook of Affective Disorder*. Churchill Livingstone: Edinburgh.

Peterson, C. and Seligman, M. E. P. (1984) Causal explanations as a risk factor for depression: theory and evidence. *Psychological Review*, *91*, 347–74.

Peterson, R. L. and Peterson, M. J. (1959) Short term retention of individual verbal items. *Journal of Experimental Psychology*, *58*, 193–8.

Philips, C. (1976) Headache and personality. *Journal of Psychosomatic Research*, *20*, 535–42.

Philips, C. (1977) Headache in general practice. *Headache*, *16*, 322–29.

Philips. C. (1978) Tension headache: theoretical problems. *Behaviour Research and Therapy*, *16*, 249–61.

Philips, C. (1980) Recent developments in tension headache research: implications for understanding the disorder. In S. Rachman (ed.) *Contributions to Medical Psychology*, vol. 2. Pergamon Press: Oxford.

Philips, C. and Hunter, M. (1981a) The treatment of tension headache: I. Muscular abnormality and biofeedback. *Behaviour Research and Therapy*, *19*, 485–98.

Philips, C. and Hunter, M. (1981b) Pain behaviour in headache sufferers. *Behavioural Analysis and Modification*, *4*, 257–66.

Philips, C. and Hunter, M. (1982) A psychophysiological study of tension headache. *Headache*, *22*, 173–9.

Pilovsky, I., Levine, S. and Boulton, D. M. (1969) The classification of depression by numerical taxonomy. *British Journal of Psychiatry*, *115*, 937–45.

Prusoff, B. A., Klerman, G. L. and Paykel, E. S. (1972) Pitfalls in the self-report assessment of depression. *Canadian Psychiatric Association Journal*, *17*, 101–7.

Rachman, S. (1974) Primary obsessional slowness. *Behaviour Research and Therapy*, *12*, 9–18.

Rachman, S. (1976a) Observational learning and therapeutic modelling. In P. Feldman and A. Broadhurst (eds) *Theoretical and Experimental Bases of Behaviour Therapies*. Wiley: Chichester.

Rachman, S. (1976b) The passing of the two stage theory of fear and avoidance: fresh possibilities. *Behaviour Research and Therapy*, *14*, 125–31.

Rachman, S. (1977) The conditioning theory of fear acquisition: a critical examination. *Behaviour Research and Therapy*, *15*, 375–87.

Rachman, S. (ed.) (1978) Perceived self efficacy: analyses of Bandura's theory of behavioural change. *Advances in Behaviour Research and Therapy*, *1*, (no. 4) 137–269.

Rachman, S. and De Silva, P. (1978) Abnormal and normal obsessions. *Behaviour Research and Therapy*, *16*, 233–48.

Rachman, S. and Hodgson, R. J. (1974) Synchrony and desynchrony in fear and avoidance. *Behaviour Research and Therapy*, *12*, 311–18.

Rachman, S. and Wilson, G. T. (1980) *The Effects of Psychological Therapy*. Pergamon: Oxford.

Rao, V. A. R. and Coppen, A. (1979) Classification of depression and response to Amitriptyline therapy. *Psychological Medicine*, *9*, 321–5.

Raps, C. S., Peterson, C., Reinhard, K. E. and Seligman, M. E. P. (1982) Attributional style among depressed patients. *Journal of Abnormal Psychology*, *91*, 102–8.

Rehm, L. P. (1977) A self-control model of depression. *Behaviour Therapy*, *8*, 787–804.

Rodnight, R. (1982) Biochemistry and pathology of schizophrenia. In J. K.

Wing and L. Wing (eds) *Handbook of Psychiatry*: *3. Psychoses of Uncertain Origin*. Cambridge University Press: Cambridge.

Rogers, C. R. (1951) *Client Centred Therapy*. Constable: London.

Rogers, C., Gendlin, E. T., Keisler, D. and Truax, C. (1967) *The Therapeutic Relationship and its Impact: A Study of Psychotherapy with Schizophrenics*. Wisconsin University Press: Madison.

Rose, G. and Barker, D. J. P. (1979) *Epidemiology for the Uninitiated*. British Medical Association: London.

Rosenhan, D. L. (1973) On being sane in insane places. *Science*, *179*, 250–8.

Rosenthal, T. L. and Zimmerman, B. J. (1978) *Social Learning and Cognition*. Academic Press: New York.

Rosenthal, T. L. and Bandura, A. (1978) Psychological modeling: theory and practice. In S. L. Garfield and A. E. Bergin (eds) *Handbook of Psychotherapy and Behaviour Change: An Empirical Analysis*. Wiley: Chichester.

Roth, M. (1955) The natural history of mental disorder in old age. *Journal of Mental Science*, *101*, 281–301.

Rowland, L. A. and Canavan, A. G. M. (1983). Is a B.A.T. therapeutic? *Behavioural Psychotherapy*, *11*, 139–46.

Rush, A. J., Weisenburger, J., Vinson, D. B. and Giles, D. E. (1983). Neuropsychological dysfunctions in unipolar nonpsychotic major depressions. *Journal of Affective Disorders*, *5*, 281–7.

Sachar, E. J. (1982) Endocrine abnormalities in depression. In E. S. Paykel (ed.) *Handbook of Affective Disorders*. Churchill Livingstone: Edinburgh.

Schacter, S. and Singer, J. (1962) Cognitive, social and physiological determinants of emotional state. *Psychological Review*, *69*, 378–99.

Scheff, T. J. (1966) *Being Mentally Ill*. Aldine: Chicago.

Scoville, W. B. and Milner, B. (1957) Loss of recent memory after bilateral hippocampal lesions. *Journal of Neurology, Neurosurgery and Psychiatry*, *20*, 11–21.

Seligman, M. E. P. (1975) *Helplessness*. W. H. Freeman: San Francisco.

Seligman, M. E. P. (1981) A learned helplessness point of view. In L. P. Rehm (ed.) *Behaviour Therapy for Depression: Present Status and Future Directions*. Academic Press: New York.

Seligman, M. E. P., Abramson, L. Y., Semmel, A. and von Baeyer, C. (1979) Depressive attributional style. *Journal of Abnormal Psychology*, *88*, 242–7.

Seligman, M. E. P. and Maier, S. F. (1967) Failure to escape traumatic shock. *Journal of Experimental Psychology*, *74*, 1–9.

Shallice, T. (1979) Case study approach in neuropsychological research. *Journal of Clinical Neuropsychology*, *1*, 183–211.

Shapiro, D. A. (1969) Empathy, warmth and genuineness in psychotherapy. *British Journal of Social and Clinical Psychology*, *8*, 350–61.

Shapiro, D. A. (1981) Comparative credibility of treatment rationales: three tests of expectancy theory. *British Journal of Clinical Psychology*, *20*, 111–22.

Shapiro, D. A. and Shapiro, D. (1982) Meta-analysis of comparative therapy outcome studies: a replication and refinement. *Psychological Bulletin*, *92*, 581–609.

Shapiro, E. S., Barrett, R. P. and Ollendick, T. H. (1980) A comparison of physical restraint and positive practice overcorrection in treating stereotypic behaviour. *Behaviour Therapy*, *11*, 227–33.

Shapiro, J. G. (1968) Relationships between visual and auditory cues of therapeutic effectiveness. *Journal of Clinical Psychology*, *24*, 236–9.

Shapiro, J. G., Foster, C. P. and Powell, T. (1968) Facial and bodily cues of genuineness, empathy and warmth. *Journal of Clinical Psychology*, *24*, 233–6.

Shapiro, M. B. (1961) A method for measuring psychological changes specific to the individual psychiatric patient. *British Journal of Medical Psychology*, *34*, 151–5.

Shapiro, M. B. (1977) An analysis of the nine stages of accurate empathy as implied by the definitions of Truax and Carkhuff. Unpublished paper. Institute of Psychiatry: London.

Shapiro, M. B., Campbell, D., Harris, A. and Dewsberry, J. P. (1958) Effects of E.C.T. upon psychomotor speed and the 'distraction effect' in depressed psychiatric patients. *Journal of Mental Science*, *104*, 681–95.

Shapiro, M. B. and Nelson, E. H. (1955) An investigation of the nature of cognitive impairment in co-operative psychiatric patients. *British Journal of Medical Psychology*, *28*, 239–86.

Shepherd, G. (1983) Introduction. In S. Spence and G. Shepherd (eds) *Developments in Social Skills Training*. Academic Press: London.

Shepherd, G. (1984) *Institutional Care and Rehabilitation*. Longmans: London.

Shepp, B. E. and Zeaman, D. (1966) Discrimination learning of size and brightness by retardates. *Journal of Comparative and Physiological Psychology*, *62*, 55–9.

Shipley, R. H. and Boudewyns, P. A. (1980) Flooding and implosive therapy: are they harmful? *Behaviour Therapy*, *11*, 503–8.

Siegler, M., Osmond, H. and Mann, H. (1969) Laing's models of madness. *British Journal of Psychiatry*, *115*, 947–58.

Slater, E. and Roth, M. (1973) *Clinical Psychiatry*. Baillière Tindall: London.

Sloane, R. B., Staples, F. R., Cristol, A. H., Yorkston, N. J. and Whipple, K. (1975) *Psychotherapy versus Behaviour Therapy*. Harvard University Press: Cambridge, Massachusetts.

Smith, M. L., Glass, G. V. and Miller, T. I. (1980) *The Benefits of Psychotherapy*. Johns Hopkins University Press: Baltimore.

Snaith, R. P., Ahmed, S. N., Mehta, S., Hamilton, M. (1971) Assessment of severity of primary depressive illness: the Wakefield self-assessment inventory. *Psychological Medicine*, *1*, 143–9.

Snaith, R. P., Bridges, G. W. K. and Hamilton, M. (1976) The Leeds scales for the self-assessment of anxiety and depression. *British Journal of Psychiatry*, *128*, 156–65.

Solomon, Z. and Bromet, E. (1982) The role of social factors in affective disorder: an assessment of the vulnerability model of Brown and his colleagues. *Psychological Medicine*, *12*, 123–30.

Spence, S. and Shepherd, G. (1983) *Developments in Social Skills Training*. Academic Press: London.

Spitzer, R. L. (1976) More on pseudoscience in science and the case for psychiatric diagnosis: a critique of Rosenhan's 'On being sane in insane places' and the contextual nature of psychiatric diagnosis. *Archives of General Psychiatry*, *33*, 459–70.

Spitzer, R. L., Endicott, J. and Robins, E. (1978) Research diagnostic criteria: rationale and reliability. *Archives of General Psychiatry*, *35*, 773–82.

Stampfl, T. G. and Levis, D. J. (1967) Essentials of implosive therapy: a learning theory based psychodynamic behavioral therapy. *Journal of Abnormal Psychology*, *72*, 496–503.

Sternbach, R. A. and Timmermans, G. (1975) Personality changes associated with reductions of pain. *Pain*, *1*, 177–81.

Sternberg, D. E., and Jarvik, M. E. (1976) Memory functions in depression: improvement with antidepressant medication. *Archives of General Psychiatry*, *33*, 219–24.

Stott, W. H. (1958) Some psychosomatic aspects of causality in reproduction. *Journal of Psychosomatic Research*, *3*, 42–55.

Straube, M. J. and Hartman, D. P. (1982) A critical appraisal of meta-analysis. *British Journal of Clinical Psychology*, *21*, 129–39.

Strauss, J. S. and Carpenter, W. T. (1972) The prediction of outcome in schizophrenia: I. Characteristics of outcome. *Archives of General Psychiatry*, *27*, 739–46.

Strauss, J. S. and Carpenter, W. T. (1974) Prediction of outcome in schizophrenia: II. Relationships between predictor and outcome variables. *Archives of General Psychiatry*, *31*, 37–42.

Strauss, J. S. and Carpenter, W. T. (1977) Prediction of outcome of schizophrenia: III. Five year outcome and its predictors. *Archives of General Psychiatry*, *34*, 159–63.

Strauss, J. S. and Carpenter, W. T. (1981) *Schizophrenia*. Plenum Press: New York.

Sturgeon, D., Kuipers, L., Berkowitz, R., Turpin, G. and Leff, J. P. (1981) Psychophysiological responses of schizophrenic patients to high and low expressed emotion relatives. *British Journal of Psychiatry*, *138*, 40–5.

Surtees, P. G. (1980) Social support, residual adversity and depressive outcome. *Social Psychiatry*, *15*, 71–80.

Szabadi, E., Bradshaw, C. M. and Besson, J. A. D. (1976) Elongation of pause time in speech: a simple, objective measure of motor retardation in depression. *British Journal of Psychiatry*, 129, 592–7.

Szasz, T. (1961) *The Myth of Mental Illness*. Harper & Row: New York.

Tarrier, N. and Barrowclough, C. (1984) Psychophysiological assessment of expressed emotion in schizophrenia. A case example. *British Journal of Psychiatry*, *145*, 197–203.

Tarrier, N., Vaughn, C. E., Lader, M. H. and Leff, J. P. (1979) Bodily reactions to people and events in schizophrenia. *Archives of General Psychiatry*, *36*, 311–18.

Taylor, M. A., Redfield, J. and Abrams, R. (1981) Neuropsychological dysfunction in schizophrenia and affective disease. *Biological Psychiatry*, *16*, 467–78.

Teasdale, J. D. and Fogarty, S. J. (1979) Differential effects of induced mood on retrieval of pleasant and unpleasant events from episodic memory. *Journal of Abnormal Psychology*, *88*, 248–57.

Teasdale, J. D. and Russell, M. L. (1983) Differential effects of induced mood on the recall of positive, negative and neutral words. *British Journal of Clinical Psychology*, *22*, 163–71.

Tennant, C. (1983) Life events and psychological morbidity: the evidence from prospective studies. *Psychological Medicine*, *13*, 483–6.

Tennant, C., Bebbington, P. and Hurry, J. (1981) The role of life events in depressive illness: is there a substantial causal relationship? *Psychological Medicine*, *11*, 379–89.

Thompson, J. K. and Adams, H. E. (1984) Psychophysiological characteristics of headache patients. *Pain*, *18*, 41–52.

Tizard, J. and Loos, F. M. (1954) Learning for a spatial relations test by adult imbeciles. *American Journal of Mental Deficiency*, *59*, 85–90.

Trethowan, W. (1979) *Psychiatry*, 4th edn. Ballière Tindall: London.

Truax, C. B. (1966a) Reinforcement and non-reinforcement in Rogerian psychotherapy. *Journal of Abnormal and Social Psychology*, *71*, 1–9.

Truax, C. B. (1966b) The influence of patient statements on judgements of therapist statements during psychotherapy. *Journal of Clinical Psychology*, *22*, 335–7.

Truax, C. B. (1968) Therapist interpersonal reinforcement of client self-exploration and therapeutic outcome in group psychotherapy. *Journal of Counselling Psychology*, *15*, 225–31.

Truax, C. and Carkhuff, R. (1967) *Toward Effective Counselling and Psychotherapy*. Aldine Press: Chicago.

Truax, C. and Mitchell, K. (1971) Research on certain therapist interpersonal skills in relation to process and outcome. In A. E. Bergin and S. L. Garfield (eds) *Handbook of Psychotherapy and Behaviour Change: An Empirical Analysis*. Wiley: New York.

Trudel, G. (1979) The effects of instructions and level of fear. *Behaviour Research and Therapy*, *17*, 113–18.

Turk, D. C. (1978) Cognitive behavioral techniques in the management of pain. In J. P. Foreyt and O. P. Rathjen (eds) *Cognitive Behavior Therapy: Research and Application*. Plenum Press: New York.

Vaughn, C. E. and Leff, J. P. (1976a) The influence of family and social factors on the course of psychiatric illness. *British Journal of Psychiatry*, *129*, 125–37.

Vaughn, C. E. and Leff, J. P. (1976b) The measurement of expressed emotion in families of psychiatric patients. *British Journal of Social and Clinical Psychology*, *15*, 157–65.

Vaughn, C. E., Snyder, K. S., Jones, S., Freeman, W. B. and Falloon, R. H. (1984) family factors in schizophrenic relapse. *Archives of General*

Psychiatry, *41*, 1169–77.

Vernon, P. E. (1964) *Personality Assessment: A Critical Appraisal.* Methuen: London.

Von Knorring, A. L., Cloninger, R., Bohman, M. and Sigvardsson, S. (1983) An adoption study of depressive disorders and substance abuse. *Archives of General Psychiatry*, *40*, 943–50.

Waters, W. E. and O'Connor, P. J. (1971) Epidemiology of headache and migraine in women. *Journal of Neurology, Neurosurgery and Psychiatry*, *34*, 148–53.

Watt, D. C., Katz, K. and Shepherd, M. (1983) The natural history of schizophrenia: a 5 year prospective follow-up of a representative sample of schizophrenias by means of a standardised clinical and social assessment. *Psychological Medicine*, *13*, 663–70.

Watts, F. N. (1975) Systematic desensitization as habituation. Unpublished PhD thesis. University of London: London.

Watts, F. N. (1979) The habituation model of systematic desensitization. *Psychological Bulletin*, *86*, 627–37.

Watts, F. N. and Bennett, D. H. (1977) Previous occupational stability as a predictor of employment after psychiatric rehabilitation. *Psychological Medicine*, *7*, 709–12.

Watts, F. N. and Bennett, D. H. (1984) *Theory and Practice in Psychiatric Rehabilitation.* Wiley: Chichester.

Weeks, D., Freeman, C. P. L. and Kendell, R. E. (1980) ECT: III Enduring cognitive deficits. *British Journal of Psychiatry*, *137*, 26–37.

Weissman, M. M. and Klerman, G. L. (1977) Sex differences in the epidemiology of depression. *Archives of General Psychiatry*, *34*, 98–111.

Wickelgren, W. A. (1968) Sparing of short-term memory in an amnesic patient: implications for strength theory of memory. *Neuropsychologia*, *6*, 235–44.

Wilkinson, I. M. and Blackburn, J. M. (1981) Cognitive style in depressed and recovered depressed patients. *British Journal of Clinical Psychology*, *20*, 283–92.

Williams, J. G. (1975) Diurnal variation in depression – is it there? *Journal of Nervous and Mental Diseases*, *161*, 59–62.

Williams, J. M. G. (1980) Generalisation in the effects of a mood induction procedure. *Behaviour Research and Therapy*, *18*, 563–72.

Williams, J. M. G. (1984a) *The Psychological Treatment of Depression.* Croom Helm: London.

Williams, J. M. G. (1984b) Cognitive-behaviour therapy for depression: problems and perspectives. *British Journal of Psychiatry*, *145*, 254–62.

Wilson, G. T. and Evans, J. M. (1977) The therapist-client relationship in behaviour therapy. In A. Gurman and A. Razin (eds) *Effective Psychotherapy.* Pergamon Press: Oxford.

Wilson, G. T. and Rachman, S. J. (1983) Meta-analysis and the evaluation of psychotherapy outcome: limitations and liabilities. *Journal of Comparative and Clinical Psychology*, *51*, 54–64.

Winefield, H. R. (1984) The nature and elicitation of social support: some implications for the helping professions. *Behavioural Psycho-therapy*, *12*, 318–30.

Wing, J. K. (1982) Course and prognosis of schizophrenia. In J. K. Wing and L. Wing (eds) *Handbook of Psychiatry, vol. 3. Psychoses of Uncertain Origin*. Cambridge University Press: Cambridge.

Wing, J. K., Cooper, J. E. and Sartorius, N. (1974) *The Measurement and Classification of Psychiatric Symptoms*. Cambridge University Press: Cambridge.

Winokur, G. (1979) Unipolar depression: is it divisible into autonomous subtypes? *Archives of General Psychiatry*, *36*, 47–52.

Winokur, G., Cadoret, R., Dorzab, J. and Baker, M. (1971) Depressive disease: a genetic study. *Archives of General Psychiatry*, *24*, 135–55.

Winokur, G., Clayton, P. and Reich, T. (1969) *Manic-depressive Illness*. Mosley: St Louis.

Wolff, H. G. (1937) Personality features and reaction of subjects with migraine. *Archives of Neurology and Psychiatry*, *37*, 895–921.

Wolff, H. G. (1962) *Headache and Other Head Pain*, 2nd edn. Oxford University Press: London.

Wollheim, R. (1971) *Freud*. Collins/Fontana: London.

Wolpe, J. (1958) *Psychotherapy by Reciprocal Inhibition*. Stanford University Press: Stanford, California.

Woodruff, R. A., Murphy, G. E. and Herjanic, M. (1967) The natural history of affective disorders: I. Symptoms of 72 patients at time of index hospital admission. *Journal of Psychiatric Research*, *5*, 255–63.

World Health Organization (1978) *Mental Disorders: Glossary and Guide to their Classification in Accordance with the Ninth Revision of the International Classification of Diseases*. WHO: Geneva.

Yates, A. (1966) Psychological deficit. *Annual Review of Psychology*, *17*, 111–44.

Yates, A. J. (1980) *Biofeedback and the modification of behaviour*. Plenum Press: New York.

Yozawitz, A., Bruder, G., Sutton, S., Sharpe, L., Gurland, B., Fleiss, J. and Costa, L. (1979) Dichotic perception: evidence for right hemi-sphere dysfunction in affective psychosis. *British Journal of Psychiatry*, *135*, 225–8.

Zeaman, D. (1965) Learning processes of the mentally retarded. In S. F. Osler and R. E. Cook (eds) *The Biological Basis of Retardation*. Johns Hopkins University Press: Baltimore.

Zeaman, D. and House, B. J. (1963) The role of attention in retardate discrimination learning. In N. R. Ellis (ed.) *Handbook of Mental Deficiency*. McGraw-Hill: New York.

Zeaman, D. and House, B. J. (1979) A review of attention theory. In N. R. Ellis (ed.) *Handbook of Mental Deficiency: Psychological Theory and Research*. Laurence Erlbaum: Hillsdale, New Jersey.

Zeigler, D. K., Hassanein, R. S. and Hassanein, K. (1972) Headache symptoms suggested by factor analysis of symptom variables in a headache prone population. *Journal of Chronic Diseases*, *25*, 353–63.

Zerbin-Rudin, E. (1979) Genetics of affective psychoses. In M. Schon and

E. Stromgren (eds) *Origin, Prevention and Treatment of Affective Disorder*. Academic Press: New York.

Zis, A. P. and Goodwin, F. K. (1982) The amine hypothesis. In E. S. Paykel (ed.) *Handbook of Affective Disorders*. Churchill Livingstone: Edinburgh.

Zubin, J. (1967) Classification of the behaviour disorders. *Annual Review of Psychology*, *18*, 373–406.

Zung, W. K. (1965) A self-rating depression scale. *Archives of General Psychiatry*, *12*, 63–70.

Index